SQL Server 2019 Revealed

Including Big Data Clusters and Machine Learning

Bob Ward
Foreword by Rohan Kumar

Apress®

SQL Server 2019 Revealed: Including Big Data Clusters and Machine Learning

Bob Ward
North Richland Hills, Texas, USA

ISBN-13 (pbk): 978-1-4842-5418-9
https://doi.org/10.1007/978-1-4842-5419-6

ISBN-13 (electronic): 978-1-4842-5419-6

Managing Director, Apress Media LLC: Welmoed Spahr
Acquisitions Editor: Jonathan Gennick
Development Editor: Laura Berendson
Coordinating Editor: Jill Balzano

Cover image designed by Freepik (www.freepik.com)

Distributed to the book trade worldwide by Springer Science+Business Media New York, 233 Spring Street, 6th Floor, New York, NY 10013. Phone 1-800-SPRINGER, fax (201) 348-4505, e-mail orders-ny@springer-sbm.com, or visit www.springeronline.com. Apress Media, LLC is a California LLC and the sole member (owner) is Springer Science + Business Media Finance Inc (SSBM Finance Inc). SSBM Finance Inc is a **Delaware** corporation.

For information on translations, please e-mail rights@apress.com, or visit http://www.apress.com/rights-permissions.

Apress titles may be purchased in bulk for academic, corporate, or promotional use. eBook versions and licenses are also available for most titles. For more information, reference our Print and eBook Bulk Sales web page at http://www.apress.com/bulk-sales.

Any source code or other supplementary material referenced by the author in this book is available to readers on GitHub via the book's product page, located at www.apress.com/9781484254189. For more detailed information, please visit http://www.apress.com/source-code.

Printed on acid-free paper

This book is dedicated to the SQL Server Community, also known as the #sqlfamily. Without the community, this amazing product would not be what it is today.

Table of Contents

About the Author xiii

About the Technical Reviewer xv

Foreword xvii

Acknowledgments xix

Introduction xxi

Chapter 1: Why SQL Server 2019? 1

  Project Seattle.. 2

  Project Aris... 3

  Seattle Becomes SQL Server 2019 6

  Modernizing Your Database with SQL Server 2019.. 7

    Data Virtualization 10

    Performance.. 11

    Security 11

    Mission-Critical Availability 12

    Modern Development Platform.. 12

    Investing in the Platform of Your Choice.. 13

    Azure Data Studio... 14

    Voice of the Customer 14

  Getting Started with SQL Server 2019 15

    Download SQL Server 2019.. 15

    Deploy SQL Server 2019.. 15

    Migrate to SQL Server 2019 15

    What's New in SQL Server 2019.. 15

    Download Book Code and Sample Databases... 16

SQL Server Workshops 16

It Is Your Grandpa's SQL Server? 16

Chapter 2: Intelligent Performance 19

Why Intelligent Performance? 19

Intelligent Query Processing 20

Prerequisites for Using the Examples for Intelligent Query Processing 22

Memory Grant Feedback Row Mode 24

Table Variable Deferred Compilation 42

Batch Mode on Rowstore 49

Scalar UDF Inlining 52

Approximate Count Distinct 57

Lightweight Query Profiling 61

Prerequisites for Using the Examples for Lightweight Query Profiling 62

Should I Kill an Active Query? 63

I Can't Catch It 68

In-Memory Database 74

Memory-Optimized TempDB Metadata 75

Hybrid Buffer Pool 81

Persistent Memory Support 82

Last-Page Insert Contention 83

Summary 85

Chapter 3: New Security Capabilities 87

Enhancing What We Have Built 87

Always Encrypted with Secure Enclaves 88

Why Enclaves? 90

Using Always Encrypted with Enclaves 91

Data Classification 92

Prerequisites for Using the Examples 95

Using Data Classification 96

Auditing and Data Classification 105

Other New Security Features 111

    TDE Pause and Resume 111

    Certificate Management 112

Summary 114

Chapter 4: Mission-Critical Availability 115

Online Index Maintenance 116

    Resumable Index Operations 117

    Prerequisites to Using the Example 118

    Try Out Resumable Index Creation 118

    Online Index Maintenance for Columnstore 123

Enhancing Always On Availability Groups 123

    Support for More Synchronous Replicas 124

    Secondary to Primary Replica Read/Write Connection Redirection 124

Accelerated Database Recovery 125

    The Challenge of Long Active Transactions 126

    How Accelerated Database Recovery Works 126

    Using Accelerated Database Recovery 135

    Accelerate Database Recovery Nuts and Bolts 139

Summary 145

Chapter 5: Modern Development Platform 147

Languages, Drivers, and Platforms 148

    Languages and Drivers 148

    Platforms and Editions 151

Graph Database 151

    What Is a Graph Database in SQL Server? 152

    Using a Graph Database in SQL Server 153

    Graph Enhancements for SQL Server 2019 155

UTF-8 Support 156

    Unicode and SQL Server 157

    Why Would You Use UTF-8? 157

SQL Server Machine Learning Services 158

How It Works 159

Security, Isolation, and Governance 163

What's New in SQL Server 2019? 165

Extending the T-SQL Language 166

The Extensibility Framework 167

Extending T-SQL with Java 168

Implementing and Using Other Languages 174

Summary 174

Chapter 6: SQL Server 2019 on Linux 175

The Amazing Story of SQL Server on Linux 175

What Is New for SQL Server 2019 on Linux 177

Platform and Deployment Enhancements 178

Platform Enhancements 178

SQL Server 2019 on Linux Deployment 180

Supporting New Linux Releases 181

Persistent Memory Support 182

SQL Server Replication on Linux 183

Change Data Capture (CDC) on Linux 184

DTC on Linux 184

Active Directory with OpenLDAP 186

SQL Server Machine Learning Services and Extensibility on Linux 187

Deployment of SQL Server ML Services on Linux 187

How It Works 189

The Extensibility Framework and Language Extensions 192

Polybase on Linux 193

Summary 193

Chapter 7: Inside SQL Server Containers 195

Why SQL Server Containers? 195

How SQL Server Containers Work 199

Container Hosting 199

Is Docker Magic? 200

Container Lifecycle 201

The SQL Server Container 203

What Is New for SQL Server 2019 206

Prerequisites for the Examples 210

Deploying a SQL Server Container 212

A New Way to Update SQL Server 225

Deploying Container As an Application 229

The docker-compose.yml File 230

Building Each Container 231

Running the Containers for Replication 233

Deploying SQL Containers in Production 236

Performance 236

Security 238

High Availability 239

Resource Control 239

Server or Database Configuration 241

Using Other Packages 242

Editions and Licensing 242

SQL Server Windows Containers 243

Summary 246

Chapter 8: SQL Server on Kubernetes 249

What Is k8s? 249

References on k8s 250

k8s Objects 250

Comment on Internals of k8s 252

k8s Deployment Options 253

Prerequisites for the Examples 255

Deploying SQL Server on k8s 257

Tips with k8s 273

SQL Server High Availability on k8s 281

Updating SQL Server on k8s 287

Using Helm Charts 292

SQL Server Availability Groups on k8s 292

Summary... 295

Chapter 9: SQL Server Data Virtualization **297**

What Is Polybase?... 297

    The History of Polybase 298

    What Is Data Virtualization?.. 300

How Polybase Works.. 302

    The Polybase Workflow 303

    SQL Server 2019 Polybase Architecture... 305

    How External Tables Work 305

    The Polybase Standalone Instance... 307

    A Polybase Scale-Out Group.. 309

    Query Processing and Polybase 310

    How Does It Work on Linux?.. 310

    How Is This Different Than Azure?... 310

Prerequisites for the Examples 311

    Setting Up and Enabling Polybase... 311

    Using the Examples 313

Using External Tables... 315

    Tools and External Tables 315

    Using an External Table with Azure SQL Database 317

    Using Built-in Connectors for External Tables 325

    Using an External Table with HDFS... 326

    Using External Tables with ODBC Connectors 326

Considerations for External Tables... 327

    A New Semantic Layer 327

External Tables vs. Linked Servers 328

Restrictions and Limitations 328

Summary 328

Chapter 10: SQL Server Big Data Clusters 331

Why Big Data Clusters? 334

What Comes with Big Data Clusters? 335

SQL Server 2019 335

Polybase 336

Hadoop Distributed File System (HDFS) 336

Spark 336

Data Cache 336

Tools and Services 337

Endpoints 337

Application Deployment 337

Machine Learning 337

Prerequisites for the Examples 338

Deploying Big Data Clusters 339

Plan the Deployment 339

The BDC Deployment Experience 344

Verify the Deployment 346

Configuring Deployment for Production 350

Big Data Cluster Architecture 351

SQL Server Master Instance 353

Controller 357

Storage Pool 359

Compute Pool 361

Data Pool 361

Application Pool 362

Using Big Data Clusters 363

Using Data Virtualization 366

Using the Data Pool 369

Using Spark 369

Deploying and Using Applications 371

Security 372

High Availability 372

Jupyter Books for SQL Server Big Data Clusters 373

Machine Learning and Big Data Clusters 374

Machine Learning Packages 375

Using Examples 375

Managing and Monitoring Big Data Clusters 376

Managing Kubernetes (k8s) 376

Managing and Monitoring Big Data Clusters 377

Summary 381

Chapter 11: The Voice of the Customer and Migration **383**

The Voice of the Customer 383

Performance Enhancements 384

User Experience 386

Diagnostics 389

What About Business Intelligence? 393

Migration to SQL Server 2019 394

The Pam and Pedro Show 394

Database Migration Assistant 395

Database Experimentation Assistant 397

Upgrading to SQL Server 2019 399

Database Compatibility 403

Query Tuning Assistant and Post Migration 407

Running in Azure Virtual Machine 408

SQL Server Migration Assistant 410

Summary 412

Index **413**

About the Author

Bob Ward is a Principal Architect for the Microsoft Azure Data SQL Server team, which owns the development for all SQL Server releases. Bob has worked for Microsoft for 26+ years on every version of SQL Server shipped from OS/2 1.1 to SQL Server 2019 including Azure. He is a well-known speaker on SQL Server, often presenting talks on new releases, internals, and performance at events such as PASS Summit, SQLBits, SQLIntersection, Red Hat Summit, Microsoft Inspire, and Microsoft Ignite. You can follow him at @bobwardms or www.linkedin.com/in/bobwardms. Bob is the author of the book *Pro SQL Server on Linux* available from Apress Media.

About the Technical Reviewer

Aaron Bertrand is a passionate technologist with over two decades of SQL Server experience. He has worked directly with several Microsoft product teams and is well known for helping improve the technical skills of the broader developer community through writing, speaking at, and moderating technical forums.

Foreword

We are truly at a unique tipping point in the history of technology, and there has never been a better time to be in the field of data, analytics, and AI. The pace of growth in data is more rapid than ever before, and digital disruption through AI and ML has created unlimited potential for companies to embrace data as a competitive advantage for their business. With the dramatic acceleration of digitization, the primary question we now face is how to take advantage of this massive volume of data to help our companies and communities transform.

We see a massive opportunity powered by the intelligent cloud and the intelligent edge. SQL Server is unparalleled in the industry in the level of consistency it provides the developers, data engineers, and administrators across the edge, on-premises, private cloud, and the public cloud. Our SQL Server community has played a very important role in this evolution, and I cannot thank them enough for their support and feedback over the last 25+ years.

SQL Server 2019 is a phenomenal release, and I am proud of what the team has delivered. SQL Server 2019 builds on the innovation that was delivered in SQL Server 2016 and SQL Server 2017. While there are several new capabilities that will serve our customers well, as is expected from every major release of SQL Server, I am most excited about the remarkable innovation that extends the skills our customers have built over multiple decades to manage and get insight from their Big Data systems. This innovation will play a critical role in driving the digital transformation for our customers.

Bob Ward has been with the SQL Server team since the very early days and has had a notable impact on the product. There are very few who have the breadth and depth of understanding that he does, and it shows in how he manages to explain complex concepts in a simple, easy-to-understand manner in this book. I hope you enjoy reading it.

Rohan Kumar
Corporate Vice President, Azure Data at Microsoft

Acknowledgments

I have so many things in my life to be thankful for, and having the ability to write this book is one of them. I believe all of my blessings come from God, and it is through His grace I have come to know the powerful message of Jesus Christ. I must first give thanks to my beautiful and talented wife Ginger. She is my partner and my soulmate. She tirelessly heard all my complaints, watched me spend very late nights on the book, and sometimes had to be the driver so I could work on the book in the passenger seat. I don't know anyone who has stronger faith than my wife Ginger, and I am so fortunate to share a wonderful life together with her. We celebrated 30 years of marriage this year, and I still love being with her as much as possible each and every day. I also want to thank my sons Troy and Ryan. Troy these days lives in Charleston, South Carolina, where I wrote the last part of the book as Hurricane Dorian approached. Troy is someone who I admire not just for his character but his quest to make this place a better world. Ryan is in his second year at Baylor Law School (Go Bears!). He continues to amaze me with this intelligence, integrity, and ability to keep it all together with confidence yet still find time to improve his golf game. I also want to thank my mother Annette Gibaud who continues to show me the example of finding a way to be kind to someone each and every day.

There are so many people who helped contribute to this book. I want first to thank Apress Media for giving me another chance to write a book. Jonathan Gennick and Jill Balzano were there again every step of the way helping me push this book to conclusion. And this book could not have been possible and on time without my Technical Reviewer Aaron Bertrand. When I thought about writing this book, Aaron was one of the first people that came to mind for a reviewer given his incredible knowledge of SQL Server and reputation as an expert in the community. Aaron was simply superhuman in how fast he cranked out reviews of each chapter.

From Microsoft, first and foremost thank you to Rohan Kumar, Gayle Sheppard, and Asad Khan for giving me the opportunity to spread the message about SQL Server 2019 which was instrumental in my detailed learning of the product to write this book. I also want to personally thank two of my closest colleagues, Buck Woody and Anna Hoffman (Thomas). I travelled the world with Buck and Anna in 2018 and 2019 telling the story of SQL Server, Big Data Clusters, and Azure. They both made me a better storyteller and teacher and are fun on the road. The Microsoft SQL Server Engineering team is nothing short of amazing. I am in awe to be working with such intelligent and professional people, many of whom helped me with details you find in this book. It all has to start with Slava Oks and Travis Wright who helped tell me the story of Seattle and Aris and were both instrumental in pushing through much of this release including Big Data Clusters. Conor Cunningham continues to amaze me with his deep knowledge of this product while being instrumental in delivering a quality release.

The true heroes of this book are the engineering team members who built this release and helped me with various parts of the book. In no particular order, I want to say thank you to Pedro Lopes, Pam Lahoud, Amit Banerjee, Brian Carrig, Tejas Shah, Vin Yu, Sourabh Agarwal, Mihaela Blendea, Nellie Gustafsson, Abiola Oke, James Rowland-Jones, Scott Konersmann, Stuart Padley, David Kryze, Robert Dorr, Mitchell Sternke, Ross Monster, Madeline MacDonald, Dylan Gray, Joe Sack, Shreya Verma, Jakub Szymaszek, Joachim Hammer, Raghav Kaushik, Parag Paul, Panagiotis Antonopoulos, Michael Nelson, Pranjal Gupta, Jarupat Jisarojito, Weiyun Huang, George Reynya, Umachandar Jayachandran (UC), Sahaj Saini, Mike Habben, Vaqar Pirzada, Rony Chatterjee, Vicky Harp, Alan Yu, Jack Li, Alexey Eksarevskiy, Jay Choe, Argenis Fernandez, Kevin Farlee, Arieh Bibliowicz, Alex Umansky, Matteo Taveggia, Kapil Thacker, Li Zhang, and Dong Cao.

I also want to thank members of Microsoft Marketing and CSS teams for their help including Anshul Rampal, Matthew Burrows, Marko Hotti, Debbi Lyons, Suresh Kandoth, and Pradeep M M.

This book and my work would not have been possible without partners such as HPE, DELL, and Red Hat who allowed me to tell the story of SQL Server 2019 to their customers. Thanks to Wendy Harms, Bill Dunmire, Urs Renggli, Robert Sonders, Louis Imershein, and Stephane Bureau (my video guy). Special thanks also to David DeWitt for your insights into the history of Polybase, Brendan Burns for your insights and my foundation for Kubernetes knowledge, and Anthony Nocentino for your great knowledge of Linux and Containers.

Finally, thank you to the SQL Server Community across the world. We now pour releases of SQL Server at you faster than ever before, yet you still exhibit immense enthusiasm and appreciation every time I present on SQL Server.

Introduction

Like my first book *Pro SQL Server on Linux*, the pages you are about to read have seen some mileage. I've travelled more in the year 2019 than any in my lifetime. That meant I needed to be prepared to write wherever and whenever I could. This includes flights, hotels, trains, and car rides across cities like Seattle, London, Manchester (UK), Nashville, Las Vegas (multiple times), San Antonio, Austin, Houston, Orlando, St. Lucia (that was on vacation), Genesee (Colorado), Charleston, Boston, Dubai, Johannesburg (South Africa), Greenville (SC), and Indianapolis and late nights in my office at my home in North Richland Hills, Texas.

I thought after finishing my first book I would not be ready to write another one, but I couldn't resist the chance to tell the story of SQL Server 2019. This book really does represent that famous saying "A labor of love." I've put my heart and soul into learning, teaching, complaining about, breaking, documenting, testing, and using SQL Server 2019. This book represents all of that and more.

I wrote this book for data professionals and developers who have a fundamental knowledge of SQL Server but want a comprehensive look at SQL Server 2019 in one book. This book has plenty of examples, figures, and references to guide you along the way. I wrote this book so it would not only be a complete understanding of SQL Server 2019 but also as a reference you can come back to at any time.

While each chapter is independent, I highly recommend you start with Chapter 1 as it gives you the history and background of the release. I also set the stage for all the key capabilities of SQL Server 2019 and why I think it is a compelling product. From there, you can go through the book in chapter sequence or skip around some. One thing is for sure, in order to get the most out of Chapter 10 on Big Data Clusters, you must read Chapters 6, 7, 8, and 9 first.

The book is essentially broken down into these major sections:

- Chapter 1 to introduce the history and the overall SQL Server 2019 release.

- Chapters 2, 3, and 4 to cover performance, security, and availability. There is a lot in these chapters alone to get you excited about SQL Server 2019.

- Chapter 5 stands on its own for developers.

- Chapters 6, 7, and 8 are all about Linux, Containers, and Kubernetes.

- Chapter 9 introduces you to Data Virtualization with Polybase.

- Chapter 10 is a big chapter for a big topic: Big Data Clusters.

- Chapter 11 concludes the book by talking about other new features and migration.

I love "learning by example" so I've included many examples for almost every chapter in the book (and in some cases, I explain how to use an example already created). You can find all the examples for this book on GitHub using the link for the book's reference at www.apress.com/9781484254189 or on my GitHub repo at https://aka.ms/bobsqldemos (https://github.com/microsoft/bobsql).

I also recommend you take a look at free training resources our team has built at https://aka.ms/sqlworkshops. This includes free hands-only lab training with SQL Server 2019!

For this book, I spent a lot of time thinking for each chapter "what would a reader want" on a particular topic or example. I hope you can see and feel that as you read the book. If you have any questions or issues with the book, I really want to hear about them. Please e-mail me directly at bobward@microsoft.com.

Bob Ward
North Richland Hills, Texas
September 2019

CHAPTER 1

Why SQL Server 2019?

In July of 2017, I made one of my regular visits to Redmond, Washington, as a member of the SQL Server engineering team. I live in North Richland Hills, Texas, and modern technology allows me to do much of my job remote from most of the SQL Engineering team. But I'm still a bit of an "old-school" person, and, in some cases, nothing beats working with people face to face. By July of 2017, I had been in the SQL Engineering team for over a year, focused mostly on SQL Server 2016 (see an example of my work on SQL Server 2016 on the Web at `https://channel9.msdn.com/Events/Ignite/2016/BRK3043-TS`).

Up until this time, I was a member of the famous Tiger Team, but, as part of my visit in 2017, I was asked to take on new tasks to focus specifically on the upcoming SQL Server 2017 release. This included SQL Server on Linux, which ultimately led to me authoring my first book, *Pro SQL Server on Linux* (`www.apress.com/us/book/9781484241271`). So on my visit, I started meeting and talking to various members of the team about SQL Server 2017 – performance enhancements, the overall set of new features, and the details behind SQL Server on Linux and Containers. One of the people I spoke with that week was Slava Oks. Slava is the lead development manager for SQL Server and one of the inventors of SQL Server on Linux. He wrote the foreword of *Pro SQL Server on Linux*, and Chapter 1 of that book talks about the history of his involvement in the project. At that time, Slava liked to come in early to the office; when I'm in Redmond I, too, try to work "Texas time" – which means I also come in very early. So we would often meet for coffee before most others were in the office, in Building 16, though now our team works in Building 43. One morning, as Slava and I talked about SQL Server 2017, he said to me, "Hey have I told you about our plans for the next version of SQL Server, the one after SQL Server 2017?" I of course pretended to know – "Sure, Slava, I've heard of it, but don't know the details." He then invited me to come to a meeting the next day where he would explain to many of our engineering team the plan for the project. I had just spent a year focusing on SQL Server 2016, was now assigned to dive into SQL Server 2017 and Linux, and here Slava wanted me to learn about the

1

release after the release that had not been shipped yet? Of course, I was not going to turn him down, because, well, it's Slava Oks. This may make it sound like Slava is some type of intimidating person, but he is one of the nicest people I've ever known at Microsoft. So while I was starting to pack my brain on the details of SQL Server 2017, I started down the path to learn about what we were doing for the future version of SQL Server, code named Project SQL Server *Seattle*.

Project Seattle

In the meeting the next day with Slava, I quickly learned in the span of a few hours we were embarking on one of the most ambitious enhancements to SQL Server I had ever seen in my career. I'm saying this with the knowledge already that we were bringing to market SQL Server on Linux, which nobody had previously thought was possible.

Slava and the team chose the code name "Seattle" because the team had used Helsinki for the code name for SQL Server 2017 and were looking for a new "city" name. Ironically, no one at Microsoft had used the name Seattle before, so it quickly stuck. I asked Slava when he first started planning Project Seattle. I was amazed to hear all the way back in January of 2017. The fact that folks like Slava, Conor Cunningham, and Travis Wright were planning Project Seattle while working on building the final pieces of SQL Server 2017 and Linux was a testament to both their dedication to the team and also their desire to keep SQL Server leading innovation in the database industry.

It was hard to believe we could so quickly plan something bigger after having delivered so many compelling and innovative features in SQL Server 2016 and SQL Server 2017.

In SQL Server 2016, we brought new performance diagnostic capabilities with Query Store. We included new features for developers such as temporal tables and JSON integration. We upped our game on security with Always Encrypted, dynamic data masking, and row-level security. And we introduced two new innovations outside the "normal" type of features for a relational database system. One of these was integration of the R language for Machine Learning models. The second was integration with Hadoop systems with a feature called *Polybase* (which will lead to something bigger in 2019, but I'm getting ahead of myself). Building features to enable new scenarios like Machine Learning and Big Data led myself and others at Microsoft to start pitching the idea that SQL Server was no longer just a relational database engine but a *data platform*.

However, to be modern and a complete data platform, we needed to be able to empower applications on systems other than just Windows Server. This led to our release of SQL Server 2017 with support for Linux and Docker Containers. Running on Linux and Containers was a very big move for Microsoft, but SQL Server 2017 also included other capabilities such as Adaptive Query Processing, automatic tuning, graph database, *clusterless* Availability Groups, and Python integration to complement R language support for Machine Learning Services.

With all of this innovation in mind, how could we in a short period of time plan and build something new, different, and exciting than SQL Server 2016 and 2017? I asked myself this question as I intently listened in my first Project Seattle meeting. In the first few minutes, I would be introduced to an idea that, when later announced to the public, would be considered quite radical. And that innovation started as the "big rock" of the Seattle project, which has a project name of its own: *Aris*.

Project Aris

In January of 2017, Slava and the leadership of the SQL Server engineering team were given direction by Rohan Kumar, Corporate Vice President of Azure Data, to look into how to integrate SQL Server with *Big Data*. Big Data is a term loosely used in the industry related to a data system that can handle *large* amounts of data, usually through a distributed, scalable computing platform. I personally like my colleague Buck Woody's definition of Big Data as, "Any data that you can't process in the time you want with the technology you have." And for many years, the preferred choice for a Big Data system has been Hadoop. So, for several months in the spring and summer of 2017, the team looked to Travis Wright for ideas on how to make the vision of Big Data integration a reality. During the summer of 2017, our Azure Data team had several projects underway with code names like Polaris, Socrates, and Plato. I asked Slava how did you decide on the name Aris? The answer: Socrates was the tutor of the famous Greek philosopher Plato, and Plato's pupil was Aristotle. Given that the word Aris is also part of the name Polaris, the name resonated with everyone on the team and our leadership.

Since integration for Big Data implied *something* to do with Hadoop, Travis spent several meetings with the team that brought Polybase to SQL Server 2016 and Azure Data Warehouse. The vision of Polybase was to allow SQL Server users to query (and ingest) data from a Hadoop system all through the T-SQL language so familiar to our existing customers. Furthermore, instead of just building a simple data extract system, Polybase could use the power of distributed computing that exists with Azure Data Warehouse and Analytics Platform System (formerly known as Parallel Data Warehouse) to *push down* computations and partition query processing to achieve scalable performance against large datasets in the target Hadoop system. I never really saw Polybase take off in SQL Server 2016 and 2017, since integrating Big Data Hadoop systems with relational systems like SQL Server was not easy. Polybase requires a significant amount of installation and configuration, and security models differ from Hadoop systems and SQL Server. In addition, the pushdown computation implementation relied on a concept called MapReduce, requiring Java to be installed on the same computer as SQL Server and Polybase services. Still, the architecture and the concepts for integrated SQL Server and Big Data systems were available to build something bigger (including a T-SQL extension called EXTERNAL TABLE). If we could simplify the deployment and configuration story for Polybase, and add in more data source support, it might become more adopted in the industry. Furthermore, Travis came to learn very quickly that, if you wanted to be taken seriously in the Big Data world of data processing, you needed to consider another technology called *Spark*.

Armed with this knowledge, Slava, Travis, and a core set of members of the team that built SQL Server on Linux had a goal to build a prototype of SQL Server integration with Big Data including Spark. They embarked on a multi-day huddle in a big conference room and dubbed it the "Aris Hackathon." Those team members were Slava Oks, Travis Wright, Scott Konersmann, Stuart Padley, Michael Nelson, Pranjal Gupta, Jarupat Jisarojito, Weiyun Huang, George Reynya, David Kryze, Umachandar Jayachandran (UC), and Sahaj Saini. By the time they were done, they had a working *cluster* that combined the existing Polybase functionality of SQL Server with Spark. Figure 1-1 shows a rough diagram of the cluster the team built.

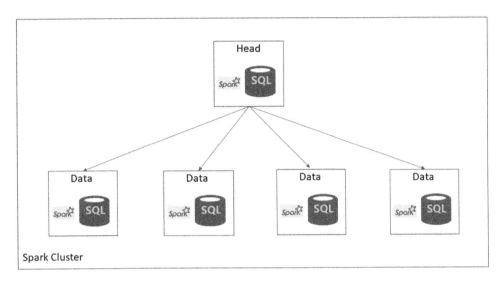

Figure 1-1. *The first Aris cluster*

In the prototype, they built a Hadoop cluster including components for Apache
Spark and HDFS, but also combined with SQL Server Polybase. They used Spark to
stream data into the *Data* nodes and then used Polybase to join data in the Head node in
SQL Server with the data ingested with Spark into HDFS. The idea behind the prototype
was to prove they could integrate Spark, Hadoop, and SQL Server together.

Around this same time, Travis had been talking to engineers who had joined
the team from a company Microsoft had acquired, called Metanautix. As part of this
acquisition, our team had technology to connect to a range of data sources, through
ODBC, including ORACLE, SQL Server, Teradata, and MongoDB. The team thought
that if we could integrate this technology with the Aris project, we could build a pretty
compelling story for *Data Virtualization*. SQL Server could now be a hub for accessing
data in different data platforms and systems without having to move the data to SQL
Server (with techniques like Extract, Transform, and Load (ETL)).

Before we could deliver software that customers could use and try, we needed to
decide on a platform to run all of these components. We needed a platform that would
allow for easy deployment of all the software, including Polybase, Hadoop, and Spark;
provide manageability and security; and enable elastic scale and high availability.
Containers seemed like a logical choice given the nature of how easy they are to deploy,
and, with SQL Server 2017, we had delivered on supporting SQL Server with containers.
The next natural choice for the team was to select Kubernetes as a platform to build out
a cluster running these containers. Kubernetes was quickly gaining momentum as a

platform for distributed computing and scalable performance. Our learnings had taught us that Linux was the preferred OS to run Kubernetes and Hadoop systems, and, since SQL Server was already supported on Linux, it was a good fit to build on.

And so, in late 2017, our team embarked on the journey of building out an *Aris* cluster that would enable the vision of Data Virtualization, but integrate with Big Data technologies such as Spark and HDFS. From the very beginning, our team decided that all of this needed to "ship in the box." That is, if you bought SQL Server, we would install all of these components as part of the license (not knowing whether this would be a new edition, but all of this would be included with SQL Server). The final product as you see now with SQL Server 2019 and what we call *Big Data Clusters* has much more than the early Aris prototypes, but the vision and concepts are the same: provide an easy-to-deploy Data Virtualization platform with built-in scalable performance, security, and manageability.

Seattle Becomes SQL Server 2019

While the concept of Aris and Big Data clusters was huge, innovative, and, quite frankly, a bit scary, every major release of SQL Server includes enhancements across several areas of the platform. This includes performance, security, and availability, the three areas Conor Cunningham often refers to as "the meat and potatoes of SQL Server." Our team had also launched SQL Server on Linux with SQL Server 2017. As amazing as that product has been, there were a few features that ship with SQL Server on Windows that needed to also be added to Linux. We also knew that containers are big, and I mean big in the sense that they are a future direction to deploy and run applications, including SQL Server. So there was some work there we know we needed to do, including exploring new scenarios with Kubernetes clusters (not just the Big Data Cluster solution).

So many teams contribute to the amazing product that is SQL Server. Our Enterprise team (aka the Tiger Team) had a pile of new features they wanted in the new release with true customer value (because that is what they do!). Our friends who build new features for performance, availability, and security for Azure SQL Database wanted to see their work in Project Seattle, since the engines that run the Azure service and SQL Server are the same. As I saw this play out in 2017, I could see the momentum for a historic release.

As the calendar year of 2017 ended, we were all set up for the next release of SQL Server, SQL Server 2018. This all made sense to me. We shipped two major versions of SQL Server in back to back years, SQL Server 2016 and SQL Server 2017, so why not SQL Server 2018?

Conor Cunningham, our product and release architect, has told me that, with our agile engineering capabilities, we could ship SQL Server every month if we wanted to. And we can do it with quality. Of course, we don't do this, because we want to ship SQL Server releases that have both quality and major value for our customers. As we started moving forward into the early months of calendar year 2018, we had to decide if we wanted to ship a major new version in that year. When we looked at the landscape of capabilities that we could put into this release, including Big Data Clusters, we made the decision in the spring of 2018 that we would ship our first preview of SQL Server vNext in calendar year 2018. (When we don't know an official name to call the next release, even if we have a project name like Seattle, we call it "vNext.") And you may have noticed we often try to make announcements for major new releases at big events. Looking at the calendar, one of the biggest global customer events for Microsoft has become Microsoft Ignite (it is now in Orlando, with ~30,000 people). So in the summer of 2018, our leadership decided to launch the preview of SQL Server vNext at Microsoft Ignite and call it SQL Server 2019, meaning that we would make this release GA (which means General Availability) sometime in calendar year 2019.

This made sense to everyone on the team. It gave us more runway to land Big Data Clusters, plus more capabilities with the "core" of SQL Server all based on customer feedback and experience. My task? Take the work I had done to evangelize and showcase SQL Server 2016 and 2017 and show our customers, the industry, and community that we have truly built a *Modern Data Platform* with SQL Server 2019.

Modernizing Your Database with SQL Server 2019

Figure 1-2 is my main "pitch" diagram when I talk about SQL Server 2019. Built by one of my colleagues in Microsoft marketing, Debbi Lyons (you may have seen myself and Debbi sometimes appearing together talking SQL Server), it represents a full picture of the new Modern Data Platform of SQL Server 2019.

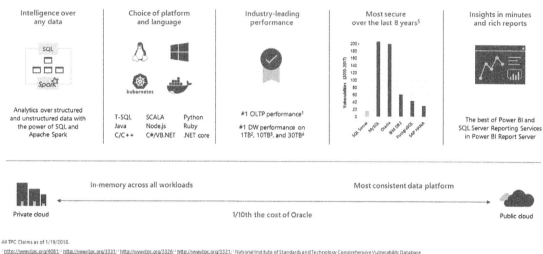

Figure 1-2. *Modernize with SQL Server 2019*

If you have ever seen me talk about SQL Server 2016 or 2017, you will notice the slide looks a bit similar, but with key differences:

- An integrated Data Virtualization solution integrating Spark, HDFS, and SQL Server in a new and innovative way (basically SQL Server "meets Big Data")

- New capabilities to continue the platform of choice value to our customers across Windows, Linux, Containers, and Kubernetes

SQL Server continues to lead the database industry in performance and is the least vulnerable data platform over the last decade. With a SQL Server license, customers have access to Business Intelligence services, such as Power BI Report Server. In addition, with the new Azure SQL Database Managed Instance service, functionality is virtually the same from SQL Server in your private cloud and Azure in the public cloud. The consistency message doesn't stop there. Your skills in T-SQL apply across SQL Server and Azure, and our tools continue to work seamlessly across SQL Server and Azure Data services.

Another set of capabilities that seems to get lost in the conversation of new features is that SQL Server (and Azure) provides in-memory features that allow you to maximize your computing resources, including In-Memory OLTP and Columnstore Indexes. All of this comes with the SQL Server 2019. Figure 1-3 is a more detailed picture of major new key functionality unique to SQL Server 2019.

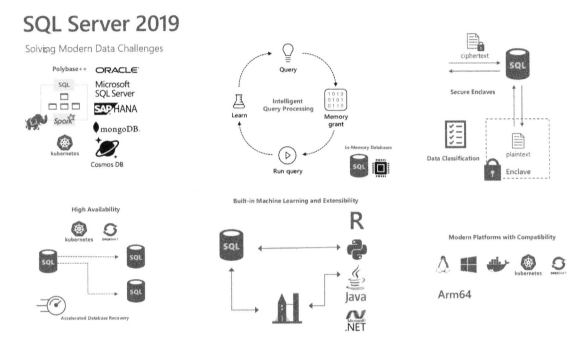

Figure 1-3. *SQL Server 2019 key functionality*

I'm going to use this diagram (going left to right, starting in the upper left-hand corner) to sketch out for you the major new features of SQL Server 2019, which will be like a blueprint for your reading for the remainder of the book. As you read through these new capabilities, keep in mind that **SQL Server powers Azure SQL Database**, which means many of the capabilities you see in this book work the same in Azure SQL Database. Furthermore, everything you see in this book can be done in Azure whether it is SQL Server in Azure Virtual Machine or containers and Kubernetes in the cloud.

Data Virtualization

Previously in this chapter, I've discussed the origins of Data Virtualization with Project Aris. SQL Server 2019 is the realization of that vision with two specific capabilities:

- **Polybase in SQL Server 2019**

  I call this Polybase++ because we have extended the functionality of Polybase that shipped with SQL Server 2016 (for more info on Polybase, see `https://docs.microsoft.com/en-us/sql/ relational-databases/polybase/polybase-guide?view=sql- server-2017`) to provide different data source connectors including Oracle, SQL Server, MongoDB (CosmosDB), and Teradata. And you can connect to these data sources without installing any client software; SQL Server has what you need built-in. In addition, you can connect to other sources such as SAP HANA by installing your own ODBC driver. I'll cover the new Polybase in SQL Server 2019 in Chapter 9.

- **Big Data Clusters**

  As I described our vision for Project Aris earlier in the chapter, we decided to build a complete solution that deploys SQL Server with the new Polybase functionality, HDFS, Spark, and other components for management, security, and availability. There is so much more to this than I can describe here, so read more on Big Data Clusters in Chapter 10.

Note   I originally wanted to come right out in the second and third chapters of this book on these topics. However, I later decided that if you need some more information about containers and Kubernetes, it would help to put those chapters ahead of this topic. So, instead, I'll "go out with a bang" with this new innovation in the book. If you can't help yourself, dive right into Chapter 9.

Performance

We always work on performance in any SQL Server release. Always. However, just making your queries run fast is not enough. We need to keep making the SQL Server engine smarter and more intelligent, adapting to your workload, hardware investments, and complex query patterns. Chapter 2 has a complete look at performance capabilities of SQL Server 2019 including but not limited to

- *Intelligent Query Processing*, which is an extension to Adaptive Query Processing introduced in SQL Server 2017.

- Query plan *insights anywhere and anytime* you need it with Lightweight Query Profiling, Last Execution Plan, and Query Store enhancements.

- A family of capabilities to provide a true *in-memory database* including enlightened I/O and Hybrid Buffer Pool for persistent memory and memory-optimized tempdb schema. Combining these technologies with our built-in Columnstore Indexes and In-Memory OLTP provides a compelling in-memory database solution.

Security

SQL Server is not only the least vulnerable database product in the industry over the last decade, but includes a wide range of features and tools to meet the modern security needs of any business. This includes the following enhancements for SQL Server 2019:

- **Always Encrypted with Secure Enclaves**

  SQL Server 2016 introduced a new end-to-end security system for data applications called *Always Encrypted*. While this system provides for encryption at rest, in-memory, and across the network, there were a few limitations, most importantly *rich computing*. In Chapter 3, I'll talk about how Always Encrypted, using a concept called *Secure Enclaves*, enables rich computing and other interesting security scenarios.

- **Data Classification and Auditing built-in**

  The General Data Protection Regulation (GDPR) took effect from the European Union (EU) in May of 2018. I've talked to many customers since that time based in the EU and companies that do business with EU customers. Our new Data Classification and Auditing built-in features, combined with our tools, can be very helpful for compliance scenarios such as GDPR and others your business may need to handle.

I'll cover these new features and more for security in Chapter 3.

Mission-Critical Availability

It is one thing to be fast and secure, but customers that rely on SQL Server to run their business need their data platform to be available all the time. SQL Server 2019 includes new capabilities to meet your highly available data needs, including

- Resumable Online Create Index and Clustered Columnstore Online Create Index to help complete the online index availability story.

- Enhances to our flagship HADR feature, Always On Availability Groups, including increase in number of replicas and primary connection redirection.

- Imagine a world where transaction rollback happens immediately, and recovery and log truncation are not dependent on large or long-running transactions. Welcome to the new world of Accelerated Database Recovery!

I'll talk more about these and other mission-critical availability solutions in Chapter 4.

Modern Development Platform

So far, I'm sure all the new things I've talked about that are coming in SQL Server 2019 seem targeted only at DBAs or IT Professionals. We definitely believe that developers are important to the success of SQL Server, so we have also invested in these new features:

- In SQL Server 2016, we introduced a new platform for in-database Machine Learning with a language called R. In SQL Server 2017, we enhanced this model by allowing for Python programs. Using this same infrastructure, we now allow developers to extend the T-SQL language using Java classes. In fact, we have built an extensibility SDK to allow other languages to be part of the SQL Server story.

- We have extended the capabilities on graph database, which was first introduced in SQL Server 2017, with new features like edge constraints and MERGE support.

- We want developers to use Unicode data types, so we have added new UTF-8 collations that can help developers manage UTF-8 data without the overhead of Unicode data types.

I'll talk more about developer-focused features in SQL Server 2019 in Chapter 5.

Investing in the Platform of Your Choice

We cranked out SQL Server on Linux in SQL Server 2017, but we had a few features on the "edge" of the engine that did not make that release. We want our users to have complete choice of what operating system to run SQL Server without worrying about features or compatibility. We have improved that now in SQL Server 2019 by adding Replication, Change Data Capture (CDC), Distributed Transactions (DTC), Machine Learning, and Polybase to SQL Server on Linux.

We also have made investments with containers including a new container registry, support for Red Hat Enterprise Linux (RHEL), and continued support for Kubernetes including OpenShift. And though not covered in this book, we have expanded the platforms for SQL Server when we announced preview support in May of 2019 for Arm processors with Azure SQL Database Edge. You can read more about Azure SQL Database Edge at `https://azure.microsoft.com/en-us/services/sql-database-edge/`.

You should stop and consider all of these platform icons, because SQL Server is not just a platform of choice. It is a *platform of choice with compatibility*. You can back up a database on any of these platforms and restore it to any of these platforms unchanged.

I'll spend time diving into SQL Server on Linux enhancements, SQL Server containers, and SQL Server on Kubernetes in Chapters 6, 7, and 8 in the book.

In addition to these major areas of investment for SQL Server 2019, there are other innovations worth calling out.

Azure Data Studio

SQL Server Management Studio (SSMS) has been the stalwart graphical user interface for SQL Server for many years. Last year we embarked on building a new tool for data exploration, extensibility, and new experiences called SQL Operations Studio. In September of 2018, we officially launched this tool and called it Azure Data Studio (ADS).

Azure Data Studio has some innovative new technology including Notebooks, Big Data Cluster deployment, External Data Wizards, and exploration of SQL Server, HDFS, and other Azure Data Services.

There is no specific chapter dedicated to Azure Data Studio. Instead you will see me use this tool (along with SSMS and others) throughout the chapters of this book.

Voice of the Customer

Having a background in customer support, I'm always interested to see our engineering team include features into new releases that can be tied to direct customer feedback or trends of support issues with our CSS team.

This release is no different and includes a series of enhancements to the database engine, including but not limited to

- A better string truncation error message with actionable context. It has been the #1 voted customer request with 1000s of votes.

- New dynamic management objects to gain insights into the internals of database page headers (yes, you too can be Paul Randal). These statements can help troubleshoot page latch contention issues.

- Scalability improvements in the engine including concurrent PFS updates, parallel bulk insert, and indirect checkpoint.

I'll show you more details about this collection of enhancements in Chapter 11.

As you look at the rest of the book, the chapters are fairly independent of each other. However, I highly recommend you first read Chapters 7 and 8 as foundational information before diving into Chapters 9 and 10 on Data Virtualization and Big Data Clusters.

Getting Started with SQL Server 2019

Here are some resources to help you deploy and configure SQL Server 2019 as you prepare to learn new features and try examples in the remaining chapters of this book.

Download SQL Server 2019

To download and try out SQL Server 2019, go to `www.microsoft.com/en-us/sql-server/sql-server-2019#Install`.

Deploy SQL Server 2019

For instructions on how to deploy SQL Server 2019 on Windows, go to `https://docs.microsoft.com/en-us/sql/database-engine/install-windows/installation-for-sql-server?view=sql-server-ver15`.

For SQL Server 2019 on Linux, go to `https://docs.microsoft.com/en-us/sql/linux/sql-server-linux-overview?view=sql-server-ver15`.

To learn how to deploy SQL Server in a Container, go to `https://docs.microsoft.com/en-us/sql/linux/quickstart-install-connect-docker?view=sql-server-linux-ver15&pivots=cs1-bash`.

Migrate to SQL Server 2019

Chapter 11 will include a discussion about migration and tools to support migration to Server 2019 from previous releases of SQL Server and other vendor database products.

What's New in SQL Server 2019

Learn all the new feature specifics about SQL Server 2019 at `https://docs.microsoft.com/en-us/sql/sql-server/what-s-new-in-sql-server-ver15?view=sqlallproducts-allversions`.

Download Book Code and Sample Databases

To be able to work with all of the examples in this book, you will want to clone the GitHub repo for the book as discussed in the book introduction.

Tip   Windows users, be sure to use the following git syntax to clone the repo to avoid any issues with CRLF for Linux scripts:

```
git clone --config core.autocrlf=false https://github.com/
microsoft/sqlworkshops.git
```

In addition, you will want to download the sample databases WideWorldImporters from `https://github.com/Microsoft/sql-server-samples/releases/tag/wide-world-importers-v1.0` and WideWorldImportersDW from `https://github.com/Microsoft/sql-server-samples/releases/download/wide-world-importers-v1.0/WideWorldImportersDW-Full.bak`. The code for the book has examples on how to restore the backup on Windows, Linux, Containers, and Kubernetes.

SQL Server Workshops

Even though I include many hands-on exercises in this book, go to `http://aka.ms/sqlworkshops` to find more free related training about SQL Server (my friend and colleague Buck Woody, who is one of the finest trainers I know, is the brainchild behind this site).

It Is Your Grandpa's SQL Server?

I enjoyed authoring this book not just because I like the technology (OK I'm biased about SQL Server) but also because our engineering team is innovating at speeds not seen by any other competitive data product or platform in the industry. And let's admit, it's fun to learn new things.

Perhaps this quote from *ITProToday* magazine says it best: "I never expected a day I'd be discussing release features of Microsoft SQL Server in the same sentence as Linux, Oracle and Apache Spark, but it's a brave new world. Microsoft's SQL Server development is moving at a pace none of its competitors is matching" (`www.itprotoday.com/sql-server/polybase-expansion-big-clusters-are-key-features-new-sql-server-2019`).

I remember my colleague Travis Wright saying about SQL Server 2019, "This is not your Grandpa's SQL Server." This is because the product has evolved from a powerful relational database engine to now include technologies like Spark, HDFS, Notebooks, Polybase, R, Python, Java, Linux, containers, and Kubernetes all as part of the product, truly a Modern Data Platform.

I remember putting this quote on Twitter. My colleague Pedro Lopes saw this and commented that SQL Server 2019 really is your grandpa's SQL Server. So who is right? They both are. SQL Server 2019 is still the incredible database engine you know and love, with scalable performance, mission-critical security, and high availability. And you will see in this book enhancements to all these core areas. But SQL Server 2019 is so much more. One of the most popular database platforms on the planet and the newest kid on the block. You can be both. Welcome to SQL Server 2019.

CHAPTER 2

Intelligent Performance

SQL Server Performance is critical to the operations of any data platform. This chapter is packed with information about how SQL Server 2019 can help you gain query performance with no application changes. This is one of the longest chapters in the book with plenty of examples so strap in and grab your favorite coffee.

Why Intelligent Performance?

To me, the most important takeaway from this book is ***why*** new capabilities in SQL Server 2019 can benefit you or solve a particular problem or challenge. For performance, the theme is to help you increase the performance of your workloads, often ***without*** making any application or query changes.

In September of 2018, I was preparing for a presentation at the Microsoft Ignite conference in Orlando, Florida. Up to this point in the year, everyone had only known our plans for SQL vNext at a high level. My colleague, Amit Banerjee, and I had the task of presenting the launch of SQL Server 2019 Preview at Ignite. As we were building out this deck, we knew we needed to showcase our new enhancements for performance. Amit had an idea for a new term, *Intelligent Database*. The idea was that SQL Server is building capabilities that include intelligence into the engine to detect, adapt, and provide insight like never before.

I've taken that same term and focused it more on performance to call it *Intelligent Performance*. This includes the following new enhancements in SQL Server 2019:

- Intelligent Query Processing

- Lightweight Query Profiling

- In-Memory Database

- Last-Page Insert Contention

© Bob Ward 2019
B. Ward, *SQL Server 2019 Revealed*, https://doi.org/10.1007/978-1-4842-5419-6_2

Each of these areas contains built-in intelligence in the SQL Server engine to help you get better performance out of your systems, in many cases without any changes at all. In some cases, SQL Server provides you insights into query performance at a level never seen before. In other situations, SQL Server has built-in capabilities to automatically take advantage of new innovations in hardware.

When you create a book, you make all types of decisions. One of them is how to organize your chapters. This chapter is very long, mostly due to examples that include many visuals. I'm a visual person, so I thought that would be a good way to show you these new features. Each section of this chapter is itself its own chapter, and you can treat it that way. I decided to include all of them in one single chapter because I wanted you to see all of the details and the sheer vastness of Intelligent Performance in SQL Server 2019.

Each section of the chapter lists the prerequisites to run any of the examples. At a high level, you are going to need

- An installation of SQL Server 2019 on Windows or Linux

- SQL Server Management Studio (SSMS) 18.0 or later

- Azure Data Studio (any OS, but the minimum version you need is 1.7.0)

Many of the examples use SSMS to view query plans, but, as you go through these examples, you can use Azure Data Studio as well (you will just need to look at the plan XML) using the new SentryOne Plan Explorer extension. Read more about this extension at `https://cloudblogs.microsoft.com/sqlserver/2019/07/11/the-july-release-of-azure-data-studio-is-now-available`.

Intelligent Query Processing

In SQL Server 2014, our engineering team made a bold decision to introduce a new set of code for the query processor within the engine that makes decisions for cardinality estimation (CE). The new "CE model" would take effect if a database used a compatibility level of 120 or later (120 is the default for SQL Server 2014). You can read all the gory details of how this works and why we made this change in our documentation at `https://docs.microsoft.com/en-us/sql/relational-databases/performance/cardinality-estimation-sql-server`.

Many have debated whether this was the right decision. One issue with the approach is that it was a broad, inflexible change. As the team was finishing SQL Server 2016 and planning SQL Server 2017, they all agreed we needed a new way to build query processing functionality. As Joe Sack, one of the lead program managers for the Query Processor (QP), tells it, "The team realized that doing one-size-fits-all changes isn't what we should do moving forward. Rather – we need to invest in features that can adapt to the vast array of customer workloads in the SQL Server ecosystem (big, small, OLTP, Hybrid, DW)."

Thus was born a new *feature family* of enhancements in SQL Server 2017 called **Adaptive Query Processing (AQP)**. The concept was to build into the query processor the ability to *adapt* as a query executed (or before it executed *again*) to provide faster execution, without any user intervention or application changes.

Note   You can see examples of SQL Server 2017 and AQP at `https://github.com/Microsoft/bobsql/tree/master/demos/sqlserver/aqp`.

As the team shipped SQL Server 2017 and AQP, they were already backlogged with new things they had wanted to put in AQP but ran out of time. They started putting new features to enhance AQP in Azure SQL Server Database, with plans to roll them into SQL Server 2019. Furthermore, the word *adaptive* didn't really reflect the vision of the work the team was producing. The SQL Server query processor has, for years, been pretty smart – using a sophisticated set of cost-based algorithms to make plan decisions. But the team wanted more; they wanted the QP to exhibit more intelligence. Thus, the name Intelligent Query Processing stuck.

Figure 2-1 shows this *family tree* of QP capabilities that includes both SQL Server 2017 and 2019.

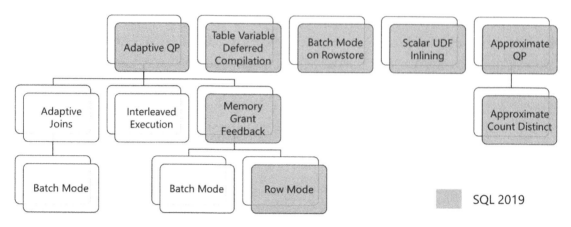

Figure 2-1. *Intelligent Query Processing family tree*

Let's take a look at each new capability you see in gray in Figure 2-1, with examples of how each works. It is so important to keep in mind as you read through this section that we built these capabilities **so you don't have to know about them**. In time, if we have done our job well, Intelligent Query Processing is "just" the query processor, and you as an application developer, DBA, or data professional are just used to an engine that is flexible, intelligent, and adaptive to your workload. You can see all the capabilities of Adaptive Query Processing as part of the new documentation on IQP at https://docs. microsoft.com/en-us/sql/relational-databases/performance/intelligent-query-processing.

Note   In all scenarios except for Approximate Count Distinct, you can enable the capabilities of Intelligent Query Processing by changing the database compatibility level of the database to 150. Approximate Count Distinct is a T-SQL function that is new to SQL Server 2019 and does not require a database compatibility level of 150.

Prerequisites for Using the Examples for Intelligent Query Processing

While many workloads will see benefits from Intelligent Query Processing (IQP), it is easy to demonstrate the performance benefits of IQP with larger datasets and databases designed for analytic queries. Therefore, for examples in this chapter, you will use the **WideWorldImportersDW** example database (you can read more about this database and its schema at `https://docs.microsoft.com/en-us/sql/samples/wide-world-importers-dw-database-catalog`).

These examples will work on SQL Server 2019 on Windows, Linux, and Containers. Given the large dataset, SQL Server is going to need at least 12Gb RAM to properly see performance differences. In addition, some of the query examples use parallelism, so installing SQL Server on a multiprocessor system is preferred.

All the scripts used for this chapter can be found on the GitHub repo under the **ch2_intelligent_performance\iqp** directory.

Complete credit to my colleague at Microsoft, Joe Sack, for all of these examples including how to extend out the WideWorldImportersDW database. These examples were modified based on Joe's GitHub repo at `https://github.com/joesackmsft/Conferences/tree/master/IQPDemos`.

In order to use the examples in this chapter, you need to go through the following steps:

1. Download the WideWorldImportersDW database backup from `https://github.com/Microsoft/sql-server-samples/releases/download/wide-world-importers-v1.0/WideWorldImportersDW-Full.bak`.

2. Restore this database to your SQL Server 2019 instance. You can use the provided **restorewwidw.sql** script. You may need to change the directory paths for the location of your backup and where you will restore the database files.

3. In order to run some of the examples, you will need larger tables than what is installed by default in WideWorldImportersDW and that are not using columnstore. Therefore, run the script **extendwwidw.sql** to create two large tables. Extending this database will increase its size, including the transaction log, to about 8Gb overall. One of these tables is called **Fact.OrderHistory**. Based on the Orders table, we will make this table much larger and not use a columnstore index. We will create another table called **Fact.OrderHistoryExtended**. This will be based on Fact. OrderHistory but will have even more rows.

Almost all the examples come with two methods:

- A set of T-SQL scripts you can use with any tool like SQL Server Management Studio, Azure Data Studio, or sqlcmd.

- A T-SQL notebook that requires Azure Data Studio. Take a close look on how to run notebooks with Azure Data Studio at `https://docs.microsoft.com/en-us/sql/azure-data-studio/sql-notebooks`.

One example requires a Windows client, as it uses the famous ostress.exe tool. Details of how to install and use ostress.exe are provided in the section "Memory Grant Feedback Row Mode." I've built all the scripts assuming you will run them as a sysadmin (I used the sa login). In normal practice, you would create other logins to use SQL Server, but I wanted to simplify examples – so just use a login with sysadmin permissions.

Memory Grant Feedback Row Mode

Before joining the SQL Server engineering team, I had a long career at Microsoft in technical support. One of the toughest problems I've seen customers face when it comes to performance is problems with *memory grants*. What is a memory grant?

SQL Server allocates memory for all kinds of reasons. When SQL Server executes a query, memory may be used to cache buffers associated with pages belonging to indexes or tables in the query. In most SQL Server instances that have been up and running, the buffer pool may be already in allocated memory so bringing in pages doesn't require additional memory.

Some query operations are intensive and require some type of temporary area to store data. Two such operations are *hash joins* (or even just hash operators) and *sorts*. To perform a hash join, SQL Server effectively has to build a mini-table in memory in order to perform the operation. Any type of data sort can require some type of array or structure to sort data. SQL Server has to have some place to perform these operations so it allocates memory outside the buffer pool. The process for allocating this memory by the query execution engine is called a memory grant.

Sounds simple enough. Here is the problem: Memory grants are based on what the optimizer knows about the query plan as it is first being executed. And the "what" for these decisions usually comes down to cardinality estimation or unique number of rows for an operation. If SQL Server thinks a sort operation as part of a query plan will be on data columns that are 100 bytes in total but with an estimated 1 billion rows, it must acquire a memory grant enough to allocate memory to sort that many rows of data of that size. The same type of concept applies for a hash operator.

Tip   There is a very old blog by the SQL Server engineering team explaining memory grants. I recommend you stop and read through this to understand more of the concepts and details. You can read the blog at `https://blogs.msdn.microsoft.com/sqlqueryprocessing/2010/02/16/understanding-sql-server-memory-grant/`.

In many scenarios, this system works just fine, and no noticeable issues can occur. However, what if the memory grants are based on cardinality estimates that are not accurate?

Two types of problems can occur:

- The memory grant can be *too small for what is really needed*, resulting in the infamous and painful "tempdb spill." SQL Server will not allow a hash join operator or sort to get all the memory it wants. If the memory request is too large (we don't document what is too large, because we might change it, and wouldn't want you to rely on it), the current allocated memory must be saved. Saved where? You guessed it… tempdb. Think of this like a paging system much like the how operating system pages memory when physical RAM is exhausted.

- The memory grant is *too large for what is really needed*. This could squeeze memory pressure for other parts of the SQL Server engine, but what is more likely is multiple users run queries that have *excessive* memory grants, and SQL Server will throttle queries. The result is some users experience bottlenecks on a wait_type called RESOURCE_SEMAPHORE.

Both of these problems can lead to performance problems. In SQL Server 2017, we introduced a concept called *memory grant feedback* for batch mode. This feature is a perfect example of *adapting*. When a query has completed execution, SQL Server knows how much memory was used for a grant vs. what was originally requested. If the memory used was far less than what was granted, why keep asking for too much memory the next time the same cached plan is executed? Same goes for if the memory used was far greater than the requested original grant. Why keep spilling to tempdb for a cached query plan over and over?

Memory grant feedback solves this problem by storing information in the cached query plan for what the correct memory grant should be for future executions. To the user, it feels like SQL Server *healed itself*. This feature was great for SQL Server 2017, but only for batch mode operations, which meant it only worked for columnstore index operations. As you will learn in a later section of this chapter titled "Batch Mode on Rowstore," SQL Server supports batch mode operations on more than just columnstore. However, why not support memory grant feedback even when batch mode is not used?

The result is an adaptive SQL Server engine for memory grant scenarios no matter what type of table or index is being used.

Enabling memory grant feedback row mode is as simple as changing the database compatibility level (dbcompat) to 150.

You can disable or enable memory grant feedback row mode even with dbcompat at 150 using the ROW_MODE_MEMORY_GRANT_FEEDBACK option for ALTER DATABASE SCOPED CONFIGURATION. You can also disable this feature at the query level using the DISABLE_ROW_MODE_MEMORY_GRANT_FEEDBACK query option. You can read examples of how to set these options at `https://docs.microsoft.com/ en-us/sql/relational-databases/performance/intelligent-query-processing? #row-mode-memory-grant-feedback`.

Underestimated Memory Grant

Let's look at some examples. Let's first look at a scenario where a memory grant is too small for the actual memory used, resulting in a spill to tempdb. All the scripts used in these examples can be found in the **ch2_intelligent_performance\iqp\rowmodemgf** directory. There are two ways to run the examples for this scenario:

- Use the T-SQL script **iqp_rowmodemfg.sql**.

- Use the T-SQL notebook in Azure Data Studio called **iqp_ rowmodemfg.ipynb**.

Let's use the T-SQL script **iqp_rowmodemfg.sql** in a step-by-step fashion. I'll use SQL Server Management Studio to explain query plan differences, but you can use any tool that can show the query plan. There are comments in the T-SQL script for each step of the example.

1. **Step 1** says to change the database compatibility level to 150, clear the procedure cache, and *warm* the buffer pool with pages from a table called Fact.OrderHistory in the WideWorldImportersDW database. Dbcompat of 150 is needed to enable memory grant feedback for rowstore. Clearing the procedure cache is just a step to ensure we are "starting clean." (Note the use of the ALTER DATABASE option to clear the procedure cache just for this database. This option is very nice!) Pulling in the pages from disk for the Fact.OrderHistory table is done just to ensure the comparison of query performance with and without memory grant feedback is a "fair fight."

```
-- Step 1: Make sure this database is in compatibility
level 150 and clear procedure cache for this database. Also
bring the table into cache to compare warm cache queries
USE [WideWorldImportersDW]
GO
ALTER DATABASE [WideWorldImportersDW] SET COMPATIBILITY_
LEVEL = 150
GO
ALTER DATABASE SCOPED CONFIGURATION CLEAR PROCEDURE_CACHE
GO
SELECT COUNT(*) FROM [Fact].[OrderHistory]
GO
```

2. **Step 2** is all about setting up conditions for an *underestimation* of a memory grant. I'll show you a trick on how to simulate this. The T-SQL UPDATE STATISTICS command has a special option to force a specific row or page count that is stored in the statistics information. You would never want to use this option normally. In fact, in the documentation of the UPDATE STATISTICS command at https://docs.microsoft.com/en-us/sql/t-sql/statements/ update-statistics-transact-sql, it says about this option, "Identified for informational purposes only. Not supported.

Future compatibility is not guaranteed." So this option is only for the purposes of this demonstration. In this case, let's force the cardinality of the statistics of this table to 1000 rows:

```
-- Step 2: Simulate statistics out of date
UPDATE STATISTICS Fact.OrderHistory
WITH ROWCOUNT = 1000
GO
```

This table actually has 3702592 rows; forcing the statistics to believe it has 1000 rows simulates a scenario where the statistics are not in sync with the actual data in the table.

3. On to **Step 3**. Now it is time to run a query using the Fact. OrderHistory table.

```
-- Step 3: Run a query to get order and stock item data
-- DO NOT select the comments here to run the query!
SELECT fo.[Order Key], fo.Description, si.[Lead Time Days]
FROM  Fact.OrderHistory AS fo
INNER HASH JOIN Dimension.[Stock Item] AS si
ON fo.[Stock Item Key] = si.[Stock Item Key]
WHERE fo.[Lineage Key] = 9
AND si.[Lead Time Days] > 19
GO
```

The query attempts to get Order and Stock Item data. Notice the use of HASH JOIN in the T-SQL syntax to force the optimizer to use a hash join. This is a simple way for demonstration purposes to induce a hash join into the query with an underestimated number of rows. I included the comments here, but it is critical **you do not execute this T-SQL fragment with the comments**. This burned me when I first started building these demos. Comments "count" when it comes to uniquely identifying a query to match a cached plan. If the next execution of the query doesn't have the same comments, the queries will not be reused. In SSMS, select the option for **Include Actual Execution Plan** (you can use Ctrl+M to enable) before executing the query. This documentation

page describes how to enable this, `https://docs.microsoft.`
`com/en-us/sql/relational-databases/performance/display-`
`an-actual-execution-plan.`

```
-- Step 3: Run a query to get order and stock item data
-- DO NOT select the comments here to run the query!
SELECT fo.[Order Key], fo.Description, si.[Lead Time Days]
FROM  Fact.OrderHistory AS fo
INNER HASH JOIN Dimension.[Stock Item] AS si
ON fo.[Stock Item Key] = si.[Stock Item Key]
WHERE fo.[Lineage Key] = 9
AND si.[Lead Time Days] > 19
GO
```

This query should take at least 30 seconds to run and returns about 66K rows (your mileage may vary). Using the SSMS option to view the execution plan, it should look something like Figure 2-2.

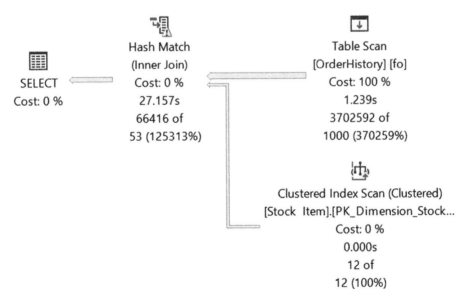

Figure 2-2. *Query plan for underestimated memory grant*

Using this plan, there are several details to observe. In SSMS, if you move your cursor over the Table Scan operator, it should look something like Figure 2-3. Notice the Estimated Number of Rows is way off the actual rows read for the scan.

Table Scan

Scan rows from a table.

Physical Operation	Table Scan
Logical Operation	Table Scan
Actual Execution Mode	Row
Estimated Execution Mode	Row
Storage	RowStore
Number of Rows Read	3702592
Actual Number of Rows	3702592
Actual Number of Batches	0
Estimated I/O Cost	69.9468
Estimated Operator Cost	69.9481 (100%)
Estimated CPU Cost	0.001257
Estimated Subtree Cost	69.9481
Number of Executions	1
Estimated Number of Executions	1
Estimated Number of Rows	1000
Estimated Number of Rows to be Read	1000
Estimated Row Size	127 B
Actual Rebinds	0
Actual Rewinds	0
Ordered	False
Node ID	1

Predicate
[wideworldimportersdw].[Fact].[OrderHistory].[Lineage Key]
as [fo].[Lineage Key]=(9)
Object
[wideworldimportersdw].[Fact].[OrderHistory] [fo]
Output List
[wideworldimportersdw].[Fact].[OrderHistory].Order Key,
[wideworldimportersdw].[Fact].[OrderHistory].Stock Item
Key, [wideworldimportersdw].[Fact].
[OrderHistory].Description

Figure 2-3. *Estimates vs. actuals for the Fact.OrderHistory table scan*

In this case, the Fact.OrderHistory table is the *build input* into a hash join. SQL Server will request a memory grant for the hash join based on this build input. This is a problem since the memory grant is based on the estimate which is only 1000 rows. Use the cursor to move over the Hash Join, which has a small warning icon with it, and notice the warning about a spill as seen in Figure 2-4.

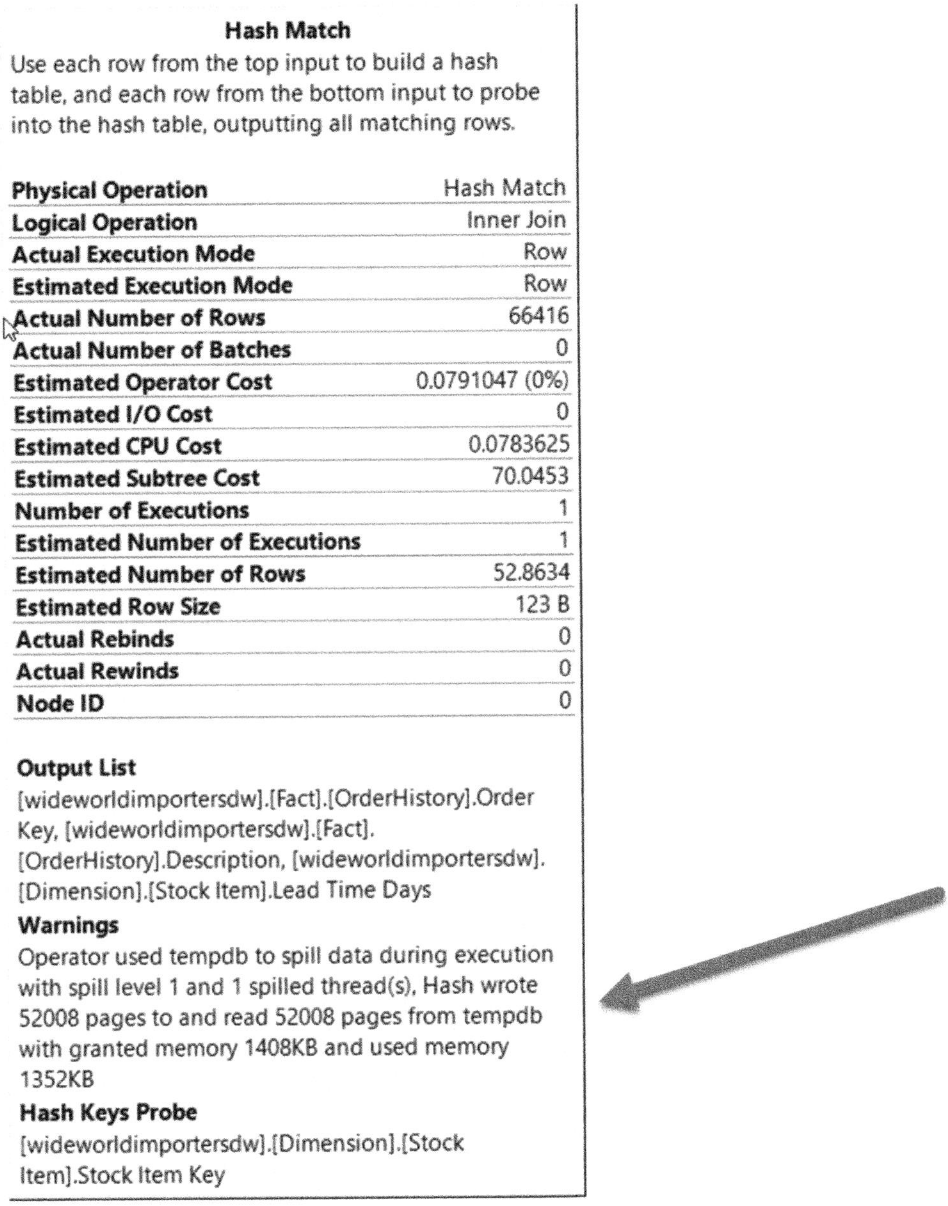

Hash Match

Use each row from the top input to build a hash table, and each row from the bottom input to probe into the hash table, outputting all matching rows.

Physical Operation	Hash Match
Logical Operation	Inner Join
Actual Execution Mode	Row
Estimated Execution Mode	Row
Actual Number of Rows	66416
Actual Number of Batches	0
Estimated Operator Cost	0.0791047 (0%)
Estimated I/O Cost	0
Estimated CPU Cost	0.0783625
Estimated Subtree Cost	70.0453
Number of Executions	1
Estimated Number of Executions	1
Estimated Number of Rows	52.8634
Estimated Row Size	123 B
Actual Rebinds	0
Actual Rewinds	0
Node ID	0

Output List

[wideworldimportersdw].[Fact].[OrderHistory].Order Key, [wideworldimportersdw].[Fact]. [OrderHistory].Description, [wideworldimportersdw]. [Dimension].[Stock Item].Lead Time Days

Warnings

Operator used tempdb to spill data during execution with spill level 1 and 1 spilled thread(s), Hash wrote 52008 pages to and read 52008 pages from tempdb with granted memory 1408KB and used memory 1352KB

Hash Keys Probe

[wideworldimportersdw].[Dimension].[Stock Item].Stock Item Key

Figure 2-4. *Hash join tempdb spill*

Notice the numbers from the warning. 52008 pages (8K per page) is ~426Mb of data I/O to tempdb files. Spills are really ugly because this is not data placed into a buffer pool page associated to tempdb. Tempdb data files become the *paging file* for memory grants for hash joins (these are not tempdb pages for temporary tables. This is yet another reason why I often call tempdb the garbage dump of SQL Server).

Tip   Want to know how a hash join works? Read this older yet classic blog post from one of our top Query Processor team engineers, the one and only Craig Freedman: `https://blogs.msdn.microsoft.com/craigfr/2006/08/10/hash-join/`.

Moving to the left in the query plan, move the cursor over the SELECT operator. In this operator are the details of the amount of memory grant for the query plan. Figure 2-5 shows ~1.4Mb of memory was requested for the grant for this query.

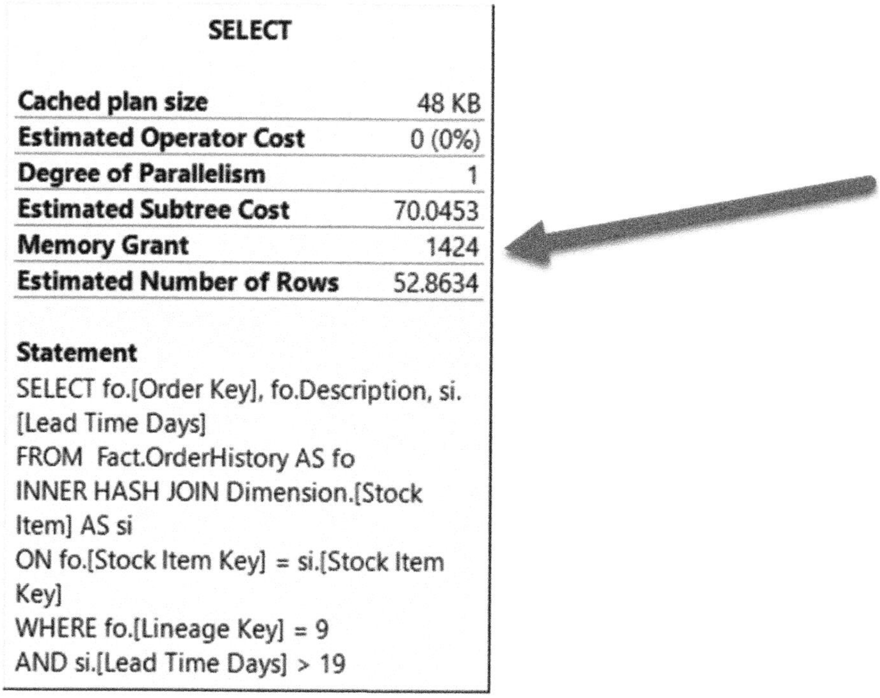

SELECT

Cached plan size	48 KB
Estimated Operator Cost	0 (0%)
Degree of Parallelism	1
Estimated Subtree Cost	70.0453
Memory Grant	1424
Estimated Number of Rows	52.8634

Statement
SELECT fo.[Order Key], fo.Description, si.[Lead Time Days]
FROM Fact.OrderHistory AS fo
INNER HASH JOIN Dimension.[Stock Item] AS si
ON fo.[Stock Item Key] = si.[Stock Item Key]
WHERE fo.[Lineage Key] = 9
AND si.[Lead Time Days] > 19

Figure 2-5. The SELECT operator showing memory grant requested

1.4Mb memory grant requested is not near enough to hold what is needed which, based on the spill, is ~400Mb.

Another piece of interesting information provided in the XML execution plan is in the Properties of the plan. To see this, right-click the SELECT operator and select Properties. Expand the option called MemoryGrantInfo, which will look like Figure 2-6.

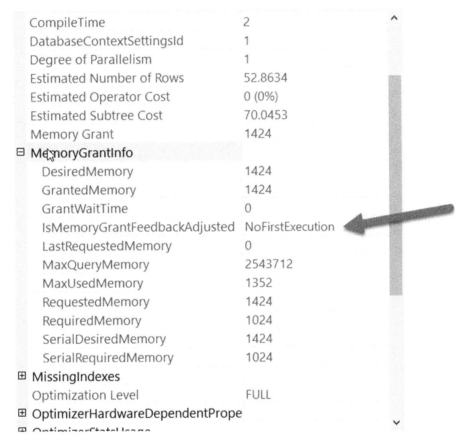

Figure 2-6. Memory grant details in the query plan properties

The most important property with respect to memory grant feedback is the field called **IsMemoryGrantFeedbackAdjusted**. The value of **NoFirstExecution** means that this is just the first execution of the query, so no feedback has been collected.

You can view the list of possible values in our documentation at `https://docs.microsoft.com/en-us/sql/relational-databases/performance/intelligent-query-processing?#row-mode-memory-grant-feedback`.

Since memory grant feedback is enabled, if the same query that is cached is executed, SQL Server will adapt and change the memory grant to accommodate the underestimation.

4. Go to **Step 4** in the script and run the same query again.
   IMPORTANT: Do not use the comments when running the query.
   Comments count when matching the exact query in plan cache.
   Be sure to keep the option in SSMS to Include Actual Execution Plan.

```
-- Step 4: Let's try this again
-- DO NOT select the comments here to run the query!
SELECT fo.[Order Key], fo.Description, si.[Lead Time Days]
FROM  Fact.OrderHistory AS fo
INNER HASH JOIN Dimension.[Stock Item] AS si
ON fo.[Stock Item Key] = si.[Stock Item Key]
WHERE fo.[Lineage Key] = 9
AND si.[Lead Time Days] > 19
GO
```

Instead of 30 seconds or more, this time the query should run in 3 seconds or less. Remember, the concept is that the plan doesn't change, so when you look at the Actual Execution Plan, it should look the same except there is no warning icon with the Hash Match Join and no spill warning. Using the cursor to move over the SELECT operator, you will see a significant difference in the memory grant as seen in Figure 2-7.

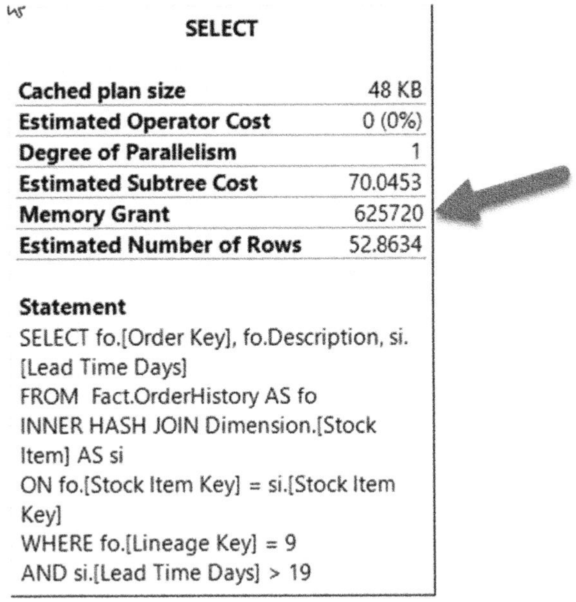

SELECT

Cached plan size	48 KB
Estimated Operator Cost	0 (0%)
Degree of Parallelism	1
Estimated Subtree Cost	70.0453
Memory Grant	625720
Estimated Number of Rows	52.8634

Statement
SELECT fo.[Order Key], fo.Description, si.
[Lead Time Days]
FROM   Fact.OrderHistory AS fo
INNER HASH JOIN Dimension.[Stock
Item] AS si
ON fo.[Stock Item Key] = si.[Stock Item
Key]
WHERE fo.[Lineage Key] = 9
AND si.[Lead Time Days] > 19

Figure 2-7.   SELECT operator showing improved memory grant.

You can see that it actually takes ~625Mb to get the correct memory grant to accommodate the Hash Join.

Right-click the SELECT operator and select Properties. The Memory Grant Feedback section now looks like Figure 2-8.

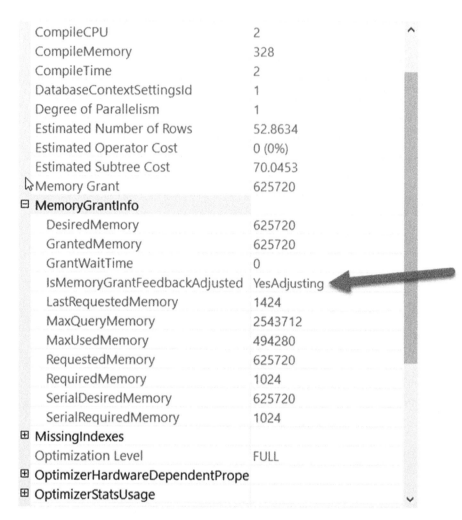

Figure 2-8. *Memory grant feedback properties after the grant is corrected*

5. We need to make sure to restore the statistics back to their original
    state by running the T-SQL for **Step 5** in the T-SQL script:

```
-- Step 5: Restore table and clustered index back to its original
state
UPDATE STATISTICS Fact.OrderHistory
WITH ROWCOUNT = 3702592;
GO
ALTER TABLE [Fact].[OrderHistory] DROP CONSTRAINT [PK_Fact_
OrderHistory]
GO
```

```
ALTER TABLE [Fact].[OrderHistory] ADD  CONSTRAINT [PK_Fact_
OrderHistory] PRIMARY KEY NONCLUSTERED
(
        [Order Key] ASC,
        [Order Date Key] ASC
)
GO
```

Excessive Memory Grant

Let's look at an example where the memory grant was too large for what memory is really needed. As I mentioned earlier, if the memory grant is very large and not what is really needed, it could be harmless – but it could also lead to unexpected memory pressure or performance problems.

This example is a little more complicated to run and requires simulation of concurrent users. Therefore, for this example, you will need the free tool called ostress, which can be downloaded at www.microsoft.com/en-us/download/details. aspx?id=4511. This tool currently requires a Windows client computer.

To see how this problem can lead to unexpected performance problems and RESOURCE_SEMAPHORE waits, use the following steps. All scripts are found in the **ch2_intelligent_performance\iqp\rowmodemgf** directory. I built all the command shell scripts to use the sa login.

1. First, we need to adjust the resource governor setting for the maximum amount of granted memory for the server by running the script **adjustrg.cmd** (which runs the T-SQL script **adjustrg. sql**). This script assumes a server name of bwsql2019 so you will need to edit this for your server. I make this adjustment in order to allow SQL Server to acquire a very large excessive grant as part of the example.

```
ALTER WORKLOAD GROUP [default]
WITH (REQUEST_MAX_MEMORY_GRANT_PERCENT = 50)
GO
ALTER RESOURCE GOVERNOR RECONFIGURE
GO
```

2. Now execute the script **turn_off_mgf.cmd** (which executes the
    T-SQL script **turn_off_mgf.sql**).

```
-- Turn off memory grant feedback
USE [WideWorldImportersDW]
GO
-- Step 2: Simulate statistics out of date
UPDATE STATISTICS Fact.OrderHistory
WITH ROWCOUNT = 5000000000
GO
ALTER DATABASE SCOPED CONFIGURATION CLEAR PROCEDURE_CACHE;
GO
ALTER DATABASE SCOPED CONFIGURATION SET ROW_MODE_MEMORY_GRANT_
FEEDBACK = OFF
GO
ALTER DATABASE SCOPED CONFIGURATION SET BATCH_MODE_MEMORY_GRANT_
FEEDBACK = OFF
GO
```

In this example script, I'll use a technique similar to the previous example for an
underestimated grant, this time changing the statistics to a number far *greater* than the
number of rows in the table.

Note   Over the years, I've seen several examples where the cardinality estimation
appears to be greater than it should be. One example is linked server queries
where there is no access to statistics for the remote data source. In these cases,
the cardinality estimates may be inaccurate and unusually large.

---

3. Now run the script **rowmode_mgf.cmd** which will run the T-SQL
    script **rowmode_mgf.sql**.

```
SELECT fo.[Order Key], fo.Description, si.[Lead Time Days]
FROM  Fact.OrderHistory AS fo
INNER JOIN Dimension.[Stock Item] AS si
ON fo.[Stock Item Key] = si.[Stock Item Key]
WHERE fo.[Lineage Key] = 9
```

```
AND si.[Lead Time Days] > 19
ORDER BY fo.[Order Key], fo.Description, si.[Lead Time Days]
OPTION (MAXDOP 1)
GO
```

This query is similar to the example from the underestimated memory grant but with an ORDER BY to add in a sort operator.

The command shell script will use ostress to run this T-SQL query with ten concurrent users, repeated ten times for each user. While this script is running, use another SQL session to run the script **dm_exec_requests.sql** to observe what type of waits queries may encounter. You will notice a significant number of waits on RESOURCE_SEMAPHORE. You can run this script repeatedly while the overall ostress script is running. These waits explain the long duration of the ostress script.

The total time of this ostress script execution should be over 40 seconds. When the script completes, your output should look like this:

```
<datetime> [0x000046CC] OSTRESS exiting normally, elapsed
time: 00:00:43.833
<datetime> [0x000046CC] RsFx I/O completion thread ended.
```

4. Execute a single query by using ***rowmode_mgf.sql*** and look at the memory grant properties of the query plan in SQL Server Management Studio. Use the same techniques as you did in the previous part of this chapter to see the Properties of the SELECT operator for the plan. Expand the ***MemoryGrantInfo*** section. The results should look similar to Figure 2-9.

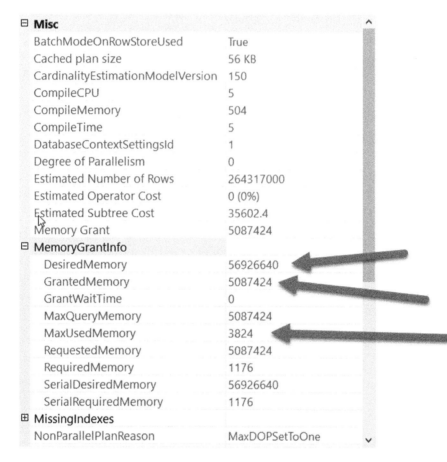

Figure 2-9. *Properties for an excessive memory grant*

Here is a description of the key properties:

DesiredMemory – This is the *ideal* memory grant based on cardinality estimates. This number is around ~56Gb. That is a crazy amount of memory!

GrantedMemory – We can't let this query have 56Gb of memory, so we only grant it around 5Gb. That is still a significant amount of memory for a grant.

MaxUsedMemory – This is the memory actually used for a grant during the query which you can see is only 3Mb. This is definitely an example of an excessive memory grant compared to what is needed.

5. Now let's turn on memory grant feedback by executing the command script **turn_on_mgf.cmd** (which runs the T-SQL script **turn_on_mgf.sql**).

6. Let's run the workload again by executing **rowmode_mgf. cmd.** The execution should complete in half the time (typically around 20 seconds). If you run **dm_exec_requests.sql** while the ostress script is running, you will see a brief blip of RESOURCE_ SEMAPHORE waits, and then it will go away because memory grant feedback has kicked in and reduced the size of the memory grant more in line with the grant actually needed for the query.

Tip   Try running rowmode_mgf.cmd a second time. Is it faster? It actually might run a bit faster now. This is because when you ran rowmode_mgf.cmd the first time, the first executions of the query were happening very quickly, and the cached plan had not been updated with the new grant. But as further executions ran, they were using the new grant. When you ran rowmode_mgf.cmd the second time, all queries were using the new memory grant.

---

7. If you look at the SELECT operator properties for the memory grant from **rowmode_mgf.sql**, you will see the memory grant numbers line up closer to what should be used for the query.

8. Restore the state of the database, table statistics, and resource governor by running the scripts **adjustrgback.cmd** and **restore_ orderhistory_state.cmd.**

Note   Even with the feedback system, in some cases, the actual needed memory grant can be very large. Large enough that concurrent users will encounter RESOURCE_SEMAPHORE waits to cause memory pressure within SQL Server. In these cases, you can use resource governor to limit the amount of memory for grants. See the documentation at `https://docs.microsoft.com/en-us/sql/t-sql/statements/create-workload-group-transact-sql` on how to change this. In SQL Server 2019, this value can now be a float value so values < 1% are valid. This could be important with systems with a large amount of memory. In addition, you can set these values at the query level. See the documentation at `https://docs.microsoft.com/en-us/sql/t-sql/queries/hints-transact-sql-query#arguments`.

This system is well designed and could really help save you time on expensive tuning for workloads requiring memory grants.

There are a few scenarios where memory grant feedback will not be enabled or will not take effect:

- There is no spill detected, or 50% of the granted memory is used.

- There is a fluctuation where the memory grant is being reduced and increased constantly.

Table Variable Deferred Compilation

When you have been at Microsoft for 26 years, you meet a lot of people. There are so many folks I've met who are smarter than me and, quite frankly, nicer than me. One of those people is Jack Li. Jack worked in CSS Technical Support with me for many years in our office in Irving, Texas. A few years back, Jack had an opportunity to work in the SQL Engineering team after I had joined. One day he humbly (as he always does) asked me whether I thought he should take the job. I didn't hesitate. I told him he had all the skills to be a top-notch developer and has a unique skill in SQL Server performance. Even though CSS lost one of their best, our engineering team gained from it.

And the first project Jack worked on in his new job was to tackle the famous problem of cardinality estimation for table variables. As long as table variables have been around, they have the inherent problem that the cardinality estimation by the SQL Server optimizer is always one row, no matter how many rows are populated into the table variable. The honest truth is that the optimizer doesn't know how many rows are actually in a table variable, since they are defined and typically populated as part of a batch or stored procedure. In fact, when Jack was in support, he blogged about this problem and trace flag solution to help at `https://blogs.msdn.microsoft.com/psssql/2014/08/11/having-performance-issues-with-table-variables-sql-server-2012-sp2-can-help/`.

This means that, when Jack joined the team, he well understood this problem. The leadership of the Query Processor team had an idea they wanted to implement in SQL Server 2019 as part of Intelligent Query Processing called *table variable deferred compilation*. They turned to Jack to build it.

As aptly described by the SQL Server documentation at `https://docs.microsoft.com/en-us/sql/relational-databases/performance/intelligent-query-processing?#table-variable-deferred-compilation`, "Table variable deferred compilation defers compilation of a statement that references a table variable until the first actual run of the statement. This deferred compilation behavior is the same as that of temporary tables. This change results in the use of actual cardinality instead of the original one-row guess."

You can read examples of how to enable and disable table variable deferred compilation, including database options and query hints, at `https://docs.microsoft.com/en-us/sql/t-sql/data-types/table-transact-sql?#table-variable-deferred-compilation`.

All the example scripts for this section can be found at **ch2_intelligent_performance\iqp\tablevariable.**

Let's walk through an example of this concept using a T-SQL notebook (Note: You can also walk through a T-SQL script of this capability from the file **iqp_tablevariable.sql**).

1. Open the T-SQL notebook with Azure Data Studio called **iqp_tablevariable.ipynb.**

2. Go through each step in the notebook to compare performance of using table variables with and without deferred compilation.

3. To compare query plans for these two scenarios, we can use a feature called Query Store, which was introduced in SQL Server 2016. You may not have realized, but when you restored the WideWorldImportersDW backup, the database already had Query Store enabled.

4. Here is how to use Query Store to compare the two queries: one using table variable deferred compilation and one not.

5. Open up SSMS, connect to the SQL Server where you ran the notebook examples, and find the Top Resource Consuming Queries report, as seen in Figure 2-10.

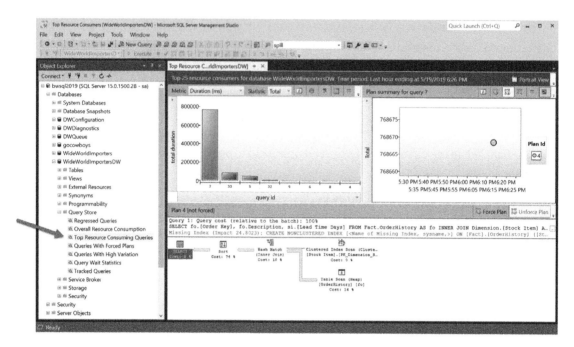

Figure 2-10. *Query Store Top Resource Consuming Query report*

6. The report in Figure 2-10 shows Query Store data after running
    the previous example of row mode memory grant feedback and
    the table variable examples in this section. Your view may look
    slightly different depending on what you have run. Each bar in the
    graph represents a unique query, so you need to find the query
    associated with the table variable example. If you click each bar,
    the query text is listed below. If you looked at the query in the
    stored procedure for this example in the notebook, it has a query
    like this:

```
SELECT top 10 oh.[Order Key], oh.[Order Date Key],oh.[Unit Price],
o.Quantity
FROM Fact.OrderHistoryExtended AS oh
INNER JOIN @Order AS o
ON o.[Order Key] = oh.[Order Key]
WHERE oh.[Unit Price] > 0.10
ORDER BY oh.[Unit Price] DESC
```

7. Click each bar in the graph until you see this query. Notice the
    two dots on the right, which represent the two query plans for
    this query. When you do, the output of the report should look like
    Figure 2-11.

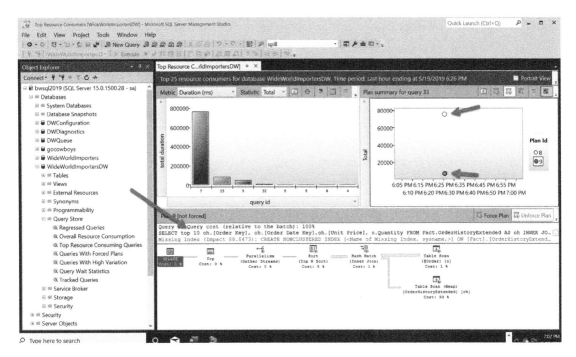

Figure 2-11. *Query plans for table variable use*

The "higher" the dot in the chart, the longer the average duration was
for that query plan. If you click each dot, you can see the query plan
visual change in the bottom window.

8. Move your cursor over the top dot to see execution statistics of the
    query plan. See statistics like the average duration like in Figure 2-12.

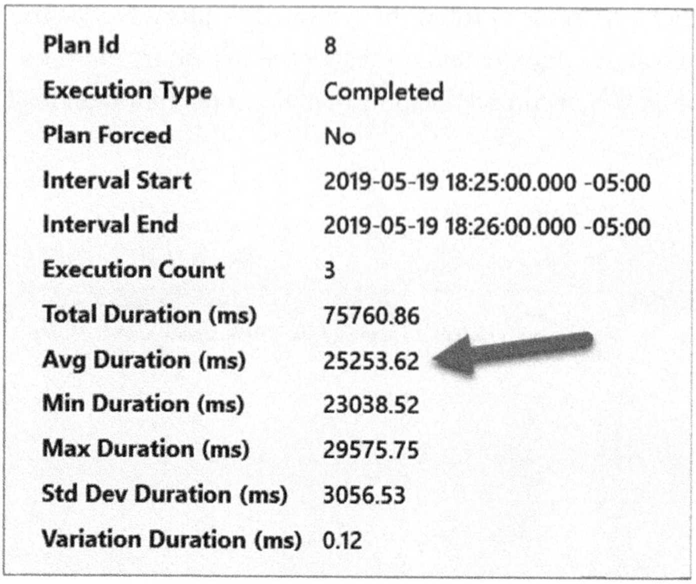

Plan Id	8
Execution Type	Completed
Plan Forced	No
Interval Start	2019-05-19 18:25:00.000 -05:00
Interval End	2019-05-19 18:26:00.000 -05:00
Execution Count	3
Total Duration (ms)	75760.86
Avg Duration (ms)	25253.62
Min Duration (ms)	23038.52
Max Duration (ms)	29575.75
Std Dev Duration (ms)	3056.53
Variation Duration (ms)	0.12

Figure 2-12. *Avg duration of the slower query plan*

If you click the dot and look at the query plan in the bottom pane, hover over the Table Scan operator. Notice the estimate of 1 as seen in Figure 2-13.

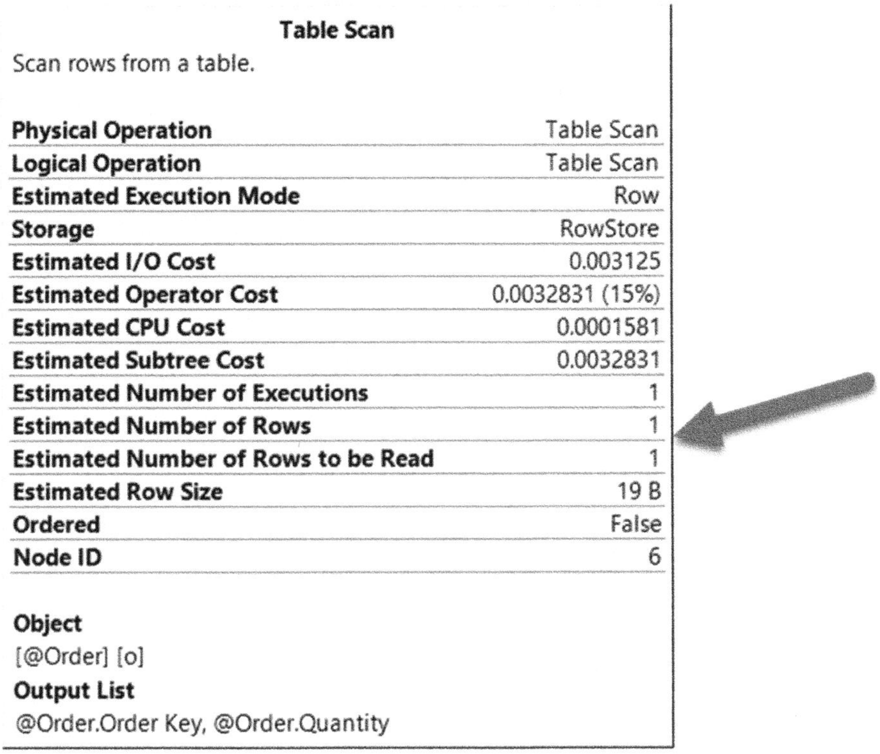

Table Scan
Scan rows from a table.

Physical Operation	Table Scan
Logical Operation	Table Scan
Estimated Execution Mode	Row
Storage	RowStore
Estimated I/O Cost	0.003125
Estimated Operator Cost	0.0032831 (15%)
Estimated CPU Cost	0.0001581
Estimated Subtree Cost	0.0032831
Estimated Number of Executions	1
Estimated Number of Rows	1
Estimated Number of Rows to be Read	1
Estimated Row Size	19 B
Ordered	False
Node ID	6

Object
[@Order] [o]
Output List
@Order.Order Key, @Order.Quantity

Figure 2-13. *Estimate of one row for a table variable*

Notice the join of the table variable and the OrderHistoryExtended table. It uses a Nested Loops Join. This makes sense for the optimizer to make this choice since it *thinks* the table variable has only one row. The problem is the table variable has ~3M rows! Using a Nested Loops Join for that many rows would be very expensive and not make sense.

9. Now click the "lower" dot in the window showing query plans. Move your mouse pointer over the dot to see the average duration. It should look something like Figure 2-14.

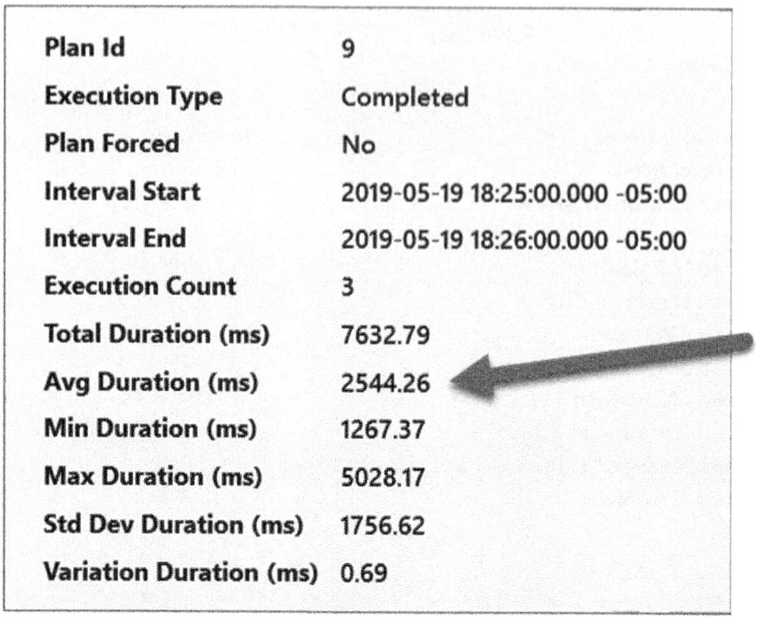

Plan Id	9
Execution Type	Completed
Plan Forced	No
Interval Start	2019-05-19 18:25:00.000 -05:00
Interval End	2019-05-19 18:26:00.000 -05:00
Execution Count	3
Total Duration (ms)	7632.79
Avg Duration (ms)	2544.26
Min Duration (ms)	1267.37
Max Duration (ms)	5028.17
Std Dev Duration (ms)	1756.62
Variation Duration (ms)	0.69

Figure 2-14. *Average duration of faster query plan*

An average of 2.5 seconds is far better than 25 seconds.

Now look at the query plan. Move your mouse pointer to the Table Scan operator. Notice the estimates are now accurate, and, since a table scan is needed, using batch mode makes sense. This is an example of multiple Intelligent Query Processing features being used at the same time. The details of this operator should look like Figure 2-15.

Table Scan

Scan rows from a table.

Physical Operation	Table Scan
Logical Operation	Table Scan
Estimated Execution Mode	Batch
Storage	RowStore
Estimated I/O Cost	7.12683
Estimated Operator Cost	8.14508 (1%)
Estimated CPU Cost	1.01825
Estimated Subtree Cost	8.14508
Estimated Number of Executions	1
Estimated Number of Rows	3702590
Estimated Number of Rows to be Read	3702590
Estimated Row Size	19 B
Ordered	False
Node ID	4

Object
[@Order] [o]
Output List
@Order.Order Key, @Order.Quantity

Figure 2-15. *Better estimates for using a table variable*

Now look at the join of the table variable and the OrderHistory
Extended table. A hash join is now used, and a table scan of the
OrderHistoryExtended table is also used.

Batch Mode on Rowstore

SQL Server 2012 added a nifty (what an understatement!), now famous capability
called **Columnstore Indexes**, through Project Apollo. See the original blog at `https://
cloudblogs.microsoft.com/sqlserver/2011/08/04/columnstore-indexes-a-new-
feature-in-sql-server-known-as-project-apollo/`. As a part of delivering this
feature, the query processor was enhanced to use *batch mode* processing of rows with
columnstore indexes. Up to this time, plan operators, like scans, execute and process
data based on a single row (and the entire row). Batch mode provides a new paradigm
to allow operators to process data based on batches of rows that are organized by
column and include vectors to identify qualify rows. This concept aligns very well with
columnstore indexes, which are organized by columns, not rows.

While columnstore indexes are very helpful for analytic query workloads where scanning and processing large number of rows is common, columnstore indexes may not fit your needs or may have restrictions preventing you from using them. Furthermore, you may have queries that fit the "analytic workload" scenario. In other words, you are not trying to query a single row or just a few rows (which many consider the normal "OLTP scenario"). Any table or index that is not organized with a columnstore index is aptly named a **rowstore**.

In SQL Server 2019, the query processor can automatically detect whether your query qualifies for batch mode processing on a rowstore. Batch mode, again, may not make sense for all queries, so a few basics must apply. For example, your query needs to process a *large* number of rows and involve operations that require aggregates (think count(∗) or sum(), joins, or sorts). In other words, batches make sense when there is a flow of data between several operators of a large number of rows to execute a query. What is large? We don't document the number (because it may make sense to change this in the future), but the threshold is generally 128K rows.

You can read all the details of batch mode on rowstore, including enabling and disabling this capability, at `https://docs.microsoft.com/en-us/sql/relational-databases/performance/intelligent-query-processing?#batch-mode-on-rowstore`. This documentation article has many details on the background of this capability, including which workloads will benefit, as well as limits and restrictions.

Tip   Do you want to really go deep on this topic? Then you will love the blog post by SQL Community Expert, Dima Pilugin, who debugged the magical 128K number. You can read this blog at `www.queryprocessor.com/batch-mode-on-row-store/`.

Using the WideWorldImportersDW database that you restored and extended in the beginning of this chapter, let's look at an example where batch mode for rowstore can accelerate query performance. Use the directory **ch2_intelligent_performance\iqp\batchmoderow** for all script examples.

You can run the following queries from the provided example script **iqp_batchmoderow.sql** or from the T-SQL notebook **iqp_batchmoderow.ipynb**.

Based on either method, let's go step by step. For this section, I encourage you to try the T-SQL notebook example. You can use iqp_batchmoderow.sql with any SQL tool, but you will need to analyze the query plans in a graphical tool like SSMS or Azure Data Studio (or read the plan XML in detail).

Open Azure Data Studio connected to your SQL Server 2019 instance and open the **iqp_batchmoderow.ipynb** notebook.

One of the beautiful aspects of notebooks is that the documentation for each step and cells are in the notebook itself. And, the notebooks that were saved under the GitHub repo for the book have all the answers already, so you know what to expect!

I've even put in image examples of query plan differences using Azure Data Studio and what you should expect to see.

Read and follow each step of the notebook. You will see that Batch Mode on Rowstore can have a significant performance difference, especially when dealing with tables of large datasets. Additionally, Batch Mode now works for both columnstore (implemented in SQL Server 2017) and rowstore, so you shouldn't need to worry about it. The query processor knows when to use it and how it can help boost performance of your query.

For a sanity check, Figure 2-16 shows what the notebook for this example looks like at the top when loaded.

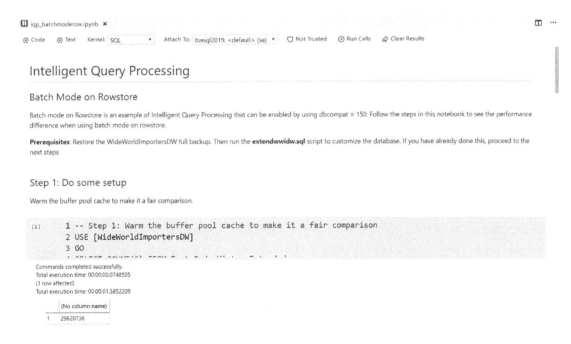

Figure 2-16. *A T-SQL notebook to demonstrate Batch Mode on Rowstore*

Scalar UDF Inlining

SQL Server has long had a concept called a user-defined function (UDF). The concept is that you build some T-SQL code inside a FUNCTION that takes one or more parameters, and this function returns a value. You could then use the function in any T-SQL SELECT statement. It is a popular way for code reuse like a stored procedure, but a function has the nice property of *being part* of the SELECT statement.

Note   There are other uses for user-defined functions, which you can read more about at `https://docs.microsoft.com/en-us/sql/t-sql/statements/create-function-transact-sql`.

There are two types of user-defined functions:

- Scalar, which returns a single value

- Table-valued, which returns a result set in the form of a TABLE type

Despite the popularity and programming advantages of UDFs, their use can lead to performance problems because of the limitations in how they are compiled and integrated into the overall query plan. For example, any time a scalar UDF is used to return a value as part of a list of columns, each row that is part of the table being accessed is applied to the code in the UDF *one row at a time*. There are other limitations in how the query processor treats UDFs that in some situations just makes them very inefficient from a performance point of view.

Now comes along scalar UDF *inlining*. The query processor can take the code (a UDF could have multiple T-SQL statements) and is able to integrate those statements with the overall query, hence the term inlining.

You can read how to enable scalar UDF inlining by using dbcompat in the documentation at `https://docs.microsoft.com/en-us/sql/relational-databases/user-defined-functions/scalar-udf-inlining?#enabling-scalar-udf-inlining`.

You can read more about how to disable and enable scalar UDF inlining without changing dbcompat at `https://docs.microsoft.com/en-us/sql/relational-databases/user-defined-functions/scalar-udf-inlining?#disabling-scalar-udf-inlining-without-changing-the-compatibility-level`.

As with all of these Intelligent Query Processing scenarios, it is best to see an example. Use the directory **ch2_intelligent_performance\iqp\scalarinlineudf** for all script examples.

As with the other examples in this chapter, you have two ways to go through scalar UDF inlining. You can use the **iqp_scalarudfinlining.pynb** T-SQL notebook or use a set of T-SQL scripts.

Note   This example is loosely based off of examples in the following blog post by Microsoft, `https://blogs.msdn.microsoft.com/ sqlserverstorageengine/2018/11/07/introducing-scalar-udf- inlining/`, which also has some really nice details on the previous limits of scalar UDF functions and how Intelligent Query Processing has enabled significant performance improvements.

For this section, let's use the T-SQL scripts along with examining the Actual Execution Plan in SSMS.

1. Open up the T-SQL script **get_customer_spend.sql**.

   The code for this script looks like the following:

   ```
   USE WideWorldImportersDW
   GO
   SELECT c.[Customer Key], SUM(oh.[Total Including Tax]) as
   total_spend
   FROM [Fact].[OrderHistory] oh
   JOIN [Dimension].[Customer] c
   ON oh.[Customer Key] = c.[Customer Key]
   GROUP BY c.[Customer Key]
   ORDER BY total_spend DESC
   GO
   ```

   This script will find the total spend per customer from the OrderHistory table. If you examine the output, you can see the range of spend for customers ranging from 2M to over 7M. Based on application requirements, we need to create a user-defined function that would take as input a customer "key" and categorize the customer into a classification based on their total spend. Anything <= 3M will be 'REGULAR'. Any customer spending between 3M and 4.5M will be 'GOLD'. Anyone spending over this amount will be considered 'PLATINUM'. Using a function has the advantage that we can change the rules for what qualifies for REGULAR, GOLD, or PLATINUM and not affect all other code using this function.

2. Open the T-SQL script **iqp_scalarudfinlining.sql** and follow each step per the comments in the script.

3. Execute the section in the script **Step 1** which will create the scalar UDF.

```
-- Step 1: Create a new function to get a customer category
based on their order spend
USE WideWorldImportersDW
GO

CREATE OR ALTER FUNCTION [Dimension].[customer_category]
(@CustomerKey INT)
RETURNS CHAR(10) AS
BEGIN
DECLARE @total_amount DECIMAL(18,2)
DECLARE @category CHAR(10)

SELECT @total_amount = SUM([Total Including Tax])
FROM [Fact].[OrderHistory]
WHERE [Customer Key] = @CustomerKey

IF @total_amount <= 3000000
  SET @category = 'REGULAR'
ELSE IF @total_amount < 4500000
  SET @category = 'GOLD'
ELSE
  SET @category = 'PLATINUM'

RETURN @category
END
GO
```

4. Set up the dbcompat, clear the procedure, and warm the buffer
   pool cache by executing **Step 2**.

```
-- Step 2: Set the database to db compat 150, clear the
procedure cache from previous executions, and make the
comparison fair by warming the cache
ALTER DATABASE WideWorldImportersDW
SET COMPATIBILITY_LEVEL = 150
GO
ALTER DATABASE SCOPED CONFIGURATION
CLEAR PROCEDURE_CACHE;
GO
SELECT COUNT(*) FROM [Fact].[OrderHistory]
GO
```

5. Let's run a query using the UDF but use a query hint to temporary
   disable scalar UDF inlining. Enable Actual Execution Plan in
   SSMS and run **Step 3** in the sequence of the script.

```
-- Step 3: Run the query but disable the use of scalar
inlining using a query hint
SELECT [Customer Key], [Customer], [Dimension].[customer_
category]([Customer Key]) AS [Discount Price]
FROM [Dimension].[Customer]
ORDER BY [Customer Key]
OPTION (USE HINT('DISABLE_TSQL_SCALAR_UDF_INLINING'))
GO
```

The query takes at least 30+ seconds. The Actual Execution Plan
should look something like Figure 2-17.

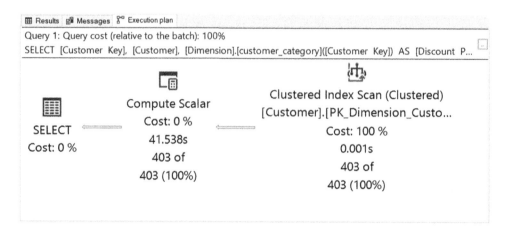

Figure 2-17. *Execution plan for scalar UDF not inlined*

If you move your mouse pointer over each operator, you will see it affects 403 rows. That doesn't seem like a lot of rows, so why does it take so long? It is because what you can't see is that the scalar function accesses the OrderHistory table, which has 3M+ rows; for each row in the Dimension.Customer table, it accesses all 3M rows in the OrderHistory table. Not efficient.

6.   Run **Step 4** in the script which will run the same query without the hint, thus enabling scalar UDF inlining.

```
-- Step 4: Run it again but don't use the hint
SELECT [Customer Key], [Customer], [Dimension].[customer_category]
([Customer Key]) AS [Discount Price]
FROM [Dimension].[Customer]
ORDER BY [Customer Key]
GO
```

The query should have executed significantly faster. If you look at the Actual Execution Plan, you will see how the operators required to run the function are exposed in the plan, and new operators to make accessing the OrderHistory table more efficient to support the query in the function. The plan will look something like Figure 2-18.

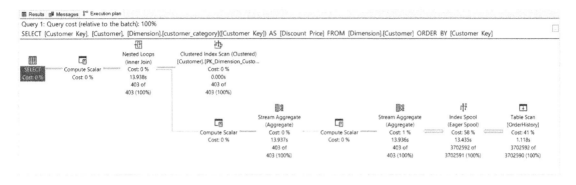

Figure 2-18. *Execution plan for scalar UDF with inlining*

You can see the power of scalar UDF inlining; now you should feel more empowered to use scalar UDFs in your applications.

You can read more about scalar UDF inlining, including all the requirements and restrictions, at `https://docs.microsoft.com/ en-us/sql/relational-databases/user-defined-functions/ scalar-udf-inlining`.

Approximate Count Distinct

There are scenarios where you need to count the number of rows in any table. That's easy. Just use SELECT COUNT(*) FROM <table> and you have your answer. But there are also situations where you need to know the number of distinct values of a column across all rows of a table. In this case, that is not that much harder. Just use SELECT COUNT(DISTINCT <col>) FROM <table>. That seems easy enough. The only problem is how the query processor must do work to figure out what are all the distinct values.

For SQL Server, this often requires the use of a *Hash Match* operator. This operator is similar to a Hash Join, in that a "hash table" is used to build a list of all the distinct values to count. If you remember, earlier in this chapter, a Hash Join requires a memory grant, so all the issues with memory grants can come into play. Furthermore, it can take a great deal of compute resources to use a hash table to count all the distinct values.

Is there a better way? Well, there is a *different* way that could be faster, at the cost of a slightly less precise answer. The solution is a **new T-SQL function** called **APPROX_ COUNT_DISTINCT**(). This is a built-in function that will count distinct values of a column based on a sample approximation. This is not an enhancement for the COUNT() function. This is an entirely new function, which is why it does not require dbcompat = 150. This function uses a concept called *HyperLogLog* (you can read more about this concept

at https://en.wikipedia.org/wiki/HyperLogLog). Using an approximation of the
count of distinct values comes with a 2% error rate on a 97% probability. This means if
you can get back an answer that you are pretty confident will be close to the real truth,
you can use this function.

Let's see an example of using this function in comparison to using COUNT and
DISTINCT.

Use the directory **ch2_intelligent_performance\iqp\approxcount** for all
script examples. You can walk through the examples using a T-SQL notebook
iqp_approxcountdistinct.ipynb. I've also provided a T-SQL script called **iqp_
approxcountdistinct.sql.** Let's use the T-SQL script and walk through step by step
examining the queries and execution plan differences.

1. Open up the **iqp_approxcountdistinct.sql** script in SSMS.

2. Run the **Step 1** set of statements to clear the procedure cache,
    change the dbcompat level to 130, and warm the buffer pool
    (make it a fair fight).

```
-- Step 1: Clear the cache, set dbcompat to 130 just to prove it
works, and warm the cache
USE WideWorldImportersDW
GO
ALTER DATABASE SCOPED CONFIGURATION CLEAR PROCEDURE_CACHE
GO
ALTER DATABASE WideWorldImportersDW SET COMPATIBILITY_LEVEL = 130
GO
SELECT COUNT(*) FROM Fact.OrderHistoryExtended
GO
```

You may wonder why I forced the dbcompat to 130 – to prove
to you that you don't have to use the latest dbcompat of 150 to
take advantage of this capability. This is because the new T-SQL
function APPROX_COUNT_DISTINCT() *just comes* with the SQL
Server 2019 engine but doesn't require a new dbcompat like other
Intelligent Query Processing features.

3. Enable Actual Execution Plan in SSMS and run **Step 2** as follows:

```
-- Step 2: Use COUNT and DISTINCT first
SELECT COUNT(DISTINCT [WWI Order ID])
FROM [Fact].[OrderHistoryExtended]
GO
```

This won't take that long to run, depending on how fast your computer is – maybe 4 to 5 seconds. Your results should be 29620736. Five seconds to count the distinct values is not too bad. However, what if this table had 100 million rows or more? That is not that out of the ordinary in large databases.

If you look at the execution plan, you will see something like Figure 2-19.

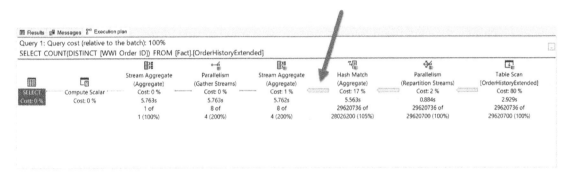

Figure 2-19. *Query plan for COUNT and DISTINCT*

Notice the Hash Match operator. If you move your mouse over that operator, you will see it uses Row Mode and has to process the entire 29M rows in the hash operator.

4. Now run **Step 3** from the script as follows:

```
-- Step 3: Use the new APPROX_COUNT_DISTINCT function to compare
values and performance
-- We should be no more than 2% off the actual distinct value
(97% probability)
SELECT APPROX_COUNT_DISTINCT([WWI Order ID])
FROM [Fact].[OrderHistoryExtended]
GO
```

This time, the query should only take a second or two – about 50% faster than before. Again, this could be significant on very large datasets.

If you look at the execution plan, it looks similar but with less operators, as seen in Figure 2-20.

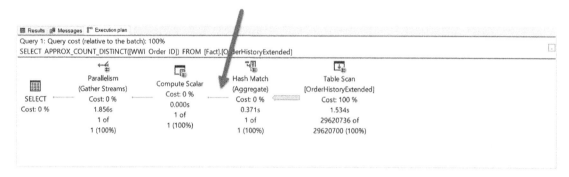

Figure 2-20. Query plan for APPROX_COUNT_DISTINCT

Notice the Hash Match operator doesn't have a "thick line" as output because the approximation operation is applied with this operator yielding only one row to the rest of the plan.

As you can see, the use of approximation for counting distinct values can provide better performance provided you need only a "close enough" value.

5. Restore dbcompat to 150 by executing **Step 4** in the script.

```
-- Step 4: Restore database compatibility level
ALTER DATABASE WideWorldImportersDW SET COMPATIBILITY_LEVEL = 150
GO
```

You can read more about the APPROX_COUNT_DISTINCT function at https://docs.microsoft.com/en-us/sql/t-sql/functions/approx-count-distinct-transact-sql.

Intelligent Query Processing is all about a smarter query processor meeting the needs of your query workloads without making major application changes. Most of the functionality is available by simply changing your database compatibility level to 150. I look forward to more enhancements in the future as the query processor takes on new scenarios powered by your feedback.

Lightweight Query Profiling

When I joined the SQL Server engineering team in 2016, I had spent a lifetime in technical support working on some of the most challenging problems ever seen by SQL Server customers. And no set of problems challenged me and others in CSS more than performance problems. Performance problems in SQL Server are tough – they are vague and time critical, and rarely do you have the information you need, when you need it.

SQL Server has amazing diagnostics for performance problems, including Dynamic Management Views (DMVs) and Extended Events. We had built DMVs to be a great mechanism to see *what is running* at any point in time. This is a great way to find out about active sessions and what queries they are running. But often, to solve a complex performance problem, you need details of the query plan.

So, the gap was going deeper. You can see what is running, but you can't dive deep into a query plan for an active query. Furthermore, if you need to find out the details of a query plan for a query that has completed, you need to use what can be *heavy* diagnostics in the form of Extended Events. Or you need to find the exact query and run it *offline* (that is away from the application) in a separate tool and turn on query plan diagnostics to get all the details.

As I joined the engineering team, I discovered there was work in progress to solve these types of problems by the famous Tiger Team. Pedro Lopes, Alexey Eksarevskiy, and Jay Choe were already working on something called the *query profiling infrastructure*. If you ask any developer about how to trace their code, they will use the term *profiling*. So how do you profile a query with SQL Server? It usually comes down to getting details about the query execution plan. It is all about gaining these insights while a query is running and obtaining the actual query execution plan when a query has completed.

This team had built the concept already of *live query stats*. (You can read more about this topic at `https://docs.microsoft.com/en-us/sql/relational-databases/performance/live-query-statistics`.) It was logical they could do more. As Alexey tells it, "I wanted this feature in the product as early as in 2009… spending so much time staring at the plans then, I wished they would come alive to easier see what's going on. So, the idea of live query stats. Those two perfectly complement each other, though of course, lightweight profiling allows to do much more."

In fact, what the team had built was a query execution statistics profile infrastructure, or *standard profiling*. This capability gives you actual execution plan statistics at the operator level for rows, CPU, and I/O. This is key information to profile a query, but there is a catch. You must enable this before running the query or enable Extended Events

61

for all queries which can be impactful to production workloads. You can read more about standard profiling at https://docs.microsoft.com/en-us/sql/relational-databases/performance/query-profiling-infrastructure?#the-standard-query-execution-statistics-profiling-infrastructure.

I love working with colleagues like Pedro, Alexey, and Jay. They are always asking, "Can we make this better?" And of course, they are all super smart. They know from experience how painful it can be to use standard profiling. They created the lightweight query execution statistics profiling infrastructure, or *lightweight profiling*. The concept is to get profiling for queries without the overhead required from standard profiling. However, to make it "light," we had to take out collecting CPU statistics so you still get "per operator" rowcount and I/O statistics. You can read more about lightweight profiling at https://docs.microsoft.com/en-us/sql/relational-databases/performance/query-profiling-infrastructure?#lwp.

This is great, but... you still need to *turn this on* to make it work. How do you know when to enable lightweight profiling? Well, often you don't. No one does. The true answer is to just have lightweight profiling running **by default**. And that is what SQL Server 2019 provides. Pedro calls this, "Performance insights anytime and anywhere." Is there a catch? Yes. You only get rowcount information from actively running queries, but often that is enough to help look at performance problems. But there is a bonus. We've added the ability to get the last actual execution plan for most cached queries.

Let's look at two scenarios so you can understand the benefit of having lightweight query profiling on by default in SQL Server 2019.

Prerequisites for Using the Examples for Lightweight Query Profiling

First, you need to perform some setup to use examples for the two scenarios. For examples in this chapter, you will use the **WideWorldImporters** example database (you can read more about this database and its schema at https://docs.microsoft.com/en-us/sql/samples/wide-world-importers-oltp-database-catalog).

These examples will work on SQL Server 2019 on Windows, Linux, and Containers. Given the large dataset, SQL Server is going to need at least 12Gb RAM to properly see performance differences. In addition, some of the query examples use parallelism, so installing SQL Server on a multiprocessor system is preferred.

All the scripts used for this chapter can be found on the GitHub repo under the **ch2_intelligent_performance\lwp** directory.

In order to use the examples in this chapter, you need to go through the following steps:

1. Download the WideWorldImporters database backup from `https://github.com/Microsoft/sql-server-samples/` `releases/download/wide-world-importers-v1.0/` `WideWorldImporters-Full.bak`.

2. Restore this database to your SQL Server 2019 instance. You can use the provided **restorewwi.sql** script. You may need to change the directory paths for the location of your backup and where you will restore the database files.

3. In order to run some of the examples, you will need larger tables than what is installed by default in WideWorldImporters. Therefore, run the script **extendwwi.sql** to create a larger table. Extending this database will increase its size including the transaction log to about 5Gb overall. One of these tables is called **Sales.InvoiceLinesExtended**. Based on the **InvoiceLines** table, we will make this table much larger and not use a columnstore index.

Should I Kill an Active Query?

Consider this scenario. You are told SQL Server is being consumed by a query that is taking up a large amount of CPU on the server. You use a DMV like **sys.dm_exec_requests** to identify the query and the user. The user is your Vice President running a report, and the query is based on a cached plan. You use the common DMVs called **sys.dm_exec_requests** and **sys.dm_exec_query_stats** to see which query is running. How do you find out whether this query will finish anytime soon or should be killed and corrected?

Let's use the following example to see this behavior and how built-in, on by default, Lightweight Query Profiling can help give you the answer.

You can run these T-SQL scripts in any tool that can connect to SQL Server, but the best experience is seeing all the details in SQL Server Management Studio (SSMS).

1. Open the T-SQL script **mysmartquery.sql** (maybe a sign it is not so smart) and execute the batch.

2. In a new connection, open up the T-SQL script **show_active_ queries.sql**.

3. Run the batch from **Step 1** in the script as follows:

```
-- Step 1: Only show requests with active queries except for
this one
SELECT er.session_id, er.command, er.status, er.wait_type,
er.cpu_time, er.logical_reads, eqsx.query_plan, t.text
FROM sys.dm_exec_requests er
CROSS APPLY sys.dm_exec_query_statistics_xml(er.session_id) eqsx
CROSS APPLY sys.dm_exec_sql_text(er.sql_handle) t
WHERE er.session_id <> @@SPID
GO
```

This code finds any active queries (other than the current connection). If you run this query over and over, you will see cpu and logical_reads values increasing and a wait_type = ASYNC_ NETWORK_IO. This pattern indicates two things:

- The query is chewing up a bunch of CPU and likely scanning a big table (logical_reads high and increasing).

- There are a great deal of results being sent back to the client (e.g., ASYNC_NETWORK_IO wait).

In my experience, this is not a "good" query and is one where an opportunity to "tune" exists. But the question is, should you kill it now, or is it "almost done"?

4.   What would be nice to know as the query is active is to see the
     progress of query plan operators (like Live Query Statistics). Run
     Step 2 from the script as follows:

```
-- Step 2: What does the plan profile look like for the active
query
SELECT session_id, physical_operator_name, node_id, thread_id,
row_count, estimate_row_count
FROM sys.dm_exec_query_profiles
WHERE session_id <> @@SPID
ORDER BY session_id, node_id DESC
GO
```

The results should look something like Figure 2-21.

	session_id	physical_operator_name	node_id	thread_id	row_count	estimate_row_count
1	146	Index Scan	5	0	228265	228265
2	146	Index Scan	4	0	0	1
3	146	Hash Match	3	0	228265	228265
4	146	Table Spool	2	0	14639940	16094965150
5	146	Index Scan	1	0	65	70510
6	146	Nested Loops	0	0	14639940	16094965150

Figure 2-21. *Query plan profile for an active query*

Notice the huge estimate_row_count for the Nested Loops and
Table Spool operators. And notice the row_count (this is the
number of rows currently processed) is far short of the estimate. It
could be the estimate is inaccurate, but, if it is right, this query is
far from completing. Run this query again to see the progression
of the row_count for these operators.

Note   When lightweight query profiling is on by default in SQL Server 2019,
row_count is the only statistics captured. It can be expensive to capture statistics
like CPU and I/O by default. You can capture these with standard profiling.

5. Let's look at the query plan itself. This is the estimated plan, but it might give a clue on these really large estimate row counts. Run **Step 3** in the script as follows:

```
-- Step 3: Go back and look at the plan and query text for a clue
SELECT er.session_id, er.command, er.status, er.wait_type,
er.cpu_time, er.logical_reads, eqsx.query_plan, t.text
FROM sys.dm_exec_requests er
CROSS APPLY sys.dm_exec_query_statistics_xml(er.session_id) eqsx
CROSS APPLY sys.dm_exec_sql_text(er.sql_handle) t
WHERE er.session_id <> @@SPID
GO
```

In SSMS, click the query_plan value, which should open up a new window with a visual query plan.

The plan should look similar to Figure 2-22.

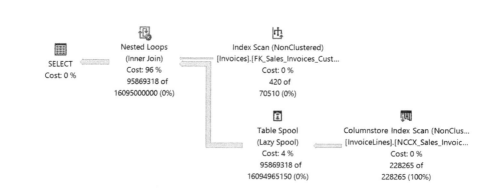

Figure 2-22. *Query plan of active query*

Notice the icon symbol with an **X** on the Nested Loops Join. If you move your mouse pointer over the Nested Loops Join operator, it will look like Figure 2-23.

Nested Loops

For each row in the top (outer) input, scan the bottom (inner) input, and output matching rows.

Physical Operation	Nested Loops
Logical Operation	Inner Join
Actual Execution Mode	Row
Estimated Execution Mode	Row
Actual Number of Rows	442589
Actual Number of Batches	0
Estimated Operator Cost	67277.038416 (96%)
Estimated I/O Cost	0
Estimated CPU Cost	67277
Estimated Subtree Cost	70181.7
Number of Executions	1
Estimated Number of Executions	1
Estimated Number of Rows	16095000000
Estimated Row Size	24 B
Actual Rebinds	0
Actual Rewinds	0
Node ID	0

Output List

[WideWorldImporters].[Sales].[Invoices].CustomerID,
[WideWorldImporters].[Sales].[InvoiceLines].InvoiceID,
[WideWorldImporters].[Sales].[InvoiceLines].LineProfit

Warnings

No Join Predicate

Figure 2-23. *Nested Loops Join warning*

What does "No Join Predicate" mean? It means there is a major problem with the JOIN operator in the query. It means there really is no "equi" join.

In the Step 3 results, look at the value of the text column of the diagnostics. It looks like this:

```
SELECT si.CustomerID, sil.InvoiceID, sil.LineProfit
FROM Sales.Invoices si
INNER JOIN Sales.InvoiceLines sil
ON si.InvoiceID = si.InvoiceID
OPTION (MAXDOP 1)
```

Since the JOIN operator has a problem, let's focus on the INNER JOIN clause:

```
INNER JOIN Sales.InvoiceLines sil
ON si.InvoiceID = si.InvoiceID
```

You will see that this query simply joins a table to itself. A simple typo of **si** vs. **sil** is the problem. This query will almost never finish. It can be killed or fixed, and your Vice President will be much happier.

6. Cancel the query from **mysmartquery.sql** if it is still running.

Lightweight query profiling also includes extended events and query hint support to enable it. You can read more about how to enable these, plus how to disable the feature per database, at https://docs.microsoft.com/en-us/sql/relational-databases/performance/query-profiling-infrastructure?#lwp.

I Can't Catch It

Consider another scenario. You have observed an increase in CPU utilization of SQL Server and don't believe it should be occurring (because it is a change from the normal behavior). You can see from a DMV like **sys.dm_exec_query_stats** where queries are taking the most CPU, but you only get the estimated plan through that DMV. You could try to run the query yourself offline and observe the actual plan, but you want to see the actual plan from the real query from the application to make sure you know you have the right details. This query runs all the time by many users but only takes a few seconds (hence the steady higher CPU all the time) so it is hard to use the new tools to capture a query in progress. You could turn on standard query profiling, but you have found that may be too heavy and cause application issues during the crucial time the query is executed.

With SQL Server 2019 comes a new capability with Lightweight Query Profiling. A new Dynamic Management Function (DMF) called **sys.dm_exec_query_plan_stats** now comes with SQL Server 2019. The idea is to capture the last actual execution plan of a cached query. You can read all the details about using this DMF at https://docs.microsoft.com/en-us/sql/relational-databases/system-dynamic-management-views/sys-dm-exec-query-plan-stats-transact-sql.

Let's see the usage of this DMF to solve a problem of finding the actual execution plan of a query that is run all the time *without* turning on any special diagnostics, knobs, and flags or running the query manually. The only catch here is that this part of Lightweight Query Profiling does require you to enable it for each database where you want this capability. You can do this with the following T-SQL statement which will be used in the example later:

```
ALTER DATABASE SCOPED CONFIGURATION SET LAST_QUERY_PLAN_STATS = ON
```

All the scripts for this example can be found also in the **ch2_intelligent_performance\lwp** directory. To make it easier to see the visual execution plans, I recommend you run this example using SSMS.

1. Open up the T-SQL script **mysmartquery_top.sql.**

2. Set up the example by running **Step 1** in the script as follows:

    ```
    -- Step 1: Clear the procedure cache and set dbcompat to 130 to
    prove you don't need 150 for last plan stats
    USE WideWorldImporters
    GO
    ALTER DATABASE SCOPED CONFIGURATION CLEAR PROCEDURE_CACHE
    GO
    ALTER DATABASE [WideWorldImporters] SET COMPATIBILITY_LEVEL = 130
    GO
    ALTER DATABASE SCOPED CONFIGURATION SET LAST_QUERY_PLAN_STATS = ON
    GO
    SELECT COUNT(*) FROM Sales.InvoiceLinesExtended
    GO
    ```

    The dbcompat is set to 130 just to prove you don't need dbcompat of 150 for this feature.

3. Now let's simulate statistics are incorrect by running **Step 2** in the script as follows:

    ```
    -- Step 2: Simulate a statistic out of date to a really low value
    UPDATE STATISTICS Sales.InvoiceLinesExtended
    WITH ROWCOUNT = 1
    GO
    ```

4. Now run the query. It should only take a few seconds, but it is all CPU. Run **Step 3** to execute the query as follows:

Note   You don't need to select actual execution plan as we are simulating how you will look at plans separately from the application.

```
-- Step 3: Run a query. This should only take a few seconds
but it is all CPU
SELECT si.InvoiceID, sil.StockItemID
FROM Sales.InvoiceLinesExtended sil
JOIN Sales.Invoices si
ON si.InvoiceID = sil.InvoiceID
AND sil.StockItemID >= 225
GO
```

5. Now let's look at the estimated query plan for this query using standard DMVs. Run **Step 4** to see the estimated plan. Remember this allows you to see the plan for the query from a different connection.

```
-- Step 4: What does the estimated plan say? Looks like the
right plan based on estimates
SELECT st.text, cp.plan_handle, qp.query_plan
FROM sys.dm_exec_cached_plans AS cp
CROSS APPLY sys.dm_exec_sql_text(cp.plan_handle) AS st
CROSS APPLY sys.dm_exec_query_plan(cp.plan_handle) AS qp
WHERE qp.dbid = db_id('WideWorldImporters')
GO
```

From the output you want to find the row where the **text** column values start with "**-- Step 3**." Click the query_plan value for that row. You should see a plan that looks like Figure 2-24.

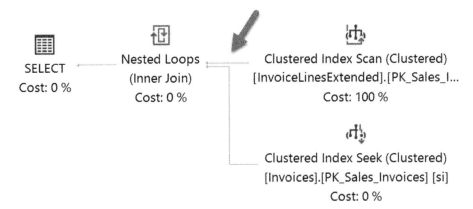

Figure 2-24. *Estimated query plan for problem query*

Notice how thin the line is coming out of the Clustered
Index Scan. That is because the optimizer estimates the
InvoiceLinesExtended table has one row. But this is only the
estimated plan, so you don't know if this is wrong (you just
simulated the estimated rows being wrong but pretend you didn't
know this).

6. Now let's use the new DMV to get the last actual plan for this
    query and see if the estimated rows are incorrect. Run **Step 5** as
    follows:

```
-- Step 5: What does the last actual plan say? Ooops. Actual vs
Estimates way off
SELECT st.text, cp.plan_handle, qps.query_plan, qps.*
FROM sys.dm_exec_cached_plans AS cp
CROSS APPLY sys.dm_exec_sql_text(cp.plan_handle) AS st
CROSS APPLY sys.dm_exec_query_plan_stats(cp.plan_handle) AS qps
WHERE qps.dbid = db_id('WideWorldImporters')
GO
```

In this example, we are using **dm_exec_query_plan_stats** instead
of dm_exec_query_plan. Find the query again in the list and click
the query_plan value. The plan should look like
Figure 2-25.

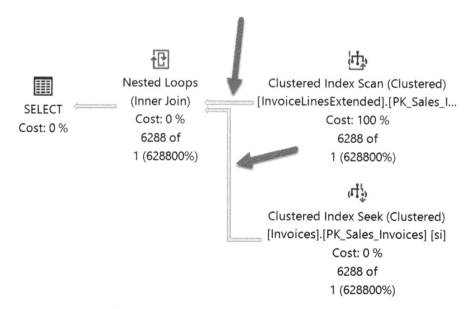

Figure 2-25. *Actual query plan for problem query*

Notice the "thicker" lines. That is because the actual number of rows to process is much larger than the estimates. This is a problem and explains why the optimizer chose to use a Nested Loops Join and make the InvoiceLinesExtended the "outer" table (because it thought there was only one row).

7. Update the statistics to correct them, so you can see what the query really should be doing. Run **Step 6** in the script as follows:

```
-- Step 6: Update stats to the correct value and clear proc cache
UPDATE STATISTICS Sales.InvoiceLinesExtended
WITH ROWCOUNT = 3652240
GO
ALTER DATABASE SCOPED CONFIGURATION CLEAR PROCEDURE_CACHE
GO
```

8. Run the query again using **Step 7** in the script and let's see the new actual plan. You will notice it runs a bit faster:

```
-- Step 7: Run the query again. Faster
SELECT si.InvoiceID, sil.StockItemID
FROM Sales.InvoiceLinesExtended sil
```

```
JOIN Sales.Invoices si
ON si.InvoiceID = sil.InvoiceID
AND sil.StockItemID >= 225
GO
```

9. Run **Step 8** to see if the new actual plan is better.

```
-- Step 8: What does the actual plan look like now? Different
because stats are up to date
SELECT st.text, cp.plan_handle, qps.query_plan
FROM sys.dm_exec_cached_plans AS cp
CROSS APPLY sys.dm_exec_sql_text(cp.plan_handle) AS st
CROSS APPLY sys.dm_exec_query_plan_stats(cp.plan_handle) AS qps
WHERE qps.dbid = db_id('WideWorldImporters')
GO
```

If you click the query_plan for the row that matches the text for
"-- Step 7: Run the query again...", you should now see a plan
that looks like Figure 2-26.

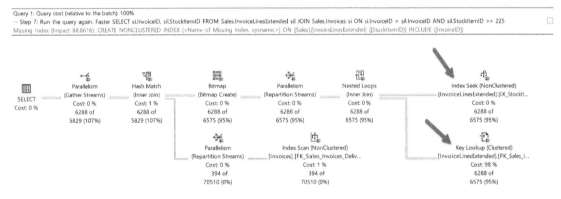

Figure 2-26. *Actual plan for better query*

The plan is radically different. You can see that, in this case,
the optimizer builds a plan to perform an index seek on the
InvoiceLinesExtended table and then join to "itself" with a Key
Lookup. For the query, based on available indexes, that is a far
more efficient way to get the results to join to the other tables and
filter the final results.

73

Now with the ability to see the actual execution plan at any time vs. having to turn on special flags that may be expensive or run the query offline, this becomes a powerful part of your toolkit for query performance tuning and troubleshooting.

Lightweight query profiling is just plain cool! If you have spent anytime supporting production SQL Servers for performance issues, having built-in diagnostics available anytime, anywhere is a breath of fresh air.

In-Memory Database

In SQL Server 2014, we introduced a feature called In-Memory OLTP, which centered on the concept of memory-optimized tables. For this feature, the entire table is stored in memory, but it is the *optimized* (read: latch-free) access that makes it special. We made significant enhancements to In-Memory OLTP in SQL Server 2016. You can read more details about that feature at `https://docs.microsoft.com/en-us/sql/relational-databases/in-memory-oltp`.

As we were working through the new features for SQL Server 2019, Slava Oks, Pam Lahoud, Brian Carrig, Argenis Fernandez, and others from the engineering team met together and collectively decided to call a new suite of features *In-Memory Database* to add to the capabilities of In-Memory OLTP.

Together, the following features have become the In-Memory Database feature suite:

- In-Memory OLTP

- Memory-Optimized TempDB Metadata

- Hybrid Buffer Pool

- Persistent Memory Support

You can see the full collection of this feature suite at `https://docs.microsoft.com/en-us/sql/relational-databases/in-memory-database?view=sqlallproducts-allversions`.

In this section, we will cover all of these new capabilities except for In-Memory OLTP (which is not new to SQL Server 2019).

Memory-Optimized TempDB Metadata

Even since I've been involved with SQL Server, the concurrency performance of workloads using temporary tables has been an issue. This has led for almost every SQL Server administrator to configure tempdb to use multiple files. You can read more about the history of this adventure with these resources:

- Inside TempDB talk by Bob Ward from the 2017 PASS Summit (https://www.youtube.com/watch?v=SvseGMobe2w)

- Paul Randal's blog on adding tempdb files (https://www.sqlskills.com/blogs/paul/correctly-adding-data-files-tempdb/)

One aspect to using tempdb files that most SQL professionals don't realize (because it is just common culture now) is that you are creating a partitioning scheme for the SQL Server engine to access allocation pages such as PFS, GAM, and SGAM pages. This type of scheme is useful because a workload using temporary tables results in a heavy create table, allocate pages, drop table cycle. This creates contention on these system allocation pages in the form of *latches*. By creating multiple files, you are spreading out the contention for latches on these pages, which increases performance for concurrent tempdb workloads.

After creating multiple files (starting with SQL Server 2016, the setup program can do this for you automatically, or you can configure it manually), you may see with a heavier concurrent tempdb-based workload more page latch waits, but these waits are on pages belonging to objects you may not recognize – objects like sysschobjs. These page latch waits are for system table pages in tempdb. When you create and drop tables at a rapid pace, SQL Server must perform internal read/write operations on pages for system tables to keep the metadata of tables consistent. These operations result in page latch pressure across users. In the past when customers would run into high page latch contention on system tables and contact me in support, I would answer, "Unfortunately you must reduce the load of tempdb usage to avoid this problem."

Pam Lahoud describes this problem very well in her blog at https://blogs.msdn.microsoft.com/sql_server_team/tempdb-files-and-trace-flags-and-updates-oh-my/.

Along comes a solution for SQL Server 2019, memory-optimized tempdb metadata. Memory-optimized tables (remember the famous project Hekaton) are latch-free by their nature, and the data for these tables all exist in memory. If the memory-optimized tables are "schema only," they don't even have durability constraints. This is a perfect platform for tempdb system tables. Since tempdb is recreated with each server restart, the system tables don't need to be durable. And since the only data being stored in memory-optimized tables is metadata (not your data in your temporary tables), the memory consumption for these should be small. Ravinder Vuppula, the lead developer for this project, called it making tempdb system tables *Hekatonized*.

Tempdb metadata does not use memory-optimized tables by default when you install SQL Server. You must run the following T-SQL command to enable this capability:

```
ALTER SERVER CONFIGURATION SET MEMORY_OPTIMIZED TEMPDB_METADATA = ON
```

You can see me demo this feature at the 2019 SQLBits keynote at `https://sqlbits.com/Sessions/Event18/Keynote`. Brent Ozar on his blog said about this feature, after seeing it demonstrated at the 2018 PASS Summit keynote, "...that TempDB improvement is just sweet. That's the kind of real-world improvement that will make a difference. People have been struggling with TempDB contention issues and latch contention issues they can't solve."

But you should try this yourself to see it in action. Let's look at an example of how memory-optimized tempdb metadata can improve the concurrency of applications using temporary tables. All the scripts for this example can be found in the **ch2_intelligent_performance\inmem\tempdb** directory. This example is a little more complicated to run and requires coordination or simulation of concurrent users. Therefore, you will need the free stress tool called ostress, which can be downloaded at `www.microsoft.com/en-us/download/details.aspx?id=4511`. This tool currently requires a Windows client computer. This example will still work with a SQL Server on Linux installation; you will just need a Windows client to drive a concurrent user workload with ostress.

In addition, I set up my SQL Server on a virtual machine with eight logical CPUs. When I ran setup for SQL Server, it automatically created eight tempdb data files. I recommend on your system you make sure you have at least eight tempdb data files if you have eight or more logical CPUs. Learn more about how to do this with this technical support article: `https://support.microsoft.com/en-us/help/2154845/recommendations-to-reduce-allocation-contention-in-sql-server-tempdb-d`.

1. Run the script **disableopttempdb.cmd** to disable memory-optimized tempdb metadata. It is off by default, but run this script in case you had this enabled at one point. You need to run this script *on the server where SQL Server is installed* (or use another

technique to restart SQL Server remotely). This script assumes
a sysadmin login and a server name. You can modify this to use
integrated authentication by changing -Usa to -E and don't forget
to replace the name of your server for the -S parameter:

```
sqlcmd -Usa -idisableopttempdb.sql -Sbwsql2019
net stop mssqlserver
net start mssqlserver
```

As you can see, this script instructs Windows Server to restart the
SQL Service. You can modify your own script on Linux to use a
command like `sudo systemctl restart mssql-server` to restart
SQL Server.

disableopttempdb.sql contains the following T-SQL statement:

```
ALTER SERVER CONFIGURATION SET MEMORY_OPTIMIZED TEMPDB_
METADATA = OFF
GO
```

2. Run the T-SQL script **tempstress_ddl.sql** to create a database and
    stored procedure that does a simple create of a temporary table:

```
DROP DATABASE IF EXISTS DallasMavericks
GO
CREATE DATABASE DallasMavericks
GO
USE DallasMavericks
GO
CREATE OR ALTER PROCEDURE letsgomavs
AS
CREATE TABLE #gomavs (col1 INT)
GO
```

You can see that the stored procedure doesn't really do anything
with the temporary table. This is to show the minimal amount
of workload that can pressure concurrency of temporary table
metadata (since any exit of the stored procedure automatically
drops the temporary table).

3. You are now ready to run a concurrent tempdb workload using ostress. Use the script **tempstress.cmd** to execute this ostress workload:

```
ostress -Usa -Q"exec letsgomavs" -n50 -r10000
-dDallasMavericks -Sbwsql2019
```

You may need to adjust a few of these parameters in the script including using -E instead of -Usa for integrated authentication on Windows. You may also want to change the name of the server with -S. The -n50 parameter is the number of users to run the workload, and -r10000 is the number of iterations for each user. Notice the use of -Q to run the stored procedure directly, a tip I learned while working on early versions of this demo. Using the -Q option for ostress to directly run a query is faster than specifying a script with -i.

You will get prompted for the password if you use -Usa, and then it is off to the races. Depending on how fast your computer is, this workload will take a few minutes.

4. While this is running, in a new connection, open up the T-SQL script **pageinfo.sql**:

```
USE tempdb
GO
SELECT object_name(page_info.object_id), page_info.*
FROM sys.dm_exec_requests AS d
  CROSS APPLY sys.fn_PageResCracker(d.page_resource) AS r
  CROSS APPLY sys.dm_db_page_info(r.db_id, r.file_id,
r.page_id,'DETAILED')
    AS page_info
GO
```

This script uses new functionality in SQL Server 2019 to *crack* page information from a *resource* as found in **sys.dm_exec_requests** and to dump out in columnar format the fields of a page header.

Why would you want to run this? This is because when you experience latch waits for tempdb, you are provided a resource in the form of a **<dbid>:<fileid>:<pageid>**. Prior to this function being exposed, you would need to manually use DBCC PAGE to find out what object the page belongs to for the latch wait, a command that is not officially supported. This technique now gives you that official support to figure out the page in a page latch wait scenario.

Your results while the query is running in the previous step should look similar to Figure 2-27.

	(No column name)	database_id	file_id	page_id	page_header_version	page_type	page_type_desc
1	sysschobjs	2	1	116	1	1	DATA_PAGE
2	sysschobjs	2	1	116	1	1	DATA_PAGE
3	sysschobjs	2	1	116	1	1	DATA_PAGE
4	sysschobjs	2	1	116	1	1	DATA_PAGE
5	sysschobjs	2	1	116	1	1	DATA_PAGE
6	sysschobjs	2	1	116	1	1	DATA_PAGE
7	sysschobjs	2	1	116	1	1	DATA_PAGE
8	sysschobjs	2	1	116	1	1	DATA_PAGE
9	sysschobjs	2	1	116	1	1	DATA_PAGE

Figure 2-27. *Page latch waits for system tables in tempdb*

As described earlier, **sysschobjs** is a system table and a common contention point as temporary tables are being created and dropped.

5. Now let's enable memory-optimized tempdb metadata. Run the script **optimizetempdb.cmd** on the server where SQL Server is installed. This script runs the following so you can use alternative methods to enable the feature and restart SQL Server:

```
sqlcmd -Usa -ioptimizetempdb.sql -Sbwsql2019
net stop mssqlserver
net start mssqlserver
```

optimizetempdb.sql contains the following T-SQL statement:

```
ALTER SERVER CONFIGURATION SET MEMORY_OPTIMIZED TEMPDB_
METADATA = ON
GO
```

6. Confirm that memory-optimized tempdb metadata is enabled by examining the SQL Server ERRORLOG file. You should see a statement in the ERRORLOG like this:

```
Tempdb started with memory-optimized metadata.
```

7. Now run the workload again using **tempstress.cmd.** This time it will only take around 30+ seconds to run the same workload, with no changes to the application.

8. Run the script **pageinfo.sql** again to see if any page latch waits are occurring. Your results should be 0 rows!

9. While this is running, in another session, run the T-SQL script **find_memoptimized_tables.sql.** Your results should look something like Figure 2-28.

	(No column name)	object_id	xtp_object_id	row_insert_attempts	row_update_attempts	row_delete_attempts
1	sysrscols	3	-2147483648	1330	0	18
2	sysseobjvalues	9	-2147483647	0	0	0
3	sysschobjs	34	-2147483644	2582	1367237	1
4	sysmultiobjvalues	40	-2147483643	0	0	0
5	syscolpars	41	-2147483640	1082	1	0
6	sysidxstats	54	-2147483639	233	4	4
7	sysiscols	55	-2147483638	506	0	8
8	sysobjvalues	60	-2147483637	181	0	4
9	syssingleobjrefs	74	-2147483634	193	0	0
10	sysmultiobjrefs	75	-2147483633	107	0	0

Figure 2-28. *Tempdb system tables as memory optimized*

You can see all the system tables that are memory optimized (your result could even include more as this feature is being enhanced). Notice the heavy changes to sysschobjs, but that is not the only system table involved.

You may wonder how much extra memory is consumed by using this feature. While you still have this environment running, run a query against the DMV **sys.dm_os_memory_clerks**. You will see a row where type = MEMORYCLERK_XTP and name = DB_ID_2. The pages_kb column is roughly the amount of memory memory-optimized tempdb metadata consumes which, based on this example, is around 200Mb.

At this point, you are free to leave this option enabled for your server, but if you want to turn it off, use the script **disableopttempdb.cmd.**

You can see the huge benefits of this feature built into the engine. You only turn on a server configuration option, restart SQL Server, and you are ready to go.

If you access to catalog views in tempdb, you will see there are a few restrictions when using memory-optimized tempdb metadata. You can read about these restrictions and all the details of this capability at `https://docs.microsoft.com/en-us/sql/relational-databases/databases/tempdb-database?view=sqlallproducts-allversions#memory-optimized-tempdb-metadata`.

Hybrid Buffer Pool

Persistent memory devices have been around for a few years but are now starting to become more popular. The concept is memory-*based* hardware that have persistence through a power source. Think the speed of RAM but any data stored is guaranteed to survive a power restart. One of the more popular persistent memory offerings is by Intel, called Optane (`www.intel.com/content/www/us/en/architecture-and-technology/optane-technology/optane-for-data-centers.html`).

Our SQL Server engineering team is always looking to find ways to optimize access to data, and, with persistent memory, there are several opportunities. In fact, SQL Server 2016 included a feature called "tail of the log caching" based on persistent memory (see Kevin Farlee's blog post on the topic `https://blogs.msdn.microsoft.com/sqlserverstorageengine/2016/12/02/transaction-commit-latency-acceleration-using-storage-class-memory-in-windows-server-2016sql-server-2016-sp1/`).

Since persistent memory is in fact memory, SQL Server can access any data stored on a persistent memory device like it is really memory. This means SQL Server can find creative ways to bypass kernel code for I/O processing when accessing data on persistent memory devices.

One such new capability is **Hybrid Buffer Pool**. The concept is that if you place your database data files on a persistent memory device, SQL Server can simply access pages on the data file from this device without having to copy data from the data file into a buffer pool page. Hybrid buffer pool uses memory-mapped kernel calls to make this a reality. If a database page is modified, it must then be copied into the buffer pool and then eventually written back to the persistent memory device.

Performance results vary on the benefits of using hybrid buffer pool, but you can typically expect some boost from this technology, especially on read-heavy workloads.

For SQL Server, provided you have placed one or more database files on a persistent memory device, you can enable Hybrid Buffer Pool for all databases for SQL Server with the T-SQL statement:

```
ALTER SERVER CONFIGURATION SET MEMORY_OPTIMIZED HYBRID_BUFFER_POOL = ON
```

Note   When you enable hybrid buffer pool for all databases, you must restart SQL Server.

You can enable hybrid buffer pool for a specific database with a T-SQL statement like this (which does not require a server restart):

```
ALTER DATABASE <databaseName> SET MEMORY_OPTIMIZED = ON
```

To read more about how to enable your devices for persistent memory for databases, how to disable hybrid buffer pool, and best practices for using hybrid buffer pool, consult the documentation at https://docs.microsoft.com/en-us/sql/database-engine/configure-windows/hybrid-buffer-pool.

Persistent Memory Support

If you don't want to enable hybrid buffer pool but would like SQL Server to take advantage of reading and writing both data and transaction log data to persistent memory devices, you can configure your device as a persistent memory device on Linux. SQL Server will automatically detect it and use memory-based operations to move data into SQL Server cache and the device, bypassing the Linux kernel I/O stack. This process is called *enlightenment*.

Dell EMC was able to see significant performance improvements with enlightenment as documented at `www.emc.com/about/news/press/2019/20190402-01.htm`. According to Dell, "With new Intel® Optane™ DC persistent memory, customers can accelerate in-memory databases, virtualization and data analytics workloads with up to 2.5 times more memory capacity for select PowerEdge Servers. The PowerEdge R740xd enables up to 2.7 times the transactions per second with an Intel® Optane™ DC persistent memory compared to NVMe drives in a virtualized Microsoft SQL Server 2019 preview environment with VMware ESXi.1."

You can read all the details about how to enable your persistent memory device on Linux for SQL Server at `https://docs.microsoft.com/en-us/sql/linux/sql-server-linux-configure-pmem?view=sqlallproducts-allversions`.

Last-Page Insert Contention

Here is a common problem for SQL Server users for a very long time. You want to build a table with a primary key that will be used in a clustered index. And this primary key is a *sequential* value. In other words, each insert of a row leads to a new value in an incrementing order. The most common form of this type of key is a column using a SEQUENCE object or an IDENTITY property.

While the design works fine in most cases, it presents a challenging problem for application performance. Each time a query needs to modify a page, SQL Server must physically protect other queries from changing or reading the page structure at the same time (even with row-level locking) using a page *latch*.

If many users were all trying to modify the same page, your application might suffer in performance due to page latch contention. If you build a clustered index on a sequential key, the data is sorted on that key. Each insert will be trying to insert a new row in the last page of the clustered index leaf level. And if many users are concurrently executing inserts, they could all end up trying to modify the last page of the index, hence the term last-page insert contention.

While this contention is not ideal, it normally is not too much of a problem, until a phenomenon called a latch *convoy* occurs. Pam Lahoud, Senior Program Manager on the team (also known as @SQLGoddess), showed me this resource on the convoy problem: `https://blog.acolyer.org/2019/07/01/the-convoy-phenomenon/`. For SQL Server and the last-page insert contention problem, a page split is an example of a scenario where a convoy can build up. A page split can easily occur when there are not enough rows on the page for a new INSERT, and a new page must be created in the clustered index. Pam also had a really great analogy to the convoy issues. According to Pam, "Traffic jams are a common analogy used to describe the problem. If you have a road that is at maximum capacity, as long as all the traffic continues to move at the same speed, throughput will be consistent, albeit slightly slower. As soon as something occurs which causes drivers to hit the brakes, such as a slow driver, hazard on the road, or a contentious interchange, traffic piles up. If cars continue to enter the road at the same rate as before, the traffic just gets worse and worse. Drivers are still making progress, but at a very slow rate. At this point, the rate of throughput won't recover until the rate of cars entering the road slows down dramatically, much lower than what the road would normally be able to handle."

Many users in the SQL community, technical support, and engineering have tackled this problem in many different ways over the years. This support article mentions many of them (`https://support.microsoft.com/kb/4460004`). What about a solution within the engine itself that doesn't require application changes? When I saw our solution show up in SQL Server 2019 CTP 3.1, I knew this problem had been discussed before by our engineering team with lots of possible solutions. I asked Wonseok Kim, the lead developer for the feature, about its history. He showed me an e-mail thread that I actually had laying around in my mail folder but forgot about. Turns out a familiar name had been working on an approach, Slava Oks, along with many other giants of the SQL Server engineering team.

The solution now exists in the form of a new option for indexes called **OPTIMIZE_ FOR_SEQUENTIAL_KEY**. By adding this option to your index or primary key constraint, you are telling SQL Server to enable new code to try and avoid the convoy problem. This option doesn't eliminate latches or prevent a latch contention problem. What it does is try to avoid the dreaded convoy problem so that your workload throughput is consistent. You can read more about this option and how to use it in our documentation at `https:// docs.microsoft.com/en-us/sql/t-sql/statements/create-index-transact- sql?view=sqlallproducts-allversions#sequential-keys`.

Note   If you use this option, you may notice a new wait_type called BTREE_ INSERT_FLOW_CONTROL. This is normal and part of the mechanism to avoid or reduce the convoy problem.

This option is not for everyone. If you don't use a sequential key for a clustered index or don't see heavy contention, then I wouldn't recommend using this option. In fact, you might experience worse performance by blindly applying this to any clustered index.

If you want to try this out yourself, make sure you have a "wide" enough table. In my testing, simply creating a table with a single IDENTITY column did not yield any performance gains. What you need to do is cause conditions where enough page splits occur to see a convoy problem.

Note   It is possible the techniques as described in article `https://support.microsoft.com/kb/4460004` may provide you better performance, but this new method for an index may give you the consistent performance you need and is far less intrusive to your application.

Summary

This chapter was very long, and it reflects the incredible capabilities of intelligent performance baked into SQL Server 2019 designed to help you improve performance without application changes. I provided many detailed examples so you can see for yourself these rich features and how they can help accelerate performance and save you time with performance tuning as you deploy SQL Server 2019 everywhere in your organization or develop with your application.

CHAPTER 3

New Security Capabilities

Security is essential to managing data. SQL Server has a proven track record of not just building a secure product but providing the necessary capabilities to help you secure your data and access to the SQL Server instance. This chapter is about what we have added in SQL Server 2019 to the story of security.

Enhancing What We Have Built

After reading and using examples for a very long chapter on performance, you may look at this chapter, see the number of pages, and ask yourself, "Hey, isn't security important?" The answer is absolutely yes! For SQL Server, security is a very important part of the overall data platform.

In SQL Server 2019, the new security capabilities and the *challenges* they are designed to meet include

- **Always Encrypted with Secure Enclaves**

  Provide an end-to-end encryption solution, but not limit application query capabilities.

- **Data Classification and Auditing**

  Provide a built-in classification system for SQL Server objects, along with auditing for viewing of data that is marked for classification.

- **Transparent Data Encryption (TDE) suspend and resume**

  Provide a mechanism to schedule expensive encryption "at rest" operations against a database.

© Bob Ward 2019
B. Ward, *SQL Server 2019 Revealed*, https://doi.org/10.1007/978-1-4842-5419-6_3

- **Certificate management**

    Make certificate management easier with SQL Server, including
    Failover Cluster Instance and Always On Availability Group
    scenarios.

This may not seem like a big set of improvements, but each new feature attempts
to solve important security problems faced by our customers and originates from their
feedback. For example, data classification was specifically built into SQL Server to
address compliance with the General Data Protection Regulation (GDPR), but can be
used for many classification and auditing needs.

It is also very important to remember that SQL Server 2019 comes with a rich set of
security features introduced in SQL Server 2016. This includes

- Always Encrypted

- Dynamic data masking

- Row-level security

- Transparent Data Encryption performance with hardware
  acceleration

You can read about all these security capabilities at `https://docs.microsoft.com/`
`en-us/sql/database-engine/whats-new-in-sql-server-2016?view=sql-server-`
`2017#security-enhancements`.

It is important to keep in mind that, for nearly a decade, SQL Server has been the
least vulnerable database and data platform – by a large percentage – as tracked by the
National Vulnerability Database (NVD) run by the National Institute of Standards and
Technology (NIST). You can see all of these details at `https://nvd.nist.gov/`.

Let's look at each of the new capabilities for security for SQL Server 2019 in more
detail, starting with Always Encrypted with Secure Enclaves.

Always Encrypted with Secure Enclaves

Prior to SQL Server 2016, you had several methods to encrypt data, including

- **Encrypting connections** – All data (the TDS protocol data)
  exchanged between a client application and SQL Server is encrypted.

- **Encrypting data** in SQL Server tables using **T-SQL** (sometimes called column-level or cell-level encryption).

- **Transparent Data Encryption (TDE)** – Encrypting data *at rest* or data encrypted at the file level for SQL Server database files.

None of these solutions provide an "end-to-end" encryption mechanism. And more importantly, SQL Server admins have control of the keys used to encrypt data. Therefore, there is no concept of *separation of duties*. In the world of today's demanding security needs, application owners (i.e., business owners) want complete control of the security of their data. They want roles like database admins to manage the data platform infrastructure but not have access to business data or the keys used to control access to that data.

In SQL Server 2016, we introduced a feature called Always Encrypted to solve these problems. Always Encrypted has its roots from projects at Microsoft Research. As Raghav Kaushik, Principal Software Engineer at Microsoft, tells it, "...there are two projects worth citing. One is the Cipherbase project at MSR-Redmond which was attempting to build query processing on encrypted data, and the Trusted Cloud project at MSR-Cambridge that focused more on the building blocks around secure hardware."

Figure 3-1 shows an example of the architecture and flow of Always Encrypted.

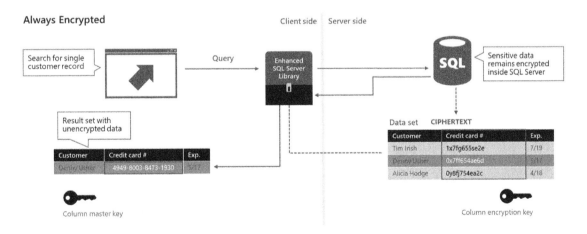

Figure 3-1. *Always Encrypted in SQL Server 2016*

The concept is the client application and their owners control the encryption lifecycle. All data is passed from the client application to SQL Server encrypted, stored in SQL Server encrypted (at the column level), and sent back to the client application encrypted. Only the client application can unencrypt the data at the application tier. In addition, the keys used to encrypt and unencrypt data are not actually stored in SQL Server. The location of the keys, owned by application owners, is stored in SQL Server. But access to those keys is controlled by the application.

It sounds like a great solution, but there is one drawback. Because all the decryption happens in the client application, some query patterns are not allowed against the data (e.g., only equality WHERE clauses are permitted). Furthermore, indexes on encrypted data with Always Encrypted are not supported. Given that the client application is the only place where decryption takes place, there is no way to truly build an index with Always Encrypted. SQL Server would have to send all the data for the columns encrypted as part of the index to the client application to build the index and then send it back to the server. So as good as the promise of Always Encrypted is, these limitations make it... well, limited in several scenarios.

Is there a solution? Yes, and it comes in the form of a concept called *Secure Enclaves*.

Why Enclaves?

Webster's dictionary defines an enclave (`www.merriam-webster.com/dictionary/enclave`) as "a distinct territorial, cultural, or social unit enclosed within or as if within foreign territory." In computer terms, it is a protective area that is secure and independent of hostile invaders. Those invaders could be hackers, but, unfortunately, they could also be administrators or DBAs.

Intel has released the concept of an enclave in their chipset known as Software Guard Extensions (SGX), which you can read about at `https://software.intel.com/en-us/blogs/2016/06/06/overview-of-intel-software-guard-extension-enclave`. SGX provide instructions in the CPU to allow for protected regions of memory that is secure for encryption and provides a safe haven from intrusion. That is interesting, but what if you don't happen to have an SGX chip? Microsoft has come along with a *virtualized* enclave solution called virtualization-based security (VBS) memory enclaves. You can read all the details about VBS at `www.microsoft.com/security/blog/2018/06/05/virtualization-based-security-vbs-memory-enclaves-data-protection-through-isolation/`.

What does that mean for Always Encrypted, and why does it matter?

Using Always Encrypted with Enclaves

Enclaves provide a unique solution for Always Encrypted for the "index problem." The data moving from the client application to SQL Server and back is still completely encrypted. And so is the data within SQL Server memory and on disk. However, when the data needs to be decrypted, for example, to build an index or support *rich computations*, the decryption can happen in the enclave on the server. The enclave is a secure region of memory in the SQL Server process space. This memory region is small and tightly integrated into the engine express services with enclave APIs. Rich computations are queries that require range queries or pattern matching (i.e., LIKE). Enclaves provide that capability now for Always Encrypted solutions.

Consider Figure 3-2 from the SQL Server documentation page (`https://docs.microsoft.com/en-us/sql/relational-databases/security/encryption/always-encrypted-enclaves`), which shows how enclaves support decryption in a secure manner but also provide more flexibility for applications.

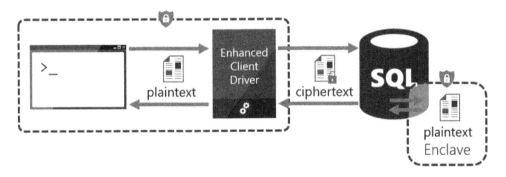

Figure 3-2. *Always Encrypted with Secure Enclaves*

Configuring Always Encrypted has never been for the mild SQL Server user. It is a complex solution for a complex problem. But it is powerful, especially now with enclaves.

Always Encrypted with Secure Enclaves requires another important component called an *attestation* Service. An attestation service is used by a client application to verify that an enclave used for encryption can be trusted. For VBS enclaves, Windows provides the **Windows Defender System Guard** runtime attestation (which uses something called the Host Guardian Service (HGS)). You can read more about Windows Defender System Guard at `www.microsoft.com/security/blog/2018/04/19/introducing-windows-defender-system-guard-runtime-attestation/`. You can also read more details about how applications communicate with Secure Enclaves at `https://docs.microsoft.com/ en-us/windows/desktop/api/enclaveapi/nf-enclaveapi-callenclave`.

In addition to setting up a VBS and configuring the Host Guardian Service, your application has to use a provider that supports communicating with an enclave. You can read the details of provider support for enclaves at `https://docs.microsoft. com/en-us/sql/relational-databases/security/encryption/always-encrypted- enclaves?view=sqlallproducts-allversions#secure-enclave-providers`.

At time of authoring this book, SQL Server has not yet officially supported hardware enclaves as provided by chip manufacturers such as Intel SGX. I expect that support to come soon, and you can stay in touch with the Always Encrypted documentation on enclaves for updates at `https://docs.microsoft.com/en- us/sql/relational-databases/security/encryption/always-encrypted- enclaves?view=sqlallproducts-allversions#why-use-always-encrypted-with- secure-enclaves`. Today Linux does not support a virtual enclave like VBS. However, once hardware enclave support is supported by SQL Server, I expect Linux support to come not long after.

I did not build an example for you to go through to set up and use Always Encrypted with enclaves. As I said earlier in the chapter, this is not a feature for the mild SQL Server user. It is an enterprise feature and takes some time to set up. But once set up, it is very powerful. Jakub Szymaszek, Senior Program Manager and lead for Always Encrypted, has provided several valuable resources on the topic.

Use the following GitHub repo to go through an example yourself with Always Encrypted using a VBS enclave, `https://github.com/microsoft/sql-server-samples/ tree/master/samples/features/security/always-encrypted-with-secure- enclaves`. Jakub also did an excellent presentation at Microsoft Ignite for you to get more details on Always Encrypted with enclaves at `https://myignite.techcommunity. microsoft.com/sessions/65357#ignite-html-anchor`.

Data Classification

With the launch of SQL Server 2017, our security group within the SQL Server engineering team built a tool in SQL Server Management Studio (SSMS) to help customers *classify* data within a SQL Server database. This tool encompassed a wizard, a set of T-SQL logic, and a report. Figure 3-3 shows the Data Classification wizard in SSMS.

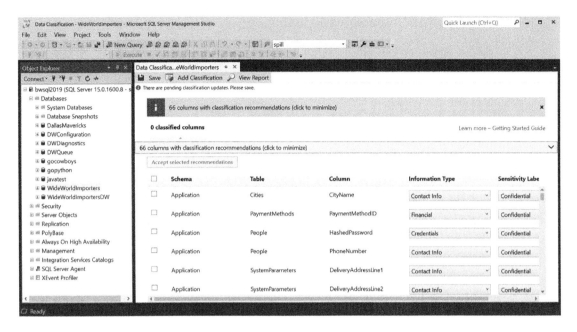

Figure 3-3. *The Data Classification wizard in SSMS*

One of the drivers behind building a tool like this was the growing trend in companies and regulatory agencies for privacy. And especially important was the pending General Data Protection Regulation (GDPR) being established by the European Union (`https://eugdpr.org/`).

Tip   GDPR regulations took effect in May of 2018. If you would like a complete guide on how to use SQL Server to meet the needs of GDPR in your organization, go to `www.microsoft.com/en-us/trustcenter/cloudservices/sql/gdpr`.

The idea of the tool was to analyze column names in your database and make recommendations on how to classify columns via a *label* and an *information_type*. The information_type could be used to tell you what kind of data exists in the column (e.g., Contact Info, Name, Financial), while the label could be used to classify the *sensitivity* of the data stored in that column (Confidential, Confidential-GDPR, HIPAA, etc.).

The tool would analyze column names and look for known patterns that matched known types of information and sensitivity. An example of a simple match would be any column with a name that contained the word Email in it. The tool would provide recommendations for labels and information_type and let you persist these within your database. Then you could use a report to view this classification information.

The tool was nice, but there were two limitations:

- The tool used a concept in SQL Server called *extended properties*. While that approach is supported and works, it is not the most efficient way to store metadata about column classification because it is a general property mechanism (you can read more about extended properties at `https://docs.microsoft.com/en-us/sql/relational-databases/system-stored-procedures/sp-addextendedproperty-transact-sql`).

- There is no built-in auditing for access to the columns that are marked for classification. Auditing is an important part of any classification system and is required to meet the needs of GDPR.

So, our team worked on a new solution for SQL Server 2019 (which also works in the Azure SQL Database suite of services) for built-in *sensitivity classifications*. Built-in means a new set of T-SQL statements, catalog views, and auditing.

The T-SQL statements now supported in SQL Server 2019 for classification are

ADD SENSITIVITY CLASSIFICATION (`https://docs.microsoft.com/en-us/sql/t-sql/statements/add-sensitivity-classification-transact-sql`)

DROP SENSITIVITY CLASSIFICATION (`https://docs.microsoft.com/en-us/sql/t-sql/statements/drop-sensitivity-classification-transact-sql`)

These T-SQL statements result in metadata stored directly into system tables (exposed by catalog views) that are specific to labels and information_types associated with columns in a table.

A new catalog view is supported to view this metadata called **sys.sensitivity_classifications** (`https://docs.microsoft.com/en-us/sql/relational-databases/system-catalog-views/sys-sensitivity-classifications-transact-sql`).

Furthermore, SQL Server Auditing now supports a new property called **data_sensitivity_information** which can be used to audit who, what, and when users are trying to view classified data.

With these capabilities, the SSMS wizard was modified to use the new T-SQL statements if working with a database in SQL Server 2019. This now provides you the capability of built-in classifications and auditing with a tool in SSMS and native T-SQL support.

> **Note**   If you have used the wizard with SSMS 17.0 or even 18.0 against a version of SQL Server prior to SQL Server 2019 and restore that database to SQL Server 2019, the classified extended properties will be migrated to the new sensitivity classification metadata.

Let's walk through an example of using the SSMS tool, the new T-SQL syntax, catalog views, and auditing.

Prerequisites for Using the Examples

First, you need to do some setup to use examples in this section of the chapter. For examples in this chapter, you will use the **WideWorldImporters** example database (you can read more about this database and its schema at `https://docs.microsoft.com/en-us/sql/samples/wide-world-importers-oltp-database-catalog`). If you have already restored the database from Chapter 2 examples, you can just keep using that database.

These examples will work on SQL Server 2019 on Windows, Linux, and Containers.

You will also need SQL Server Management Studio (SSMS) version **18.2** or higher to complete all the steps in the example. You can complete some of the steps using the T-SQL scripts provided, but some of the examples rely on the tools built into SSMS. You can download the latest version of SSMS from `https://docs.microsoft.com/en-us/sql/ssms/download-sql-server-management-studio-ssms`.

All the scripts used for this chapter can be found on the GitHub repo for this book under the **ch3_new_security_capabilities\dataclassification** directory.

In order to use the examples in this chapter, you need to go through the following steps (skip these steps if you have already restored the database from Chapter 2):

1. Download the WideWorldImporters database backup from `https://github.com/Microsoft/sql-server-samples/releases/download/wide-world-importers-v1.0/WideWorldImporters-Full.bak`.

2. Restore this database to your SQL Server 2019 instance. You can use the provided **restorewwi.sql** script. You may need to change the directory paths for the location of your backup and where you will restore the database files.

Using Data Classification

Walk through the following steps to see data classification in action. In the next section, you will learn how to set up auditing to track users who try to view columns set up with classification.

1. First you may run these examples more than once so run the following script **setup_classification.sql**:

```
-- Step 1: In case you have run these demos before drop existing
classifications
USE WideWorldImporters
GO
IF EXISTS (SELECT * FROM sys.sensitivity_classifications sc
WHERE object_id('[Application].[PaymentMethods]') = sc.major_id)
BEGIN
     DROP SENSITIVITY CLASSIFICATION FROM [Application].
     [PaymentMethods].[PaymentMethodName]
END
GO
IF EXISTS (SELECT * FROM sys.sensitivity_classifications sc
WHERE object_id('[Application].[People]') = sc.major_id)
BEGIN
     DROP SENSITIVITY CLASSIFICATION FROM [Application].
     [People].[FullName]
     DROP SENSITIVITY CLASSIFICATION FROM [Application].
     [People].[EmailAddress]
END
GO
```

2. Now use the SSMS Data Classification tool to add classifications for two columns in the WideWorldImporters database. Launch SSMS and find the WideWorldImporters database in Object Explorer. Right-click and choose Tasks ➤ Data Discovery and Classification ➤ Classify Data as seen in Figure 3-4.

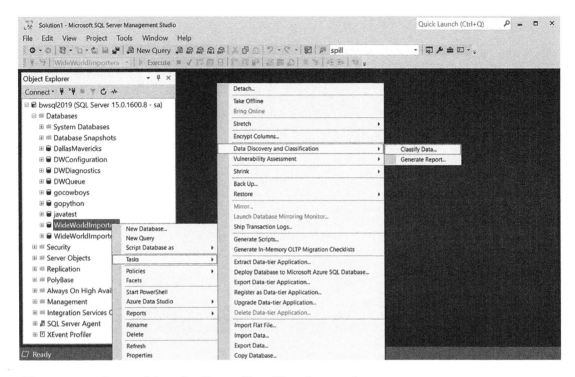

Figure 3-4. *Launching the Data Classification tool*

3. The tool analyzes column names in objects in the WideWorldImporters database and creates recommendations for which columns to classify and what labels and information_type to use. When you launch the tool with WideWorldImporters, you should get 66 columns with recommendations. Click the recommendations to see the result as in Figure 3-5.

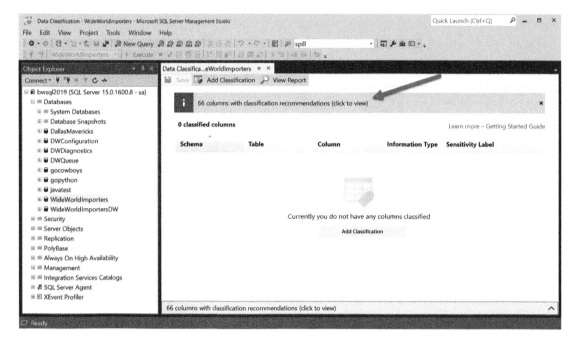

Figure 3-5. *Classification recommendation from SSMS*

4. What you will see now is a list of columns with suggested information_type and (sensitivity) label choices. The values for these recommendations are baked into the tool and cannot be configured. However, I'll show you with T-SQL how to "use your own system." Save some of these recommendations by checking the PaymentMethodName and FullName columns, then click **Accept selected recommendations**. Before you click Accept, your screen should look like Figure 3-6.

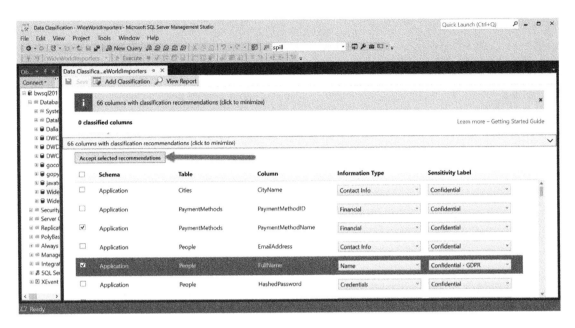

Figure 3-6. *Accept classification recommendations*

Notice that PaymentMethodName has a recommendation of Financial and Confidential (if you query this table, you will see the values are Cash, Check, Credit-Card, and EFT). For FullName, the recommendation is Name and Confidential-GDPR.

Note   The tool does not guarantee GDPR compliance or even look specifically at the details of GDPR. These are simply recommendations based on our knowledge of GDPR. If you need to use this system for GDPR purposes, be sure to follow your company policies and procedures.

---

5. After you click Accept, the tool will show you which columns were selected and allow you to save the choices. The "garbage can" icons allow you to delete your choices and choose again. Notice the number of columns to recommend has been reduced by 2. For now, select Save, as seen in Figure 3-7.

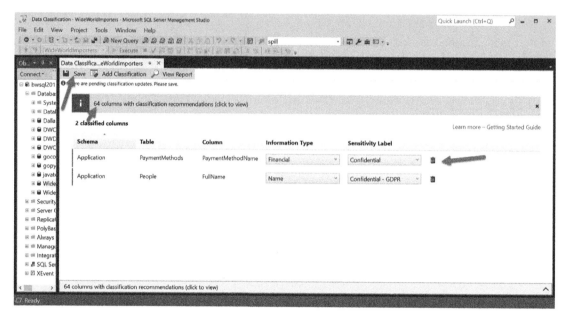

Figure 3-7. *Saving accepted recommendations*

6. After you have saved, you can select the option called View Report to see a visual of classifications saved with your database. A new tab in SSMS is created for the report. Be sure to click the + next to the Application schema to see all the classified columns. The report should look like Figure 3-8.

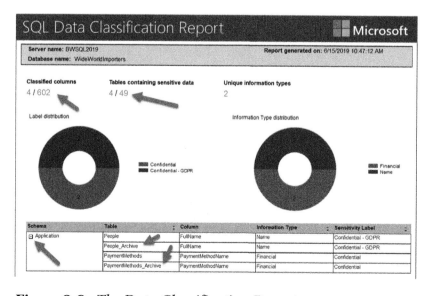

Figure 3-8. *The Data Classification Report*

The report will query the sys.sensitivity_classifications catalog view along with other metadata in the database. The report shows how many columns and tables are marked for labels out of all possible columns and tables. The report also shows a distribution of label and information_type values in the database. Notice at the bottom of the report, in the list of columns, that the People_Archive and PaymentMethods_Archive tables appear. Why? This is because these tables have system-versioned temporal tables built with them. Temporal tables, introduced in SQL Server 2016, provide point-in-time information about changes to a table in a database (you can read more about temporal tables at `https://docs.microsoft.com/en-us/sql/relational-databases/tables/temporal-tables`).

Since you accepted recommendations for columns in a table that has a temporal table, we want to be sure to also classify columns in the "hidden" archive table. You don't access those columns directly, but SQL Server persists the archive table. So, any access to temporal data can also be audited.

Note   You are not allowed to add sensitivity classifications directly to archive tables from temporal data. When you drop a sensitivity classification for a column, the classification for the archive table is also dropped.

---

7. If you go back to the tab with the saved recommendations, you will see an option for Add Classification. This is a way for you to manually add sensitivity classifications through the tool to either override the recommendations or choose a column that was not recommended. You still get the choices provided by the tool for labels and information_type. If you clicked Add Classification, it would look like Figure 3-9.

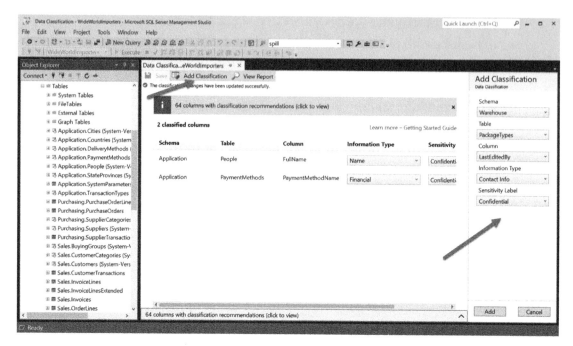

Figure 3-9. *Manually adding a classification through the tool*

8. The tool is great, but you may also want to use T-SQL directly
    to add your own classifications and system. First, use the script
    findclassifications.sql to see how you can use T-SQL to view all
    existing classifications.

```
USE WideWorldImporters
GO
SELECT o.name as table_name, c.name as column_name,
sc.information_type, sc.label
FROM sys.sensitivity_classifications sc
JOIN sys.objects o
ON o.object_id = sc.major_id
JOIN sys.columns c
ON c.column_id = sc.minor_id
AND c.object_id = sc.major_id
ORDER BY sc.information_type, sc.label
GO
```

Your results should look the same as from the report.

9. To add your own classification from T-SQL, use the script
    addclassification.sql. Run each step to add the classification
    and see the new results. You can put in whatever label and
    information_type values you want for your purposes. For this
    example, I chose different labels and types from the tool. Since
    this is an e-mail address, I called the type **Email** and the label
    PII (which stands for Personally Identifiable Information). In
    essence, these are just string values we are storing associated with
    columns. But like any system that is being built and designed, a
    good classification system will have some structure on what label
    and information_type labels should be used for a company and
    a database, and this metadata will show up that way in audits, as
    we'll see shortly.

```
-- Step 1: Add the classification
ADD SENSITIVITY CLASSIFICATION TO
[Application].[People].[EmailAddress]
WITH (LABEL='PII', INFORMATION_TYPE='Email')
GO
-- Step 2: View all classifications
USE WideWorldImporters
GO
SELECT o.name as table_name, c.name as column_name,
sc.information_type, sc.information_type_id, sc.label, sc.label_id
FROM sys.sensitivity_classifications sc
JOIN sys.objects o
ON o.object_id = sc.major_id
JOIN sys.columns c
ON c.column_id = sc.minor_id
AND c.object_id = sc.major_id
ORDER BY sc.information_type, sc.label
GO
```

Your result should look like Figure 3-10.

	table_name	column_name	information_type	information_type_id	label	label_id
1	People	EmailAddress	Email	NULL	PII	NULL
2	People_Archive	EmailAddress	Email	NULL	PII	NULL
3	PaymentMethods	PaymentMethodName	Financial	c44193e1-0e58-4b2a-9001-f7d6e7bc1373	Confidential	331f0b13-76b5-2f1b-a77b-def5a73c73c2
4	PaymentMethods_Archive	PaymentMethodName	Financial	c44193e1-0e58-4b2a-9001-f7d6e7bc1373	Confidential	331f0b13-76b5-2f1b-a77b-def5a73c73c2
5	People_Archive	FullName	Name	57845286-7598-22f5-9659-15b24aeb125e	Confidential - GDPR	989adc05-3f3f-0588-a635-f475b994915b
6	People	FullName	Name	57845286-7598-22f5-9659-15b24aeb125e	Confidential - GDPR	989adc05-3f3f-0588-a635-f475b994915b

Figure 3-10. *Classifications from the tool and T-SQL*

In these results, notice that the columns added by the tool have values for **information_type_id** and **label_id**. The T-SQL statement ADD SENSITIVITY CLASSIFICATION supports a GUID value to tag the strings for labels and types. This could be particularly valuable if your company builds a classification system to store all the accepted labels and types. You can now refer to any label or type through a GUID value, though it is up to you to generate GUID values.

Tip   The T-SQL function NEWID() can be used to generate unique GUID values within SQL Server. You can find more details at `https://docs.microsoft.com/en-us/sql/t-sql/functions/newid-transact-sql`.

So far so good. It seems like a fairly simple and straightforward system, which it is. But it is only as good as the labels and information_type values you choose to use. The beauty of T-SQL support is that any application that supports T-SQL can now build a classification system and query it since catalog view support also exists through T-SQL.

What about auditing? Proceed to the next section to see how it works. Leave everything as is to use these previous steps to show how auditing works.

Auditing and Data Classification

Having sensitivity classification metadata about columns is valuable, but an even more valuable feature would be for auditing to automatically pick up when users view columns marked with those classifications.

Modern versions of SQL Server include a built-in feature called **SQL Server Audit**. Based on Extended Events technology, Audit has many options and provides a rich auditing system. You can read more about the complete functionality of SQL Server Audit at https://docs.microsoft.com/en-us/sql/relational-databases/security/auditing/sql-server-audit-database-engine.

Audits are produced in a record format with all types of properties for each *audit event*. SQL Server 2019 adds a new audit event property called *data_sensitivity_ information*. So, for example, if you are auditing SELECT statements on certain tables where you have added sensitivity classification to columns, if the columns are part of the SELECT "list" to view data, the data_sensitivity_information column will show this access.

Let's continue with the example from earlier to look at how auditing works with sensitivity classifications.

1. Because you may run these examples more than once and don't want to have to restore the database, first run the script **dropsqlaudit.sql**.

```
-- Step 1: Disable the audits and drop them
USE WideWorldImporters
GO
IF EXISTS (SELECT * FROM sys.database_audit_specifications WHERE
name = 'People_Audit')
BEGIN
      ALTER DATABASE AUDIT SPECIFICATION People_Audit
      WITH (STATE = OFF)
      DROP DATABASE AUDIT SPECIFICATION People_Audit
END
GO
USE master
GO
```

```
IF EXISTS (SELECT * FROM sys.server_audits WHERE name = 'GDPR_
Audit')
BEGIN
      ALTER SERVER AUDIT GDPR_Audit
      WITH (STATE = OFF);
      DROP SERVER AUDIT GDPR_Audit
END
GO

-- Step 2: Remove the .audit files from default or your path
-- del C:\program files\microsoft sql server\mssql15.mssqlserver\
mssql\data\GDPR*.audit
```

Notice that Step 2 is a comment in the script to delete files. When you run an audit, it creates files in a path you specify. When you disable and drop the audit, the files remain in that directory. To keep the example clean, manually delete any leftover files from previous executions.

2. Open up the script **setupsqlaudit.sql** to create and start the audit. I won't go into the details of how auditing and specifications work. You can see through the syntax I've provided that an audit is set up to track SELECT statements against the [Application].[People] table in the WideWorldImporters database. Check out the documentation on auditing to learn more at https://docs.microsoft.com/en-us/sql/relational-databases/security/auditing/sql-server-audit-database-engine.

```
USE master
GO
-- Create the server audit.
CREATE SERVER AUDIT GDPR_Audit
    TO FILE (FILEPATH = 'C:\program files\microsoft sql server\
mssql15.mssqlserver\mssql\data')
GO
-- Enable the server audit.
ALTER SERVER AUDIT GDPR_Audit
```

```
WITH (STATE = ON)
GO
USE WideWorldImporters
GO
-- Create the database audit specification.
CREATE DATABASE AUDIT SPECIFICATION People_Audit
FOR SERVER AUDIT GDPR_Audit
ADD (SELECT ON Application.People BY public )
WITH (STATE = ON)
GO
```

3. Now let's run some queries and look at what is audited. Open up the script **findpeople.sql** and run Steps 1 and 2 as guided by comments in the script:

```
-- Step 1: Scan the table and see if the sensitivity columns were
audited
USE WideWorldImporters
GO
SELECT * FROM [Application].[People]
GO
-- Step 2: Check the audit
-- The audit may not show up EXACTLY right after the query but
within a few seconds.
SELECT event_time, session_id, server_principal_name,
database_name, object_name,
cast(data_sensitivity_information as XML) as data_sensitivity_
information,
client_ip, application_name
FROM sys.fn_get_audit_file ('C:\program files\microsoft sql
server\mssql15.mssqlserver\mssql\data\*.sqlaudit',default,default)
GO
```

Your results should look like Figure 3-11.

	event_time	session_id	server_principal_name	database_name	object_name	data_sensitivity_information	client_ip	application
1	2019-06-15 17:42:01.6702752	53	sa				10.0.0.50	Microsoft S
2	2019-06-15 17:43:29.7592877	53	sa	WideWorldImporters	People	<sensitivity_attributes> <sensitivity_attribute la..	10.0.0.50	Microsoft S

Figure 3-11. *Audit of a single table scan of a table with classifications*

In this example, you have run a query selecting all columns from the People table. The **fn_get_audit_file** T-SQL function is used to retrieve audit results in a row/column format. I've pulled only certain columns from the result set of this function. You can see the entire list of arguments and output columns for this function at https://docs.microsoft.com/en-us/sql/relational-databases/system-functions/sys-fn-get-audit-file-transact-sql.

The first row is a record that an audit has been started. The second row is an audit of the SELECT statement. Notice the data_sensitivity_information column value is an XML data type. Click that value and SSMS will bring up a new window with the complete XML data. Your results should look like Figure 3-12.

Figure 3-12. *Data sensitivity details*

The details of the XML include an attribute for any unique label and information_type accessed by the SELECT statement. You can now take this information and look up what columns are associated with these details with the **sys.sensitivity_classifications** catalog view.

4. Now execute statements in **findpeople.sql** for Steps 3 and 4:

```
-- Step 3: What if I access just one of the columns directly?
SELECT FullName FROM [Application].[People]
GO
```

```
-- Step 4: Check the audit
-- The audit may not show up EXACTLY right after the query but
within a few seconds.
SELECT event_time, session_id, server_principal_name,
database_name, object_name,
cast(data_sensitivity_information as XML) as data_sensitivity_
information,
client_ip, application_name
FROM sys.fn_get_audit_file ('C:\program files\microsoft sql
server\mssql15.mssqlserver\mssql\data\*.sqlaudit',default,default)
GO
```

The results from Step 4 should look like Figure 3-13.

	event_time	session_id	server_principal_name	database_name	object_name	data_sensitivity_information	client_ip	application
1	2019-06-15 17:42:01.6702752	53	sa				10.0.0.50	Microsoft S
2	2019-06-15 17:43:29.7592877	53	sa	WideWorldImporters	People	<sensitivity attributes><sensitivity attribute la...	10.0.0.50	Microsoft S
3	2019-06-15 17:53:45.6213307	53	sa	WideWorldImporters	People	<sensitivity attributes><sensitivity attribute la...	10.0.0.50	Microsoft S

Figure 3-13. *Audit including a SELECT for one column marked for classification*

A third row in the audit exists (you will get one row for each SELECT). If you click the data_sensitivity_information column, you will see only one label because only the FullName column was selected.

5. The audit will only track access to classifications if a column from the classification is part of the SELECT *list* or output of a query. Let's prove it. Run Steps 5 and 6 from **findpeople.sql**:

```
-- Step 5: What if I reference a classified column in the WHERE
clause only?
SELECT PreferredName FROM [Application].[People]
```

```
WHERE EmailAddress LIKE '%microsoft%'
GO
-- Step 6: Check the audit
-- The audit may not show up EXACTLY right after the query but
within a few seconds.
SELECT event_time, session_id, server_principal_name,
database_name, object_name,
cast(data_sensitivity_information as XML) as data_sensitivity_
information,
client_ip, application_name
FROM sys.fn_get_audit_file ('C:\program files\microsoft sql
server\mssql15.mssqlserver\mssql\data\*.sqlaudit',default,default)
GO
```

The results of Step 6 should look like Figure 3-14.

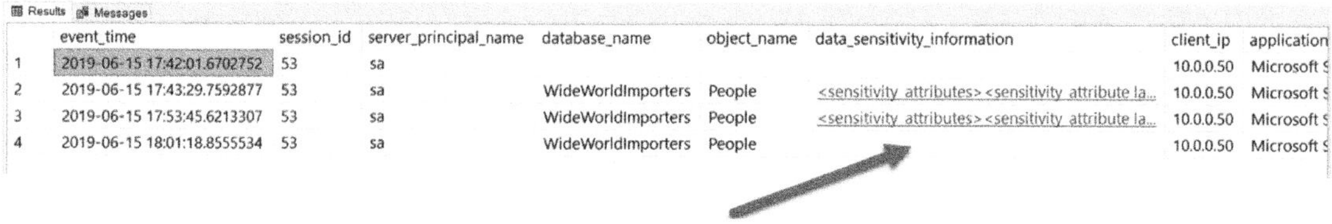

Figure 3-14. *Audit results for classified column in WHERE clause*

In this example, the query produces results for the PreferredName column using the EmailAddress column as criteria. PreferredName is not included in a classification but EmailAddress is. But because EmailAddress is not part of the SELECT list, the data_sensitivity_ information column is not populated.

Data classification is a simple but very powerful new capability in SQL Server 2019 you can add to your toolkit for keeping data secure and your organization compliant to any regulatory policies. The feature works both in SQL Server 2019 and Azure SQL Database. Take a look at the complete guide from our team on Information Protection at https://docs.microsoft.com/en-us/azure/sql-database/sql-database-data-discovery-and-classification.

Other New Security Features

There are a few other minor but important new security features in SQL Server 2019, including pause and resume for TDE, and simpler certificate management for encryption for SQL Server.

TDE Pause and Resume

Transparent Data Encryption (TDE) is all about data encryption *at rest.* This allows you to encrypt the SQL Server database and log files independent of the SQL Server engine. This way, if someone attempts to obtain access to your database and/or transaction log files, the data in the files will be encrypted. TDE has been a feature for several releases; you can read more about how to use it at https://docs.microsoft.com/en-us/sql/ relational-databases/security/encryption/transparent-data-encryption.

When you enable TDE for an existing database, SQL Server must read ***every*** database page from disk into the buffer pool and write it back out to the database file encrypted. The encryption happens in a background worker thread so it doesn't directly impact user workloads, but reading and writing all database pages can be intensive and consume CPU and I/O resources. For a very large database, this can impact a mission-critical application.

SQL Server 2019 introduces the concept of *pause* and *resume* for TDE encryptions. Now you can enable TDE for a database but then suspend the encryption at any point and resume the encryption from the last point it was suspended. This allows you to effectively schedule the full encryption of the database using TDE per your application needs.

Suspending TDE is as simple as running the following T-SQL statement:

```
ALTER DATABASE <db_name> SET ENCRYPTION SUSPEND
```

Resuming the encryption process where it was suspended can be done with the following T-SQL statement:

```
ALTER DATABASE <db_name> SET ENCRYPTION RESUME
```

To help with diagnostics for this new capability, the DMV **sys.dm_database_ encryption_keys** has three new columns to see the state of the TDE scan:

- **encryption_scan_state** – A number indicating if the TDE scan is in progress, suspended, or completed

- **encryption_scan_state_desc** – A string description of the scan state such as RUNNING, SUSPENDED, COMPLETE

- **encryption_scan_modify_date** – A date/time for the last time the scan state changed

This is a minor but important enhancement to using TDE with very large SQL Server databases. You can read more about TDE pause and resume at `https:// docs.microsoft.com/en-us/sql/relational-databases/security/encryption/ transparent-data-encryption`.

Certificate Management

Let's say you want to encrypt connections to SQL Server, a common practice to ensure the Tabular Data Stream (TDS) protocol between client applications and SQL Server is encrypted. When you set encryption with a protocol like TLS, you need certificates. SQL Server on Windows provides a mechanism to use certificates through the popular program SQL Server Configuration Manager. However, you must first do all the work to install the certificate on the server or even on multiple servers for a Failover Cluster Instance (FCI) or an Always On Availability Group.

Figure 3-15 shows a SQL Server Configuration Manager dialog box to choose an installed certificate to use with SQL Server 2017.

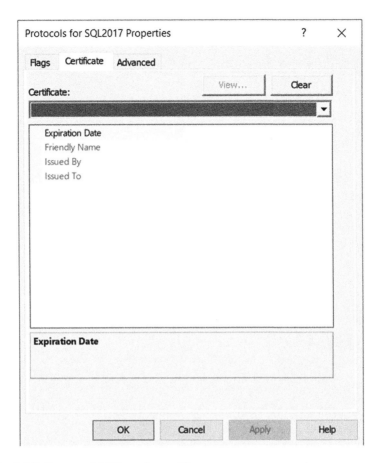

Figure 3-15. *SQL Server 2017 and certificate management*

SQL Server 2019 now includes the ability through SQL Server Configuration Manager to import a certificate and even import certificates across nodes of a Failover Cluster Instance or Availability Group – and you can perform it all from the primary instance. Figure 3-16 shows a dialog box for SQL Server Configuration Manager on SQL Server 2019.

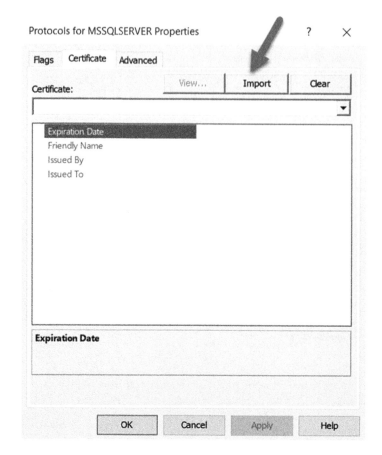

Figure 3-16. *SQL Server 2019 and configuration management*

Notice the new Import button on this dialog box. You can read all the instructions for how to use this on a single server or cluster at https://docs.microsoft.com/en-us/ sql/database-engine/configure-windows/manage-certificates.

Summary

Built on the rich capabilities of SQL Server 2016 such as Always Encrypted, row-level security, and dynamic data masking, SQL Server 2019 introduces new security features such as Secure Enclaves, data sensitivity classification, TDE suspend/resume, and easier certificate management. All of this, combined with all the security features built into SQL Server from previous releases, provides the right platform to keep your data secure, trusted, compliant, and manageable.

CHAPTER 4

Mission-Critical Availability

In the previous two chapters, you learned about new capabilities in SQL Server 2019 to solve modern challenges involving performance and security. For many enterprise customers, there is a third piece to the puzzle to ensure a database platform meets the challenges of today's applications and business: *availability*.

SQL Server provides availability by default because almost everything you do with SQL can be done **online**. SQL Server 2019 enhances the online availability for your data with the following new features designed to solve new challenges:

- **Online index enhancements**
  Users "want their cake and eat it too." They want administrators to keep indexes healthy and up to date but want complete access to their data all the time. SQL Server 2019 enhances previous online index features with **resumable online index creation** and **online clustered columnstore index** maintenance.

- **Availability Group enhancements**

  The flagship HADR feature of SQL Server, Always On Availability Groups, continues to be enhanced with each release of SQL Server including more replicas and better application connection redirection.

- **Accelerated Database Recovery**

  Anyone reading this book may have encountered this situation. Someone tries to kill a long-running transaction and gets frustrated eventually restarting SQL Server. But then they come to you and are even more frustrated that recovery of a database is taking forever.

115

© Bob Ward 2019
B. Ward, *SQL Server 2019 Revealed*, https://doi.org/10.1007/978-1-4842-5419-6_4

Why didn't SQL Server just bring the database back up immediately? You explain because recovery has to roll back the transaction you killed, or the database won't be consistent. Imagine none of that has to happen anymore. Welcome to Accelerated Database Recovery (ADR), one of the most innovative technologies I've seen come to the core SQL Server engine in some time. ADR is designed to make rollback instant, allow the transaction log to be aggressively truncated, and provide for "constant time recovery" for a user database. I wanted to start off with this topic, but I'll hold your curiosity until the end of the chapter.

Online Index Maintenance

Indexes can be such an important aspect to database performance. Therefore, maintaining indexes is a common task to keep your database healthy. One issue with creating indexes is the availability to access your data given the locks that are required on the table. The creation or rebuild of a clustered index effectively locks the table for the duration of the index operation. A nonclustered index create or rebuild can still be intrusive because it requires a shared (SH) table lock.

SQL Server 2005 (yes it has been around that long) introduced the concept of an *online* index create or rebuild. An online index build provides better availability to the application because a table lock is not required during the index build process.

Note   There is some locking against the table, but these are shorter in length and performed in phases during the online index build. To read more about how an online index is built, read the documentation at `https://docs.microsoft.com/en-us/sql/relational-databases/indexes/how-online-index-operations-work`. A useful resource for understanding the original online index implementation is at `https://docs.microsoft.com/en-us/previous-versions/sql/sql-server-2005/administrator/cc966402(v=technet.10)`.

While an online index build can help with availability, building an index can be resource intensive, which could still affect overall application availability depending on the nature of the queries of the application. Furthermore, there could be situations where building an index on a large table in one operation could be problematic, such as if the index failed before completing. A failure during an index build (e.g., you run out of space in the database) requires you to fix the problem and restart the index build from the beginning. Wouldn't it be nice to be able to take any index build operation and "start where it left off" should it fail? It would also be nice to schedule an index build into multiple segments, say, to spread across maintenance windows.

Resumable Index Operations

In SQL Server 2017, we introduced the concept of a *resumable* index *rebuild* operation. The idea is that you start rebuilding an index with the T-SQL statement **ALTER INDEX REBUILD**, and then you can use ALTER INDEX with the **PAUSE** option to suspend the index rebuild. All the progress to rebuild the new online index is saved so you can resume the index rebuild with ALTER INDEX using the **RESUME** option. You also have the option to abort an online index rebuild in progress with an ALTER INDEX command using the **ABORT** option. You can read the full syntax of how to use ALTER INDEX for a resumable index in the documentation at `https://docs.microsoft.com/en-us/sql/t-sql/statements/alter-index-transact-sql`. You can also read more specific details of how resumable rebuild index works and any restrictions at `https://docs.microsoft.com/en-us/sql/t-sql/statements/alter-index-transact-sql#online-index-operations`.

SQL Server 2019 introduces the concept of resumable indexes when *creating* the index with **CREATE INDEX**. You can read the syntax for how to create a resumable index in the documentation at `https://docs.microsoft.com/en-us/sql/t-sql/statements/create-index-transact-sql`. You can also read more details about resumable index creation at `https://docs.microsoft.com/en-us/sql/t-sql/statements/create-index-transact-sql#online-option`.

In addition, SQL Server 2019 introduces the concept of a **default database scoped setting** for online and resumable index operations. These new options are called ELEVATE_ONLINE and ELEVATE_RESUMABLE. You can read the details of using these options in the documentation at `https://docs.microsoft.com/en-us/sql/relational-databases/indexes/guidelines-for-online-index-operations?#online-default-options`.

Instead of just reading about resumable index creation, let's try an example using the new database scoped options.

Prerequisites to Using the Example

To execute the example presented in this chapter, you must install SQL Server 2019. In SQL Server 2017, resumable index rebuild requires Enterprise Edition. Therefore, you will need to install either Enterprise, Evaluation, or Developer Edition for these examples.

All of the scripts and files for this example can be found in the GitHub repo for the book under the **ch4_mission_critical_availability\resumableindex** directory.

There are three options to use the example:

- A T-SQL notebook called **resumableindex.ipynb** which requires Azure Data Studio (you need the June 2019 or later version). The T-SQL notebook has all the instructions for the complete example.

- Load the T-SQL script **resumableindex.sql** in SQL Server Management Studio (SSMS) or Azure Data Studio and go through each step as commented in the script.

- Run each set of T-SQL statements separately as seen in the T-SQL script **resumableindex.sql** and as I'll walk you through in the next section.

Try Out Resumable Index Creation

Let's walk through step by step on how to use a resumable online index.

1. Run Step 1 in the **resumableindex.sql** script to create the database for this example:

```
-- Step 1: Create the database
USE master
GO
DROP DATABASE IF EXISTS gotexasrangers
GO
CREATE DATABASE gotexasrangers
GO
```

2. Run Step 2 to create a table and populate it with some data. I chose this number of rows so that the index build will take over a minute. This is because when I show you how to use the

MAX_DURATION option, the minimum value for that option is 1 minute. Be patient with this step as it could take as long as 10–15 minutes to run. Go get a cup of coffee and come back to see this finish and proceed to Step 3.

```
-- Step 2: Create a table as a heap with no clustered index
-- Make the table fairly big so an index build takes at least
-- a few minutes. The resumable index option for MAX_DURATION has
-- a minimum value of 1 minute.
USE gotexasrangers
GO
DROP TABLE IF EXISTS letsgorangers
GO
CREATE TABLE letsgorangers (col1 int, col2 char(7000) not null)
GO
SET NOCOUNT ON
GO
BEGIN TRANSACTION
GO
INSERT INTO letsgorangers values (1, 'I would love to win the
World Series')
GO 750000
COMMIT TRANSACTION
GO
SET NOCOUNT OFF
GO
```

3. Run Step 3 to create an online, resumable clustered index. Notice the use of the option called MAX_DURATION. This means that the index build will be paused if it has not completed after 1 minute.

```
-- Step 3: Try to create the index as online, resumable, and a
max_duration of one minute
CREATE CLUSTERED INDEX rangeridx ON letsgorangers (col1) WITH
(ONLINE = ON, RESUMABLE = ON, MAX_DURATION = 1)
GO
```

When the duration has expired, the CREATE INDEX will experience a failure. Normally, this would require you to "start over" since the entire index build would be rolled back. But since you created the index as resumable, the index build is merely paused.

When the failure occurs, your output should look something like the following:

```
Msg 3643, Level 16, State 1, Line 31
The operation elapsed time exceeded the maximum time
specified for this operation. The execution has been
stopped.
The statement has been terminated.
Msg 596, Level 21, State 1, Line 29
Cannot continue the execution because the session is in the
kill state.
Msg 0, Level 20, State 0, Line 29
A severe error occurred on the current command.   The
results, if any, should be discarded.
```

This message means the statement has failed and terminated the connection. This seems like a problem but, again, the progress of the create index is simply paused.

Note   Another way to pause a resumable index build is to use the ALTER INDEX command with the PAUSE option on another connection while the create index is running.

---

4. Run Step 4 to check on the progress of the index build using the Dynamic Management View (DMV) **sys.index_resumable_ operations**.

```
-- Step 4: Check the progress of the index build
USE gotexasrangers
GO
SELECT * FROM sys.index_resumable_operations
GO
```

In your result set, the **state_desc** should be **PAUSED**, and the **percent_complete** should be around 30%. This means that when you resume the index build, it should only have about 70% left to finish.

5. To resume the index build operation and complete it, you can use the ALTER INDEX statement like in Step 5.

```
-- Step 6: Resume the index build
ALTER INDEX rangeridx on letsgorangers RESUME
GO
```

While this is running, you could use ALTER INDEX with the PAUSE option to pause the index build again (and then resume it again).

6. Let's try creating a resumable index a different way. First, use Step 6 to drop the existing index and set two database scoped options to make creating indexes online and resumable the default, where supported.

Note   Not all indexes can be built online and resumable. For example, XML indexes are not supported. You can see a list of indexes that are not supported for online operations at `https://docs.microsoft.com/en-us/sql/relational-databases/indexes/guidelines-for-online-index-operations`.

```
-- Step 6: Drop the first index. Use the default scoped
option for resumable and online
USE gotexasrangers
GO
ALTER DATABASE SCOPED CONFIGURATION SET ELEVATE_RESUMABLE =
WHEN_SUPPORTED
GO
ALTER DATABASE SCOPED CONFIGURATION SET ELEVATE_ONLINE =
WHEN_SUPPORTED
GO
DROP INDEX IF EXISTS letsgorangers.rangeridx
GO
```

7. Now create the index using Step 7 with no special options. **Let the CREATE INDEX run for about 30 seconds and then cancel it.** Use whatever technique to cancel a query from your tool (for SSMS hit the red stop button):

```
-- Step 7: Create the index again. Notice there are no options
used.
-- CANCEL this after about 30 seconds
CREATE CLUSTERED INDEX rangeridx ON letsgorangers (col1)
GO
```

Your output will be something like this:

```
The statement has been terminated.
Query was canceled by user.
```

Normally, cancelling a CREATE INDEX would cause it to roll back. But since the default options for indexes that are supported are ONLINE and RESUMABLE, the index build is only paused, even though you didn't have to explicitly specify those options.

8. Check the status of the paused index build using Step 8.

```
-- Step 8: Check the index progress
USE gotexasrangers
GO
SELECT * FROM sys.index_resumable_operations
GO
```

As seen earlier in this example, the state_desc should be PAUSED, and the percent_complete should be around 20–30%.

9. Use Step 9 to resume and complete the index build.

```
-- Step 9: Resume the index build
ALTER INDEX rangeridx on letsgorangers RESUME
GO
```

Keep this possible scenario in mind when you think of resumable indexes. Let's say creating or rebuilding an index takes 4 hours, and, during that time, building the index takes a certain amount of memory, CPU, and I/O resources that can be somewhat impactful to your application. You could now use a technique of CREATE and then PAUSE/RESUME in multiple segments. Choose the segments to create or resume the index build when application usage is at its lowest; you are now scheduling an index build into multiple phases. You could even use a SQL Server Agent job to schedule these phases for whatever time best meets your application requirements.

Online Index Maintenance for Columnstore

Clustered columnstore indexes are critical for high-performance analytic queries, especially in data warehouse scenarios. Building (or rebuilding) a clustered columnstore index may be a lengthy operation given the size of tables where a clustered columnstore index is typically built. Since the build or rebuild of a clustered columnstore index is *offline*, the entire table must be locked from other transactions, which is not the availability you likely need.

SQL Server 2017 introduced the ability to build and rebuild nonclustered columnstore indexes online. In SQL Server 2019, clustered columnstore indexes can now be built and rebuilt online. You can read the details of the syntax for online clustered columnstore build at `https://docs.microsoft.com/en-us/sql/t-sql/statements/create-columnstore-index-transact-sql`. The syntax to rebuild a clustered columnstore index online will be the same as with a standard index using the ALTER INDEX syntax at `https://docs.microsoft.com/en-us/sql/t-sql/statements/alter-index-transact-sql`. Resumable indexes are not yet supported for online clustered or nonclustered columnstore indexes.

Enhancing Always On Availability Groups

Always On Availability Groups (I will refer to this as Availability Groups for the rest of the chapter) are the flagship High Availability Disaster Recovery (HADR) feature in SQL Server. First shipped in SQL Server 2012, each release has come with new enhancements to expand the capabilities of Availability Groups.

For example, in SQL Server 2016, we introduced the concept of database health for failover with Availability Groups (you can read more about this concept at `https://docs.microsoft.com/en-us/sql/database-engine/availability-groups/windows/sql-server-always-on-database-health-detection-failover-option`). We also boosted the internal performance of Availability Groups, which you can read about at `https://blogs.msdn.microsoft.com/bobsql/2016/09/26/sql-server-2016-it-just-runs-faster-always-on-availability-groups-turbocharged/`.

In SQL Server 2017, one key new capability for Availability Groups is the concept of *clusterless* Availability Groups. This allows you to set up an Availability Group with no clustering software. Any failover is manual, but this capability could allow you to set up a read scale-out replica platform or even set up Availability Groups across Windows and Linux. You can read more about this capability at `https://docs.microsoft.com/en-us/sql/database-engine/availability-groups/windows/read-scale-availability-groups`.

For SQL Server 2019, we have introduced two new capabilities for Availability Groups, based on customer feedback and technology trends:

- Support for more replicas

- A new method to ensure your application is connected to the primary replica

Support for More Synchronous Replicas

We now support up to **five synchronous replicas** in an Availability Group, and a total of nine overall replicas. See the documentation at `https://docs.microsoft.com/en-us/sql/database-engine/availability-groups/windows/always-on-availability-groups-sql-server` for more information.

Secondary to Primary Replica Read/Write Connection Redirection

Secondary to primary replica read/write connection redirection is a new capability to solve the challenge for your application to always be directed to the primary replica no matter what SQL instance is hosting the primary replica for the Availability Group.

In previous versions of SQL Server, the only way as a developer to ensure you were connected to the primary replica of an Availability Group was to use the concept of a *listener*. However, a listener may not always be available when you configure SQL Server Availability Groups such as a *clusterless* Availability Group as I described earlier in this section.

SQL Server 2019 now provides T-SQL settings for Availability Groups and connection string options for client applications to ensure the application will always be connected to the primary replica no matter what server in the Availability Group the application is connected to. SQL Server provides the built-in logic for this concept and uses a concept of redirection if an application connected to a server that was a secondary replica.

You can read all the details of how to set up primary connection redirection for SQL Server and your application in the documentation at `https://docs.microsoft.com/en-us/sql/database-engine/availability-groups/windows/secondary-replica-connection-redirection-always-on-availability-groups`.

Accelerated Database Recovery

One of the aspects of my job at Microsoft I still find very exciting is to learn about new innovations that start as projects and then see them make it into a new feature of a released product, sometimes years later.

As an example, I remember seeing in 2016 when I joined engineering about a project called constant time recovery (CTR). I remember taking some time to see what this project was about, because I saw the name of my long-time colleague Peter Byrne involved in the project. CTR has become Accelerated Database Recovery (ADR) with SQL Server 2019 and Azure SQL Database.

CTR actually started as a project in 2015 initiated by Hanuma Kodavalla, Distinguished Engineer at Microsoft. Hanuma recruited others to join a project including Peter Byrne, Panagiotis Antonopoulos, and Srikumar Rangarajan, among others. The project was trying to attack one very large problem with SQL Server: *long-running transactions*. When these engineers finished the work, they decided to write a paper on the concept. As you read through the rest of this chapter and use the examples, consider also reading all the details of the paper for the CTR project at `www.microsoft.com/en-us/research/publication/constant-time-recovery-in-azure-sql-database/`. I call this the **CTR Paper** and will refer to it that way for the rest of this chapter. I recommend you do what I did when I wrote this chapter. Bring up this paper and refer to it back and forth as you read the chapter and use the examples.

The Challenge of Long Active Transactions

Long-running transactions can cause **recovery to "run out of control"** (effectively take a very long time that you can't predict) and affect application availability to data. This isn't some type of bug or problem with the SQL Server engine; it is doing exactly as it is told by the application. SQL Server can't prevent an application from running a large number of modifications within a transaction or a transaction that makes few modifications but does not commit or roll back for long periods of time. That is the classic definition of a *long-running transaction*.

In addition, rolling back a long transaction requires something called *compensation* operations. Rollback requires logical undo. A DELETE of 1 million rows requires 1 million DELETE log records. A rollback of this delete transaction would require SQL Server to undo all the deletes and also log 1 million INSERT log records. This **slows down the time it takes to roll back a transaction**. I've often seen customers try to KILL a session with a long-running active transaction and wonder why the KILL doesn't have immediate effect. It is usually because the transaction must be rolled back before the session can be safely terminated (or you would have data inconsistency).

Another consequence of a long-running transaction is its impact on **transaction log truncation**. The transaction log can only be truncated up to the oldest active transaction. You can't remove transaction log records for a transaction that is still not committed or rolled back. But since the transaction log is serial, a single "old" active transaction (and it may not have any activity associated with it) can hold up the truncation of the transaction log for every other transaction after it. This means to you the appearance of a transaction log that seems to "grow out of control" (and often you can't figure out why).

Accelerated Database Recovery was designed to solve all of these problems.

How Accelerated Database Recovery Works

Accelerated Database Recovery (ADR) is designed to tackle the problems with long-running transactions through the following capabilities, as listed in the documentation at https://docs.microsoft.com/en-us/azure/sql-database/sql-database-accelerated-database-recovery:

- **Fast and consistent database recovery**

  With ADR, long-running transactions do not impact the overall recovery time, enabling fast and consistent database recovery irrespective of the number of active transactions in the system or their sizes.

- **Instantaneous transaction rollback**

  With ADR, transaction rollback is instantaneous, irrespective of the time that the transaction has been active or the number of updates that it has performed.

- **Aggressive log truncation**

  With ADR, the transaction log is aggressively truncated, even in the presence of active long-running transactions, which prevents it from growing out of control.

SQL Server Normal Recovery

In order to understand how Accelerated Database Recovery can solve these problems, it is first important) to understand how traditional recovery works for SQL Server.

Consider this diagram in Figure 4-1 as provided in the CTR paper (`www.microsoft.com/en-us/research/publication/constant-time-recovery-in-azure-sql-database/`).

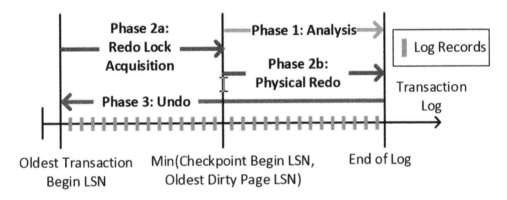

Figure 4-1. *The normal SQL Server recovery process*

The recovery process for SQL Server consists of three phases:

1. **Analysis**

   Start from the log record when a CHECKPOINT was recorded and scan log records until the end of the log.

   This analysis allows SQL Server to know:

   - Which transactions were not committed (active) at the time the database was last taken offline (could just be a SQL Server shutdown). These are likely the transactions that need to be rolled back to ensure consistency.

- The log record containing the oldest modified or "dirty" page. SQL Server needs this so it can redo, if necessary, any committed transactions where pages associated with the committed transactions do not reflect the transaction state.

In other words, analysis is all about setting up recovery to perform the next two phases: **redo** and **undo**.

2. **Redo**

In order for your data to be consistent, SQL Server must ensure that any committed transactions are accurately reflected during recovery. The method to achieve this involves finding the log record from the oldest modified or "dirty" page in the transaction log and comparing the Log Sequence Number (LSN) for each log record in the committed transaction with the LSN on the affected page. If the page LSN is smaller than the log record LSN, the log record operation (INSERT, UPDATE, DELETE, etc.) must be *redone*. Each log record for committed transactions is examined this way until the end of the log.

However, the redo phase, phase 2, actually starts at the log record with the oldest active transaction. The redo phase starts here because it needs to acquire locks for active transactions so that the database can be made available to users (who would be blocked on these locks so they cannot touch active transaction data) after the redo phase. However, this means the redo phase is affected by the size of log records from the oldest active transaction. Can you see now why the length of recovery time can be affected by a long active transaction? Once redo is finished, the third and final phase, undo, takes place.

3. **Undo**

Just like ensuring committed transactions are accurately reflected on database pages, SQL Server must make sure that any transactions that are **not** committed are **not** reflected in database pages. You may be wondering how could SQL Server have database pages hardened to disk for transactions that were not committed? This is because SQL Server can at any time write a modified or dirty page to disk if it needs a page for another user and no free pages are available.

Or a checkpoint (including indirect checkpoint) operation could take place, which will write modified pages to disk, whether the transaction is committed or not. Therefore, if SQL Server was shut down with active transactions that were not committed, the engine must ensure during recovery that no database pages have any modifications associated with the uncommitted transaction. Any active transactions in this state need to be rolled back, just like if a ROLLBACK TRANSACTION was executed at runtime.

SQL Server does this by scanning the log backward, from the end of the log to the log record with the oldest active transaction, to perform the necessary rollback operations. Now the time for undo is proportional to the length of the oldest active transaction. This is also why customers are surprised when they kill SQL Server in hopes of getting the database up quickly when a long-running transaction can't be killed (because it is in rollback) and recovery takes a long time. It is because SQL Server must keep your data consistent and has to finish the rollback it was previously running.

This recovery system, based on a design called ARIES (see this paper for more details `https://dl.acm.org/citation.cfm?id=128770`), has served SQL Server well for 25 years and works perfectly fine (and is still needed and used) except for the one scenario I have called out: a long-running active transaction which lengthens the time for both redo and undo processing.

Now let's look at how Accelerated Database Recovery (ADR) changes the game.

SQL Server Using Accelerated Database Recovery (ADR)

I won't attempt to give you every detail of what the CTR paper describes, but I'll describe the basic components that make ADR work and how it is different from the standard ARIES recovery approach and then use an example to give you more insight.

ADR introduces the concept of a Persistent Version Store (PVS). SQL Server has a concept called a version store which is used for snapshot isolation, but that version store is kept in tempdb. PVS is a similar concept in that versions of modifications are kept for rows, but this version store is persistent, because it is stored in the user database (the version store for snapshot isolation) is not persistent because it is kept in tempdb, and tempdb is recreated after a server restart). Once you enable ADR, SQL Server will start

129

tracking modifications using versions. Versions can be stored either in the row (*in-row*) of a database page or in *off-row* storage within the database. Versions have the previous state of the data before the modification and a transaction ID that caused the version, to easily identify whether a version of the data should be visible to other transactions.

Now with PVS, transaction operations like rollback get interesting and *easy*. If a transaction is rolled back, SQL Server simply marks the transaction as ABORTED. Now any query looking at the row for data can determine if a version of the row is visible and should be used. If the latest version of a row is associated with an ABORTED transaction, the query can ignore this version and look for a previous version. If the version of the row is associated with a committed or active transaction, isolation level rules apply to see if the row is visible.

SQL Server maintains the state of transactions to make all this work through the concept of an *Aborted Transaction Map*. This is discussed in more detail in the CTR paper.

Note   One aspect of versions with ADR that can be confusing is isolation levels. The current feature of versions (in tempdb) is specifically built to support snapshot isolation levels. Versions for ADR are not built to support snapshot isolation but can be used to support them along with the other benefits of ADR.

PVS also provides benefit to fast recovery (hence the term constant time recovery). The redo phase just needs to make sure the version store is consistent within rows of pages of tables. Undo just needs to mark any active transaction as aborted, and the process of versioning as described earlier does the rest. This makes recovery very quick.

Some transactions, mostly system transactions (e.g., page allocation, updating statistics), cannot use the new PVS scheme. Therefore, when ADR is enabled, SQL Server maintains a secondary log (*Slog*, which is stored in the transaction log) for any transactions that cannot use versioning. Transactions associated with the Slog must use the normal ARIES recovery mode. Fortunately, system transactions are almost always short-lived so won't cause issues as seen with long-running user transactions.

Figure 4-2, extracted from the CTR paper, shows the new recovery process when ADR is enabled.

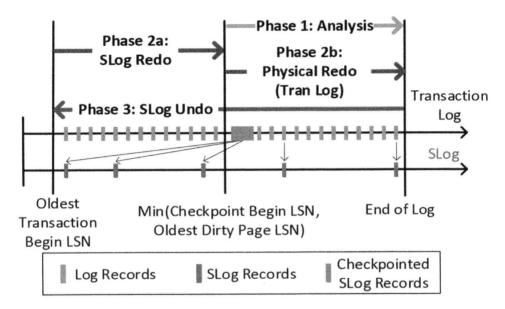

Figure 4-2. SQL Server using Accelerated Database Recovery

As you can see in the diagram, SQL Server still has three phases of recovery: analysis, redo, and undo. But now the process is much faster, hence the term accelerated.

Analysis still must do the work as it has done in the past, starting from the last log record for a CHECKPOINT, but redo and undo are significantly different.

Redo will ensure log records for Slog operations are redone from the oldest active transaction to the log record from the oldest dirty page operation. From this point, redo will perform the same operations of ensuring data is correctly committed as with ARIES recovery. But this sequence should usually be short, assuming standard checkpoint configurations are used for the database.

Undo just needs to mark any uncommitted transaction as aborted but will need to undo Slog transaction operations similar to ARIES user transactions. But system transactions are short in nature and represent a very small subset of all transactions, so this process should always be fast.

The result is a new, incredibly fast recovery system all based on a version store kept in the user database.

Let's use an example to look more into how transaction logging is different when using ADR. This example is all self-contained. You just need SQL Server 2019 and SQL Server Management Studio (SSMS) or Azure Data Studio (ADS) to run this example. You will use the script **alookatadr.sql** as found in the **ch4_mission_critical_availability\adr** directory.

1. Open up the script **alookatadr.sql** and execute Step 1 in the script to create the database.

```
-- Step 1: Create the database and make it simple recovery.
Default for ADR is OFF
USE master
GO
DROP DATABASE IF EXISTS gocowboys
GO
CREATE DATABASE gocowboys
GO
ALTER DATABASE gocowboys SET RECOVERY SIMPLE
GO
```

Tip   This example uses a SIMPLE recovery model for the database to make it easier to examine log records.

---

2. Run Step 2 in the script to create a table and insert rows. Note that the script inserts 1000 rows. Because of an optimization with ADR, you can't just use one row (you will learn more about this optimization later in the chapter):

```
-- Step 2: Create a very basic table and insert 1000 rows
USE gocowboys
GO
DROP TABLE IF EXISTS howboutthemcowboys
GO
CREATE TABLE howboutthemcowboys (col1 int, col2 char(100) not
null)
GO
INSERT INTO howboutthemcowboys VALUES (1, 'Whitten has returned')
GO 1000
```

3. Use Step 3 to truncate the log via a CHECKPOINT (to make it easier to see existing log records) and delete the 1000 rows in a transaction. Roll back the transaction and examine the log using the system function **sys.fn_dblog**:

```
-- Step 3: Truncate the log, delete all rows, roll it back, and
look at the tlog records
CHECKPOINT
GO
BEGIN TRANSACTION;
DELETE FROM howboutthemcowboys
ROLLBACK TRANSACTION
GO
SELECT * FROM sys.fn_dblog(NULL, NULL)
GO
```

The results of querying the log should yield some 2000+ rows. If you scroll to the bottom of the results, you should see log records such as in Figure 4-3.

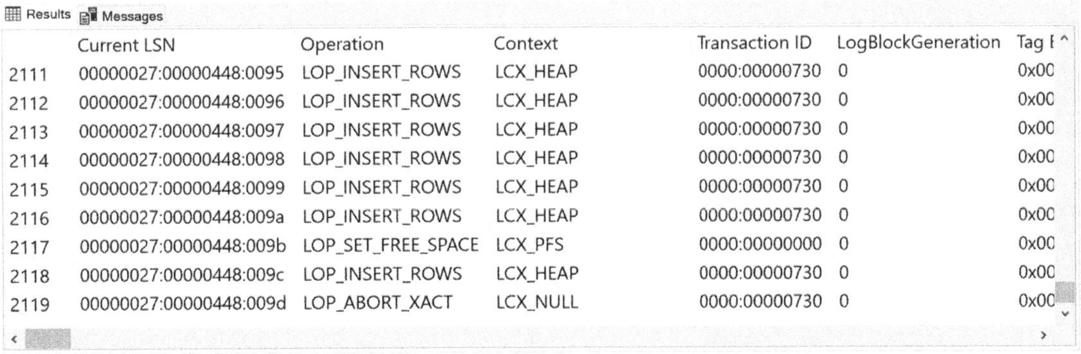

	Current LSN	Operation	Context	Transaction ID	LogBlockGeneration	Tag F ^
2111	00000027:00000448:0095	LOP_INSERT_ROWS	LCX_HEAP	0000:00000730	0	0x00
2112	00000027:00000448:0096	LOP_INSERT_ROWS	LCX_HEAP	0000:00000730	0	0x00
2113	00000027:00000448:0097	LOP_INSERT_ROWS	LCX_HEAP	0000:00000730	0	0x00
2114	00000027:00000448:0098	LOP_INSERT_ROWS	LCX_HEAP	0000:00000730	0	0x00
2115	00000027:00000448:0099	LOP_INSERT_ROWS	LCX_HEAP	0000:00000730	0	0x00
2116	00000027:00000448:009a	LOP_INSERT_ROWS	LCX_HEAP	0000:00000730	0	0x00
2117	00000027:00000448:009b	LOP_SET_FREE_SPACE	LCX_PFS	0000:00000000	0	0x00
2118	00000027:00000448:009c	LOP_INSERT_ROWS	LCX_HEAP	0000:00000730	0	0x00
2119	00000027:00000448:009d	LOP_ABORT_XACT	LCX_NULL	0000:00000730	0	0x00

Figure 4-3. *Log records from an aborted DELETE*

Notice all the log records called LOP_INSERT_ROWS before the LOP_ABORT_XACT to make the transaction aborted. These LOP_INSERT_ROWS records are compensation log records for the DELETE. The logical rollback of a DELETE is an INSERT. All the LOP_INSERT_ROW log records and the final LOP_ABORT_XACT were generated as part of the ROLLBACK TRANSACTION statement.

4. In Step 4, enable ADR with ALTER DATABASE, recreate the table, and insert rows again:

```
-- Step 4: Change to use ADR for the db. Recreate the table again
ALTER DATABASE gocowboys SET ACCELERATED_DATABASE_RECOVERY = ON
GO
USE gocowboys
GO
DROP TABLE IF EXISTS howboutthemcowboys
GO
CREATE TABLE howboutthemcowboys (col1 int, col2 char(100) not
null)
GO
INSERT INTO howboutthemcowboys VALUES (1, 'Whitten has returned')
GO 1000
```

5. With Step 5, repeat the same exercise to truncate the log, roll back a DELETE, and look at log records in the transaction log:

```
-- Step 5: Delete and rollback and look at the tlog again
CHECKPOINT
GO
BEGIN TRANSACTION
DELETE FROM howboutthemcowboys
ROLLBACK TRANSACTION
GO
SELECT * FROM sys.fn_dblog(NULL, NULL)
GO
```

You should now see only 1000+ log records. Scroll down again to the bottom of the results and look at the last log records. It should look like Figure 4-4.

	Current LSN	Operation	Context	Transaction ID	LogBlockGeneration	Tag Bits ^
10...	00000029:000004e0:00f2	LOP_DELETE_ROWS	LCX_HEAP	0000:00000b32	0	0x0000
10...	00000029:000004e0:00f3	LOP_DELETE_ROWS	LCX_HEAP	0000:00000b32	0	0x0000
10...	00000029:000004e0:00f4	LOP_DELETE_ROWS	LCX_HEAP	0000:00000b32	0	0x0000
10...	00000029:000004e0:00f5	LOP_DELETE_ROWS	LCX_HEAP	0000:00000b32	0	0x0000
10...	00000029:000004e0:00f6	LOP_DELETE_ROWS	LCX_HEAP	0000:00000b32	0	0x0000
10...	00000029:000004e0:00f7	LOP_DELETE_ROWS	LCX_HEAP	0000:00000b32	0	0x0000
10...	00000029:000004e0:00f8	LOP_DELETE_ROWS	LCX_HEAP	0000:00000b32	0	0x0000
10...	00000029:000004e0:00f9	LOP_DELETE_ROWS	LCX_HEAP	0000:00000b32	0	0x0000
10...	00000029:000004e0:00fa	LOP_ABORT_XACT	LCX_CTR_ABORTED	0000:00000b32	0	0x0000

Figure 4-4. *Log records from an aborted DELETE with ADR*

Notice there are no INSERT compensation records, and the LOP_ABORT_XACT has Context of LCX_CTR_ABORTED. All the LOP_DELETE_ROWS log records were generated with the DELETE statement. The ROLLBACK TRAN T-SQL statement only generated the LOP_ABORT_XACT record.

6. SQL Server 2019 includes diagnostics to examine the PVS. Use Step 6 to see statements for the PVS in this database.

```
-- Step 6: Look at the PVS stats
SELECT * FROM sys.dm_tran_persistent_version_store_stats
WHERE database_id = db_id('gocowboys')
GO
```

Now that you have seen how ADR works, let's look at two examples to see how ADR improves rollback performance, log truncation, and faster recovery.

Using Accelerated Database Recovery

As you saw from the example you just completed, using Accelerated Database Recovery (ADR) requires no application changes. You simply use the following T-SQL statement to enable ADR and you are off and running:

```
ALTER DATABASE <dbname> SET ACCELERATED_DATABASE_RECOVERY = ON
```

Let's walk through two examples to see:

- How fast rollback now executes and how the transaction log is aggressively truncated

- How fast recovery completes, allowing you fast access to the database

Everything you need to run these examples can be found in the notebooks and scripts for each example.

Fast Rollback and Aggressive Log Truncation

Use the following example to see how fast rollback can be executed using ADR, and how aggressive the transaction log is now truncated, avoiding excessive log growth scenarios. In this example, we will compare the speed of rollback and the growth of the transaction log with and without ADR.

You can run through this example using the T-SQL script **adr.sql** in the **ch4_mission_critical_availability\adr** directory.

I recommend in this situation to use the T-SQL notebook **adr.ipynb** in the **ch4_mission_critical_availability\adr** directory. The notebook has all the instructions to create a database, create a table, and insert data. Then with ADR disabled, you will delete all the rows in the table in a transaction. Then you will examine the amount of log space that has been used but can't be truncated even after a checkpoint. Then you will observe the speed of a rollback of the entire delete (or lack of speed, to be more precise).

Then, in the notebook, you will repeat those steps, but this time with ADR on. The T-SQL script has all the same steps. After going through this example, let's do something a bit more advanced. Let's see the speed of recovery using the same T-SQL example but with more rows to see the impact of recovery.

Speeding Up Recovery

In order to show how fast recovery works, you have to create an example where the undo phase of recovery needs to attempt to roll back a large number of modifications or transactions.

So how do you create a scenario where SQL Server has to run the undo phase on a certain transaction? In order to do this, you need to craft a scenario for an active transaction that does NOT get rolled back or committed before SQL Server is shut down. There are three methods to make this happen:

- Execute the T-SQL statement **SHUTDOWN WITH NOWAIT**.

- Shut down the SQL Server service (e.g., net stop mssqlserver).

- Terminate the SQLSERVR.EXE process (for Windows, use "End Task" from Task Manager).

Any of these techniques will stop SQL Server without affecting the active transaction. There is one additional consideration. For SQL Server to roll back the active transactions, there "has to be something to roll back." If the database pages affected by the active transaction were never flushed to disk, when SQL Server runs recovery, it can't "undo" something that was never there. Therefore, you should execute a CHECKPOINT against the database when using one of these methods (shutting the SQL Server service down gracefully does run a checkpoint against all databases). Note, it is possible that the Recovery Writer or Lazy Writer have flushed these pages, but this is not something you can rely on for a demo.

Tip   What if you wanted to force redo? It is a bit of the opposite approach. You have to have a committed transaction, but the pages affected by the transaction cannot be flushed to disk. Run a transaction similar to the examples found in this chapter but commit the transaction. Then "crash" the server, but you must do this without a checkpoint, so use the "End Task" method.

Armed with this knowledge, you can go through the T-SQL script **adr_recovery. sql** or the T-SQL notebook **adr_recovery.ipynb** as found in the **ch4_mission_critical_ availability\adr** directory. I recommend using the notebook, as it has documentation explaining each step with guidance on when to "crash" SQL server.

You will want to examine the ERRORLOG when going through the steps of the notebook or script. I have examples here for what you should see when recovery runs without and with ADR enabled.

Here is an example ERRORLOG when ADR is not enabled.

```
spid25s     Recovery of database 'gocowboys' (6) is 2% complete
            (approximately 697 seconds remain). Phase 2 of 3. This is an
            informational message only. No user action is required.
spid25s     Recovery of database 'gocowboys' (6) is 5% complete
            (approximately 682 seconds remain). Phase 2 of 3. This is an
            informational message only. No user action is required.
spid25s     Recovery of database 'gocowboys' (6) is 7% complete
            (approximately 667 seconds remain). Phase 2 of 3. This is an
            informational message only. No user action is required.
spid25s     Recovery of database 'gocowboys' (6) is 7% complete
            (approximately 667 seconds remain). Phase 3 of 3. This is an
            informational message only. No user action is required.
spid8s      Recovery of database 'gocowboys' (6) is 40% complete
            (approximately 113 seconds remain). Phase 3 of 3. This is an
            informational message only. No user action is required.
spid8s      Recovery of database 'gocowboys' (6) is 50% complete
            (approximately 94 seconds remain). Phase 3 of 3. This is an
            informational message only. No user action is required.
spid8s      Recovery of database 'gocowboys' (6) is 59% complete
            (approximately 79 seconds remain). Phase 3 of 3. This is an
            informational message only. No user action is required.
spid8s      Recovery of database 'gocowboys' (6) is 68% complete
            (approximately 65 seconds remain). Phase 3 of 3. This is an
            informational message only. No user action is required.
spid8s      Recovery of database 'gocowboys' (6) is 76% complete
            (approximately 48 seconds remain). Phase 3 of 3. This is an
            informational message only. No user action is required.
spid8s      Recovery of database 'gocowboys' (6) is 84% complete
            (approximately 32 seconds remain). Phase 3 of 3. This is an
            informational message only. No user action is required.
spid8s      Recovery of database 'gocowboys' (6) is 93% complete
            (approximately 15 seconds remain). Phase 3 of 3. This is an
            informational message only. No user action is required.
```

spid8s	1 transactions rolled back in database 'gocowboys' (6:0). This is an informational message only. No user action is required.
spid8s	Recovery is writing a checkpoint in database 'gocowboys' (6). This is an informational message only. No user action is required.
spid8s	Recovery completed for database gocowboys (database ID 6) in 211 second(s) (analysis 15 ms, redo 56340 ms, undo 154549 ms.) This is an informational message only. No user action is required.

Note   The redo is needed here for some system transactions involved with index statistics for this example.

Here is the ERRORLOG when ADR is enabled. Recovery when ADR is enabled happens so fast; SQL Server doesn't even bother writing how long recovery took!

spid25s	1 transactions rolled back in database 'gocowboys' (6:0). This is an informational message only. No user action is required.
spid25s	Recovery is writing a checkpoint in database 'gocowboys' (6). This is an informational message only. No user required.

Accelerate Database Recovery Nuts and Bolts

This all sounds too good to be true, and I'm sure you are wondering if there are any side effects to this. If ADR is so great, why don't we just make it the default?

Performance and Size

There are two questions that come up when I've talked to customers about ADR:

Does the database get larger?

The short answer to this question is yes. The more important question is by how much. Since we are keeping versions of rows in the database for a period of time, naturally the size required for PVS is bigger than without it.

The problem, as with any feature like this, is the dreaded answer, "it depends." Depends on what? The factors are

- Is the application write-intensive with a lot of modifications? The bigger the number of modifications, the more size will be required to hold versions.

- How long are transactions that need to read version data? Once versions are not needed by any query, they can be removed.

Accelerated Database Recovery has built-in optimizations to keep the version store as small as possible, including the following:

- **"on-demand"**

  When updating a row, SQL Server can "reuse" a version of a row that was aborted and write in a new version in its place. This happens during the process of a data modification.

- **Background cleanup**

  What about if versions are still around that are no longer needed (e.g., aborted transactions) and an update has not occurred yet? SQL Server uses the existing background worker thread architecture to schedule cleanup (every "few" minutes) on any versions that can be discarded both for in-row and off-row versions. SQL Server uses a concept called *logical revert* to clean up these versions. Logical revert is the process of ensuring the committed version of the row is the "main" row for the page, thereby making the "list" of versions shorter to traverse. Section 3.3 of the CTR paper (`www.microsoft.com/en-us/research/publication/constant-time-recovery-in-azure-sql-database/`) has an excellent detailed description of how logical revert works. In addition, Section 3.7 of this same paper describes the entire cleanup process.

Section 4 of the paper has results from experimental testing on growth, using an example of 50 million insert, update, and delete operations. The team found after 50M updates, the PVS grew the database by about 1Gb. You should look through these results as it also shows the significant size reduction of the transaction log due to the use of ADR (and you observed this during the activity in this chapter using the **alookatadr.sql** script).

140

Does using ADR cause any performance impact?

This is probably the most common question asked about ADR. And like the growth factor, the answer is, "Maybe, and it depends." Since ADR is tracking every modification with versions, write-intensive workloads will see the biggest impact. And read operations for write-intensive workloads may also be affected some to find a version of a row.

As part of the CTR paper, the engineering team performed some testing using benchmarks derived from the industry standard TPC-C and TPC-E benchmarks (see `www.tpc.org` for more information about these benchmarks). TPC-C is an older benchmark but very write-intensive. TPC-E is a more balanced but still "OLTP" write workload benchmark. You can see the results in the paper in **Section 4.2**, but, effectively, the run of TPC-C encountered about a 14% (in-row version) impact, and TPC-E encountered a 2.5% (in-row version) impact.

I did my own "quick and dirty" testing using the open source tool HammerDB (see `www.hammerdb.com` for more details). This tool comes with a variation of the TPC-C benchmark. Using a 10 warehouse/10 virtual user execution over a 5-minute period, I saw about 15% impact from using ADR.

Note   None of these test results means that you will see these exact numbers or any performance impact if you enable ADR for your database. This is because these tests use benchmarks of a certain type of workload that may or may not match your application. Find a standard way to test the performance of your application with and without ADR to know the true impact of performance.

Look over the results in all of Section 4 of the paper, because it also shows some of the amazing recovery time results the team has seen in Azure (you have already seen the possible impact with a simple database).

Another major benefit of Accelerated Database Recovery is that failover time for Always On Availability Groups can be faster and a better version story exists for read-only queries on replicas.

Unexpected Scenarios

In some cases, the Persistent Version Store (PVS) cannot be stored in-row, because it does not fit on a page. In this case, the versions are stored in an internal system table. These are called "off-row" scenarios. As you can imagine, when PVS is stored off-row, it is not the ideal situation. Therefore, these scenarios should be avoided if possible.

Off-row versions can occur mostly when the modification is a substantial change to the current version of the row. If an update is so significant, it is not possible or does not make sense to store a version in-row; the version will be stored in an internal system table as an off-row version. I did some poking around in a database with ADR on, and the PVS is kept in a table called **persistent_version_store** in each database. This table is marked as a type INTERNAL_TABLE which is similar to other tables like ones for Query Store. This system table has the version data and metadata to link it back to the actual row in the page of a table.

If you are concerned whether your application is generating a lot of off-row versions, there are performance counters and extended events you can use which I describe in the next section called Tracking ADR.

Note   At the time I wrote this chapter, the off-row PVS is stored in the PRIMARY filegroup of your database, and there is no choice on this. The engineering team was discussing whether they could add an option to move the off-row PVS to another filegroup chosen by the user through ALTER DATABASE. Consult the documentation for ALTER DATABASE to see if this enhancement made its way into the final SQL Server 2019 release.

Another unexpected situation is called *short-transaction optimization*. This situation is a good thing. It doesn't make sense to use PVS when transactions are very short in nature. Therefore, when testing ADR, don't expect a transaction that deletes a few rows to use ADR. If you are examining the log with fn_dblog(), you can see transactions where ADR will not apply with the following Operation and Context, LOP_FORGET_XACT and LCX_XACT_DOES_NOT_SUPPORT_CTR.

Tracking ADR

Like many new features of SQL Server, the ADR team has wait types, Extended Events, and performance monitor counters to track the execution of ADR, the use of the Persisted Version Store (PVS), and cleanup processing.

Figure 4-5 shows some of the performance counters available to track the use of the Persisted Version Store (PVS), including tracking how many off-row versions are being generated.

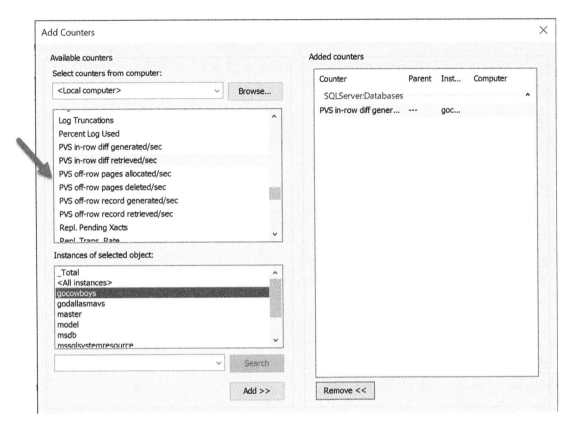

Figure 4-5. *PVS performance counters*

There are several Extended Events that can also be used to track specific generation of versions and for cleanup tasks. You can find all of these events by executing the following queries against the XE Dynamic Management Views:

```
select * from sys.dm_xe_objects where name like '%pvs%'
select * from sys.dm_xe_objects where name like '%ctr%'
```

One of these that might be interesting is the **pvs_add_record** event. You could use this event along with an action sql_text to find out what queries are generating off-row versions.

Note   I have not done any testing using these Extended Events, so I cannot speak to the performance impact they may have on your application.

Finally, for those who really want to go deep, there are several wait types listed in the sys.dm_os_wait_stats DMV which apply to ADR. You could monitor these to track execution of activities like cleanup. Use the following T-SQL statement to find these wait types:

```
select * from sys.dm_os_wait_stats
where wait_type like '%pvs%' or wait_type like '%ctr%'
```

Should I Use ADR?

If you don't have long-running transactions, ADR will likely not help you and may negatively impact your application. If your application generates a lot of off-row versions, the impact may be too high to see the benefit of ADR. Keep in mind, though, that this could still be of big benefit for failover scenarios, such as with Always On Availability Groups.

My recommendation is to find a way to test this with your application. We didn't make this the default (yet) for SQL Server 2019, because there are too many types of workloads out there, and not all – as I've discussed in this chapter – will see a benefit. But keep these final thoughts in mind:

- This is one of those features you may not know you need now but when you need it… you need it. You may not be able to predict when a long-running recovery is going to bring your business down. Wouldn't it be nice to have this enabled so that just doesn't happen?

- Most workloads are not like TPC-C which are really, really write-intensive. Our testing results with a more balanced read/write workload like TPC-E did not show a huge impact.

- Consider this quote from the engineering team in the CTR paper as they used a "cloud-first" approach to roll out this capability first in Azure, "…CTR has already been enabled in five regions and approximately one million databases with very promising results."

Summary

Ensuring your data and application are available is an important aspect of any respectable data platform product. SQL Server 2019 continues to enhance core availability functionality like resumable online indexing and Availability Groups. Furthermore, SQL Server 2019 brings to the industry a very innovative approach to solving downtime due to long-running active transactions with Accelerated Database Recovery.

CHAPTER 5

Modern Development Platform

Just about any developer needs data, and a product like SQL Server has the capabilities, languages, drivers, and platforms you need. A *modern* data developer needs a database platform to meet the challenges of today's applications. SQL Server 2019 meets these challenges with the following capabilities:

- Support for a **wide variety of languages and drivers** across **multiple operating system platforms** such as Windows, macOS, and Linux with compatibility. Editions of SQL Server provide a common surface area to minimize application logic.

- **Graph databases** integrated with SQL Server allow developers to implement data models, such as social networks, without an additional product – and query against it using a familiar language like T-SQL.

- Developers need the ability to build applications to handle Unicode data using encoding systems widely used across the industry. SQL Server 2019 supports **UTF-8** encoding through new collations.

- Developers need a database platform to support new types of applications integrating Machine Learning that are scalable, secure, and integrated with the database. **SQL Server Machine Learning Services** includes new enhancements in SQL Server 2019.

- The T-SQL language provides many capabilities, but developers may need more. They want the ability to extend the T-SQL language integrated with the database. **SQL Server Language Extensions** in SQL Server 2019 allow developers to install and use new languages such as **Java** integrated with SQL Server data.

147

© Bob Ward 2019
B. Ward, *SQL Server 2019 Revealed*, https://doi.org/10.1007/978-1-4842-5419-6_5

Languages, Drivers, and Platforms

When I started with Microsoft in 1993, developers writing applications for SQL Server primarily used languages like Visual C or Visual Basic with a driver called DB-Library. The clients were all running DOS (yes, DOS) or Windows, while SQL Server was a Windows NT mainstream database server. C++ and ODBC soon followed, but the choice of languages, drivers, and platforms was pretty restricted. Today, the choice of language, drivers, and platforms for both client applications and SQL Server is way beyond anything I ever thought I would see.

Languages and Drivers

SQL Server 2019 is a modern database platform, and along with it comes a wide set of choices of programming languages, including modern languages popular with developers who traditionally have not used SQL Server.

Along with these language choices are drivers to access SQL Server that match the requirements and needs of each language. Furthermore, these drivers work on a variety of client platforms including macOS, Linux, and Windows.

Additionally, choices of drivers such as ODBC, OLE-DB, and .Net have become more focused, instead of the wide variety and sometimes confusing choices from the past.

So how do you choose a language and/or driver? First, the language choice in some cases dictates the driver you will use. For example, if you want to write code in PHP and access SQL Server, you must use the PHP Driver for SQL Server.

Fortunately, Microsoft has created a very nice web site to help you make decisions on language, choose the right driver, choose one or more client platforms, and see examples of writing code to access SQL Server in that language.

To see this in action, go to the web site `http://aka.ms/sqldev`. The main web page looks like Figure 5-1.

Figure 5-1. *The SQL Server development hub*

If you hover over one of the language choices, you can pick a client platform language to get details of using that language with the appropriate driver and a code sample tutorial (Figure 5-2 shows an example using Go).

Figure 5-2. *Using the Go language with SQL Server*

Choosing the option for Windows, you will be presented with a complete tutorial to build your first Go application for Windows (your SQL Server could be running on Windows, Linux, or even containers) with SQL Server Developer Edition. Each language and platform choice has a similar template like Figure 5-3 for Go.

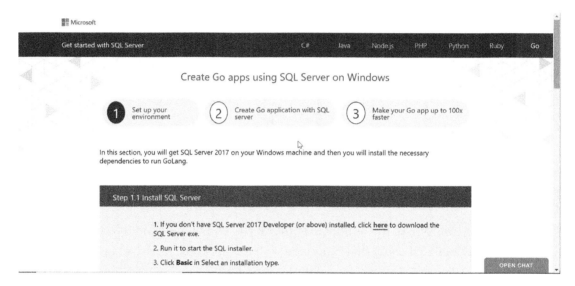

Figure 5-3. *Creating a Go application for SQL Server*

Many developers who use languages such as C++ or C# have seen, to be honest, a confusing list of driver choices for SQL Server.

After SQL Server 2012, we consolidated the list of drivers and versions you should be using for ODBC, OLE-DB, or ADO.Net. I have found this documentation page `https://docs.microsoft.com/en-us/sql/connect/connect-history` to show a very good history of past drivers and which ones to use now if you are using SQL Server 2014 or newer.

In addition, to get a complete list of language and appropriate driver choices to build a SQL Server application, I find this documentation page to be an excellent resource: `https://docs.microsoft.com/en-us/sql/connect/sql-connection-libraries`. (This includes driver for object-relational mapping (ORM) framework applications.)

I am a bit of an "old-school" developer, so ODBC is my primary choice for a driver. And we have built an ODBC driver for SQL Server that keeps up with new features of SQL Server and is available for Linux, macOS, and Windows. You can read the complete documentation for the latest SQL Server ODBC Driver at `https://docs.microsoft.com/en-us/sql/connect/odbc/microsoft-odbc-driver-for-sql-server`.

Platforms and Editions

Starting with SQL Server 2017, SQL Server is now supported on Windows, Linux, and with Docker Containers. This opens up the platform to developers who have never considered SQL Server before. Regardless of what operating system hosts the production SQL Server, developers can now test their applications with SQL Server Developer Edition on Windows, Linux, or with Containers. And because the SQL Server engine codebase is the same on all of these platforms, developers can write applications local to their SQL Server deployment and be assured it is compatible with the production SQL Server. This includes former feature gaps for SQL Server on Linux, such as replication and Distributed Transactions (DTC), which now are available in SQL Server 2019.

Although not new to SQL Server 2019 (this was introduced in SQL Server 2016 SP1), SQL Server editions other than Enterprise Edition contain similar "surface area" features to make it easier to build a single application than can work across editions. For example, In-Memory OLTP is now available as a feature for SQL Server Enterprise and Standard Edition, and even SQL Server Express Edition (although the scale of this feature is not the same across editions). You can now build your application using In-Memory OLTP on Developer Edition and be assured it can work across various editions without putting logic to detect editions in your application.

Graph Database

The concept of a relational database handles all types of design models, data patterns, and applications. However, there are certain types of data models designed after a real-world problem that don't necessarily fit well with a standard relational system and the SQL language. The models typically involve hierarchical, "network," or complex many-to-many relationships of data. Wikipedia has a good description of this problem and solutions at `https://en.m.wikipedia.org/wiki/Graph_database`.

Some developers have tried to still use a relational database to "fit" in a graph model and use complex T-SQL statements to "navigate" the graph. In some cases, dedicated projects to graph data have been built, such as the popular open source graph database Neo4j (`https://github.com/neo4j/neo4j`). Other database platforms have included an "add-on" to their relational database to provide graph capabilities.

In 2016, members of the SQL Engineering team, including Hanuma Kodavalla, Craig Freedman, Devin Rider, and Shreya Verma, formed a project to look into building graph database capabilities into SQL Server and Azure SQL Database. Their goal was to include graph capabilities *built into the SQL Server engine* and find a way to use the T-SQL language to create *graph tables* and manipulate and search them with T-SQL. This is another great example of leveraging the power of T-SQL by extending it.

The result of this effort was the release of graph database capabilities in SQL Server 2017 and Azure SQL Database. One of the huge benefits of a graph database in SQL Server is that it comes along with the power of SQL Server. This includes HADR, security, performance, and all the features of the engine. Rather than incorporate them into the engine, other platforms treat features like this as add-ons or completely separate products altogether.

What Is a Graph Database in SQL Server?

A graph database in SQL Server is using tables to represent *nodes* and *edges* in a graph model using T-SQL extensions. The term "database" is logical as it is not a different database in the SQL Server sense. In a graph database, a node is an entity or object, and an edge is a relationship between nodes.

A graph database, therefore, is a collection of node and edge tables and the data and metadata that bind them together. SQL Server supports extensions to the T-SQL language to define a node or edge table through the **AS NODE** or **AS EDGE** syntax for **CREATE TABLE**. The complete syntax to create a node or edge table can be found at `https://docs.microsoft.com/en-us/sql/t-sql/statements/create-table-sql-graph`.

Additionally, SQL Server supports a new T-SQL keyword called **MATCH** to navigate the node and edge tables as part of a SELECT statement. The syntax for how to use a MATCH keyword can be found in the documentation at `https://docs.microsoft.com/en-us/sql/t-sql/queries/match-sql-graph`.

You can read the complete set of documentation for graph database in SQL Server and Azure SQL Database at `https://docs.microsoft.com/en-us/sql/relational-databases/graphs/sql-graph-overview`. You can also see a nice presentation from Kevin Farlee from Microsoft on YouTube at `www.youtube.com/watch?v=xirfl_t4Gqs`.

The best way to see how a node or edge table works with SQL Server is to run through an example.

Using a Graph Database in SQL Server

Many of you as readers will likely be new to using a graph database in SQL Server, so I'll use a simple example to demonstrate the power of this capability. In fact, I'll use the example provided in the documentation as found at `https://docs.microsoft.com/en-us/sql/relational-databases/graphs/sql-graph-sample`, but put in a few variations and add commentary to explain the example.

Consider the concept of a *social network*. Many of you experience this every day on platforms like Facebook or LinkedIn. A network by its nature is a connection of things typically modeled in a graph. Consider a network of friends as seen in Figure 5-4.

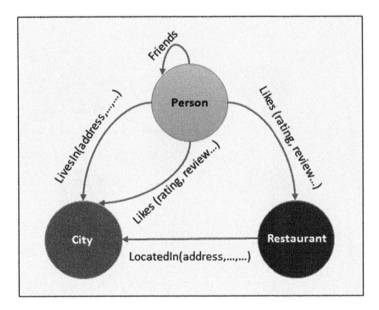

Figure 5-4. *A network of friends*

In this model of a graph, the nodes are Person, City, and Restaurant. The arrows represent the relationships between the nodes; these are the edges. Notice the particular relationship called Friends where Persons are related to each other. Building out this model in a pure set of relational tables is not all that difficult, but traversing the graph using traditional T-SQL queries gets complex.

Let's build an example of a graph database using the preceding model, so you can get the feel of the basics, and then look at what is new in SQL Server 2019.

Note   There is no special prerequisite to use the examples for Graph database except to install SQL Server 2019 (Windows, Linux, or a Container) and use a tool like SQL Server Management Studio (SSMS) or Azure Data Studio (ADS) (June 2019 version or later). The graph example in this specific section is designed for SQL Server 2019.

For this example, consider John in this social network. He already knows he is friends with Mary and Julie, but he doesn't know whom they are friends with (and who their friends are friends with, and so on). He wants to expand his social network and also discover which restaurants his friends like.

Consider the "social network of friends" in Figure 5-5.

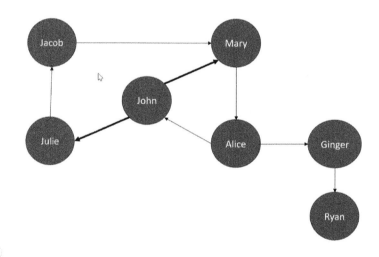

Figure 5-5. *The social network of friends*

John doesn't know the entire network, so he needs to use a graph database to navigate.

All scripts for graph database examples can be found in the **ch5_modern_development_platform\sqlgraph** directory. Using the model in Figure 5-4 as a guide, follow Steps 1-7 in the T-SQL notebook **socialnetwork.ipynb** using Azure Data Studio. These steps will show you how to build graph tables as nodes and edges, populate data, and then traverse the graph using the T-SQL MATCH syntax.

There is also a T-SQL script **socialnetwork.sql** you can use to follow Steps 1-7 using SSMS or ADS.

Graph Enhancements for SQL Server 2019

SQL Server 2019 comes with a few enhancements to help make graph database a more powerful and compelling platform for graph data compared to other products. This includes

- Traversing a graph path using the new SHORTEST_PATH() syntax

- Support for derived tables and views in a graph database

- Edge constraints to enforce proper graph relationships

- Using the T-SQL MERGE statement to support scenarios like *upsert*

Let's review some of these new enhancements.

SHORTEST_PATH

One of the more common challenges to solve with a graph database is to traverse the graph data recursively without having to manually navigate to each level. SQL Server 2017 did not support this concept, but SQL Server 2019 provides support for this through the new **SHORTEST_PATH**() T-SQL syntax.

Using **Steps 8 and 9** examples in **socialnetwork.ipynb** and **socialnetwork.sql**, see how SHORTEST_PATH allows John and Jacob to traverse the social network of friends.

You can see the details of using SHORTEST_PATH() in the documentation at `https://docs.microsoft.com/en-us/sql/relational-databases/graphs/sql-graph-shortest-path` or in this blog post by Shreya Verma at `https://techcommunity.microsoft.com/t5/SQL-Server/Public-Preview-of-Shortest-Path-on-SQL-Server-2019/ba-p/721240`.

Edge Constraints

While the NODE and EDGE T-SQL syntax provides a very nice new way of building graph data using SQL Server tables, in SQL Server 2017 there was no way to enforce *integrity* of node and edge data. Just like the concept of foreign key constraints in SQL Server tables, SQL Server 2019 provides the ability to enforce data integrity with nodes and edges.

Consider the social network you just built using the examples in this chapter. It would be nice to ensure that any data for the friendOf edge table has to be from a valid row in the Person table. Edge constraints provide this capability.

In addition, edge constraints enforce proper network relationships. In our social network model, a Person can like a Restaurant, but a Restaurant cannot like a Person. An edge constraint can enforce this, too. Furthermore, edge constraints ensure that edges are not left *dangling*. With edge constraints, you cannot delete a node that is part of an edge relationship if data exists in the edge table. Again, this behavior is similar to foreign keys in traditional relational tables.

You can read more about edge constraints in the documentation at `https://docs.microsoft.com/en-us/sql/relational-databases/tables/graph-edge-constraints` or in another blog post by Shreya at `https://blogs.msdn.microsoft.com/sqlserverstorageengine/2018/09/28/public-preview-of-graph-edge-constraints-on-sql-server-2019/`.

Using MERGE with Graph Tables

SQL Server provides a T-SQL statement called **MERGE** which performs insert, update, or delete operations on a target table based on the results of a join with a source table. In SQL Server 2017, you can use the MERGE statement to consolidate DML operations on node tables, but not on edge tables. SQL Server 2019 now provides the capability to use MERGE with edge tables as well.

Take a look at some great examples by Shreya in her blog post on this topic at `https://blogs.msdn.microsoft.com/sqlserverstorageengine/2018/07/16/match-support-in-merge-dml-for-graph-tables/`.

UTF-8 Support

Applications and databases have been using Unicode as a standard to encode character data as far back as the early 1990s. SQL Server on Windows has included data types and collations to support Unicode encoding of character data almost as long as the product has existed. SQL Server 2019 introduces a new method for Unicode encoding called UTF-8, which is widely used by applications and databases normally on Linux systems.

If you would like to read more about the basics of Unicode before reading this section, you can use these resources:

`https://docs.microsoft.com/en-us/windows/win32/intl/unicode`
`https://en.wikipedia.org/wiki/Unicode`
`https://unicode.org/standard/WhatIsUnicode.html`

Unicode and SQL Server

The normal way SQL Server supports Unicode encoding is through the **nchar** and **nvarchar** data types. SQL Server supports Unicode encoding of these data types using the UTF-16 encoding scheme. UTF-16 requires a minimum 2 bytes per "character" to store data. The ASCII character using UTF-16 "a" requires 2 bytes of storage. When you define a column like the following:

```
col1 nchar(10) not null
```

SQL Server requires 20 bytes of storage for this column, even if you are using just standard ASCII characters.

This is opposed to the following column definition:

```
col1 char(10) not null
```

which requires 10 bytes but can only store characters from the ASCII character set.

Note   It is a very common mistake for developers and data professionals to use nchar, char, and so on and assume the length is the number of characters not byte storage.

UTF-16 allows for the entire spectrum of Unicode characters because many characters for language support outside of just ASCII characters require 2 bytes to represent the character.

Why Would You Use UTF-8?

While the majority of applications and databases like SQL Server use UTF-16 for Unicode character encoding, many in the Linux community use an encoding called UTF-8. UTF-8 is similar to UTF-16, in that it supports the entire Unicode character set, but uses a different encoding and byte storage scheme depending on which character is being stored. For example, ASCII characters only require 1 byte of storage in UTF-8 but require 2 bytes in UTF-16.

Consider an application that was only developed for the ASCII character set but needs to be updated to support all Unicode characters. It is possible this application uses **char** and **varchar** data types in SQL Server. Before SQL Server supported UTF-8, the data professional would need to change the data types of all SQL Server columns from **char** to **nchar** and **varchar** to **nvarchar**. Using ALTER TABLE to change data types in this fashion for ASCII characters practically doubles the storage requirements for these columns even if you initially are only using ASCII characters.

Now with SQL Server 2019, an alternative is to leave your data types as char and varchar but change the collation of the columns to use the new UTF-8 collations, such as LATIN1_GENERAL_100_CI_AS_SC_UTF8. ALTER TABLE allows you to change the collation at the column level. UTF-8 encoding for characters only requires 1 byte of storage for ASCII characters.

Make these decisions carefully, as there are some restrictions for UTF-8, and, for certain characters, the storage requirements are larger for UTF-8 (not ASCII) than UTF-16.

UTF-8 is supported for SQL Server for Windows, Linux, and containers (remember "Windows" collations are supported for SQL Server on Linux because of the SQLPAL architecture. The documentation says UTF-8 is only supported for Windows collations not SQL collations).

Use these resources to study whether UTF-8 is for you:

```
https://cloudblogs.microsoft.com/sqlserver/2018/12/18/introducing-utf-8-
support-in-sql-server-2019-preview/
https://docs.microsoft.com/en-us/sql/relational-databases/collations/
collation-and-unicode-support
https://docs.microsoft.com/en-us/sql/relational-databases/collations/
collation-and-unicode-support#utf8
```

SQL Server Machine Learning Services

When I joined the SQL Engineering team in 2016, after working in Microsoft support for 20+ years, Joseph Sirosh was the VP in charge of SQL Server. SQL Server 2016 had just shipped, and I knew Joseph was particularly proud of the work the SQL Server team had done to integrate Machine Learning through the R programming language with the product.

Joseph is a data scientist and has an incredible passion for Machine Learning and Data. As an open source language, R is one of the most popular programming languages for data science and Machine Learning, so integrating this with SQL Server seemed like a natural fit. In addition, in 2015, Microsoft had acquired a company called Revolution

Analytics, which had built a commercial version of R, including changes to make it more scalable, called **RevoScaleR**. (See this resource for the history of R, `https://en.wikipedia.org/wiki/R_(programming_language)`.) Joining these forces to build a Machine Learning platform for data with SQL Server was now possible. This original feature was called **SQL Server 2016 R Services**. SQL Server 2017 introduced integration with the Python programming language, using the same concepts and architecture. With this change, the new capability of R and Python together became **SQL Server Machine Learning Services**.

While the changes for SQL Server Machine Learning Services (ML Services) for SQL Server 2019 are not significant, this capability may be something new you are looking at, so I'll spend some brief time talking about how it works. This is important for several reasons:

- Understanding how ML Services works and the benefits of using it will allow you to make decisions on whether this capability is right for you and your application.

- You can gain more confidence in allowing ML Services to be used with SQL Server if you know more about the integration, security, and governance of this capability.

- The architecture, called the **Extensibility Framework**, used for ML Services is the same one used for what is called SQL Server Language Extensions, new for SQL Server 2019.

Before you read the rest of this chapter, consider reviewing the documentation of SQL Server ML Services at `https://docs.microsoft.com/en-us/sql/advanced-analytics/sql-server-machine-learning-services`.

How It Works

Prior to SQL Server ML Services, data scientists developed and executed their *models* (a term often used for a Machine Learning program) on separate computers (workstations or servers) where all data, such as SQL Server, was accessed remotely. In many cases, R or Python programs used for these models would simply "pull back" an entire table and filter the results in the program, thus not taking advantage of the power of languages like SQL.

SQL Server ML Services offers a new capability to execute scalable Machine Learning programs under the following concepts:

- Machine Learning programs are executed on the same computer as SQL Server, but in independent processes from SQLSERVR.EXE.

- SQL Server provides a T-SQL interface through a system stored procedure, **sp_execute_external_script**, to execute Machine Learning code.

- SQL Server provides an architecture for intelligent data exchange and scalability with Machine Learning code.

Consider Figure 5-6 for the SQL Server ML Services architecture, called the **Extensibility architecture in SQL Server Machine Learning Services**, as found in the SQL Server documentation at https://docs.microsoft.com/en-us/sql/advanced-analytics/concepts/extensibility-framework#architecture-diagram.

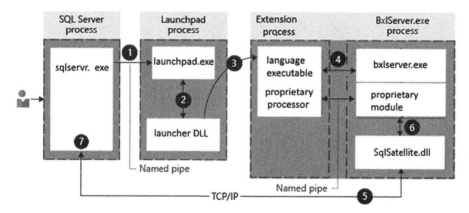

Figure 5-6. *The SQL Server ML Services architecture*

Unfortunately, the documentation does not provide the details of the numbers in the diagram, so I'll do so here, which will help you understand more how it works.

Note I've spoken on this topic in the past and have a very detailed architecture diagram and explanation. You can see this in Figure 5-7 or the details at `www.youtube.com/watch?v=y52oBaI32Jo` and `www.slideshare.net/BobWard28/sql-server-r-services-what-every-sql-professional-should-know`. These resources show the architecture for SQL 2016 R Services, but it is the same architecture to include Python. An updated slide that includes Python can be found at `https://aka.ms/bobwardms`. Search in the SQL2017 folder for a deck called *Inside SQL Server Machine Learning Services*.

Here is my version of the architecture at a deeper dive (Figure 5-7).

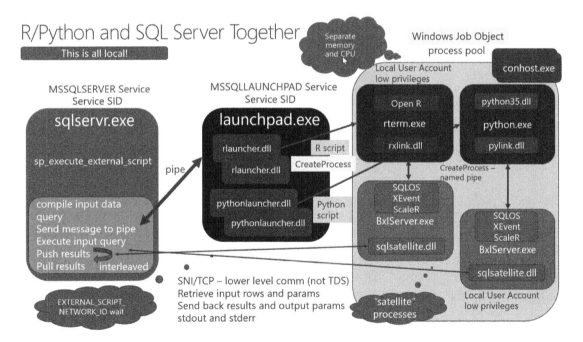

Figure 5-7. *A deeper dive into SQL Server ML Services*

1. User executes sp_execute_external_script with a language chosen (R or Python), a script, and other parameters like what T-SQL query to execute. SQL Server communicates to a separate program called the Launchpad (a service in Windows or daemon in Linux) via named pipes, passing in all the relevant details (such as the R or Python script).

2. Launchpad has the code to execute a DLL corresponding to the R or Python language. Launchpad uses a worker thread model similar to the SQL Server engine. In fact, it loads the SQLOS system that SQL Server uses for OS services.

3. The Launchpad DLL will fork or create a new process for the corresponding language (**rterm.exe** for R or **python.exe** for Python).

4. Another process is forked called **bxlserver.exe** (often referred to as a *satellite* process). This program will interact with rterm.exe or python.exe to exchange data.

5. bxlserver.exe communicates with the SQL Server engine on a private TCP channel (not the same as connecting as a client into SQL Server) to receive data from the T-SQL query executed to feed the R or Python program. This execution happens in an *interleaved* fashion. This means the engine can get rows for the T-SQL query to feed the Machine Learning program and at the same time get results back. The DLL that supports this exchange is called **sqlsatellite.dll**.

6. sqlsatellite.dll works with a module in bxlserver.exe to exchange data with rterm.exe or python.exe.

7. All results (including stdout messages) from the rterm.exe or python.exe program are streamed back to SQL Server through the TCP channel.

The result of this is that a user executes sp_execute_external_script and receives back results in the form of a table (like a SELECT result set) along with stdout messages. There are also options for output parameters and more.

The key concept for a better solution is that the R or Python code is running on the same computer as SQL Server (close to the data), and SQL Server can exchange data with the code in an efficient manner (there is no network traffic to exchange data).

The best way to understand how the T-SQL query (aka "the input query") and the R or Python program interact is to try an example. Instead of going through an example here, I highly recommend you use the example at `https://aka.ms/sqldev` or directly for Python at `https://microsoft.github.io/sql-ml-tutorials/python/rentalprediction/`. One reason I recommend you use this example is that it also includes an example of how to use **native scoring** through T-SQL (`https://docs.microsoft.com/en-us/sql/advanced-analytics/sql-native-scoring`).

My colleague Buck Woody also has an excellent workshop to try all of this and see it in action at `https://github.com/Microsoft/sqlworkshops/tree/master/SQLServerMLServices`. What is nice about this workshop is that you will learn a bit about data science along the way (for those of us who, unlike Buck, are mere mortals at data science).

Security, Isolation, and Governance

One of the first assignments Joseph Sirosh had for me was to boost confidence with the SQL community at large on SQL Server R Services. He had discussed this capability with several big companies using SQL Server, and the data professionals at these companies were leery of running R scripts with SQL Server.

One of the first things I did was explain the architecture as I've described in the previous section and described in the deck at `www.slideshare.net/BobWard28/sql-server-r-services-what-every-sql-professional-should-know`. This architecture helped explain the *isolation* model of SQL Server ML Services. All R and Python scripts run in separate processes from SQLSERVR.EXE, so any issues with these scripts would not cause any issues with the database engine. This is in contrast with other "extension" models of SQL Server, such as extended procedures and SQLCLR, which all run "in-process" of SQLSERVR.EXE. Furthermore, the satellite processes run isolated from each other so can't interfere with R or Python processing for each user. In addition to these running as separate processes, any process created from Launchpad runs in an isolation model using the concept of an **AppContainer** in Windows (`https://docs.microsoft.com/en-us/windows/win32/secauthz/appcontainer-isolation`) and a **namespace** in Linux (`https://en.wikipedia.org/wiki/Linux_namespaces`).

The second concept I needed to explain was security. Consider the security model of executing R or Python for SQL Server ML Services:

- This feature is only enabled if it is first installed and then configured with sp_configure. You can read about how to install SQL Server ML Services on Windows at `https://docs.microsoft.com/en-us/sql/advanced-analytics/install/sql-machine-learning-services-windows-install` and for Linux at `https://docs.microsoft.com/en-us/sql/linux/sql-server-linux-setup-machine-learning`. You can read about the sp_configure option at `https://docs.microsoft.com/en-us/sql/database-engine/configure-windows/external-scripts-enabled-server-configuration-option`.

- The T-SQL system procedure, sp_execute_external_script, requires the EXECUTE ANY EXTERNAL SCRIPT database permission. This permission is only given by default to those users or roles with CONTROL permissions or logins or roles with CONTROL SERVER permissions. Any other user or login trying to execute an R or Python script must be granted explicit permissions.

- Users will also need permission to access objects referenced in the "input query" of the sp_execute_external_script.

- The processes forked for execution of R and Python (rterm.exe and python.exe) all run in a specific low privilege account. For Windows, you can read more about this at `https://docs.microsoft.com/en-us/sql/advanced-analytics/security/create-a-login-for-sqlrusergroup`. For Linux, these programs run under the **mssql_satellite** account.

- By default, satellite processes do not have access to connect to a network outside of the computer running SQL Server.

The third concept to give more confidence to control the execution of R and Python is *governance*. SQL Server has had the concept of governance since SQL Server 2008, with a capability called **Resource Governor**. Resource governor provides a mechanism to control resources for SQL Server execution for CPU, memory, and I/O resources. Therefore, resource governor is a natural interface to control resource usage for ML Services programs.

The concept of an external resource pool has been added to SQL Server to explicitly control resource usage for processes that are created through sp_execute_external_script, including rterm.exe, python.exe, bxlserver.exe, and others. In Windows, external resource groups are implemented by a concept called Windows *Jobs* or Job Objects. You can read more about Windows Job Objects at `https://docs.microsoft.com/en-us/windows/win32/procthread/job-objects`. For Linux, the concept of control groups (cgroups) is used to control resource usage. You can read more about cgroups at `https://en.wikipedia.org/wiki/Cgroups`.

Not only can external resource groups help you control CPU and memory for external processes, but you can also specify CPU affinity. This way you can affinitize satellite processes to a specific node or set of CPUs and keep SQL Server processing affinitized to other CPUs or nodes. This is the exact architecture used to achieve the now famous 1 million predictions per second proof point, which you can read about at `https://cloudblogs.microsoft.com/sqlserver/2016/10/11/1000000-predictions-per-second/`.

What's New in SQL Server 2019?

SQL Server Machine Learning Services is *radical*, and helps take SQL Server from a database engine to a true data platform. SQL Server 2019 enhances SQL Server ML Services with these new features:

- External libraries can now be installed for new R or Python packages using the T-SQL statement CREATE EXTERNAL LIBRARY. You can read more about this at `https://docs.microsoft.com/en-us/sql/t-sql/statements/create-external-library-transact-sql` (SQL Server 2017 allowed this for R).

- The Launchpad service (or daemon on Linux) is critical to the SQL Server ML Services architecture. Now in SQL Server 2019, SQL Server ML Services can be part of an Always On Failover Cluster Instance including the Launchpad service.

- SQL Server Machine Learning Services is now supported on Linux. I'll discuss this further in Chapter 6.

- SQL Server ML Services now supports creating and training models over partitioned data using new parameters for sp_execute_external_ script. Read more to learn an example of this new feature at `https://docs.microsoft.com/en-us/sql/advanced-analytics/tutorials/r-tutorial-create-models-per-partition`.

I think SQL Server Machine Learning Services is a "gamechanger." I asked my colleague Buck Woody, Applied Data Scientist at Microsoft, his thoughts on the significance of SQL Server integration with Machine Learning. According to Buck, "Running predictive and categorical Machine Learning workloads on SQL Server allows not only performance gains by placing the compute directly over the data, but also has advantages for security. SQL Server maintains one of the highest levels of security in the industry, and with the addition of traditional Machine Learning languages such as

R and Python along with various libraries, leverages that security transparently. There's another advantage for using SQL Server as a Machine Learning platform – it provides the Data Scientist a place to experiment and operationalize workloads, and the Database Developer the control of implementing the R and Python Machine Learning code in Transact-SQL, allowing an effective separation of duties."

Extending the T-SQL Language

In the late summer of 2018, I was at Redmond, Washington, at Microsoft corporate HQ preparing to build a presentation to help launch the official preview of SQL Server 2019 at the Microsoft Ignite conference. As part of this effort, I was interviewing various program managers to ensure I had the content accurate, and talking to them about building demos.

One of these program managers (PM) is Nellie Gustafsson. Nellie is one of the lead PMs for SQL Server Machine Learning Services, among other things. I had been talking to Nellie about what other languages the team was thinking about including for SQL Server ML Services for SQL Server 2019. In our meeting, she caught me by surprise by telling me that **Java** would be the next language. She went further: She said that ideally the team would like to open up the architecture for ML Services with an SDK (Software Development Kit). This way anyone with enough technical knowledge could *bring their own language* to extend T-SQL using the same architecture used to run R and Python for SQL Server ML Services.

However, at the time we launched CTP 2.0 for SQL Server 2019, we decided to hold back the SDK and just release Java as the third language for SQL Server ML Services. Java is not necessarily a common language for Machine Learning, so we launched this feature with examples that simply demonstrated how to extend T-SQL for functionality not built into the language (in fairness, we were also using Java to demonstrate Machine Learning with Big Data Clusters).

The concepts would be the same as SQL Server ML Services. You would use the same sp_execute_external_script system stored procedure but specify "Java" as the language and supply a compiled Java class. Even though this was not the complete extensibility open architecture, integrating Java with SQL Server 2019 opened up some eyes to more radical work from Microsoft.

The Extensibility Framework

By the time we released SQL Server 2019, we had decided to *open up* the ML Services architecture. We called this the *extensibility framework.* The way to access the extensibility framework is through something called a *language extension.* Java would simply be an *example* of using this new framework, and we would ship the language extension to use it in the product.

To make the extensibility framework viable, we had to make additions to the existing SQL Server ML Services architecture, including

- We need to keep R and Python "as is" so these languages are considered "built into" SQL Server. R and Python are not considered language extensions but are just part of SQL Server as SQL Server ML Services.

- The "launcher" for R and Python in the Launchpad service specifically launches rterm.exe and python.exe. bxlserver.exe was also designed to specifically work with R and Python. We built a "common" launcher within the Launchpad server to launch any language (you will see this is tied into the CREATE EXTERNAL LANGUAGE concept).

- We need a new "host" program to run other languages. Therefore, we supply a host program called **Extension Host.** On Windows, this program is called **exthost.exe**.

- The Extension Host has to include sqlsatellite.dll (or sqlsatellite.so on Linux) and provide a way for the language extension to interact with it to exchange data with SQL Server.

Figure 5-8 shows a rough picture of this architecture for Windows (the Linux architecture diagram is there as well) from the documentation at `https://docs.microsoft.com/en-us/sql/language-extensions/concepts/extensibility-framework`.

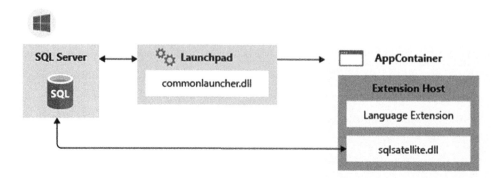

Figure 5-8.   *The Extensibility architecture for external languages on Windows*

Now with these enhancements in SQL Server 2019, you can

- Use sp_execute_external_script to run R or Python scripts for Machine Learning programs.

- Extend T-SQL with sp_execute_external_script with other languages such as Java, provided you have installed a language extension. In SQL Server 2019, we provide all the software to extend T-SQL with Java.

To be clear, the language extension (which is a DLL on Windows or a shared object library, .so, on Linux, typically written in C++) is a key piece of software to support a language extension. Microsoft provides the language extension for Java when you install SQL Server. Since the language extension is built for Java, it will load a Java Virtual Machine (JVM) to run your Java classes. How do you get a JVM to run these? You'll learn about this in the next section.

In addition, you will need an SDK library native to your language. As you will read in the next section, Microsoft provides an SDK library for Java. The SDK will implement a set of known classes and methods so that your class can be executed, and you can exchange data with SQL Server.

Extending T-SQL with Java

One question you may be asking is what is an example of extending the T-SQL language? Using R and Python for Machine Learning makes sense. T-SQL has no built-in Machine Learning functions or capabilities. So why might you need Java? Have you heard of the term regular expression or regex (https://en.wikipedia.org/wiki/Regular_

expression)? Regex is all about searching patterns in string or character data based on an expression. A regex expression can be very powerful – a lot more powerful than the LIKE clause and other T-SQL string functions.

Since there are no built-in full regex capabilities in T-SQL, you could build a Java class that supports regex and integrate it into T-SQL using the extensibility framework and the Java extension shipped with SQL Server 2019. Since the framework allows a language extension to exchange data with SQL Server in a unique way, you can use a Java class with sp_execute_external_script to apply a regex expression on data based on a T-SQL query.

This is in fact what the supplied tutorial does in the documentation as found at https://docs.microsoft.com/en-us/sql/language-extensions/tutorials/search-for-string-using-regular-expressions-in-java.

Instead of supplying you with a step-by-step example, I encourage you to go through the tutorial yourself. I went through this tutorial on Windows, and it works just as well for Linux. I have some tips plus some scripts I used to go through it.

This tutorial will show you the following:

- Create a database and sample data.

- Create a Java class to implement a regex expression engine.

- Build your code so it can be installed with SQL Server using the SQL Server Java SDK.

- Create an external language and libraries to enable Java and install your code. The external language will map to the language extension DLL or .so file. The external libraries will be the SQL Server Java SDK and your code.

- Call your Java class with sp_execute_external_script.

Technically, you can build your code on a separate computer than SQL Server. But if you do this, you will need the SQL Server Java SDK which is called **mssql-java-lang-extension.jar** (Windows and Linux). One way to get the SDK is to install SQL Server with the Java extensibility feature. Therefore, I recommend you run this tutorial on the same computer where you install SQL Server. You can also build it on, say, your laptop, with SQL Server Developer Edition, and then install the final result of your code (which will be a .jar file) to a production SQL Server.

> **Note**   At the time of the writing of this book, we had published a GitHub repo at `https://github.com/microsoft/sql-server-language-extensions` for language extensions, including the SQL Server Java SDK. But the mssql-java-lang-extension.jar file was not available. The plan is to make the SDK available on GitHub so you can build your own Java class independent of a SQL Server installation.

Prerequisites for the Tutorial

The prerequisites to use the tutorial are called out in the documentation at `https://docs.microsoft.com/en-us/sql/language-extensions/tutorials/search-for-string-using-regular-expressions-in-java#prerequisites`.

One of the steps for the prerequisites is to install a Java Runtime Engine (JRE). Here is more radical stuff for you. In SQL Server 2019, we ship a JRE from the Zulu Open JRE. That's right. **SQL Server 2019 ships Java for free**!

Here is what the install screen looks like on Windows to choose your JRE (Figure 5-9).

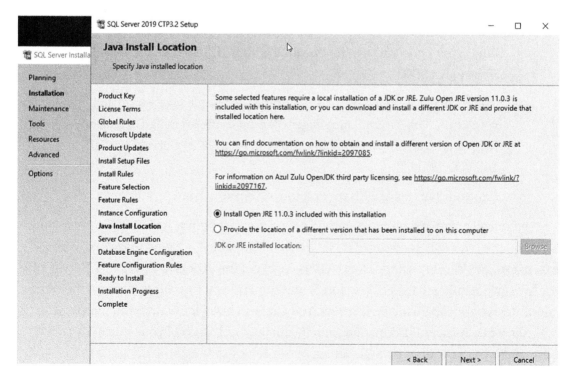

Figure 5-9.   *Choosing a JRE for SQL Server*

> **Note**   Even though Zulu Open JRE is free and shipped with SQL Server, it is fully supported by Microsoft. You also have the option to install your own JRE. If you install your own JRE, there are some additional steps for configuration, which the installation documentation calls out.

Don't forget to properly set the JRE_HOME environment variable on Windows and restart the Launchpad service after you install SQL Server. You can read more about this at `https://docs.microsoft.com/en-us/sql/language-extensions/install/install-sql-server-language-extensions-on-windows#add-the-jre_home-variable`. (For Linux, it is JAVA_HOME, but the install process should have added this for you.) Note the tutorial mentions an example of C:\Program Files\Zulu\zulu-8\jre\ when in fact SQL Server installs the Azul Open JRE at C:\Program Files\Microsoft SQL Server\MSSQL15.MSSQLSERVER\AZUL-OpenJDK-JRE.

As part of the installation process, Microsoft will also install the Java language extension file. For Windows, it is called **javaextension.dll** and packaged in a file called **java-lang-extension.zip**. On Linux, it is called **javaextension.so** and packaged in a file called **java-lang-extension.tar.gz.** The tutorial shows you the location for these files, as you will need this path to create an external language.

Now you can go through the tutorial to create a database and data, build your Java class, install an external language, install your code, and then call your Java class.

Tips for the Tutorial

Here are some tips for using the tutorial. I have provided a set of sample scripts I used in the **ch5_modern_development_platform\java** directory.

- **Picking a JDK to compile your code**

  The tutorial shows you example code for a regex class and the instructions for including the SQL Server Java SDK. Unfortunately, the tutorial doesn't give a lot of details about how to build something in Java. I installed the Zulu Open JDK to get my Java compiler, javac, to use with this tutorial from `www.azul.com/downloads/zulu-community`. Since I was on Windows, I chose these options as seen in Figure 5-10.

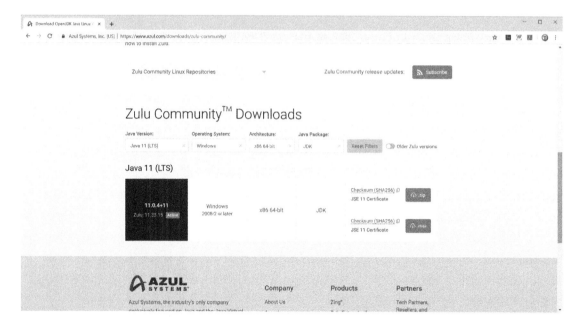

Figure 5-10. *Installing the Zulu JDK for Windows*

You may already have a Java SDK for your computer. You could be using Visual Studio Code, IntelliJ, or Eclipse, which are some of the more popular ones. I just wanted a simple way to compile my Java code from the command line, so I picked the Zulu JDK.

The Zulu JDK comes as a zip file, and I pulled this into my Downloads folder. I then extracted the zip file into the current directory. I wanted javac and the jar program in my path, so I extracted the zip file in place and added this directory to my system path, C:\Users\Administrator\Downloads\zulu11.33.15-ca-jdk11.0.4-win_x64\zulu11.33.15-ca-jdk11.0.4-win_x64\bin.

- **Building your code**

    I recommend following the instructions in the tutorial to build a .jar file for your code but use the package concept. Using this method will assume a subdirectory of pkg for your class. I've provided a **buildclass. cmd** script I used that does it all. It will compile the RegexSample. java code along with the SQL Server Java SDK file mssql-java-lang-extension.jar. Then it uses the jar program to build a package from the code in the pkg subdirectory. (The tutorial example uses a package which will assume a pkg subdirectory when you build the .jar file.) The result of the entire build process is a **sqlregex.jar** file. This is your class code and will be installed as an **external library**.

- **Installing your code**

  The T-SQL script **setuplanguage.sql** is used on Windows to create an external language for Java and to create two external libraries: (1) for the SQL Server Java SDK and (2) your code.

  It is important to note that external language and libraries are installed in a user database.

- **Executing your code**

  The T-SQL script **sqlregex.sql** shows an example like in the tutorial to execute your Java class.

  I will be transparent to you that if you miss a step here, including all the prerequisites, you will hit an error executing sp_execute_external_script. It can be frustrating to debug problems with this feature.

Here are a few things to remember:

- You have to enable external script execution with the configuration option *external scripts enabled*.

- If you pick the Zulu Open JRE during install, make sure to set JRE_HOME if using Windows and restart the Launchpad service.

- If you use your own JRE, you have extra steps to perform for permissions to the JRE binaries. The documentation shows how to do this on Windows and Linux.

- When you build your .jar file for your code, you must put the compiled code (the .class file) in the subdirectory where you are building the code called pkg. That is the convention for using a package name (the package name could be anything in your code, and then your subdir needs to match that name). The docs talk about how much easier it is with a Java IDE to do all of this; I did try out IntelliJ and Visual Studio Code; I just preferred a scriptable method from the command line with javac and jar.

173

Implementing and Using Other Languages

Since we built the extensibility framework and concept of external languages, now programming languages other than Java are possible with T-SQL. Java is just an example we shipped to let you use an extension "out of the box" but also show others how to integrate other programming languages. Imagine if external languages were available for .Net or Go.

The key is the language extension. The language extension is a DLL on Windows or shared library object on Linux that understands how to communicate with the Extension Host. Once a language extension is available, then an SDK set of classes can be built in the native language of the extension. Your code will use the classes implemented by the SDK along with the class to be executed by the call to sp_execute_external_script.

The required set of classes for an SDK to enable a language extension is shown through the Java example at `https://docs.microsoft.com/en-us/sql/language-extensions/how-to/extensibility-sdk-java-sql-server`.

In addition, as I described in the previous section, the source code and documentation for how to write a language extension will be available on GitHub at `https://github.com/microsoft/sql-server-language-extensions`.

It will be interesting to see how language extensions take off within the SQL Server community. For you, imagine scenarios where you cannot implement something in T-SQL today, but would like to extend the language and take advantage of all the capabilities of SQL Server including security, availability, and resource governance without having to write code outside of T-SQL.

All of the process isolation, security, and governance capabilities that exist for SQL Server ML Services apply language extensions and the extensibility framework.

Summary

In this chapter, you have learned how SQL Server 2019 provides features and tools for the modern data developer, including support for just about any programming language you need, updated data providers, graph database, UTF-8 support, Machine Learning, and T-SQL extensions. This is combined with the already powerful performance capabilities of Intelligent Query Processing and tempdb metadata optimizations to provide a complete package needed by any modern data developer.

CHAPTER 6

SQL Server 2019 on Linux

In this chapter, I'll describe what is new for SQL Server 2019 on Linux. However, if you are new to SQL Server on Linux, I'll start the chapter by reviewing the amazing story of how and why we built SQL Server to run on Linux.

The Amazing Story of SQL Server on Linux

In October of 2017, our SQL Server engineering team rocked the industry by shipping SQL Server for Linux on platforms such as Red Hat, Ubuntu, and SUSE. Our engineering team was able to bring SQL Server to market using a very innovative strategy and architecture with software known as the SQL Platform Abstraction Layer (SQLPAL).

Figure 6-1 shows the fundamental architecture of SQL Server on Linux with SQLPAL.

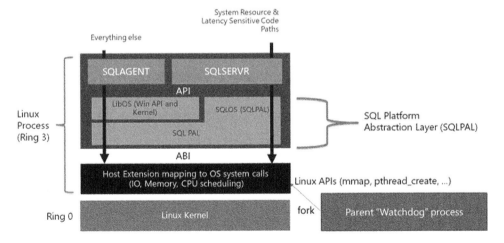

Figure 6-1. *The SQL Server Linux architecture*

© Bob Ward 2019
B. Ward, *SQL Server 2019 Revealed*, https://doi.org/10.1007/978-1-4842-5419-6_6

I go into a very deep detail of this architecture in my book *Pro SQL Server on Linux* by Apress Media, so I won't repeat that in this book (I know; shameless plug for a different book). However, I include this figure and a brief discussion because it tells the story of **choice with compatibility**. The SQL Server core engine and its code are the same codebase for SQL Server on Windows and Linux. The SQLPAL provides the software so that the SQL Server engine doesn't care on what OS platform it is running. This means you can take a database backup on SQL Server on Windows and restore it on Linux with complete compatibility.

For the most part, the feature set of SQL Server 2017 on Linux was completely the same as on Windows. Slava Oks once told me, "Bob, the Query Processor is... the Query Processor, whether it is on Windows or Linux." What he means is that the exact same binary code for the Query Processor runs on both Windows and Linux. Even features like SQL Server Agent and SSIS are available for SQL Server on Linux.

We "timebox" almost every release of SQL Server, trying to maximize the value of what we put into a major release with the balance of getting it shipped in the timeframe we need it to go to market.

While we would have loved that every feature of SQL Server on Windows was included in SQL Server 2017 on Linux, there were some features on the *edge of the engine* that we didn't have time to put into the release – features like Replication and Distributed Transaction Coordinator (DTC). Furthermore, there were a few platform enhancements that we made to ensure SQL Server on Linux was as robust and ready for enterprise customers as our software on Windows.

Before I go deeper into this subject, I should come clean and tell you that there are no examples in this chapter. You might be reading this and be stunned, given I wrote an entire book on SQL Server on Linux. Most of the contents of this chapter either require some complex configuration or are part of using SQL Server independent of Linux. Having said that, consider these options for SQL Server examples and demos:

- *Pro SQL Server on Linux* **GitHub repo** – `https://github.com/Apress/pro-sql-server-on-linux`

- **Demos and examples on the bobsql GitHub repo** – `https://github.com/microsoft/bobsql`

- **Microsoft hands-on lab for SQL Server on Linux** – `https://docs.microsoft.com/en-us/learn/paths/sql-server-2017-on-linux/`

- **The SQL Server Workshop site** – `https://aka.ms/sqlworkshops`.
  While I don't have a specific workshop there yet for SQL Server on
  Linux, don't be surprised if one shows up at some point. There are
  labs to use SQL Server on Linux Replication with containers in these
  workshops.

- Finally, I will let you try out SQL Server Replication on Linux in action
  in Chapter 7, using containers.

What Is New for SQL Server 2019 on Linux

Taking the momentum of delivering SQL Server on Linux, in SQL Server 2019 we added
several enhancements to solve challenges for the data professional and bring **feature
parity** with SQL Server on Windows, including

- **Platform and deployment enhancements** to ensure SQL Server
  on Linux responds correctly to current resource availability and to
  include deployment options for parity with SQL Server on Windows.
  In addition, we have worked to ensure we support the most up-to-
  date version of Linux distributions, which includes enhancements for
  Linux I/O influenced by the SQL Server engineering team.

- **I/O Accelerated Performance** with Persistent Memory Support to
  keep up with advancements in hardware technology.

- **SQL Server Replication** is now supported on Linux to provide data
  synchronization capabilities – this has been a popular SQL Server
  feature for years.

- **Change Data Capture (CDC)** provides a method for developers
  and data professionals to track changes to structure and data from
  SQL Server tables. This has been a popular feature on SQL Server on
  Windows for many releases and is now available on Linux.

- Ensure **Distributed Transactions** are supported so developers have
  options to write distributed data applications as they have for years
  on SQL Server on Windows.

- **Simplified Active Directory deployment** using OpenLDAP
  providers.

- Support **SQL Server Machine Learning Services and Extensibility** on Linux to enable new application scenarios, bring Machine Learning models close to the data in a secure and scalable fashion, and extend the T-SQL language.

- Bring **Data Virtualization** to SQL Server on Linux by supporting Polybase queries to external data sources, with no data movement, such as Hadoop, SQL Server, Oracle, Teradata, and MongoDB.

I'll devote a major section in the rest of this chapter to each of these enhancements.

Platform and Deployment Enhancements

For SQL Server 2019, we made enhancements to the core engine and SQLPAL to make sure SQL Server was "enterprise ready" as it has been on Windows. In addition, we invested in deployment improvements to support new packages for new capabilities and provide users with similar functionality as setup on Windows. We also want to make sure SQL Server on Linux is supported on the latest Linux releases, such as Red Hat Enterprise Linux 8.0, Ubuntu 18.04, and SUSE Linux Enterprise Server 15. These new Linux releases include enhancements to the Linux kernel for I/O performance with durability which was influenced by the importance of I/O in SQL Server.

Platform Enhancements

While it is completely true that the core SQL Server engine on Linux is the same codebase as SQL Server on Windows, the SQLPAL (and a component called the Host Extension) is designed to allow SQL Server to interact with the Linux kernel when necessary. We discovered after we shipped SQL Server on Linux that a few areas needed to be enhanced to ensure our database platform behaved in the same fashion as SQL Server on Windows. Because these were core database engine capabilities integrated with the operating system, we backported these changes to SQL Server 2017 – if you install the latest Cumulative Update for SQL Server 2017, you will have these changes.

Memory Notifications

The SQL Server memory management system has always been built to be resilient and responsive to both memory needs within SQL Server and demands outside the engine in the overall operating system environment.

While the core engine of SQL Server is the same as on Windows, concepts such as responding to memory pressure are specific to the operating system. We discovered some issues with the concept of "memory notifications" in SQL Server 2017 on Linux and have enhanced our Linux integration to ensure this works as it does on Windows in SQL Server 2019.

Note   We also made changes in the latest Cumulative Update to ensure these enhancements are also in SQL Server 2017 on Linux.

Our enhancement will ensure our "target," which is the ceiling of memory allocations for SQL Server, and will be adjusted if there is memory pressure from the operating system. In other words, if the overall operating system is low on physical memory, SQL Server will adjust the "target" down to attempt to avoid OS memory swaps or the dreaded "OOMKiller" scenario (you can read more about oomkiller at `https://unix. stackexchange.com/questions/153585/how-does-the-oom-killer-decide-which- process-to-kill-first`).

The way to see the SQL Server target memory get adjusted with memory pressure (i.e., low physical memory) is to monitor the **committed_target_kb** column in the **dm_os_sys_info** Dynamic Management View (DMV).

Ring Buffer Dynamic Management Views

SQL Server has a DMV called **dm_os_ring_buffers** that can be used to track CPU utilization for the server and SQLSERVR.EXE process. This DMV is not supported officially, but it is used for one key monitoring tool, the Performance Dashboard in SQL Server Management Studio (SSMS). You can read more about how to use the Performance Dashboard at `https://docs.microsoft.com/en-us/sql/relational- databases/performance/performance-dashboard`.

One of the nice features of the dashboard is to show the overall CPU utilization of the computer and SQLSERVR.EXE (even over the last hour of time) to help narrow down CPU issues specific to SQL Server. This report relies on data from dm_os_ring_buffers.

The problem is that, on Linux, we always reported CPU usage as 100% fixed, so the report would not show correct data. With SQL Server 2019 (and the latest CU on SQL Server 2017), this DMV reports the correct usage, and now the Performance Dashboard can be used against a SQL Server on Linux.

SQL Server 2019 on Linux Deployment

If you are familiar with installing SQL Server on Windows, you will be completely amazed at the simplicity of deploying SQL Server on Linux. You can start at this documentation page https://docs.microsoft.com/en-us/sql/linux/sql-server-linux-overview to see the "quickstarts" for deploying SQL Server on Linux.

There were a few changes for SQL Server on Linux deployment worth calling out:

- **New packages** were created to support new features. One of the reasons why SQL Server on Linux deployment is lighter and faster is the product is deployed in a series of packages. While the **mssql-server** package includes the core database engine, SQL Agent, Replication, CDC, and Distributed Transactions, the following packages are required to enable new functionality:

    mssql-mlservices-mlm-py∗ and **mssql-mlservices-mlm-r**∗ – Software for Machine Learning services. There are other packages for ML Services which I will describe later in this chapter.

    mssql-server-extensibility – Software to enable external languages for the extensibility framework.

    mssql-server-extensibility-java – Software to enable Java support for external languages. This package will install the mssql-server-extensibility package.

    mssql-server-polybase – Software to enable the Data Virtualization feature of Polybase for SQL Server on Linux.

- Just as with SQL Server on Windows, SQL Server on Linux will now automatically create **more than one data file for tempdb** (up to 8) based on the number of cores discovered during installation. This option can help avoid page latch contention on system allocation pages.

- **mssql-conf** options have been added to support new features for SQL Server 2019. For example, mssql-conf options for DTC support have been added, which you can read more about at `https://docs.microsoft.com/en-us/sql/linux/sql-server-linux-configure-msdtc`.

Supporting New Linux Releases

It is important for SQL Server to be supported on the latest release of major Linux distributions. Therefore, with SQL Server 2019, we want to ensure we support these major Linux versions:

- Red Hat Linux Enterprise 8.0

- Ubuntu 18.04

- SUSE Linux Enterprise Server 15

Note   At the time of the writing of this book, it was our intention to officially support these Linux releases with SQL Server 2019. SQL Server does work on all of them, but we had to make some changes to the deployment packaging and ensure they were well tested. It is possible issues could come up to prevent us from being 100% ready at the time SQL Server 2019 ships, but, if it isn't announced then, I expect it to be formally announced shortly thereafter.

Along with the support of the latest Linux releases comes a benefit to I/O performance. My long-time colleague Bob Dorr noticed after the release of SQL Server 2017 that I/O performance of SQL Server on Linux with *complete durability* could be a problem. This led to the addition of some SQL Server configuration options for a concept called "forced flush," as documented in the Microsoft article at `https://support.microsoft.com/en-us/help/4131496/enable-forced-flush-mechanism-in-sql-server-2017-on-linux`. We decided to ensure SQL Server, by default, prioritized durability over performance. But customers want both, of course. Any customer could change from the default and achieve durability with performance, if they knew their disk system could support proper flushed writes.

During the calendar year of 2018, Bob Dorr and others on the SQL Server engineering team worked with Linux open source engineering, especially those at Red Hat. The result of this work was changes to the Linux kernel for the XFS file system *upstream*. Red Hat Enterprise Linux (RHEL) 8.0 includes these kernel changes. Other Linux releases are to follow incorporating these changes. Now a user can "turn off" our enforced flush changes for SQL Server on Linux, but still achieve maximum performance with durability.

As with other experiences in our career, Bob Dorr wanted to tell the "story behind the story." And he did so in this detailed blog post at `https://bobsql.com/sql-server-on-linux-forced-unit-access-fua-internals/`. I demonstrated these changes at the Red Hat Summit in May of 2019 and showed the incredible 100%+ performance improvements using RHEL 7.6 vs. RHEL 8.0 configuring SQL Server to use the FUA enhancements. It seems like a small story, but stop and think about this: **Microsoft assisted in contributing to the open source Linux kernel to improve I/O for all applications!**

Persistent Memory Support

One of the things I love about the SQL Server engineering team is that they are always looking to the future. Always looking at the latest advances in technology to ensure SQL Server stays ahead of the curve.

It doesn't surprise me to see that SQL Server on Linux can take advantage of persistent memory devices. Persistent memory (pmem) is a *byte-addressable* storage device. This means persistent memory can be accessed like standard RAM but have the properties of a storage device – so data stored on it can survive computer power outages and restarts.

Persistent memory devices can always be treated in both Windows and Linux as *block* devices. In other words, they can be presented by the operating system as a standard disk drive, and SQL Server can access them like any drive. In block mode, persistent memory devices can be faster to access than even some of the fastest SSDs on the market. However, because pmem devices are byte addressable, an application like SQL Server could transfer data between the device and standard RAM as though it was memory, using API calls like memcpy(), resulting in even faster I/O performance.

SQL Server 2019 has been enhanced to recognize database and transaction log files stored on pmem devices and to *bypass* the Linux kernel I/O stack to transfer data from these devices. You can read more about how applications can take advantage of pmem devices, using a concept called DAX (`www.kernel.org/doc/Documentation/filesystems/dax.txt`) at `https://docs.pmem.io/getting-started-guide/installing-ndctl`.

You can read how to configure a pmem device with SQL Server in our documentation at `https://docs.microsoft.com/en-us/sql/linux/sql-server-linux-configure-pmem`. As I described in Chapter 2, DELL EMC was able to achieve faster performance of SQL Server using pmem support, which you can read about at `www.emc.com/about/news/press/2019/20190402-01.htm`. In addition, HPE engineers have demonstrated I/O performance improvements with SQL Server 2019 in this YouTube video at `www.youtube.com/watch?v=8WUix125tQO`.

SQL Server Replication on Linux

One of the most popular technologies for copying and distributing data to other SQL Server instances is SQL Server Replication. Because SQL Server Agent was included in SQL Server 2017, and the core database engine provides much of the functionality of SQL Server Replication, we wanted this capability to be part of SQL Server 2017 on Linux. But time ran out before we could hook everything together and ensure it was well tested, so SQL Server Replication for Linux is now available in SQL Server 2019.

To continue the great story of compatibility, almost all of the functionality of SQL Server Replication for Windows exists on Linux. This includes snapshot, transaction, merge, and peer-to-peer replication. Furthermore, you can configure replication to use publishers and subscribers across Windows and Linux.

To know about the complete set of SQL Server Replication features on Linux, read through the documentation at `https://docs.microsoft.com/en-us/sql/linux/sql-server-linux-replication`.

In Chapter 7 on containers, I'll show you an example of how to use SQL Server Replication on Linux using containers. The documentation also includes a tutorial at `https://docs.microsoft.com/en-us/sql/linux/sql-server-linux-replication-tutorial-tsql`.

Change Data Capture (CDC) on Linux

Similar to the story for SQL Server Replication, all the components for Change Data Capture (CDC) are in SQL Server on Linux. However, we could not release this feature in SQL Server 2017 on Linux just because of time constraints. In SQL Server 2019, CDC is fully supported.

If you are not familiar with CDC, it is an excellent technology to capture changes of data from tables and is especially useful for Extract, Transform, and Load (ETL) applications.

All of the functionality to track and query changes is provided within SQL Server. CDC uses some of the same internal technology as SQL Server Replication to capture changed data. You can read all about CDC at `https://docs.microsoft.com/en-us/sql/relational-databases/track-changes/about-change-data-capture-sql-server`.

DTC on Linux

After we released SQL Server 2017 on Linux, I asked my friend Bob Dorr what his new focus would be. He said "everything" of course, but one task Slava Oks gave him was to work on getting feature parity for SQL Server on Linux. One of those features was Distributed Transaction support, including support for the Microsoft Distributed Transaction Coordinator (MSDTC).

Along with Kapil Thacker and others in the engineering team, we were able to leverage the SQLPAL architecture to get the core MSDTC service and software working on Linux without having to write a "new" DTC for Linux. (That SQLPAL is a thing of beauty. We should one day find a way to open up the SQLPAL architecture so others can just get their Windows apps to work on Linux.)

One of the most common methods to use DTC for SQL Server is with a distributed transaction across linked servers, from one SQL Server to the other, using the T-SQL **BEGIN DISTRIBUTED TRANSACTION** statement. Linked server queries across SQL Server instances worked on Linux in SQL Server 2017, but not for distributed transactions. As Bob Dorr calls out in this blog post, `https://bobsql.com/sql-server-linux-distributed-transactions-requiring-the-microsoft-distributed-transaction-coordinator-service-are-not-supported-on-sql-server-running-on-linux-sql-server-to-sql-server-distributed-tr/`, you will get an error if you attempt this (wait for it... it will work on SQL Server 2017 now, with the latest Cumulative Update).

If you ever want to know the internals of how DTC works and interacts with SQL Server (or any XA transaction), read this incredibly detailed blog post by Bob Dorr at `https://bobsql.com/how-it-works-sql-server-dtc-msdtc-and-xa-transactions/`.

While distributed linked server transactions were the number one goal for this team to bring DTC transactions to SQL Server on Linux, there are other scenarios for developers the team wanted to enable including

- OLE-TX Distributed Transactions against SQL Server on Linux for ODBC providers. You can read more about building applications with OLE-TX at `https://docs.microsoft.com/en-us/sql/relational-databases/native-client-odbc-how-to/use-microsoft-distributed-transaction-coordinator-odbc`.

- XA Distributed Transactions against SQL Server on Linux using JDBC and ODBC providers. You can read more about XA transactions at `https://docs.microsoft.com/en-us/sql/connect/jdbc/understanding-xa-transactions`.

To enable this functionality, Kapil, Bob, and the team had to build the MSDTC service in such a manner with SQLPAL to support the existing port communication structure as it runs on Windows today. The resulting architecture looks like Figure 6-2 (Tejas Shah and I tag teamed to build this diagram, with help from Kapil and Bob).

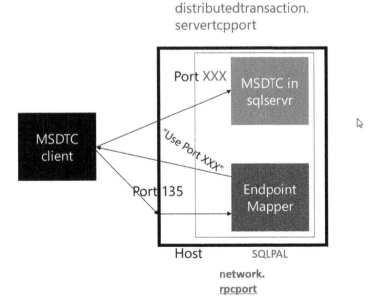

Figure 6-2. *MSDTC on Linux*

This diagram definitely needs some explaining. Imagine the MSDTC client is a SQL Server distributed transaction through a linked server (so another SQL Server running Linux or Windows). In the box on the right, there are two components running in the SQLSERVR Linux process using SQLPAL: the endpoint mapper and MSDTC. The overall host is the operating system on Linux hosting the SQLSERVR process.

MSDTC relies specifically on port 135, and we could not change that unless we modified the MSDTC code for Linux. The MSDTC client tries to communicate first on port 135. We built an "endpoint mapper" which will map port 135 to a port we can listen on. That is configured by the mssql-conf option **network.rpcport**. This endpoint mapper will then communicate back to the MSDTC client which port to use to communicate with the MSDTC Linux service, which then integrates with SQL Server. The port for the MSDTC service can be randomly generated, but you need firewall access to this port, so you should configure this with the mssql-conf option **distributedtransaction. servertcpport.**

The complete configuration experience is available to you at `https://docs. microsoft.com/en-us/sql/linux/sql-server-linux-configure-msdtc`. Once you complete these configurations, you can now just fire up a **BEGIN DISTRIBUTED TRANSACTION** across a SQL Server linked server. In fact, I have an example for you to try just that using containers at `https://github.com/microsoft/sql-server-samples/ tree/master/samples/containers/dtc`.

Active Directory with OpenLDAP

In order to have enterprise credibility for SQL Server on Linux, we had to make sure we supported Active Directory (AD) authentication. Like other aspects of SQL Server on Linux, the *configuration experience is different* than on Windows, but the *experience and compatibility are the same.*

We document an overview of the process to set this up on Linux at `https://docs. microsoft.com/en-us/sql/linux/sql-server-linux-active-directory-auth- overview`, and I talk about the architecture of this in Chapter 7 of my book *Pro SQL Server on Linux.*

One of the steps to configure AD support for SQL Server on Linux is to have the Linux server hosting SQL Server join an Active Directory domain. And when we released SQL Server 2017 on Linux, we document how to do this using a Linux package called **SSSD** and a program called **realmd**. We heard feedback from customers that they wanted alternate methods to join the domain – specifically, a simpler experience, with third-party packages like PBIS, VAS, or Centrify. Turns out SQL Server doesn't do anything to prevent using these packages; we just needed to make a few minor configuration changes to make them work. We outline and document these at `https://docs.microsoft.com/en-us/sql/linux/sql-server-linux-active-directory-join-domain`. Tejas Shah and the team spent some time cleaning up all the documentation for these options. It is important to know this is not a new enhancement for SQL Server 2019, as this will also work for SQL Server 2017. However, the concept is new enough I wanted to call it out in this book.

SQL Server Machine Learning Services and Extensibility on Linux

As I described in detail in Chapter 5, SQL Server Machine Learning Services is *radical* – it allows you to combine the power of R and Python, integrated with SQL Server, to build scalable and powerful Machine Learning models and applications.

While this has been a great story for SQL Server on Windows, we needed to complete the compatibility story by bringing this technology to Linux. In addition, as we introduced the new extensibility framework and language extensions, including Java, we needed to ensure this also works with Linux.

Deployment of SQL Server ML Services on Linux

Like SQL Server on Windows, for SQL Server Machine Learning on Linux, we help you install the necessary packages to deploy R and Python scripts with SQL Server.

We give you choices on how to deploy SQL Server ML Services – minimal, full, or combo. These function as follows:

> **full** – All the packages for R or Python and includes pretrained models to use for Machine Learning. This package is called **mssql-mlservices-mlm-r** or **mssql-mlservices-mlm-py**. All dependent packages are also installed (such as R Open) when you use this option.

minimal – All the packages for R or Python, but no pretrained models. This package is called **mssql-mlservices-packages-r** or **mssql-mlservices-packages-py**. All dependent packages are also installed (such as R Open).

combo – Install SQL Server 2019 (the database engine) with SQL Server ML Services in one step. You can read about how to do this at https://docs.microsoft.com/en-us/sql/linux/sql-server-linux-setup-machine-learning#install-all.

When I installed the full version for SQL Server ML Services for R, these packages were installed as seen in Figure 6-3.

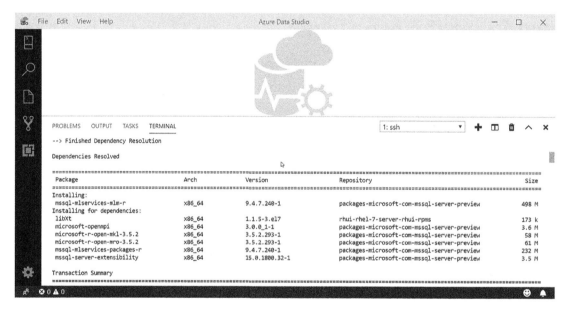

Figure 6-3. *Installation of full SQL Server ML Services for R*

Tip   If you are looking for a great way to use ssh against your SQL Server on Linux, you can use the Terminal option in Azure Data Studio, as you will see in examples in this chapter.

Note that one of the packages installed is **mssql-server-extensibility**, which I'll describe later in this chapter, and is required for the extensibility framework for language extensions (the same framework is used for both SQL Server ML Services and language extensions).

Once you have deployed, you have some post-install steps to perform, such as accepting the EULAs for R or Python. Follow these steps in the documentation at https://docs.microsoft.com/en-us/sql/linux/sql-server-linux-setup-machine-learning#post-install-config-required.

I also recommend, just like on Windows, you use the "hello world" example to verify the installation was successful. The example for R looks like this T-SQL statement:

```
EXEC sp_execute_external_script
@language =N'R',
@script=N'
OutputDataSet <- InputDataSet',
@input_data_1 =N'SELECT 1 AS hello'
WITH RESULT SETS (([hello] int not null));
GO
```

It is also possible you, data scientists, or data engineers need additional R or Python libraries to use for your applications. Use the following guidance in the documentation on how to add this code at https://docs.microsoft.com/en-us/sql/linux/sql-server-linux-setup-machine-learning#add-more-rpython-packages.

Note   If you have used this feature with SQL Server 2019 CTP builds, be sure to remove all of those packages before trying to use the SQL Server 2019 RTM feature.

How It Works

I described in Chapter 5 the architecture of SQL Server ML Services including the Launchpad service and satellite processes.

SQL Server ML Services on Linux has the same concept. On Linux, the Launchpad process is a systemd unit service called **mssql-launchpadd**. You can view or control this service using systemctl. Figure 6-4 shows an example of the status of this service on Linux.

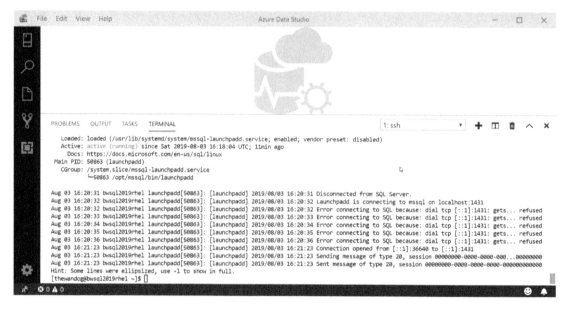

Figure 6-4. *The Launchpad on Linux*

The Launchpad service is represented by a daemon process on Linux called
launchpadd. The same concept of forking processes on Windows for satellite processes
works on Linux, including the R program and bxlserver. Figure 6-5 shows the processes
forked off the launchpadd service to run an R script.

```
91949 ?        Sl     19:21 /opt/microsoft/omsagent/ruby/bin/ruby /opt/microsoft/omsagent/bin/omsagent -d /var/opt/microsoft/omsagent/2ccb3c4a-2e2a-45e
50863 ?        Ssl    0:01 /opt/mssql/bin/launchpadd
53620 ?        Sl     0:00  \_ /opt/mssql/bin/launchpad -hostname fe80::5eea:5d6d:0:187e%eth0 -sandboxWorkingDir /var/opt/mssql-extensibility/data/ef2
54040 ?        S      0:00       \_ /opt/mssql/mlservices/runtime/R/bin/exec/R --slave --no-restore --no-save -e library(RevoScaleR);~+~RevoScaleR:::rx
54059 ?        Sl     0:00            \_ /opt/mssql/mlservices/libraries/RServer/RevoScaleR/rxLibs/x64/BxlServer /var/opt/mssql-extensibility/data/ef232
52148 ?        Ssl    0:00 /opt/mssql/bin/sqlservr
52152 ?        Sl     0:30  \_ /opt/mssql/bin/sqlservr
53986 ?        Sl     0:00 /usr/sbin/abrt-dbus -t133
[thewandog@bwsql2019rhel ~]$
```

Figure 6-5. *Satellite processes for an R script on SQL Server on Linux*

You may be asking how I was able to capture these processes in-flight? Use these steps:
From another ssh session, run the following T-SQL script:

```
EXEC sp_execute_external_script
@language =N'R',
@script=N'
OutputDataSet <- InputDataSet
Sys.sleep(10)',
```

```
@input_data_1 =N'SELECT 1 AS hello'
WITH RESULT SETS (([hello] int not null));
GO
```

Note the Sys.sleep() call to make the R script pause during execution.

From your other ssh session, run the following commands from the Linux shell:

```
ps -axf
```

SQL Server ML Services (and the extensibility framework) uses namespaces for process isolation for satellite processes. You can use the same example earlier to cause the R script to pause and run the command on Linux:

```
sudo lsns
```

You will see a separate namespace created for the launchpad process (which forks the satellite processes). Figure 6-6 shows an example of this separate namespace.

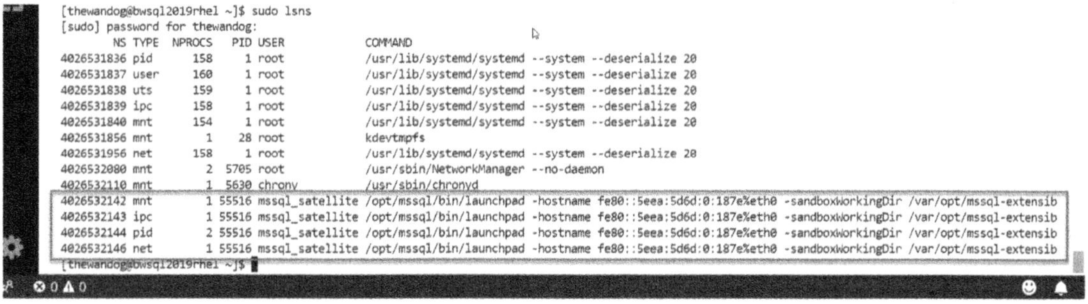

Figure 6-6. *Namespace for satellite processes on Linux*

Figure 6-6 shows something else important about SQL Server ML Services (and the extensibility framework). The user account that satellite processes runs under is called the **mssql_satellite** login. This is important for any permissions required by R or Python scripts (and extensibility languages).

Note   Don't forget that the native scoring feature of SQL Server is built into the SQL Server engine, so can be used on SQL Server on Linux (even on SQL Server 2017). Read more at `https://docs.microsoft.com/en-us/sql/advanced-analytics/sql-native-scoring`.

The Extensibility Framework and Language Extensions

Based on the same framework as SQL Server ML Services, we introduced the concept of language extensions, which I described in detail in Chapter 5. As part of this capability, we shipped Java as an example of a language extension in the box.

To deploy SQL Server language extensions on Linux, you can install one of these packages:

> **mssql-server-extensibility** – This is the core software to use the extensibility framework for any language. It is a dependent package, as you saw earlier in this chapter, installed when you install SQL Server ML Services.

> **mssql-server-extensibility-java** – This will install the extensibility framework and the java language extension and SDK so you can run your Java code.

Just like SQL Server ML Services, you also have the option to perform a combo install of SQL Server with language extensions, which you can read about at https://docs.microsoft.com/en-us/sql/linux/sql-server-linux-setup-language-extensions. In addition, SQL Server will install the Java Runtime Engine (JRE) Version 8 if it is not already installed on Linux (as with Windows, we will install the Zulu JRE).

The process to deploy your Java class is almost identical to SQL Server on Windows and how I described how to use the regex tutorial in Chapter 5. In fact, Java is very compatible, so you can take the same java class you built in Chapter 5 and compile/build a jar file on Linux. You use the same steps to create an external language, external library for the SDK, and external library for your Java class (in the form of a jar file).

When you run your code, the same Launchpad architecture is used to fork a process for satellite processing. Like SQL Server on Windows, this process is called Extension Host and looks like Figure 6-7 from a process output on Linux.

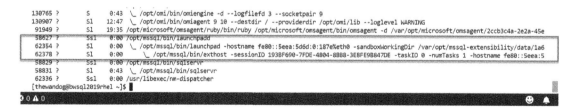

Figure 6-7. *The exthost satellite process to run Java for SQL Server on Linux*

Polybase on Linux

It is difficult to arrange everything in a book in the exact right order. Chapter 9 is dedicated to the concept of Data Virtualization and Polybase in SQL Server 2019. I wanted to briefly mention it here because it is new to SQL Server on Linux.

Polybase was introduced in SQL Server 2016 for Hadoop connectors and enhanced in SQL Server 2019 with connectors for SQL Server, Oracle, Teradata, and MongoDB.

As you will read in Chapter 9, Polybase uses some of the components of our Analytics Platform System (APS, formerly known as Parallel Data Warehouse) to perform scale-out query processing. These exist as services in Windows and use the SQLPAL for SQL Server 2019 on Linux.

We have introduced the **mssql-server-polybase** package to enable Polybase for SQL Server on Linux. You can read the complete deployment steps at `https://docs.microsoft.com/en-us/sql/relational-databases/polybase/polybase-linux-setup`.

The same T-SQL statements and concepts apply for Polybase for SQL Server on Linux as with Windows, with these exceptions for SQL Server 2019:

- Polybase for SQL Server on Linux does not support scale-out groups.

- The generic ODBC connector is not supported.

Our plans for the future are to get complete feature parity for Polybase for SQL Server on Linux past SQL Server 2019. You will learn more about how to use Polybase in Chapter 9.

Summary

SQL Server on Linux is all about choice with compatibility. In SQL Server 2017, the core database engine for Linux was compatible with SQL Server on Windows. With SQL Server 2019, we have included enhancements for capabilities on the edge of the engine including Replication, Change Data Capture, Distributed Transactions, Machine Learning Service and Language Extensions, and Polybase.

In addition, we have made enhancements to platform integration with Linux, supported the latest Linux releases, included enhanced I/O performance with durability, added persisted memory support, and clarified how OpenLDAP providers can be used to configure Active Directory authentication.

The story for SQL Server on Linux is a strong one. I was invited by Red Hat in May of 2019 to not just attend the Red Hat Summit, but to present the story of SQL Server on Linux with several of my colleagues (and in one case copresent with Red Hat). I had also attended the Red Hat Summit in 2018, and, as the event ended in 2019, I no longer felt like Microsoft SQL Server "was the new kid on the block." I felt we were now a mainstream part of the Linux ecosystem and community.

CHAPTER 7

Inside SQL Server Containers

Why SQL Server Containers?

When I thought about how I would approach this chapter, I thought about only talking about what is new for containers for SQL Server 2019. While that alone would be worth a chapter, I decided to go bigger and be more inclusive to talk about the concept of containers, why it is important as a new way of deploying SQL server, and of course what are new capabilities for containers with SQL Server 2019. I could write an entire book on containers so you will not walk away from this chapter with an exhaustive knowledge on the subject. There are many great resources on containers (one I still find value is still `www.docker.com`!) to supplement this chapter. My goal for this chapter is to give you enough information about containers to see how SQL Server containers work and why you should consider using them. I do promise you will leave this chapter understanding how to deploy, manage, and use SQL Server containers.

If you feel like you know the concept of containers fairly well, you are more than welcome to skip down to the section called "What Is New for SQL Server 2019." After that section is a series of examples you will find valuable to dive more into containers. I should say even if you know the basics of containers, you might consider starting at the section "How SQL Server Containers Work," specifically at the subsection "The SQL Server Container" as I'll disclose some internals of the unique aspects of SQL Server using containers.

Containers solve a challenge that virtual machines cannot provide today. Virtual machines have been such an amazing technology to *abstract applications from underlying hardware*, but they require an entire operating system to be loaded and run for your application. Virtual machines do allow applications to run isolated from each other on the host and for SQL Server that has been a great solution for consolidation scenarios (even though SQL Server does allow for multiple instances to be hosted on the same computer). Containers provide the same concept of isolation, but they are far more lightweight than using a virtual machine. Containers are often considered an abstraction from the operating system.

Here is an important concept to remember as I describe containers. Containers don't replace virtual machines. Containers *complement* them. In fact, one of the most common environments to run containers is inside a virtual machine. Let me provide the definition of a container by first defining a *container image*. A container image is a binary file that describes a set of files organized in a file system and a **program** to run from those files. A *container* is an instance of running the container image program along with the file system from the image in an **isolated manner**.

Consider the following diagram in Figure 7-1 I often use to talk about what are containers and why they can solve certain challenges for modern applications.

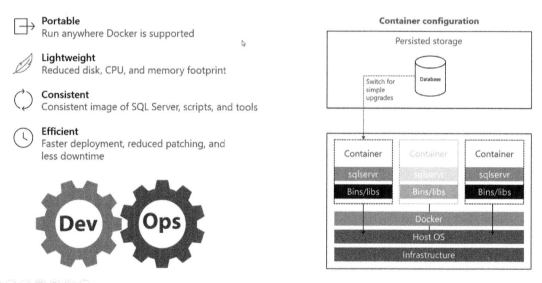

Figure 7-1. *The promise of SQL Server containers*

Let me unpack this figure starting on the left side of the diagram:

Portable

Containers are portable because a container image can be run anywhere docker can be run which is almost everywhere including Windows, Linux, and macOS computers or in cloud systems supporting these operating systems or Kubernetes (you will learn more about Kubernetes in Chapter 8). You can take a SQL Server container image as a binary file and "pull it" into any of the systems, and it will operate the same.

Note   Calling all macOS users. Please take a look at the following blog post I wrote showing how you can now run SQL Server and tools with no Windows software required! `https://bobsql.com/take-the-sql-server-mac-challenge/`

Lightweight

A container is a running instance of a container image, and it in the end is just a process based on a program running in an isolated manner. That makes it far more lightweight than an entire virtual machine to host a program. The footprints of containers are also optimized because if you run more than one container from an image, a portion of the image files (called the *readable* layer which I'll explain later in the chapter) is shared across the containers. This will reduce the footprint and resources required to run multiple SQL Server instances on a host or virtual machine.

Note   SQL Server on Linux does not support multiple instances, but you can achieve the same solution using containers.

Consistent

This is one of the aspects about containers I absolutely love, and it helps solve a big challenge for SQL Server. For years, companies have set up *development* servers with SQL Server to host a test and development playground for developers. This causes major pain as so many developers using the same SQL Server (and they usually need a higher level of access for SQL Server) can result in inconsistencies and major pains for folks like database administrators.

Containers provide a consistent way for developers to use SQL Server without having to share a SQL Server instance. For example, if you want all developers to use a specific image of a SQL Server version along with a specific database, you can build a container image to achieve this. And because containers are portable and SQL Server now supports Linux, you can give the same SQL Server container image for developers that are using different platforms. Your macOS developers can use the same SQL Server image as your Windows developers. Now that is a consistent story! The symbol in the bottom left-hand corner of the figure for *DevOps* simply describes how important the container story is to support a DevOps model.

Efficient

Containers provide a new and quite frankly mind-opening experience for updating software like SQL Server. If you have ever had to apply a cumulative update or patch for SQL Server, you will find the container experience amazing. You will experience less downtime and a faster experience to roll back updates should that be needed.

In Figure 7-1 on the right side, the diagram shows a picture of how this works. The container in the middle which is "grayed" out represents a SQL Server container that is stopped. The container on the left is a new version of SQL Server that is started but pointed to the same system and user databases which are stored in *persisted storage* (in a concept called a volume which I'll explain later in this chapter). This is a technique I'll show you later in this chapter I call "switching" containers to apply or roll back a cumulative update of SQL Server.

While you are looking at the diagram, I want to call out the following observations:

- The black boxes that say **Bin/libs** represent the minimum binaries required to run SQL Server. This represents the "lightweight" aspect of a container vs. an entire virtual machine. And what is not really represented in the diagram is that if the containers are from the same image, these files are shared across containers.

- The box that says **Docker** represents the docker software that is used to run and manage containers. In reality this should say Container Runtime as Docker is just an example of a container runtime.

- Notice the arrows that point down *through* Docker to the **Host OS**. Docker is not a layer in between a container and the host operating system. In other words, SQL Server doesn't have to communicate through some layer to execute kernel OS operations. This is why containers are also considered more lightweight because they have a program that talks directly to the host OS. The unique aspect of container execution is that they run in isolation from each other, hence the term container.

With these fundamentals of container in mind, let's spend time learning how containers work. Understanding how things work often allows you to use things more efficiently.

How SQL Server Containers Work

Before you begin your journey of trying out SQL Server containers, let me spend time explaining how they work. To first explain how they work, I need to spend some time talking about *container hosting*, the magic behind docker, and the *container lifecycle*.

Container Hosting

I just finished the last section talking about how containers are really programs that work directly with the host operating system. The host operating system could be in a virtual machine or directly with a host *bare metal* computer.

Given the program interacts directly with the host operating system like any program on the system (except of course they run in a special isolated manner), they must be compiled and executed to run on the host operating system.

When we shipped SQL Server 2017 on Linux, we also introduced SQL Server container images based on Linux, namely, Ubuntu Linux. Almost every container image in the world is based on a host operating system, and most of them are based on Linux. For Linux host systems, running a SQL Server container based on Linux is no problem. Whether the Linux system is a bare metal computer or a virtual machine, SQL Server Linux containers are a natural fit.

What about Windows and macOS? Docker as a container runtime is the key. Docker supports containers running on Windows through a program called Docker Desktop for Windows. Any container based on a Linux image will be run in the context of a Virtual Machine that runs Linux called **DockerDesktopVM**. Docker Desktop for macOS uses a concept called HyperKit (`https://github.com/moby/hyperkit`). You can read more about Docker Desktop at `www.docker.com/products/docker-desktop`.

Recently, there have been some advances in containers with Docker for Windows to support a concept called Linux Containers for Windows (LCOW). The Windows team describes this concept as a lighter method to run Linux containers in Windows than a full virtual machine. You can read more about LCOW at `https://docs.microsoft.com/en-us/virtualization/windowscontainers/deploy-containers/linux-containers`. In addition, Docker Desktop for Windows can use a more optimized method using the new Windows Subsystem for Linux (WSL). You can read more about how Docker Desktop can use WSL2 at `https://engineering.docker.com/2019/06/docker-hearts-wsl-2/`.

What about containers based on images for Windows or macOS? If a container image is based on an operating system like Linux, are there container images based on Windows or macOS? The answer is yes for Windows. Windows does have a concept of a container image based on Windows. You can read more about Windows containers at `https://docs.microsoft.com/en-us/virtualization/windowscontainers/about/`. SQL Server has not produced a supported version of a Windows container. But in the summer of 2019, we announced a private preview program for SQL Server Windows Container. I'll talk more about SQL Server Windows Containers at the end of this chapter. As of the time I wrote this book, I've yet to see a container image based on macOS. Since SQL Server is not built for macOS natively, this is not an issue, but as I've stated SQL Server supports Linux which will run using Docker Desktop for macOS (using HyperKit).

Is Docker Magic?

What I've described so far seems kind of magical to anyone familiar with computer systems. Anytime someone mentions the word container, the name Docker comes up in the same sentence. As it turns out, the concept of operating system virtualization, which defines the concept of what containers are all about, has been around for some time (read `https://en.wikipedia.org/wiki/OS-level_virtualisation` for more info). Anyone that has worked with me when I research how something works knows I always want to know "What is the API?" In other words, what is the programming interface used to achieve a goal. For containers, using APIs provided by the kernel OS provides the answer behind the magic.

Docker (as well as other container runtimes in the market) has taken the concept of containers and built a platform and ecosystem and that is universally used. But Docker itself uses the capabilities of the operating system to enable the concept of containers, namely, these main constructs (on Linux but similar concepts apply to Windows containers):

Namespace – Namespaces provide a mechanism for processes to run isolated from each other. You can read more about namespaces at `https://en.wikipedia.org/wiki/Cgroups#NAMESPACE-ISOLATION`.

Control groups (cgroups) – cgroups provide a mechanism to control resource usage for processes or a set of processes. Containers by default have access to all computing resources such as memory and CPU, but cgroups provide a method to limit resource usage for a container.

Union file system – A union file system allows multiple directories to be presented as one. This concept is key to keeping the footprint of containers small and supporting a

readable and **writeable** layer. In Linux system, the OverlayFS file system supports a union file system. You can read more about how this works for containers at `https://docs.docker.com/storage/storagedriver/overlayfs-driver/#how-the-overlay-driver-works`.

Let me stop and explain a key concept I just introduced for containers:

readable layer – A container image is read-only and consists of a set of files presented in a file system. For SQL Server, this includes the minimum files supported from the base operating system image and the files for SQL Server including binaries and system databases.

writeable layer – The writeable layer is any changes made to the file system of a container after it is started. This could include any changes to files from the readable layer or new files added. The writeable layer is persisted for the lifetime of the container. Once the container is removed, the writeable layer is also removed. As you can imagine for SQL Server user databases, this presents a problem.

volume – A volume is a location of persisted storage on the host that is mapped to a directory location in the writeable layer of the container. You will see for SQL Server a common practice is to use a volume to map to a directory in the container to store databases. Volumes persist outside the lifetime of the container, so if a container is removed, the volume still exists.

One thing I love docker has done is to introduce their own API abstracting the OS concepts that support containers called **libcontainer**. You can read more about libcontainer at `https://github.com/opencontainers/runc/tree/master/libcontainer`. Another interesting read about the open source nature of containers is the Open Container Initiative (OCI), which Microsoft is a founding member (`www.opencontainers.org/`).

It is important to note that Docker is an example of a container runtime and one of the most popular in the industry. There is an open-source access container runtime called containerd which you can read about at `https://containerd.io/`.

Container Lifecycle

When you install Docker whether it is on Linux, Windows, or macOS, the following components are installed which enable containers:

Docker engine – This consists of the docker daemon which is a "service" that controls all the operations for building and running containers. The docker engine supports an API for programs to interact with the engine for building and running containers. You can read more about the docker engine at `https://docs.docker.com/engine/`. You can read more about the engine API at `https://docs.docker.com/develop/sdk/`.

docker client – This is a program called **docker** which uses the engine API to build and run containers. The docker client is a consistent program in that it supports options and behaves the same across Windows, macOS, and Linux. You will use the docker client throughout this chapter in the examples.

docker compose – This is a program called **docker-compose** which allows you to build and run multi-container applications. You will use docker-compose in an example later in this chapter with SQL Server Replication.

Using these components, consider the following workflow I call the container lifecycle as seen in Figure 7-2.

Figure 7-2. *The container lifecycle*

Let's look at each of these in more detail:

build – The **docker build** command is used to build a new container image. Even though an SDK is supported, the standard approach is to define the image to build using a file called **Dockerfile**. You can read more about docker build at `https://docs.docker.com/engine/reference/commandline/build/`. The reference for the syntax of a Dockerfile can be found at `https://docs.docker.com/engine/reference/builder/`. Microsoft builds the images containing SQL Server so you in many cases will never build your own image. However, there are circumstances where you will build a customized image *based on SQL Server*. I'll show you examples later in this chapter.

push – Once you build an image, you probably want others to use it so you can push or publish your container image to a registry using the **docker push** command. That registry can be on a local server or in the public domain. One of the most common public domain registries is the Docker Hub or hub.docker.com. Microsoft, including SQL Server, publishes their container images at mcr.microsoft.com (called the Microsoft Container Registry). I'll talk later in this chapter on how to find the various SQL Server images on the Microsoft Container Registry. You can read more about docker push at `https://docs.docker.com/engine/reference/commandline/push/`.

pull – Anyone wanting to consume a container image must pull it even if it is stored on a local server. A container image is pulled using the **docker pull** command. The docker engine will store a copy of the image locally on the host computer. You can

read more about the docker pull command at `https://docs.docker.com/engine/`
`reference/commandline/pull/`.

run – To run a container based on an image, you use the **docker run** command. If
you run a container based on an image that is not already pulled, docker will first pull
the image and then run the container. You will learn all the parameters and details
required in this chapter to run a SQL Server container.

After you run a container, you will want to **manage** it. The docker client will allow
you to stop, start, restart, and remove a container. In addition, the docker client will let
you manage images including removing them.

The docker client can also be used to **monitor** and manage the container ecosystem
by listing out running containers and stopped containers and dumping out stats and logs
from running and stopped containers.

Finally, the docker client allows you to **interact** with running containers by copying
files into the writeable layer from the host system and running a program that exists
in the containers' file system (which will be run in the same namespace as the main
container program. These commands will be very useful for SQL Server containers as
you will see in the examples in this chapter.

The SQL Server Container

The SQL Server container images contain the necessary files for the SQL Server engine,
SQL Server Agent, all the features included with the engine like Replication, and the SQL
Server command-line tools (sqlcmd and bcp). When you run a SQL Server container,
SQL Server is pre-installed! In other words, when you pull and run a SQL Server
container, you are ready to use it. This is one of the major benefits of using a SQL Server
container. There is no install of SQL Server required once you start a container.

I mentioned in the previous section that an image is built with docker build using
a file called a Dockerfile. To understand how the SQL Server container is pre-installed,
here is a rough outline of the commands in the Dockerfile for SQL Server:

```
FROM <ubuntu or rhel base image>
LABEL < Microsoft label information >
EXPOSE 1433
COPY < SQL Server binaries and libraries >
RUN ./install.sh
CMD ["/opt/mssql/bin/sqlservr"]
```

The FROM command specifies the base OS image the SQL Server container image is built on. One of the great things about containers is the ability to build new images based on others, creating a layering effect of images. In fact, later in the chapter, I'll show you how to build your own image based on the SQL Server image (which is based on the base OS image).

The EXPOSE command allows the SQL Server container to have programs connect to port 1433 inside the container. This is important since by default containers are isolated. You will see that often this port will be mapped to another port in the host, allowing multiple SQL Server containers to run on the same host (which normally would fail since two programs can't be listed on the same port).

The COPY and RUN commands are just part of the build process to copy in all of the SQL Server binary files into the container image file system and install any software dependencies.

All of these commands in the SQL Server Dockerfile so far are part of building the container image. When a docker build command is executed, each of these statements is used to build the image. The CMD statement indicates to docker the name of the program to run when the container starts up, which is sqlservr. This means that a SQL Server container doesn't run like a "service" (e.g., systemd unit service in Linux). When I've described this to some people, they have asked "How does SQL Server then stay running?" Turns out the SQL Server program (this is the same on Windows) is built to be a *daemon* program, which means it runs in the background until it gets a signal to be stopped.

With this in mind, let's see how you run a SQL Server container and then talk about internally how we "pre-install" SQL Server.

The basic syntax to run a SQL Server container looks like this with the docker run command (note: on Linux you typically need to preface the command with sudo):

```
docker run
-e 'ACCEPT_EULA=Y' -e 'MSSQL_SA_PASSWORD=Sql2017isfast'
-p 1401:1433
-v sqlvolume:/var/opt/mssql
--hostname sql2019latest
--name sql2019latest
-d
mcr.microsoft.com/mssql/rhel/server:2019-latest
```

Let me explain each of these arguments:

```
-e 'ACCEPT_EULA=Y' -e 'MSSQL_SA_PASSWORD=Sql2017isfast'
```

The -e parameters specify environment variables that the container needs to execute. In the case of SQL Server, you need at minimum to accept the EULA agreement and the sa password. Other environment variables can be used as well to specify the SQL Server edition or enable SQL Server Agent. Any environment variable supported by SQL Server can be used to preconfigure the installation of SQL Server when starting the container. You can get a complete set of environment variables at `https://docs.microsoft.com/en-us/sql/linux/sql-server-linux-configure-environment-variables`.

```
-p 1401:1433
```

This is not required if you are only going to run one SQL Server container on the host (and assumes you don't have SQL Server installed on the host). If you do have more than one SQL Server, you need to map port 1433 to a different port. Any application wanting to connect to this SQL Server container will use port 1401 now instead of just the default port.

```
-v sqlvolume:/var/opt/mssql
```

This specifies what volume to use to map to the SQL Server directory where databases are stored. This is not required, but if you want your databases to persist independent of the lifetime of the container, you will want to use a volume. For any production SQL Server container, you will want to use a volume.

```
--hostname sql2019latest
```

This parameter is also not required but very convenient. This is because the hostname you specify will become @@SERVERNAME within SQL Server.

```
--name sql2019latest
```

This parameter is also not required but is convenient for you to manage the container. By using a name, you can now easily identify a container by name and manage it. For example, after starting this container, you can stop it by running `docker stop sql2019latest`.

```
-d
```

This parameter says to run the container in the background. You normally want to use this parameter for a SQL Server container. However, a nice debugging technique is to remove this parameter if you cannot start a SQL Server container. This is because when the sqlservr program is run from the command line, the default behavior is to dump the contents of the ERRORLOG to stdout which would then show up when you run the container. You can also use the `docker logs` command to dump out the ERRORLOG of a SQL Server container.

```
mcr.microsoft.com/mssql/rhel/server:2019-latest
```

This is the *tag* of the container image you want to run. I'll show in the next section how to figure out which tags to use for a particular SQL Server container. If the tagged image doesn't exist locally, docker will pull that image first and then run the container.

One interesting aspect of how a SQL Server container works is the startup sequence. When the sqlservr program runs in the container, the /var/opt/mssql directory does not exist. However, the sqlservr program has the intelligence to create this directory and extract the system databases from the installed files of the container image at startup. In addition, sqlservr understands how to take the environment variables and use them as startup parameters to bind in the EULA agreement, sa password, and other environment variables. In other words, the sqlservr program understands how to install itself!

Let's look at what is new in SQL Server 2019 with containers before diving into some examples.

What Is New for SQL Server 2019

Now that you have a perspective on how containers work and how they work with SQL Server, let's review the new capabilities with containers for SQL Server 2019:

- We now provide SQL container images with a **base OS image of Red Hat Enterprise Linux (RHEL)** for SQL Server 2019. See the next point here on how to find out what these images look like. I'll use mostly RHEL images in this chapter for the examples.

- SQL Server 2019 containers by default run as non-root allowing SQL Server to be officially supported on Red Hat OpenShift.

- All SQL Server container images are now stored in the Microsoft Container Registry at **mcr.microsoft.com**.

When we released SQL Server 2017 and container images, we published our images in the Docker Hub repository at `https://hub.docker.com/_/microsoft-mssql-server`. Since that time within Microsoft, we established a standard that official Microsoft container images would now be published in the Microsoft Container Registry at mcr.microsoft.com. We continue to "syndicate" or list our images on the Docker Hub, but the images themselves are found only on mcr.microsoft.com.

Let me stop here and explain about the naming convention for container images:

The SQL container images will follow this naming convention:

mcr.microsoft.com/mssql/server:<tag> – Ubuntu images

mcr.microsoft.com/mssql/rhel/server:<tag> – Red Hat Enterprise Linux images

---

Note   While we don't currently package container images for SUSE, you can build one yourself using this example provided by Vin Yu from Microsoft at `https://github.com/microsoft/mssql-docker/tree/master/linux/preview/SLES`.

The <tag> syntax is based on the specific build you are looking for or the "latest" build.

For example, to get the latest build container image for SQL Server 2017 for Ubuntu, you would use this container image name:

`mcr.microsoft.com/mssql/server:2017-latest-ubuntu`

or for SQL 2017 CU10 for Ubuntu, you would use

`mcr.microsoft.com/mssql/server:2017-CU10-ubuntu`

Note   You can also use a tag of 2017-latest for the latest Ubuntu image, but that is not recommended. That was the original tags we used when we first shipped SQL 2017. It is best to explicitly state the base image by name.

We did not ship any RHEL container images for SQL Server 2017. They are all listed for SQL Server 2019. For example, to get the latest SQL Server 2019 RHEL container image, you would use:

```
mcr.microsoft.com/mssql/rhel/server:2019-latest
```

If you pull a SQL container image and are not sure what version of SQL Server the image was built for, use the **docker inspect** command. Run the following command first:

```
docker images
```

This will list out the images that are stored locally on your server. The TAG column may give you a clue on the version of SQL Server. But if the TAG has a value of something like **2017-latest-ubuntu**, you wouldn't know what CU build of SQL Server 2017 this is without running a container based on this image. But if you run a command like

```
docker inspect <IMAGE ID>
```

where IMAGE ID is the GUID from the docker images command.

the result is a JSON file that describes the image. This can be very useful for any container image. If you search the JSON text for a section called Labels, you will get a result that looks like the following:

```
"Labels": {

                "com.microsoft.product": "Microsoft SQL Server",
                "com.microsoft.version": "14.0.3223.3",
                "vendor": "Microsoft"
```

The version number is the build of SQL Server. You can do a simple search on the Internet and find the version number matched to a SQL Server build. In this example, 14.0.3223.3 matches SQL Server 2017 CU16.

This is nice of course, but how can you know the entire possible list of container images from mcr.microsoft.com? This tip which I've seen provided by my colleague Umachandar Jayachandran (he goes by UC) will save you a great deal of time.

Use this URL to find a list of all Ubuntu images:

`https://mcr.microsoft.com/v2/mssql/server/tags/list`

For RHEL images, you can use

`https://mcr.microsoft.com/v2/mssql/rhel/server/tags/list`

Tip   If you install the Docker extension with Azure Data Studio or Visual Studio Code, you can use the extension to browse mcr.microsoft.com including the mssql/server images. This blog post talks about the extension at `https://jeeweetje.net/2019/07/10/exploring-containers-in-the-microsoft-container-registry-with-visual-studio-code/`.

- We now support **non-root containers** with SQL Server 2019. Up to this time, all containers for SQL Server are run in the context of the root user in Linux. While Containers run in isolation, some in the industry don't think running as root is a secure model and prevents SQL Server from being officially supported in environment such as RedHat OpenShift.

- Up to this point, SQL Server containers only support SQL Server authentication. It is our intention to support **Active Directory authentication with containers** in SQL Server 2019. At the time I wrote this chapter, it was somewhat up in the air on whether this would be officially supported for the SQL Server 2019 release. I'll talk more about this concept later in the chapter in the section "Deploying SQL Containers in Production."

- As we marched close to releasing SQL Server 2019, we announced preview support for SQL Server containers based on a **base image of Windows**. I call this **SQL Server container Windows images**. I have a separate section at the end of this chapter discussing this topic.

As with many topics related to computer technology, you can only read so much about how something works. Only by using something can you truly put together all the pieces of the puzzle. Let's go through a series of topics about SQL Server containers by using examples.

Prerequisites for the Examples

After perhaps disappointing you in the previous chapter with no examples, in this chapter I have more than enough. This was one of the chapters I enjoyed writing the most because I love the topic of containers.

I am going to show you several different ways to run containers in this chapter on Windows and Linux. I have provided you scripts where you can run all the examples on either platform (or macOS), but in the examples I may talk more in detail about how to use an example on a specific platform.

My goal when I wrote this chapter is that all examples would be based on Bash shell scripts and use the new Windows Subsystem for Linux (WSL2) for Windows users. However, at the time of this writing, this would have required an *insider* build of Windows 10, and I didn't want to put that risk on you as the reader. For Windows users, I have examples to use in PowerShell (but remember as I just discussed in the previous section, this will still use the Docker Desktop VM). WSL2 will change this game, but the next major production build of Windows 10 will be required to use WSL2 (unless you are game for the insider builds).

For all examples on all platforms, you will need

- An Internet connection as these examples will pull docker images from the Microsoft Container Registry.

- The WideWorldImporters sample database backup which can be found at `https://github.com/Microsoft/sql-server-samples/releases/download/wide-world-importers-v1.0/WideWorldImporters-Full.bak`.

- The SQL Server command-line tools need to be installed on your computer if not already. Windows users can find the download from `https://docs.microsoft.com/en-us/sql/tools/sqlcmd-utility`. Linux users can use the following documentation: `https://docs.microsoft.com/en-us/sql/linux/sql-server-linux-setup-tools`. macOS users refer to the following documentation: `https://docs.microsoft.com/en-us/sql/linux/sql-server-linux-setup-tools#macos`.

- Azure Data Studio or ADS (minimum June 2019 edition) from `https://docs.microsoft.com/en-us/sql/azure-data-studio/download`. ADS is perfect for these examples since it is a cross-platform tool. For ADS users, I recommend you install this extension: `https://marketplace.visualstudio.com/items?itemName=ms-azuretools.vscode-docker`. For ADS you need to choose the Download Extension option on the install page. Download the VSIX file to your local computer and then follow the docs for ADS to install it. Here is how you add an extension for ADS: `https://docs.microsoft.com/en-us/sql/azure-data-studio/extensions`.

Here is a list for each platform of what you will need to install:

Windows users

Install Docker Desktop for Windows at `https://hub.docker.com/editions/community/docker-ce-desktop-windows`. Windows Server users can also install Docker by reading `https://docs.docker.com/install/windows/docker-ee/`.

Here is another important point for Windows users. You will likely use **git** to clone the repo for the book for all the samples. To do this, you will have likely installed Git for Windows. Be sure when you install Git for Windows to **turn off the autocrlf option**. Otherwise, Linux shell scripts that are needed for this chapter will fail. If you don't know what option, you should use a syntax like the following when cloning the repo:

```
git clone --config core.autocrlf=false <github URL>
```

Linux users

Docker comes in the free or Community Edition (CE) or paid Enterprise Edition (EE). For the CE, there are various install options depending on your Linux distribution. For example, Ubuntu users can install docker from `https://docs.docker.com/install/linux/docker-ce/ubuntu/` or `https://hub.docker.com/search/?type=edition&offering=community`.

If you have Docker EE, there are specific install instructions for Ubuntu, RHEL, and SUSE at `www.docker.com/products/docker-enterprise`.

macOS users

Install Docker Desktop for Mac from `https://hub.docker.com/editions/community/docker-ce-desktop-mac`. The scripts I've built for Linux and macOS users preface all docker commands with sudo. Although not required on macOS, using sudo works just fine and allows for a single set of scripts for either platform.

Deploying a SQL Server Container

You really need to see containers in action to appreciate the power of what they bring and how they work. If you remember the container lifecycle I discussed earlier in the chapter, Microsoft has already completed the build and push steps for SQL Server containers. I will discuss later in the chapter how you will build your own images based on SQL Server, but for now I'll show you the **pull ➤ run** sequence and **stop ➤ start ➤ remove** manage sequence. And I will show you other docker commands you can use to explore containers.

IMPORTANT: You must copy the WideWorldImporters backup file into a local directory where you run these scripts to go through this activity. You can download this backup from `https://github.com/Microsoft/sql-server-samples/releases/download/wide-world-importers-v1.0/WideWorldImporters-Full.bak`.

All the examples in this section can be found at **ch7_inside_sql_containers\deploy**. Use the **dockerpowershell** directory for Windows. For Linux and macOS users, use the **dockerbash** directory (be sure to make your scripts executable with chmod u+x <script>). I'll walk you through in this chapter the PowerShell examples.

1. Run the following command from PowerShell to start a SQL Server container. (I choose to use the Terminal option in Azure Data Studio (ADS) to run the scripts or script **step1_dockerrunsql.ps1**.) Since the image for SQL Server 2019 is not locally on my computer, docker will do a pull first and then start the container:

```
docker run -e "ACCEPT_EULA=Y" -e "SA_PASSWORD=Sql2019isfast"
-p 1433:1433 --name sql2019latest --hostname sql2019latest
-d mcr.microsoft.com/mssql/rhel/server:2019-latest
```

Figure 7-3 shows an example in ADS for this script to pull the SQL Server 2019 RHEL image.

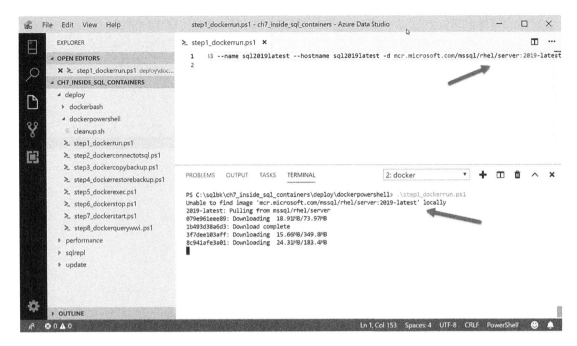

Figure 7-3. *Deploying a SQL Server RHEL container*

You may want to see more about the SQL Server 2019 image. You can do that with a command like the following:

```
docker inspect mcr.microsoft.com/mssql/rhel/server:2019-latest
```

The output will be a very long JSON file. Take note of this interesting section of the output:

```
"Cmd": [
              "/bin/sh",
              "-c",
              "#(nop) ",
              "CMD [\"/opt/mssql/bin/sqlservr\"]"
        ],
```

This shows you the CMD from the Dockerfile which is to just run sqlservr. Unfortunately, there is not a proven way to confirm what the base image of a container image is. I've seen lots of programs out there, and the docker history command for our containers doesn't give the name of the base image.

When the container is run, unfortunately you will not know if SQL Server started correctly or not. The command will dump out a long "guid" value and come back to the command prompt. We can use the docker tool to see if the container started plus try to connect to SQL Server.

2. Run the following command to see the status of the container that was run for SQL Server:

```
docker ps
```

Your output will look something like the following if SQL Server was started successfully.

```
CONTAINER ID        IMAGE
    COMMAND                     CREATED             STATUS
        PORTS                       NAMES
95345f25b901        mcr.microsoft.com/mssql/rhel/server:
2019-latest   "/opt/mssql/bin/sqls..."   About a minute ago
Up About a minute        0.0.0.0:1401->1433/tcp   sql2019latest
```

The only true way to see if SQL Server started is to try and connect to it. You can connect with a program outside the container or inside the container. Let's use a way outside the container first by executing the following command or use the script **step2_dockerconnecttosql.ps1**:

```
sqlcmd -Usa -PSql2019isfast '-Slocalhost,1401' '-Q"SELECT
@@VERSION"'
```

Your output should look something like the following (the version may be different since I did this with SQL Server 2019 CTP 3.2):

```
-------------------------------------------------------------
Microsoft SQL Server 2019 (CTP3.2) - 15.0.1800.32 (X64)
        Jul 17 2019 21:29:33
        Copyright (C) 2019 Microsoft Corporation
        Developer Edition (64-bit) on Linux (Red Hat Enterprise
        Linux Server 7.6 (Maipo)) <X64>
```

Notice SQL Server thinks it is running on RHEL 7.6. I've also mentioned that the container is a program running in an isolated manner. You can prove that if you are running on Linux systems by running the following command on the host.

```
ps -axf
```

Your output should look something like this (the PID values will likely be different):

```
/usr/bin/containerd
  22846 ?       Sl    0:02   \_ containerd-shim -namespace
                                  moby -workdir /var/lib/containerd/
                                  io.containerd.runtime.v1.linux/
                                  moby/4f5c
  22864 ?       Ssl   0:00      \_ /opt/mssql/bin/sqlservr
  22909 ?       Sl    31:37        \_ /opt/mssql/bin/sqlservr
```

Windows and macOS users: I have a trick for you to see this same type of information. Since the SQL Server Linux container is running in a Linux VM, how can you access the VM itself?

Try this out. Run the following commands either from PowerShell or your macOS terminal (complete credit to this blog post https://nickjanetakis.com/blog/docker-tip-70-gain-access-to-the-mobylinux-vm-on-windows-or-macos):

```
docker container run --rm -it -v /:/host alpine
```

You should get a root prompt. Now run this command:

```
chroot /host
```

You are now in a Bash shell in the context of the Linux VM on Windows. You are limited in what you can do, and the ps command earlier does not work. But you can run this command:

```
ps -o ppid,pid,comm
```

This will dump out a bunch of processes, and since sqlservr was just started, it should be near the end of the list. There will be two sqlservr processes like this (your values will likely be different):

```
2922   2946  sqlservr
2946   2991  sqlservr
```

For the first sqlservr process, the value on the left side is the ppid or parent pid. Now run this command (substitute in your ppid value):

```
ps | grep 2922
```

You should see a result like this:

```
2922 root      0:00 containerd-shim -namespace moby -workdir
/var/lib/docker/containerd/daemon/io.containerd.runtime.v1.linux/
moby/a0c005ccefe8c8a716e066b0a857e919bded6f50ac791cb82f6de2b0dbe
f220e -address /var/run/docker/containerd/containerd.sock
-containerd-binary /usr/local/bin/containerd -runtime-root /var/
run/docker/runtime-runc -debug
```

This is a docker process that is used to fork the container program which in this case is sqlservr.

3. To restore the WideWorldImporters backup, you must copy this into the writeable layer of the container. Run the following command or script **step3_dockercopybackup.ps1**:

   ```
   docker cp c:\sql_sample_databases\WideWorldImporters-Full.bak
   sql2019latest:/var/opt/mssql
   ```

   By copying the backup file into /var/opt/mssql, the backup file is immediately accessible by SQL Server in the container.

4. With the backup in the writeable layer, SQL Server in the container context can access this backup so you can restore it. To restore the database, you can use the sqlcmd tool that *exists in the container*. For this you can use the docker exec command like the following or in the script **step4_dockerrestorebackup.ps1**:

```
docker exec -it sql2019latest /opt/mssql-tools/bin/sqlcmd
-S localhost -U SA -P "Sql2019isfast" -Q "RESTORE DATABASE
WideWorldImporters FROM DISK = '/var/opt/mssql/WideWorldImporters-
Full.bak' WITH MOVE 'WWI_Primary' TO '/var/opt/mssql/data/
WideWorldImporters.mdf', MOVE 'WWI_UserData' TO '/var/opt/mssql/
data/WideWorldImporters_userdata.ndf', MOVE 'WWI_Log' TO '/var/
opt/mssql/data/WideWorldImporters.ldf', MOVE 'WWI_InMemory_Data_1'
TO '/var/opt/mssql/data/WideWorldImporters_InMemory_Data_1'"
```

The WideWorldImporters backup was built with SQL Server 2016 so you would see an output that the database is being restored and upgraded to 2019.

5. You probably want to see the ERRORLOG of the SQL Server running in the container. One way to do this is to use **docker exec** and navigate the directory structure of the container using the following command or the script **step5_dockerexec.ps1**:

```
docker exec -it sql2019latest bash
```

When this command is successful, your cursor will be at a Bash shell prompt in the context of the container like the following:

```
root@sql2019latest:/#
```

You can now change to the /var/opt/mssql/log directory and display the ERRORLOG with the command cat ERRORLOG.

Remember that one of the benefits of a container is a smaller footprint that is running in a VM with the entire OS loaded. In addition, I've told you a container is really just a program running in an isolated manner sharing the host operating system resources. You can see this behavior by running the following command:

```
ps -axf
```

Your output should look something like

```
[root@sql2019latest /]# ps -axf
   PID TTY      STAT    TIME COMMAND
   268 pts/0    Ss      0:00 bash
   561 pts/0    R+      0:00  \_ ps -axf
     1 ?        Ssl     0:00 /opt/mssql/bin/sqlservr
     7 ?        Sl      1:25 /opt/mssql/bin/sqlservr
```

You can see that only bash and sqlservr are running. You can
compare this to running the following command on a RHEL 7.6
server or VM in the host (not the container):

```
ps -axf | wc -l
```

which counts the number of processes. On a "fresh" RHEL
7.6 server I installed in Azure, I got a number of 122! The bash
program is run in the same namespace as the SQL Server
container, so it is isolated to only access files in the readable and
writeable layer of this specific container.

Exit the shell by typing in the command exit.

Note   You may be asking how it is possible to be able to run these Linux
commands if the container is just the sqlservr program. That is because the docker
exec is able to run a program in the namespace of the container program (similar
to how sqlcmd works with a SQL Server container). A docker exec would fail if the
program itself did not exist in the directory structure of files for the container. Bash
works because it is in the base image. sqlcmd works because we install sqlcmd in
the SQL Server image.

Let me stop and call out how nice the Docker extension is to use
with Azure Data Studio (or Visual Studio Code). I mentioned
in the Prerequisites that you may want to install this extension.
Figure 7-4 is an example of managing a running SQL Server
container to "attach" a Bash shell.

Figure 7-4. *Using the Docker extension in Azure Data Studio*

As you can see from the "explorer" options from this extension, you can look at running containers (or stopped ones) and images that have been pulled or even browse registries like mcr.microsoft. com or your own Azure Container Registry or Docker Hub.

6. If you need to shut down SQL Server in the container, technically you could issue a T-SQL SHUTDOWN command. This would stop the SQLSERVR process and would shut down the container since it is the main program from the container. Or you could run the following command to stop the container or the script **step6_dockerstop.ps1**:

```
docker stop sql2019latest
```

When the command is successful, it will print the name of the container to std output.

When you stop a container, the program that started the container is killed. For SQL Server, this will lead to a detection of the kill and a SQL Server clean shutdown.

You can prove SQL Server was shut down by running the following command after the container is stopped:

```
docker logs sql2019latest
```

The output of the ERRORLOG from the SQL Server container will be displayed to the console with output showing a statement like the following:

```
<datetime> spid<n>s     SQL Server is terminating in response
to a 'stop' request from Service Control
```

At this point, the writeable layer of the container is preserved (in this case, the WideWorldImporters database is part of this since it was restored) for the container, and the container is considered *idle* but available to start again. You can see any containers that are stopped but not removed by running the following command:

```
docker ps -a
```

Your output should look like the following:

```
CONTAINER ID        IMAGE
   COMMAND                  CREATED
      STATUS                    PORTS             NAMES
95345f25b901          mcr.microsoft.com/mssql/rhel/server:
2019-latest        "/opt/mssql/bin/sqls..."    10 hours ago
      Exited (0) 11 seconds ago                sql2019latest
```

7. You can start the container again with the following command or script **step7_dockerstart.ps1**:

```
docker start sql2019latest
```

Once again, the name of the container will be displayed in the console, and you will be returned to the prompt.

8. You can query the WideWorldImporters database using the following command or script **step8_dockerquerywwi.ps1**:

```
sqlcmd -Usa -PSql2019isfast '-Slocalhost,1401' '-Q"SELECT
COUNT(*) FROM [WideWorldImporters].[Application].[People]"'
```

You should get back a number of 1111 for number of rows in the People table.

9. If you stop the container and now remove it, the writeable layer will be gone and so is your database (not good). You can stop and remove a container with the following commands or the script **step9_dockerstopandremove.ps1**:

```
docker stop sql2019latest
docker rm sql2019latest
```

Think of stopping and removing SQL Server as uninstalling SQL Server. But the good news is that any other SQL Server containers (even based on the same image) are unaffected by this.

10. As I described on how SQL Server container works, use a volume to store your databases on persisted host storage that can survive when the container is removed.

Run the container with a volume using the following command or script **step10_dockerrunvolume.ps1**:

```
docker run -e "ACCEPT_EULA=Y" -e "SA_PASSWORD=Sql2019isfast"
-p 1401:1433 --name sql2019latest --hostname sql2019latest -v
sqlvolume:/opt/mssql/data -d mcr.microsoft.com/mssql/rhel/
server:2019-latest
```

Note   Because the image for SQL 2019 is still on your local computer, docker will not try to pull it again.

In this example, the name **sqlvolume** will be automatically mapped to a directory in the host server or VM that is not part of the writeable layer. Any writes to the /var/opt/mssql directory in the writeable layer are redirected to the host folder for sqlvolume.

You can find out the directory for sqlvolume by running the following command:

```
docker inspect sqlvolume
```

Your output should look like the following:

```
[
    {
        "CreatedAt": "2019-08-07T02:24:50Z",
        "Driver": "local",
        "Labels": null,
        "Mountpoint": "/var/lib/docker/volumes/sqlvolume/_data",
        "Name": "sqlvolume",
        "Options": null,
        "Scope": "local"
    }
]
```

On Windows, /var/lib/docker/volumes/sqlvolume/_data is a
directory inside the Linux VM but still persisted.

Note   As part of writing this book, we had discovered a problem with our SQL
Server containers and Windows volumes. I wanted the examples for Windows
users to see a volume map of something like

-v c:\data:/var/opt/mssql

But we have discovered a problem that started in SQL Server 2017 CU14
that breaks that model. Others have reported this same problem on GitHub at
`https://github.com/microsoft/mssql-docker/issues/441`. I believe
we will have this problem solved by the time this book is published. You track our
fix for this issue on the GitHub page.

11. Copy the WideWorldImporters backup and restore the database
    again as you did in earlier steps by executing the script **step11_
    dockercopyandrestore.ps1** or these commands:

```
docker cp c:\sql_sample_databases\WideWorldImporters-Full.bak
sql2019latest:/var/opt/mssql
docker exec -it sql2019latest /opt/mssql-tools/bin/sqlcmd
-S localhost -U SA -P "Sql2019isfast" -Q "RESTORE DATABASE
WideWorldImporters FROM DISK = '/var/opt/mssql/WideWorld
Importers-Full.bak' WITH MOVE 'WWI_Primary' TO '/var/opt/mssql/
data/WideWorldImporters.mdf', MOVE 'WWI_UserData' TO '/var/opt/
mssql/data/WideWorldImporters_userdata.ndf', MOVE 'WWI_Log' TO
'/var/opt/mssql/data/WideWorldImporters.ldf', MOVE 'WWI_InMemory_
Data_1' TO '/var/opt/mssql/data/WideWorldImporters_InMemory_
Data_1'"
```

12. Now stop and remove the container. Then start it again with the same volume name using the following commands or script **step12_dockerrestart.ps1**:

```
docker stop sql2019latest
docker rm sql2019latest
docker run -e "ACCEPT_EULA=Y" -e "SA_PASSWORD=Sql2019isfast"
-p 1401:1433 --name sql2019latest --hostname sql2019latest
-v sqlvolume:/var/opt/mssql -d mcr.microsoft.com/mssql/rhel/
server:2019-latest
```

In this situation, when the new SQL 2019 container starts, all system and user databases already exist. SQL Server recognizes this and just "uses" these databases and starts up.

13. Make sure your data is still there by running a query against WideWorldImporters as in a previous step using the following command or script **step13_dockerquerywwi.ps1**:

```
sqlcmd -Usa -PSql2019isfast '-Slocalhost,1401' '-Q"SELECT
COUNT(*) FROM [WideWorldImporters].[Application].[People]"'
```

You should get back a number of 1111 for number of rows in the People table.

Let's use the Azure Data Studio (ADS) tool to connect to the container. Launch Azure Data Studio (if you have not already). Start a new connection and in the **Server** field put in **localhost,1401** (or the <servername>,1401). Put in your sa password you used to start the container. ADS should connect and interact with the container just like any other SQL Server.

Figure 7-5 shows a connection and query against the WideWorldImporters database with ADS.

Figure 7-5. *Connecting to a container with Azure Data Studio*

14. Let's clean up all the resources by stopping the container, removing it, removing the volume, and removing the image using the following commands or script **cleanup.sh**:

```
sudo docker stop sql2019latest
sudo docker rm sql2019latest
sudo docker volume rm sqlvolume
sudo docker rmi mcr.microsoft.com/mssql/rhel/server:2019-latest
```

Now that you know the fundamentals of deploying and managing a container with SQL Server including persisting a user database in a volume, let's use these skills to learn a new and unique way to update SQL Server with containers.

A New Way to Update SQL Server

I mentioned very early in this chapter how containers provide a new and amazing way to update SQL Server. Let's see it in action. Because SQL Server 2019 was in preview as I wrote this book, there were no cumulative updates available to show you an update with containers for 2019. Therefore, in this example, I'll show you how to update containers using SQL Server 2017. Once SQL Server 2019 ships and we start shipping cumulative updates, you will be able to use the same approach.

Imagine this scenario to understand the example. You are currently running SQL Server 2017 Cumulative Update (CU) 10 with a container in production. You need to apply the latest CU for SQL Server 2017. With Windows or Linux, the process is to patch or update the current SQL Server instance which requires a restart of SQL Server.

Containers offer a new approach which also require a restart but are faster to update and provide a huge benefit for rollback. Remember SQL Server containers are pre-installed. Therefore, when you run a SQL Server container based on any cumulative update, you are not patching existing software.

All the examples to see updates in action can be found at **ch7_inside_sql_ containers\update**. Windows users can use the **dockerpowershell** directory, and Linux and macOS users can use the **dockerbash** directory (be sure to make your scripts executable with chmod u+x <script>).

I'll walk you through the PowerShell experience in this section.

1. Run the following command or script **step1_dockerrun.ps1** to deploy a SQL Server 2017 CU10 container:

   ```
   docker run -e "ACCEPT_EULA=Y" -e "SA_PASSWORD=Sql2017isfast"
   -p 1401:1433 --name sql2017CU10 --hostname sql2017CU10 -v
   sqlvolume:/var/opt/mssql -d mcr.microsoft.com/mssql/server:
   2017-CU10-ubuntu
   ```

   It is unlikely you have already pulled the SQL 2017 CU10 image so it will be pulled first. Notice the use of a volume here which is a key to this method of updating SQL Server.

2. Connect to SQL Server to find the version you have installed with the following command or script **step2_dockerconnecttosql.ps1**:

   ```
   sqlcmd -Usa -PSql2017isfast '-Slocalhost,1401' '-Q"SELECT
   @@VERSION"'
   ```

Your output should look like the following:

```
Microsoft SQL Server 2017 (RTM-CU10) (KB4342123) - 14.0.3037.1 (X64)
        Jul 27 2018 09:40:27
        Copyright (C) 2017 Microsoft Corporation
        Developer Edition (64-bit) on Linux (Ubuntu 16.04.5 LTS)
```

3. Run the following commands to update the container or use the
    script **step3_dockerupdate.ps1**:

```
docker stop sql2017CU10
docker run -e "ACCEPT_EULA=Y" -e "SA_PASSWORD=Sql2017isfast"
-p 1401:1433 --name sql2017latest --hostname sql2017latest -v
sqlvolume:/var/opt/mssql -d mcr.microsoft.com/mssql/server:
2017-latest-ubuntu
```

Let me describe what is happening here. The first container
is stopped and no longer has access to the system databases
on the volume. The second container starts up *using the same
volume and port* but a different image for the latest CU build. The
new container starts SQL Server which recognizes the system
databases already exist. The engine is smart enough to recognize
when the system databases exist to just use them. Furthermore,
SQL Server is smart enough to perform any necessary "update"
steps on system and user databases to ensure they are compatible
with the specific CU build.

4. Run the following commands to connect to the container
    (remember the same port) to verify the version of SQL Server has
    been updated or use the script **step4_dockerconnecttosql.ps1**:

```
sqlcmd -Usa -PSql2017isfast '-Slocalhost,1401' '-Q"SELECT
@@VERSION"'
```

Depending on how soon you run this step after the update, you
may receive this error:

```
Sqlcmd: Error: Microsoft ODBC Driver 17 for SQL Server : Login
failed for user 'sa'. Reason: Server is in script upgrade mode.
Only administrator can connect at this time..
```

This is because SQL Server is performing any necessary steps to update system and user databases to ensure they are compatible with the new CU. No user data is affected.

Technically not every CU update requires any changes to metadata for system and user databases. However, we have discovered we "attempt" to run these update steps for any CU change. This can slow down the update process, but it is far faster than having to actually patch the SQL Server. There is a trick to avoid this, but it is only for debugging purposes. Trace flag 902 can bypass any of these CU update steps.

This means you could run your container by adding this statement to the end of the docker run commands you have used to this point.

```
/opt/mssql/bin/sqlservr -T902
```

This is an interesting trick docker provides. I have shown you that the CMD statement is what docker uses to run the program for the container. Turns out you can override this for a container image by specifying a program to run instead. By running SQL Server with this trace flag, you can start a container with sqlservr using the trace flag to override the default. I use this when I demo this new way to update containers, but it is only for demo purposes. I've discussed in our engineering team with one of our development leads Li Zhang that perhaps in the future we can get clever to only run the update steps when needed.

Eventually, the query to connect will work, and your output should look like this:

```
Microsoft SQL Server 2017 (RTM-CU16) (KB4508218) - 14.0.3223.3 (X64)
        Jul 12 2019 17:43:08
        Copyright (C) 2017 Microsoft Corporation
        Developer Edition (64-bit) on Linux (Ubuntu 16.04.6 LTS)
```

You may get a different version because when you try these steps, there are probably other later CU builds for SQL Server 2017. The key is that the version should be later than CU10, and you didn't have to patch SQL Server.

5. While the update in itself is nice, the true compelling story is rollback. In fact, it is not really a rollback story but a *switch* story. This is because **SQL Server CU builds are compatible with each other**. By using the same volume and port, you can now switch back to CU10 by simply running these statements or the script **step5_dockerrollback.ps1**:

```
docker stop sql2017latest
docker start sql2017CU10
```

Since the parameters for the containers are saved, you are really just switching to installed versions of SQL Server against the same set of system and/or user databases.

6. Run the following command or script **step6_dockerconnecttosql. ps1** to prove you are now back and running SQL 2017 CU10:

```
sqlcmd -Usa -PSql2017isfast '-Slocalhost,1401' '-Q"SELECT @@VERSION"'
```

Again, you might get the script upgrade error, but fairly quick your results should show SQL 2017 CU10 as the version.

You could now just switch back and forth per your needs. Imagine even a world where you pre-pull images for a series of CU builds you want to use for production on your local server. Then you can start containers with any CU build you need per your application or company requirements.

What is really compelling is to use containers to test a specific CU on a test server and then bring it to your production server to update at the right time.

7. Clean up all your resources with the **cleanup.ps1** script. If you want to remove all resources but keep the images to test this sequence faster, use the **reset.ps1** script.

Deploying Container As an Application

There are situations where you may want to *customize* the SQL Server container image. Customized containers involve using the SQL Server container image as the base and adding files to the container image. In many cases, these files are database backups and/or script files.

One scenario to customize the SQL container image is to deploy multiple containers as an application. An example of this, which my colleague Vin Yu often demonstrates, deploys a SQL Server container with a database and an ASP.Net application. You can view an example of building a containerized application with SQL Server like this at `https://docs.docker.com/compose/aspnet-mssql-compose/`.

One tool that is very helpful to build multiple container images and run containers based on those images is **docker-compose**. Docker-compose allows you to declare the definition of container images to build along with parameters to run containers based on those images.

A great example of an application involving SQL Server that needs multiple containers is SQL Server Replication. Since SQL Server Replication is now supported in SQL Server 2019, containers provide an interesting deployment method. In 2018, Vin Yu and I had to present at various conference new features coming for SQL Server on Linux. I asked Vin to present the replication story. As we were preparing our demos, he asked me to look over what he had built. He said he used containers to deploy snapshot replication with a publisher, distributor, and subscriber with a single command. My first reaction to Vin was "you can't do that." I loved that he proved me wrong. Let's use the example he built for that demo (which you can also find on our samples on GitHub at `https://github.com/microsoft/sql-server-samples/tree/master/samples/containers/replication`).

All files for this example can be found at **ch7_inside_sql_containers\sqlrepl**. Because we will use docker-compose for this example, we don't need a PowerShell vs. bash version of the scripts. We will provide a set of Bash shell and T-SQL scripts, but they *run in the context of each container*.

Since this example will only take a single command to deploy and run the containers to deploy SQL Server replication, let's take a look at all the files provided for this example before you run it.

The docker-compose.yml File

docker-compose relies on a declarative text file called **docker-compose.yml** (which is a YAML file. YAML stands for Yet Another Markup Language). You can use a different file name, but by default docker-compose looks for a file called docker-compose.yml.

Let's look at the docker-compose.yml file for this example. The version tag at the top of the file declares what version of docker-compose should be used (3 is the latest but you can read about compose versioning at `https://docs.docker.com/compose/compose-file/compose-versioning/`).

```
services:
    db1:
        build: ./db1
        environment:
            SA_PASSWORD: "MssqlPass123"
            ACCEPT_EULA: "Y"
            MSSQL_AGENT_ENABLED: "true"
        ports:
            - "2500:1433"
        container_name: db1
        hostname: db1
    db2:
        build: ./db2
        environment:
            SA_PASSWORD: "MssqlPass123"
            ACCEPT_EULA: "Y"
            MSSQL_AGENT_ENABLED: "true"
        ports:
            - "2600:1433"
        container_name: db2
        hostname: db2
```

There are two "services" or containers that will be built and executed by docker-compose. One called db1 and one called db2.

The method in which docker-compose works is to first build a container image (if the build clause is provided) and then run a container based on that image using the other parameters in the docker-compose.yml file.

The clause

```
build: ./db1
```

indicates docker-compose should change to the db1 directory from the current directory and execute a docker build in that directory. The same concept applies for db2.

The rest of the definition in the yml file defines how to run the built container in each directory.

```
environment:
    SA_PASSWORD: "MssqlPass123"
    ACCEPT_EULA: "Y"
    MSSQL_AGENT_ENABLED: "true"
ports:
    - "2500:1433"
    container_name: db1
    hostname: db1
```

Each of these values is passed to the docker run command used to run the container after it is built. Note the use of MSQL_AGENT_ENABLED in this example because SQL Server Replication relies on SQL Server Agent.

Building Each Container

Let's look at what is in each directory provided in the example to build and run the containers for replication. I call the scenario of using these files the "Vin Yu method" to build a SQL Server custom container image as a tribute to my colleague Vin Yu who taught me how to do this.

Each directory contains the following files:

Dockerfile – Contains the definition of how to build the custom image based on the SQL Server container image.

entrypoint.sh – This becomes the main program to run for the container. It launches a script called db-init.sh and the sqlservr program.

db-init.sh – This script is called by entrypoint.sh and will pause for a period of time and then execute the db-init.sql script.

db-init.sql – This contains T-SQL code to create the publisher, distributor, subscriber, and the snapshot publication on db1. It will create the subscriber database for db2. Effectively what Vin did was script out what SQL Server Management Studio builds to set up replication and save it to execute with T-SQL in a clever way.

If you look at the Dockerfile for db1 and db2, it looks like this:

```
FROM mcr.microsoft.com/mssql/rhel/server:2019-latest

COPY . /

RUN chmod +x /db-init.sh
CMD /bin/bash ./entrypoint.sh
```

When docker-compose executes the "build" phase for each container, the definition of the Dockerfile says to

- Use the latest SQL Server RHEL container image as the base (which uses the RHEL OS image as its base)

- Copy the entrypoint.sh, db-init.sh, and db-init.sql scripts into the file system of the container image

- Modify the db-init.sh script so it is an executable script (you don't need to do this for the entrypoint.sh script)

- Make the default program to run the Bash shell executing the entrypoint.sh script

Now let's look at the **entrypoint.sh** script:

```
#start SQL Server, start the script to create/setup the DB
#You need a non-terminating process to keep the container alive.
#In a series of commands separated by single ampersands the commands to the
left of the right-most ampersand are run in the background.
#So - if you are executing a series of commands simultaneously using
single ampersands, the command at the right-most position needs to be non-
terminating
 /db-init.sh & /opt/mssql/bin/sqlservr
```

This script will execute the db-init.sh script first and while it executes start the sqlservr program (that is what the & symbol means, start one program and then run the next one).

db-init.sh for db1 looks like this:

```
#wait for the SQL Server to come up
sleep 45s

mkdir /var/opt/mssql/ReplData/
chown mssql /var/opt/mssql/ReplData/
chgrp mssql /var/opt/mssql/ReplData/

echo "running set up script"
#run the setup script to create the DB and the schema in the DB
/opt/mssql-tools/bin/sqlcmd -S localhost -U sa -P MssqlPass123 -d master -i
db-init.sql
```

Since db-init.sh starts first, it must wait for SQL Server to start before executing any T-SQL scripts.

Then it creates some directories required to store snapshots for replication in the containers' writeable layer.

Finally, this script executes the db-init.sql T-SQL script using sqlcmd which exists in every SQL Server container.

db-init.sql for db1 is quite long but effectively contains the T-SQL code to set up a publisher, distributor, subscriber, and snapshot publication.

db-init.sh for db2 will also pause for its SQL Server to start and then execute the db-init.sql script in its directory. db-init.sql for db2 only needs to create the database to hold the data for the subscriber.

It is quite an interesting method to customize a SQL Server container. This same method can be used to customize a SQL Server container to create a database and run your own T-SQL scripts. In the long term, we want a better method to achieve this type of goal so that you don't have to manually "sleep" in a shell script to execute custom code. For now, this method works quite well.

Running the Containers for Replication

Try it for yourself with one of two methods:

- Run the following command (preface with sudo on Linux). You must be in the **ch7_inside_sql_containers\sqlrepl** directory to run this.

  docker-compose up

> If you use this option, the containers are not started in the background so you will see a dump of information to the console including SQL Server ERRORLOG files. DO NOT hit <ctrl>+<c> at this point or you will shut down the containers.

- If you have the Docker extension installed, you can right-click the docker-compose.yml file and select Compose Up. This method run the containers in the background.

Note   On some Windows 10 systems, I have seen the following pop-up in Figure 7-6 for the Windows Defender Firewall for a service that is required for networking for Docker. If you see this, click Allow Access.

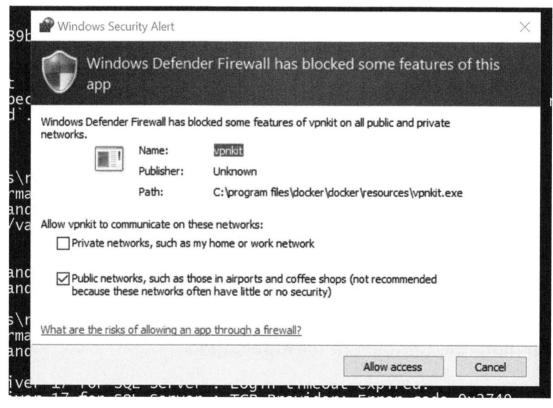

Figure 7-6. *Windows Firewall warning for Docker*

To ensure your containers deployed correctly and SQL Server Replication is running, first check to see if the subscriber has the data replicated. Use Azure Data Studio or SQL Server Management Studio (SSMS) to connect to localhost,2600 and see if the [Sales].[dbo].[customer] table has data. It should have three rows.

Also, you can verify the snapshot agent job was applied successfully by using SSMS connecting to the subscriber. Use Object Explorer like in Figure 7-7 to check the snapshot job status.

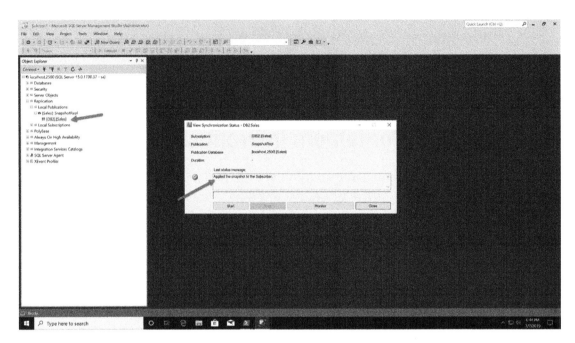

Figure 7-7. *Snapshot job for a SQL Server Replication container*

When Vin first showed me this, I had to stop and think about this method. I've worked on a complex system like Replication since it was first invented in SQL Server 6.0. I never thought I would see a way to deploy it so easily. Of course, SQL Server Replication can be more complex so using containers for your scenario could involve more. But look at the promise of what containers can provide for a distributed system like SQL Server Replication.

- If you ran docker-compose up from the command line, hit Ctrl+C which will stop the containers.

- You will want to clean up resources, so when you are done, run the following command (preface with sudo on Linux). You must be in the **ch7_inside_sql_containers\sqlrepl** directory to run this.

  docker-compose down

  This will stop and remove the running containers.

  This will not remove the docker custom images, so to clean up all resources, use the **cleanup.ps1** or **cleanup.sh** script to remove the customized images.

Deploying SQL Containers in Production

I've been presenting and talking about containers ever since we started supporting them with SQL Server 2017. As I've presented this topic even with the story about how containers are really just the sqlservr program running in a unique way, I've faced some skepticism that SQL Server containers can be used for a production workload. I hope I'll convince some of the skeptics with information in this section about performance, security, availability, resource control, and server configuration related to SQL Server containers.

Performance

As I've talked about containers, one of the myths I've heard is that SQL Server containers may not perform as well as a SQL Server instance not running in a container. You have seen that I've presented the story that a SQL Server container is just a program running in an isolated manner and has *direct* access to operating system resources. Therefore, the performance you can expect for SQL Server Linux containers is exactly the same performance for SQL Server on Linux not running in a container.

If you are like me though, you want some proof. Therefore, I took the open source benchmark tool called HammerDB (`www.hammerdb.com`) and ran a test using the analytic performance test derived from TPC-H. I compared the performance with HammerDB for SQL Server on Linux running in a container and SQL Server outside of a container on the same host Linux virtual machine. **I found the performance 100% identical** using these deployments.

I encourage you to try this yourself. Here are the details of how I used HammerDB for this test:

- I installed the HammerDB tool in a Windows 10 Virtual Machine in Azure.

- I created an Azure VM with RHEL 7.4. using a size of DS13 v2 (8 vcpus, 56GB RAM).

- I created a Premium SSD of 2TB to host the databases for HammerDB. I mounted this drive in a directory on Linux and called it /data. This is the guide I use to add a data disk to Linux in Azure VM (`https://docs.microsoft.com/en-us/azure/virtual-machines/linux/attach-disk-portal`).

- Installed SQL Server 2019 CTP 3.2 in the host Linux Virtual Machine.

- I precreated the tpch database of a size of 35Gb and 5Gb log. I used a scale factor of 10 with 16 virtual users (the Windows VM client is an 8-core VM).

Tip   Change the driver to "ODBC Driver 17 for SQL Server" when using the latest version of HammerDB and use a clustered columnstore index.

- I then ran the TPC-H test using 16 virtual users. I was able to achieve ~160,000 qph when running HammerDB against both the SQL Server container and SQL Server outside the container installed on the same VM (I only run one of these at a time).

I encourage you to run a test like this for yourself or any other performance test with SQL Server containers. Just make sure you are running a fair comparison between a container and SQL Server outside of a container.

Security

Since SQL Server containers are just SQL Server on Linux as an isolated program, all the security capabilities and features of SQL Server on Linux work for containers. This includes all SQL Server engine security capabilities for logins, securables, and principles. Features like dynamic data masking, row-level security, Transparent Data Encryption (TDE), and others all work with containers.

Active Directory Authentication

The only exception to a complete secure feature set is Active Directory (AD) Authentication. During the lifecycle of building SQL Server 2019, it was our intention to document and support Active Directory authentication for containers. And it still may make our final release. But at the time I was writing this chapter, Dylan Gray, one of our lead developers for Linux and containers, and I were discussing this support. If at the time we ship SQL Server 2019 AD support was not documented and available, I expect it to be shortly close after SQL Server 2019 ships.

Dylan and I discussed what the documented process will look like, and it is very similar to setting up AD authentication for SQL Server on Linux without containers which you can read at `https://docs.microsoft.com/en-us/sql/linux/sql-server-linux-active-directory-authentication`. The key differences will be to pass into the container information about the Kerberos SPN via a keytab file in a volume that the SQL Server container can use. I've had several customers tell me that having AD authentication is a key element to using SQL Server containers in a production environment, and we intend to deliver on that request and requirement.

Non-root Containers

Ever since we shipped SQL Server containers, the container program runs under the context of the root user in the container namespace. Even though a root container program does not have complete root privileges to the host computer, it is a best practice to run a container program not as root.

SQL Server 2019 will support non-root containers, and in fact when I spoke to Madeline McDonald, one of our lead developers for containers, about support for non-root containers, she told me the intention as we shipped SQL Server 2019 was to ship any SQL Server 2019 container as non-root by default but leave SQL Server 2017 containers "as is."

I asked Madeline what the procedure was to run a SQL Server 2017 or SQL Server 2019 CTP container as non-root, and she gave me an example to try it.

Try out the scripts and files I've provided in the **ch7_inside_sql_containers\ nonroot** folder. You will use the Dockerfile to build a customer container. The Dockerfile looks like the following:

```
FROM mcr.microsoft.com/mssql/rhel/server:2019-latest
RUN useradd -u 10001 -g root mssql
RUN mkdir -p -m 770 /var/opt/mssql && chgrp -R 0 /var/opt/mssql
USER mssql
CMD ["/opt/mssql/bin/sqlservr"]
```

Notice the RUN commands which will add a user and group for mssql and precreate the SQL Server directories for permissions for the mssql group. The Dockerfile USER command indicates which user context to run the container program under. Everything else is the same as running a SQL Server container today. Build the docker image using docker build and then use the scripts I've provided to run the container.

High Availability

SQL Server Containers support the basics of backup and restore, and even log shipping can work. I've shown you an example of using SQL Server Replication which can be a high available solution for some customers.

Even though it is possible to set up an Always On Availability Group between containers, the preferred method for high availability for containers is to use Kubernetes. I'll discuss how to make SQL Server highly available using Kubernetes in Chapter 8.

Resource Control

By default, SQL Server containers (as do all containers) have access to all CPU and memory resources on the host server. Docker provides a way to control and govern access to those resources for any container. For example, the docker run command provides these options:

-m – Controls the amount of memory the container can access.

-cpuset-cpus – Controls which CPU the threads within the container can run on. Be careful with this option. SQL Server will not restrict the number of schedulers based on this option. However, docker (using cgroups) will enforce which CPUs all SQL Server threads run on. If you do this option, I recommend you combine with this SQL Server affinity using ALTER SERVER CONFIGURATION.

You can read more about resource usage for docker containers at `https://docs.docker.com/config/containers/resource_constraints/`.

While these options do work, for SQL Server I recommend you use the built-in capabilities of SQL Server configuration to control memory and CPU resources.

For example, consider these options at your disposal:

memorylimitmb – This controls the amount of physical memory exposed to SQL Server on Linux to use. You can read more about this option at `https://docs.microsoft.com/en-us/sql/linux/sql-server-linux-configure-mssql-conf#memorylimit`.

"max server memory" – This sp_configure option is very familiar to SQL Server users and controls the amount of memory used by the SQL Server engine within the memorylimitmb space.

ALTER SERVER CONFIGURATION – This T-SQL command allows you to affinitize which NUMA nodes and/or CPUs SQL Server will run on. You can read more about this option at `https://docs.microsoft.com/en-us/sql/t-sql/statements/alter-server-configuration-transact-sql`.

Resource Governor – Resource governor can help control CPU, memory, and I/O resources especially at the application or workload level. You can read more about resource governor at `https://docs.microsoft.com/en-us/sql/relational-databases/resource-governor/resource-governor`.

In fairness, not everything that runs in sqlservr on Linux (using the SQLPAL) is controlled by these T-SQL options. Processing by SQL Agent, DTC, Polybase, or other code outside the SQL Engine runs in the SQLPAL may need some resource control when running as a container, and the docker options listed in this section could be useful should you need them. However, the majority of CPU and memory consumption comes from the database engine, and SQL provides the options for you to have the desired control.

Server or Database Configuration

I've listed in this section several SQL Server configuration options that you may want to consider. There are many others provided by the mssql-conf script, T-SQL sp_configure, and ALTER SERVER CONFIGURATION. In addition, databases have many other configuration options when you create the database or through ALTER DATABASE.

While a running SQL Server container can be modified using T-SQL statements, you should think carefully when using containers whether that is the right strategy. For example, if you applied an sp_configure change to a container that requires a restart, you will have to restart the container for the change to take effect. Furthermore, you will need to make sure you use a persisted volume for system databases, so your changes are not lost.

Another option is to build a customized image (much like I showed you with the container example in this chapter for replication) running any configuration scripts you need after SQL Server starts.

For example, let's say you want to ensure your SQL Server enforces a specific **max degree of parallelism** value for any SQL Server container in your environment. One way to do this is to build a custom container image with a script that sets the desired maxdop value. You can even tag and name this, so you know what the options you used for a certain SQL container. Now these scripts to build the container along with the T-SQL scripts can become part of your change control and CI/CD lifecycle.

The only downside to this approach is for any configuration change that does not require a restart of SQL Server for the instance of your database. For these scenarios, you may still build a specific container image with the new desired configuration changes but also directly apply your configuration changes to a running SQL Server.

Another interesting problem is applying configuration changes that do require a restart (there are less of these than you may think). However, if you do have this scenario, you will have to restart the container immediately after starting it up with your applied configuration changes.

For any mssql-conf changes, you should use environment variables that match the setting you want as seen with docker run examples in this chapter. A great example of using this option for DTC can be found at `https://github.com/microsoft/sql-server-samples/tree/master/samples/containers/dtc`. If, for some reason, there is an mssql-conf setting where an equivalent environment variable setting does not exist, you could create a customized image with a precreated mssql.conf file. You would use a Dockerfile like the following:

```
FROM microsoft/mssql-server-linux:latest
COPY ./mssql.conf /
RUN mkdir /var/opt/mssql
RUN mv ./mssql.conf /var/opt/mssql
CMD ["/opt/mssql/bin/sqlservr"]
```

where your mssql.conf had all the needed config values. You can learn about the protocol format of this file at `https://docs.microsoft.com/en-us/sql/linux/sql-server-linux-configure-mssql-conf#mssql-conf-format`.

Using Other Packages

I've told you the SQL Server container image comes with the database engine, SQL Server Agent, and includes capabilities such as Replication and DTC. SQL Server on Linux was built on the concept of packages. Features like Polybase don't come with the standard SQL Server package and are not in the SQL Server container image.

We have built a series of examples for you to learn how to build your own customized image based on the SQL Server image adding in the packages you would like in your container. You can find these examples at `https://github.com/microsoft/mssql-docker/tree/master/linux/preview/examples`.

Editions and Licensing

By default, when you pull and run a SQL Server container image as I've shown you in this chapter, we automatically assume the Developer Edition of SQL Server. As you may know, the Developer Edition is not supported for production use.

Therefore, when running a SQL Server container, you can use the MSSQL_PID environment variable to indicate the edition of SQL Server. You can read more about using this option at `https://docs.microsoft.com/en-us/sql/linux/sql-server-linux-configure-docker#production`.

One of the most common questions I have received about containers is how containers are licensed.

With the release of SQL Server 2017, we modified our licensing guide to include a discussion on containers. You can download the guide from `www.microsoft.com/en-us/sql-server/sql-server-2017-pricing`. Look specifically in the section "**Licensing SQL Server 2017 in Containers**" (there will be a new guide for SQL Server 2019 when it is released). Licensing for containers works similar to virtual machines. For many users, the full core licensing model applies. One interesting exception you should read is that customers with Software Assurance (SA) along with Enterprise Edition get a benefit. According to the guide, "…With the addition of Software Assurance (SA) coverage on all Enterprise Edition core licenses (for a fully licensed server), customers' use rights are expanded to allow any number of containers to run on the licensed server. This valuable SA benefit enables customers to deploy an unlimited number of containers to handle dynamic workloads and fully utilize hardware computing capacity."

SQL Server Windows Containers

All the discussion around containers in the chapter to this point is a discussion of SQL Server containers based on Linux images. You have seen that these containers can run on any platform including Linux, Windows, and macOS.

However, the Windows team has built the capability of running containers natively in Windows based on Windows images. We announced in the summer of 2019 a private preview program to support SQL Server containers based on Windows images.

Many of the same concepts will apply to just about everything I've discussed in this chapter. A lot of that is due in part to the great compatibility story of SQL Server on Windows and Linux. The key differences will be in certain aspects that are different from Windows and Linux, such as configuration for Active Directory. Furthermore, when you want to interact directly with the container, you typically will use PowerShell or the command shell.

Windows supports the same concepts as in Linux to make containers a compelling story including isolation through namespaces. You can read more about Windows containers' work at `https://docs.microsoft.com/en-us/virtualization/windowscontainers/about/`.

Windows offers an option with containers that is slightly different than Linux. Containers can run in two isolation modes:

Process isolation – Containers run as isolated processes using namespaces.

Hyper-V isolation – Containers run in a "special" virtual machine (that is the term the docs use, not mine).

You can read more about these isolation models at `https://docs.microsoft.com/en-us/virtualization/windowscontainers/manage-containers/hyperv-container`.

On Docker for Desktop for Windows, you can only run **either** Windows containers or Linux containers. (Note: this should change when Docker for WSL2 is available to use. You can read more about this at https://engineering.docker.com/2019/06/docker-hearts-wsl-2/.)

By default, Docker for Desktop supports Linux containers. To switch to use Windows Containers, select the option from the docker icon in the Windows tray as seen in Figure 7-8.

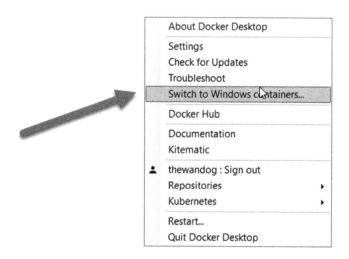

Figure 7-8. *Switching to Windows containers with Docker Desktop*

Hyper-V and process isolation are supported for Windows containers on latest builds of Windows 10 and Windows Server 2019. You can read more about Windows containers on Windows Server 2019 at https://docs.microsoft.com/en-us/virtualization/windowscontainers/quick-start/quick-start-windows-server. I also encourage you to read the FAQ on Windows containers at https://docs.microsoft.com/en-us/virtualization/windowscontainers/about/faq.

In addition, Windows Server 2019 supports Linux Containers on Windows (LCOW) which supports Linux containers using Hyper-V isolation. You can read more about LCOW at https://docs.microsoft.com/en-us/virtualization/windowscontainers/deploy-containers/linux-containers. This makes Windows Server just about the only platform to run both Windows and Linux containers simultaneously (you could run Windows containers by installing a Windows VM on macOS, but Windows Server is the only one to "natively" support these scenarios).

I tried Windows containers in its early form for private preview on a Windows Server 2019 system.

Here is an example syntax for a docker run command for both Hyper-V and process isolation for a SQL Server Windows container:

```
docker run -e 'ACCEPT_EULA=Y' -e 'MSSQL_SA_PASSWORD=SafePassw0rd' -p
1401:1433 --isolation=process -d -e 'MSSQL_PID=Developer' --name sql1
private-repo.microsoft.com/mssql-private-preview/mssql-server:windows-
ctp3.1
```

```
docker run -e 'ACCEPT_EULA=Y' -e 'MSSQL_SA_PASSWORD=SafePassw0rd' -p
1402:1433 --isolation=hyperv -d -e 'MSSQL_PID=Developer' --name sql2
private-repo.microsoft.com/mssql-private-preview/mssql-server:windows-
ctp3.1
```

You can see the syntax is almost exactly the same as with Linux containers. Notice the syntax for the --isolation parameter.

I used the famous sysinternals tool Process Explorer (https://docs.microsoft.com/en-us/sysinternals/downloads/process-explorer) to see what the sqlservr program looks like for process isolation. You can see in Figure 7-9, similar to the docker daemon, a program called CExecSvc is responsible for forking the sqlservr container program.

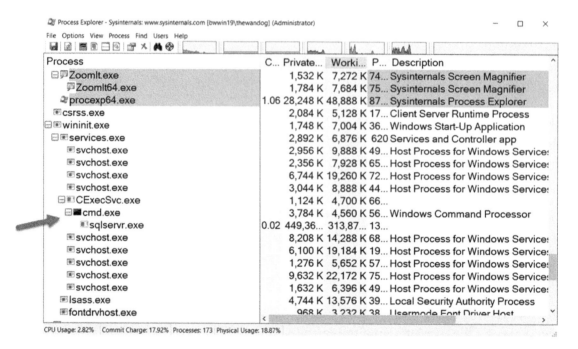

Figure 7-9. A SQL Server Window container in process isolation

There is not much documented about Hyper-V isolation except that the container programs are hosted in a Windows program called **vmwp.exe.**

My hope is that by the time you read this book, we will have progressed our work with SQL Server Windows containers as many customers I believe want the promise of containers but for several different reasons do not or cannot use containers based on Linux. I personally believe if LCOW containers can perform well, then many customers may end up with a mixed environment of both Windows and Linux containers on their Windows Server.

Summary

It has been a very long chapter to read and go through. I have covered what a container is and why it can solve modern challenges to host products like SQL Server and develop applications. Containers are portable, lightweight, consistent, and efficient.

I described and showed you that containers are really just programs running in an isolated and unique way. You learned the new enhancements for SQL Server containers in SQL Server 2019 including RHEL images and the new Microsoft Container Registry.

If you went through the rest of the chapter, you were able to try out yourself several examples including deploying containers, seeing the new amazing way to update (and rollback) SQL Server, and deploying a multi-container application like SQL Server replication.

You learned how containers are ready for production despite what you might have been told including SQL Server container performance, security, and availability.

And you finished up the chapter getting a sneak peak on what SQL Server Windows containers will look like.

I hope you have a strong grasp of SQL Server containers and are ready to learn about a platform built to deploy and scale containers called Kubernetes.

CHAPTER 8

SQL Server on Kubernetes

If containers are the new virtual machines, then Kubernetes are the new servers. You will see in this chapter that Kubernetes is an important technology to the future of containerized applications, especially running enterprise workloads like SQL Server.

What Is k8s?

If you have not read Chapter 7, you might go back and at least browse it before you read this chapter. Why? Because Kubernetes or k8s is all about *hosting containers*. k8s is actually much more than just hosting. I'll use k8s for Kubernetes for the rest of the chapter because that is the popular acronym for it (and it is sure faster to type). k8s stands for k<8 letters>s in the word Kubernetes (I had to research it myself when I first saw the term).

Unlike Chapter 7, I will not go into exhaustive detail on the internals of k8s because that would really take an entire book. What I will do is introduce you to some of the terms, add in some comments about how the internals work, and point you to some excellent references.

After going through the basics of k8s in this chapter, I'll talk about how k8s solves important challenges for the deployment of containers in a scalable platform that provides built-in high availability (HA). I'll also show how to update all the SQL Server containers in a k8s environment, similar to the process of updating a single container, which I described in Chapter 7. I'll introduce you to an intriguing concept to deploy SQL Server in k8s, called Helm Charts. Finally, I'll talk about the future of availability with SQL Server 2019 and k8s and how we are looking to integrate Always On Availability Groups with k8s.

© Bob Ward 2019
B. Ward, *SQL Server 2019 Revealed*, https://doi.org/10.1007/978-1-4842-5419-6_8

References on k8s

Let's start with the references, because you may want to go read or browse those first:

The Brendan Burns Videos on k8s – This is my term and not an official name. Brendan Burns, one of the founders of k8s and now a Distinguished Engineer at Microsoft, built a series of learning videos on k8s. I personally think you can watch these and learn what you need for k8s for most scenarios. You can watch these at `www.youtube.com/playlist?list=PLLasXO2E8BPCrIhFrc_ZiINhbRkYMKdPT`. I had the privilege of presenting with Brendan at the Microsoft MVP Summit in the spring of 2019, and I was truly amazed at how he can simplify the story of k8s through drawings (he can do it on his Surface Go device with a pen).

Another resource that uses these videos is on our Azure site at `https://azure.microsoft.com/en-us/topic/what-is-kubernetes`.

Managing Kubernetes – This is a book by Craig Tracey and Brendan Burns. I found this an excellent resource on the internals of k8s. You can find this book at `https://learning.oreilly.com/library/view/managing-kubernetes/9781492033905/`.

AKS documentation – This is the documentation for Azure Kubernetes Service (AKS), and there are great videos and documentation about not just AKS but the core of k8s. You can find these resources at `https://azure.microsoft.com/en-us/services/kubernetes-service/`.

`https://kubernetes.io/` – This is the main web site for k8s open source, and it is full of examples, details, and visualizations of k8s. There is also an excellent link for k8s online training courses at `https://kubernetes.io/docs/tutorials/online-training/overview/`.

Here are two other online training courses I would recommend:

`www.pluralsight.com/courses/getting-started-kubernetes`

`www.pluralsight.com/courses/kubernetes-installation-configuration-fundamentals` – This course is from my friend and technical editor of *Pro SQL Server on Linux*, Anthony Nocentino.

k8s Objects

Whether you read over these resources or not, let me describe in this chapter some of the terminology of k8s from my point of view, and a few comments about internals I found interesting as I've learned the topic. The fundamental terms and objects you need to know about k8s as you read this chapter are

Cluster – Think of the k8s cluster as a server or computer. This is the *main host* for all software running on k8s. It is common to refer to the host of all objects as a k8s cluster.

Node – Think of a node as a virtual machine running on the cluster. A node will be a host for running *pods* (which have containers) within the cluster. It is very common to have more than one node on a k8s cluster. You can read more about a node at `https://kubernetes.io/docs/concepts/architecture/nodes/`.

Pod – A pod is a logical collection of containers running on a node in the cluster. A pod will be a unit of deploying, managing, and failing over containers running in the cluster. You can read more about a pod at `https://kubernetes.io/docs/concepts/workloads/pods/pod-overview/`.

Service – The Kubernetes documentation describes a service as "abstraction which defines a logical set of Pods and a policy by which to access them." For the purposes of SQL Server, a service will serve as a *load balancer* and an abstraction of the private IP address of the pod hosting SQL Server. It is very much like a listener for clustering for SQL Server. k8s provides the concept of a service built into the k8s software, and applications like SQL Server can bind to them so that no matter where the SQL Server pod is hosted in the cluster, applications can always connect to the service using the same IP address and port. You can read more about a k8s service at `https://kubernetes.io/docs/concepts/services-networking/service/`.

secret – A secret is a k8s object that allows you to store sensitive information, like a password. This is very convenient for SQL Server to store the sa password. You can read more about k8s secrets at `https://kubernetes.io/docs/concepts/configuration/secret/`.

storage class – A storage class is a k8s object to expose storage like a disk system. You can read more about k8s storage classes at `https://kubernetes.io/docs/concepts/storage/storage-classes/`.

Persistent Volume Claim – A Persistent Volume Claim (PVC) is a request for storage backed up by a Persistent Volume which is mapped to a storage class. For me, this is like asking for a volume on a disk drive for storage. In the case of SQL Server, this will work quite well for database files.

There are other terms I will introduce and talk about as you go about using examples in the rest of the chapter.

Comment on Internals of k8s

You can use the references I provided earlier in the chapter to truly dive into the internals, but I will say that one aspect of k8s you should understand is **API**. I love it when I can look at how something works by reviewing the Application Programing Interface (API). Everything at the core of k8s is based on an **API server.** You can read about all the components that power a k8s cluster, but the API server is a piece of software that accepts requests and "does stuff." Think of the API server like SQL Server. The API of SQL Server is T-SQL, and applications can submit T-SQL commands to SQL Server, and it "does stuff." k8s works in a similar way. You can read more about the k8s API at `https://kubernetes.io/docs/concepts/overview/kubernetes-api/`. The API server is part of the k8s *control plane*, which you can read more about at `https://en.wikipedia.org/wiki/Kubernetes#Kubernetes_control_plane_`(primary). Keep in mind the concept of a control plane and API server as you use k8s and then start to learn about **SQL Server Big Data Clusters** in Chapter 10.

This means that, if you like to write code, you can deploy and manage containers in k8s using the API; or, you can use a very convenient command-line interface (CLI) called **kubectl** (Buck Woody always pronounces this "kubecuttle") which interacts with the k8s API for you. The way you will program to the k8s API with kubectl is with a declarative protocol using YAML files. You can read more about the kubectl program at `https://kubernetes.io/docs/reference/kubectl/overview/`. Use this "cheatsheet" for a quick reference at `https://kubernetes.io/docs/reference/kubectl/cheatsheet/`.

Take a look at the components that make up a k8s cluster at `https://kubernetes.io/docs/concepts/overview/components/`. And if you are wondering how containers are deployed and managed in the k8s cluster, Docker is a component that is installed by k8s and runs within each node of the cluster. I consider k8s a simple yet complex system to deploy, schedule, manage, scale, and power container applications, like SQL Server.

Since k8s is open source, it is possible to deploy a cluster in many different ways, platforms, and systems. Let's look at the various k8s deployment options that meet your needs or requirements.

k8s Deployment Options

k8s was founded by Google back around 2014, when Brendan worked there, to build a system to scale containerized applications for internal applications. In 2015, k8s 1.0 became open source, and is still an open source project today. (The k8s Wikipedia has an interesting origin story at `https://en.wikipedia.org/wiki/Kubernetes#History`.) Kubernetes is from a Greek word for "pilot" or "helmsman" and is a fitting name for something to steer the ship of a world of containers.

Since k8s became open source, several companies have taken the k8s project and built a commercial k8s system for customers to use. You can read the k8s documentation site for a list of partners at `https://kubernetes.io/partners/#kcsp`.

At the time I wrote this book, my experiences with the k8s landscape break down to these deployment choices:

Open source k8s – I've talked to some customers thinking about SQL Server with k8s, and they have said that they are going to deploy their own k8s in their data center, or in virtual machines in the cloud, using the latest open source build of k8s. If you go down this path, you typically use a deployment tool called **kubeadm** (`https://kubernetes.io/docs/setup/production-environment/tools/kubeadm/install-kubeadm/`). Another popular option is a tool called **kubespray** (`https://kubernetes.io/docs/setup/production-environment/tools/kubespray/`). If you are thinking of deploying your own k8s in your data center, it does give you maximum control, but *you own it*. In other words, you will have to own both maintaining and managing the k8s cluster, along with SQL Server running in it.

Minikube – Want to get a quick and easy single node k8s running on your laptop or in a virtual machine? Minikube is your friend; it is meant for small testing and development purposes, and you can get up and running in no time. You can read about how to set up Minikube at `https://kubernetes.io/docs/setup/learning-environment/minikube/`.

Tip Docker Desktop can automatically deploy Minikube for you. Look at the example at `https://docs.docker.com/docker-for-windows/#kubernetes`.

Azure Kubernetes Service (AKS) – If you want the feel of a *managed k8s cluster*, then consider a cloud service like Azure Kubernetes Services (AKS). Brendan owns the team that builds and runs this service, so I feel pretty confident when using AKS that I am getting the latest innovations of k8s along with the power of the cloud. The examples in this chapter will use AKS, but they are compatible with any k8s distribution. Since AKS is a cloud service, they can innovate at the speed of the cloud (sorry, I couldn't resist). For example, AKS can support both Linux and Windows Containers (see `https://azure.microsoft.com/en-us/blog/announcing-the-preview-of-windows-server-containers-support-in-azure-kubernetes-service/`). And AKS supports the concept of virtual nodes (`https://docs.microsoft.com/en-us/azure/aks/virtual-nodes-cli`). Dive into AKS at `https://azure.microsoft.com/en-us/services/kubernetes-service`.

Azure Stack – Azure Stack is an appliance system providing customers with Azure services in their own data centers. k8s is a deployment option with Azure Stack, which you can read about at `https://docs.microsoft.com/en-us/azure-stack/user/azure-stack-solution-template-kubernetes-deploy`. You should think of k8s on Azure Stack as equivalent to AKS running in your data center. As AKS evolves, so will k8s on Azure Stack.

Red Hat OpenShift – OpenShift has become a very popular platform in the industry. OpenShift is a k8s platform that can be run in your data center or in public clouds, which you can read more about at `www.openshift.com/`. While OpenShift is very compatible to open source k8s, there are differences in using the system and platform. You probably won't believe this, but I led a team of Microsoft Engineers at the May 2019 Red Hat Summit to proctor a lab on SQL Server 2019 on OpenShift. Check it out for yourself at `https://github.com/Microsoft/sqlworkshops/tree/master/SQLonOpenShift`. Several of the examples in this chapter have an OpenShift version on that GitHub site for you to use in your OpenShift environment. Microsoft offers a managed OpenShift platform (think AKS) called Azure Red Hat OpenShift. You can read more about this service at `https://docs.microsoft.com/en-us/azure/virtual-machines/linux/openshift-get-started#azure-red-hat-openshift`.

Windows Server – How did that platform get into this chapter? Everything I've described about k8s so far is all based on Linux. k8s got its start on Linux, so that all makes sense. To give you more flexibility, though, we wanted Windows Server to be a part of the k8s world, so it is possible now to use Windows Server to host a k8s cluster. Not everything in the cluster will be "pure" Windows, but Windows container–based nodes are supported. You can read more about Kubernetes with Windows at `https://docs.microsoft.com/en-us/virtualization/windowscontainers/kubernetes/getting-started-kubernetes-windows`.

Other k8s cloud providers – Azure is not the only cloud k8s provider in town. Amazon has Elastic Kubernetes Service (EKS), Google has the Google Kubernetes Engine (GKE), and there are others as well.

Other k8s providers – There are other k8s providers in the market. SUSE has several k8s solutions, which you can read about at `www.suse.com/solutions/kubernetes/`. One of the more popular ones I've seen my customers talk about is Rancher (`https://rancher.com/`). I'm sure you may have heard of others that customers want to use. Another k8s provider I'm going to pay particular attention to in the future is VMWare PKS (`https://cloud.vmware.com/vmware-enterprise-pks`).

Ultimately, your choice for k8s is based on whether you want to deploy k8s in your data center or in a public cloud. Your other decisions should be based on what kind of support you will receive, is the k8s cluster managed or do you need to manage everything, and whether the k8s distribution will last and be relevant in the future. SQL Server will work on just about all of the k8s platforms and providers. Working for Microsoft, I will be interested to see the popularity of k8s on AKS and Windows Server. In my experience with Linux, OpenShift is a major force and a k8s platform that many customers are using or evaluating.

It's time to learn by example, so let's go over the prerequisites to use the examples for deployment, HA, and updates with k8s and SQL Server 2019.

Prerequisites for the Examples

All the examples for this chapter rely on the cross-platform CLI kubectl program. You should be able to use the examples in this chapter with any k8s distribution using kubectl.

I used Azure Kubernetes Service (AKS) to deploy my k8s cluster for all of the examples. Therefore, there will be two possible differences in your use of my examples for your k8s distribution:

- **Storage class** – My examples use a storage class for Azure disks. You will need to put in the storage class specific to your platform.

- **Load Balancer** – My examples use a load balancer type for the service, but that is implemented only in k8s cloud providers. If you are not using a cloud provider for k8s, you will want to use a type of service called a NodePort. You can read more about NodePort at `https://kubernetes.io/docs/concepts/services-networking/#nodeport`.

Other than that, these examples in the chapter should run on just about any k8s platform you have configured.

If you are using AKS, I used the following steps to create my AKS cluster, per the documentation at `https://docs.microsoft.com/en-us/azure/aks/kubernetes-walkthrough`.

createaksrg.sh

```
az group create --name bwaks --location eastus2
```

createaks.sh

```
az aks create \
    --resource-group bwaks \
    --name bwsqlaks \
    --node-count 2 \
    --enable-addons monitoring \
    --generate-ssh-keys
```

connectoaks.sh

```
az aks get-credentials --resource-group bwaks --name bwsqlaks
```

You can see the scripts and commands I used to create the resource group, create the cluster, and connect to the cluster in the **ch8_sql_on_k8s** directory. Even though these are Bash shell scripts, you can run these following commands where the Azure CLI is supported. I like to use the Azure Cloud Shell which I'll show you in these examples because the Azure CLI is built-in. If you want to use a platform, you will need to install the Azure CLI at `https://docs.microsoft.com/en-us/cli/azure/install-azure-cli?view=azure-cli-latest`.

I also recommend you install the Kubernetes Visual Studio Code extension to assist in using k8s clusters and objects. I wanted to install this on Azure Data Studio. To do this, you need to download these extensions:

```
https://marketplace.visualstudio.com/items?itemName=redhat.vscode-yaml
https://marketplace.visualstudio.com/items?itemName=ms-kubernetes-tools.
vscode-kubernetes-tools
```

To use this extension, you also need to install kubectl from `https://kubernetes.io/docs/tasks/tools/install-kubectl/`.

To learn more about how to install extensions with Azure Data Studio, refer to the documentation at `https://docs.microsoft.com/en-us/sql/azure-data-studio/extensions`.

As I said, for me, I like to use these examples with the Azure Cloud Shell. The Azure Cloud Shell supports both PowerShell and bash and includes many built-in tools like the Azure CLI, kubectl, and even sqlcmd. You can read more about the Azure Cloud Shell at `https://azure.microsoft.com/en-us/features/cloud-shell`.

No matter what client or k8s distribution you use, if you can run kubectl, you can use these examples.

Deploying SQL Server on k8s

For examples in this section, let me show you how to deploy a pod with a single SQL Server container.

You will need a secret for the sa password, storage for databases, and a load balancer to connect to SQL Server. All of this will be done with a series of kubectl commands and declarative YAML files.

In addition, I recommend you create your own pods using the concept of namespaces in k8s. A namespace gives you a scope for the objects (e.g., pods) you create in the k8s cluster to be separated from other objects. Namespaces provide a very nice mechanism to organize and manage your k8s objects.

Let's go step by step through the process of deploying and connecting to a SQL Server container in a pod. These steps assume you have an existing k8s cluster. I created a two-node cluster using AKS as I've described in the Prerequisites, but even a single node cluster will work.

When I went through these examples, I used the Azure Cloud Shell, which can be run from any browser as seen in Figure 8-1.

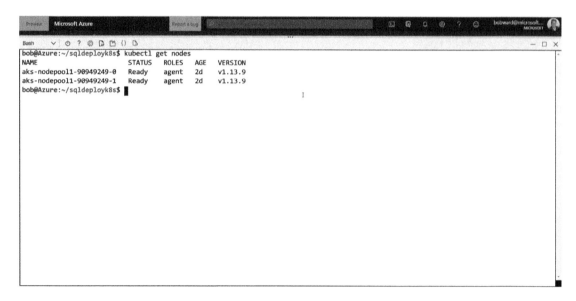

Figure 8-1. *Using Kubernetes with the Azure Cloud Shell*

I love the Azure Cloud Shell. One time I was on a plane trip back to Texas, and battery ran out on my laptop. I needed to do some work with AKS for a demo I was building. My iPhone still had power, and I had heard about the Azure app (`https://apps.apple.com/us/app/microsoft-azure/id1219013620`). I installed the app, connected with my subscription, and browsed my Azure resources. I then noticed the app had a cloud shell option. I selected this and now I was back in business. Figure 8-2 shows an example of using the Azure Cloud Shell from my phone.

Figure 8-2. *The mobile k8s user*

I remember sitting next to a passenger who was playing Candy Crush on their phone. They saw what I was doing and said, "what game are you playing?" My response was, "I'm deploying a Kubernetes cluster using the Cloud Shell." They went back to their game, no doubt wondering what strange person was playing the "Kubernetes game."

The example scripts for deployment can be found at **ch8_sql_on_k8s\deploy**. Make sure to set execution permissions for the shell scripts with chmod u+x <script>. Also, if you would like to run these in the Azure Cloud Shell, read the following documentation on uploading these example scripts (https://docs.microsoft.com/en-us/azure/cloud-shell/persisting-shell-storage#transfer-local-files-to-cloud-shell). Remember, the big advantage of the Azure Cloud Shell is that it only requires a browser, and all the tools like kubectl, az, and sqlcmd are already installed.

On to the examples to deploy SQL Server in AKS:

1. Create a namespace using the following command or script
    step1_create_namespace.sh:

    ```
    kubectl create namespace mssql
    ```

    You should get back this message indicating that the namespace
    was created:

    ```
    namespace/mssql created
    ```

    You can also verify the namespace was created by running this
    command:

    ```
    kubectl get namespaces
    ```

    On my cluster, I got back these results. The other namespaces
    come with a k8s cluster.

    ```
    NAME            STATUS    AGE
    default         Active    2d10h
    kube-public     Active    2d10h
    kube-system     Active    2d10h
    mssql           Active    56s
    ```

2. I'd like all of my objects to be created in the new mssql
    namespace. I can explicitly use the namespace as I create
    objects, or I can set a default context of the new namespace with
    the following commands (or use the script **step2_setcontext.
    sh**). Substitute in your cluster and username. You can find this
    information using the command `kubectl config view`.

    ```
    kubectl config set-context mssql --namespace=mssql
    --cluster=bwsqlaks --user=clusterUser_bwaks_bwsqlaks
    kubectl config use-context mssql
    ```

    If this command is successful, you should see output like the
    following:

```
Context "mssql" created.
Switched to context "mssql".
```

To verify your context is correct or to view it at any time, run the following command:

```
kubectl config current-context
```

3. Now, let's create the load balancer service to be used for the SQL Server pod. I will caution you about load balancers and cloud services like Azure. Azure is effectively providing you a public IP endpoint that won't change, so you can bind this into the private IP address of the pod regardless if it changes. I've seen scenarios where the load balancer service takes some time to create. Therefore, I recommend that, once you create them, don't remove them, unless you are doing tests like the demo from this chapter.

Run the following command or script **step3_create_service.sh** to create the load balancer:

```
kubectl apply -f sqlloadbalancer.yaml --record
```

Here is an example of using a YAML file to access the k8s API server in a declarative fashion. What you are effectively doing with kubectl apply is sending API commands to the API server, just like if you had written code using the API directly (yes, you are now a k8s programmer).

Let's look at the **sqlloadbalancer.yaml** file to understand an example of the format:

```
apiVersion: v1
kind: Service
metadata:
  name: mssql-service
spec:
  selector:
    app: mssql
```

```
ports:
  - protocol: TCP
    port: 31433
    targetPort: 1433
type: LoadBalancer
```

The protocol uses a label and value syntax. One of the references you can use to determine the exact set of labels and values for various k8s objects is at `https://kubernetes.io/docs/concepts/overview/working-with-objects/kubernetes-objects/`. Personally, I look at examples, copy them, and modify them for my own scenarios.

Let's use this YAML file to explain a few of the values.

```
apiVersion: v1
```

Every YAML file needs this apiVersion field. This tells the API server which "version" of the API you are using for various uses of k8s. You should typically stick with v1, but some new concepts of k8s may require a "beta" or other versions. Read more about API versioning at `https://kubernetes.io/docs/reference/using-api/api-overview/#api-versioning`.

```
kind: Service
```

This tells the API server what kind of object you are interacting with. In this case, it is a Service object that will help us deploy a load balancer. You can read more about a k8s Service at `https://kubernetes.io/docs/concepts/services-networking/service/`.

```
metadata:
  name: mssql-service
```

This is the name of the service. You will use this to manage the object and also bind this to another object like a pod.

```
spec:
  selector:
    app: mssql
  ports:
    - protocol: TCP
      port: 31433
      targetPort: 1433
  type: LoadBalancer
```

The spec label allows you to define more details about the Service object. A selector allows you to use a "label" to group and identify an object. In this case, using the **app:mssql** label will allow you to manage and view objects in k8s based on a label. I'll show you an example of using this label as part of this exercise. The label of app: mssql is also critical for a LoadBalancer, since it binds the LoadBalancer to any pod that uses the same label (which will be our SQL Server pod).

The port section allows you to map a port that will be viewed externally with a port inside the pod. This makes sense for SQL Server since, just like you learned in Chapter 7 on containers, you can't have more than one SQL Server listening on port 1433 at the host level. In this example, when applications want to connect to SQL Server, they will use the IP address of the Service with a port of 31433. I'll show you a clever trick to connect to the Service for SQL Server later in the example.

The type is the type of Service which, in this case, is a LoadBalancer service implemented by a cloud provider. The various service types can be found at `https://kubernetes.io/docs/concepts/services-networking/service/#publishing-services-service-types`.

When you execute a kubectl with the apply option and a YAML file, the execution is often *asynchronous*. This means the kubectl command will return immediately, but the operation declared in the YAML file is scheduled by the API server in the background.

In this case, when you execute the kubectl apply command for this service, your result should look like:

```
service/mssql-service created
```

This result actually means the service creation has been *scheduled* to be created. How can you know whether the service is ready to use? There are a few ways. First, you can run the following command:

```
kubectl get service
```

Your result may look like this:

```
NAME                TYPE          CLUSTER-IP      EXTERNAL-IP
    PORT(S)             AGE
mssql-service   LoadBalancer   10.0.150.233   <pending>
        31433:32010/TCP    61s
```

The CLUSTER-IP is the private IP address within the k8s cluster. The EXTERNAL-IP will be the static public IP you can use to connect to SQL Server. Notice the PORT has a value of 31433:32010. Even though SQL Server listens on port 1433 in the container, port 32010 is mapped to port 1433 within the cluster. Port 31433 is mapped to 32010, allowing you to connect to <EXTERNAL-IP>,<31433> to connect to SQL Server, no matter where the pod with SQL Server lives within the k8s cluster.

Notice the value of EXTERNAL-IP is <pending> when you look at it right after running this kubectl apply command. You will not be able to use the LoadBalancer until that value is a valid IP address; this could take several minutes to complete.

4. Now that the LoadBalancer has been scheduled to create, let's create a secret to hold the sa password for SQL Server. Use the following command or script **step4_create_secret.sh**:

```
kubectl create secret generic mssql-secret --from-literal=
SA_PASSWORD="Sql2019isfast"
```

When this command completes, you should see the following results, and the secret should be immediately created:

```
secret/mssql-secret created
```

Note   In Chapter 7, I mentioned that Active Directory authentication for SQL Server containers is coming for SQL Server 2019. Once this support is finalized, we should be able to also support AD Authentication for SQL Server in k8s.

5. The next step is to create storage for the SQL Server databases using the concept of a **PersistentVolumeClaim** (PVC). A PVC is like a volume defined on top of a core disk system which we can use to map to directories for databases for the SQL Server pod.

    Use the following command to create the PVC to be used for the SQL Server pod or script **step5_create_storage.sh**:

    ```
    kubectl apply -f storage.yaml
    ```

    You should see this message come back quickly, and the PVC is scheduled to be created in the background:

    ```
    persistentvolumeclaim/mssql-data created
    ```

    While that is being created (which may be fast), let's look at the **storage.yaml** file to see what is happening behind the scenes:

    ```
    apiVersion: v1
    kind: PersistentVolumeClaim
    metadata:
      name: mssql-data
      annotations:
        volume.beta.kubernetes.io/storage-class: azure-disk
    spec:
      accessModes:
      - ReadWriteOnce
      resources:
        requests:
          storage: 8Gi
    ```

The metadata is interesting because the annotations label binds the PVC to a disk called a storage class. How did I know to use azure-disk? That is because when you create an AKS cluster, you automatically get an Azure disk based on premium storage with a storage class called azure-disk. You can create others, but this is the standard one created by AKS. You can read more about storage with AKS at `https://docs.microsoft.com/en-us/azure/aks/concepts-storage`. If you are not using k8s, you would have created storage classes already, or you can find out which ones are available with your k8s administrator, or the following command:

```
kubectl get StorageClass
```

You can find more about the details of azure-disk by running this command:

```
kubectl describe StorageClass azure-disk
```

The spec section of this storage.yaml describes what access is allowed for PVC as well as the size of the volume. The AccessModes of ReadWriteOnce means that the volume is read/write and only one pod/node is allowed to access the volume at any time. It doesn't mean that a pod can't be moved to another node and the volume accessed (this will be a fundamental concept for HA, as you will learn later in the chapter). It just means two pods, or two nodes, cannot access the volume at the same time. This makes sense for a SQL Server database. 8Gi means a volume with a size of 8Gb.

You can see whether the PVC was successfully created by running this command:

```
kubectl describe PersistentVolumeClaims mssql-data
```

At the bottom of the output, a successful PVC creation looks like this:

Type	Reason	Age	From
		Message	
----	------	----	----

Normal ProvisioningSucceeded 9m16s persistentvolume-controller Successfully provisioned volume pvc-b8c9225e-c038-11e9-b5fa-c6f80bad26d8 using kubernetes.io/azure-disk

I've seen some scenarios where there might be some temporary timeouts or errors, but eventually the PVC is created.

6. You now have a load balancer service, a secret for the sa password, and storage. It's time to put this all together and create a pod that has a single container for SQL Server. Run the following command or script **step6_deploy_sql2019.sh** (the --record option provides more details from behind the scenes of the deployment):

```
kubectl apply -f sql2019deployment.yaml --record
```

You should see these results, which indicate that a *deployment* has been scheduled:

```
deployment.apps/mssql-deployment created
```

A *deployment* is going to allow us to create a pod with a concept of a *ReplicaSet* for the SQL Server pod. I'll define ReplicaSet later when I show you the built-in HA capabilities of k8s.

To see the status of the deployment and the objects related to the pod, run the following command:

```
kubectl get all
```

This will show all objects in the current context (namespace mssql) including status of the pod, LoadBalancer, and deployment.

When you run this immediately, you might see results like this:

```
NAME                                      READY   STATUS
RESTARTS   AGE
pod/mssql-deployment-7bb4c5f5d7-rpw45  0/1     ContainerCreating
0          4s
```

```
NAME                         TYPE            CLUSTER-IP
EXTERNAL-IP      PORT(S)             AGE
service/mssql-service    LoadBalancer    10.0.150.233
13.77.103.119       31433:32010/TCP     55m
```

```
NAME                                  READY   UP-TO-DATE   AVAILABLE   AGE
deployment.apps/mssql-deployment   0/1     1            0           4s
```

```
NAME                                          DESIRED   CURRENT   READY   AGE
replicaset.apps/mssql-deployment-7bb4c5f5d7   1         1         0       4s
```

The first line has the STATUS of the pod creation. A STATUS of **ContainerCreating** means the container defined for the pod is in the process of being created. If this is the first time you have created a pod with the SQL Server container image, it may take longer, as the container image must be pulled into the local docker registry of k8s.

The deployment STATUS indicates when the overall deployment is successful. The STATUS of the LoadBalancer is independent of the deployment. This means you need to wait for the pod to have a status of **Running**, the LoadBalancer to have a valid EXTERNAL-IP address, and the deployment to have AVAILABLE = 1 before you can start connecting to SQL Server. The status of the Replica should match the status of the pod or deployment.

While the pod is still being created, let's look at the **sql2019deployment.yaml** file in various parts.

```
kind: Deployment
metadata:
  name: mssql-deployment
```

This section tells the API server we are creating a deployment of a pod and the name.

The rest of the YAML is the specification for the deployment, so let's break that down.

```
replicas: 1
  selector:
    matchLabels:
      app: mssql
  strategy:
    type: Recreate
```

This defines the number of replicas for the pod (one) and to recreate the pod should any updates be needed. I'll explain the significance of these terms later in this chapter. The matchLabels is to associate the label of the deployment with the pod label (which are both mssql).

The next big section is called a template, which defines more details about the containers for the pod and volumes used for storage.

You can see in the template section we use another label for app of mssql so we can manage, view, or control objects with the deployment using a label.

Next comes the specification for the pod, which contains details about the container to deploy in the pod.

```
spec:
    terminationGracePeriodSeconds: 10
    containers:
    - name: mssql
      image: mcr.microsoft.com/mssql/rhel/server:2019-latest
      env:
      - name: MSSQL_PID
        value: "Developer"
      - name: ACCEPT_EULA
        value: "Y"
      - name: MSSQL_SA_PASSWORD
        valueFrom:
```

```
            secretKeyRef:
               name: mssql-secret
               key: SA_PASSWORD
        volumeMounts:
        - name: mssqldb
          mountPath: /var/opt/mssql
```

You can see in the spec a few things that look familiar once you have used containers. You see the image the container will be based on and the environment variables used to supply to the SQL Server container. Notice how the sa password is mapped to the secret you already created.

The value of **terminationGracePeriodSeconds** defines how long k8s will allow the container to shut itself down should it need to be terminated. It is possible for a SQL Server to need more or less time, but I chose 10 seconds in our examples. SQL Server is resilient for consistency whether or not it is shut down gracefully.

The volumeMount entry is a name called mssqldb, which maps to the directory to store all SQL Server databases. mssqldb is defined right below this spec as part of the deployment:

```
volumes:
    - name: mssqldb
      persistentVolumeClaim:
        claimName: mssql-data
```

Here is the mapping to the PVC that was created. Now, when the SQL Server container is started in the pod, all system and user databases by default will live in persisted storage with the PVC. You will see how this can become important when you learn about HA and updating in other sections of this chapter.

You can run `kubectl get all` again to see if everything is ready to use for SQL Server.

You also have a few other interesting kubectl commands at your disposal to examine the state of the pod and SQL Server. To see a complete list of option, you can run the command `kubectl help` or look at the kubectl reference documentation at `https://kubernetes.io/docs/reference/kubectl/overview`.

7. Run the following command to see the logs of the pod (and container in the pod) which happens to be the ERRORLOG of SQL Server. You can also use the script **step7_getlogs.sh**:

```
kubectl logs -l app=mssql --tail=100000
```

Normally, the kubectl logs command requires a pod name, but you can use the mssql label instead of having to look up the name of the pod.

Your results should literally be a dump of the SQL Server ERRORLOG.

8. You can also see a detailed view of events related to operations in k8s you have completed so far in this namespace, by running the following command or script **step8_getevents.sh**:

```
kubectl get events
```

Your output should show you a timeline for events that have occurred in this namespace. If all worked well, it should look something like the following:

```
LAST SEEN    TYPE      REASON                    KIND
   MESSAGE
29m          Normal    ProvisioningSucceeded     PersistentVolumeClaim
   Successfully provisioned volume pvc-c18b530f-c040-11e9-b5fa-
   c6f80bad26d8 using kubernetes.io/azure-disk
25m          Normal    Scheduled                 Pod
   Successfully assigned mssql/mssql-deployment-7b6565d684-8r7cc
   toaks-nodepool1-90949249-0
25m          Normal    SuccessfulAttachVolume    Pod
   AttachVolume.Attach succeeded for volume "pvc-c18b530f-c040-11e9-
   b5fa-c6f80bad26d8"
```

```
24m           Normal   Pulled                  Pod
   Container image "mcr.microsoft.com/mssql/rhel/server:
   2019-latest" already present on machine
24m           Normal   Created                 Pod
   Created container
24m           Normal   Started                 Pod
   Started container
25m           Normal   SuccessfulCreate        ReplicaSet
   Created pod: mssql-deployment-7b6565d684-8r7cc
25m           Normal   ScalingReplicaSet       Deployment
   Scaled up replica set mssql-deployment-7b6565d684 to 1
30m           Normal   EnsuringLoadBalancer    Service
   Ensuring load balancer
29m           Normal   EnsuredLoadBalancer     Service
   Ensured load balancer
```

9. You can also get more details about the deployment using the
    following command or script **step9_describe_deployment.sh**:

    ```
    kubectl describe deployment mssql-deployment
    ```

    You will get all types of details about the deployment, including
    the most recent events specifically related to the deployment.

10. You can also get more details about the pod that was deployed
    using the following command or script **step10_describe_pod.sh**:

    ```
    kubectl describe pod -l app=mssql
    ```

    This is where using the label of mssql pays off again. You will get
    more details of the pod, containers within the pod, and events
    related to the pod, and all you have to remember is the mssql
    label.

    This command, along with kubectl get events, can be useful for
    troubleshooting purposes for pod deployment.

11. Now (finally) it is time to connect to SQL Server running in a
    container in the pod. Here is a trick I learned from Anthony

Nocentino (known expert on Linux, Containers, and k8s and my technical reviewer for *Pro SQL Server on Linux*). Run the following command or script **step11_testsql.sh** to connect to SQL Server through the LoadBalancer:

```
SERVERIP=$(kubectl get service | grep mssql-service |
awk {'print $4'})
PORT=31433
sqlcmd -Usa -PSql2019isfast -S$SERVERIP,$PORT -Q"SELECT
@@version"
```

Your results should show you the version of SQL Server installed. If you look carefully at this command, it dynamically extracts the EXTERNAL-IP of the LoadBalancer and parses out the IP address to be used as part of the connection string. You could also go further and add in parsing logic for the port from the output of `kubectl get service`.

This was more detailed than just having you run each step, because I wanted to describe to you what is happening behind the scenes and learn more about how YAML works as an API for programming interface for k8s.

Tips with k8s

Before you move on to the next section, since you have a deployed SQL Server pod, let me show you some tips on using other resources with k8s.

k8s Extension

I discussed in an earlier section of the chapter called "Prerequisites for the Examples" the Kubernetes Extension for Visual Studio Code and showed how to install this for Azure Data Studio (ADS).

Let me show you some examples of using this extension with your deployed SQL Server pod.

First, one thing about using the k8s extension, along with the dependency for YAML, are the tips it provides for using YAML files. Find the sql2019deployment.yaml file in the **ch8_sql_on_k8s\deploy** directory with the samples. Use the Explorer feature of ADS to find the file.

Hover over any of the YAML syntax and get tips about the various statements in the file. For example, Figure 8-3 shows a tip for the terminationGracePeriodSeconds declaration.

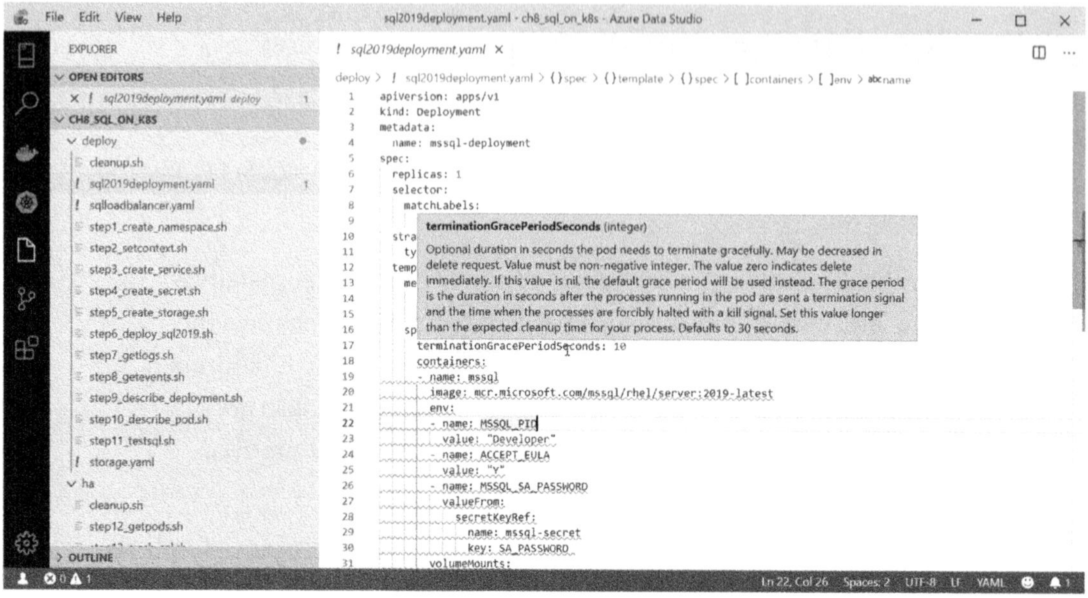

Figure 8-3. *Using the k8s extension to explore a YAML file*

The ADS extension also includes a "live" explorer to look at k8s resources. I used this to connect to my AKS cluster (if you use AKS, you will need to provide some login information when you use the tool). Once connected, I could browse objects and even perform some interesting operations.

Since my pod was deployed in a namespace, I first needed to change context to that namespace, as seen in Figure 8-4.

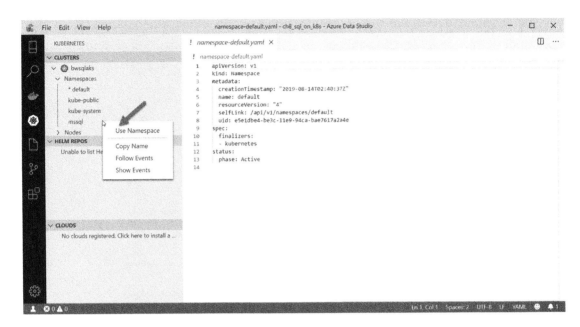

Figure 8-4. *Setting the namespace with the k8s extension*

One cool thing I can do is to attach to a running pod and run a Bash shell to view the ERRORLOG. First, I found my deployment in the k8s explorer, and used the right-click option to select Terminal, as seen in Figure 8-5.

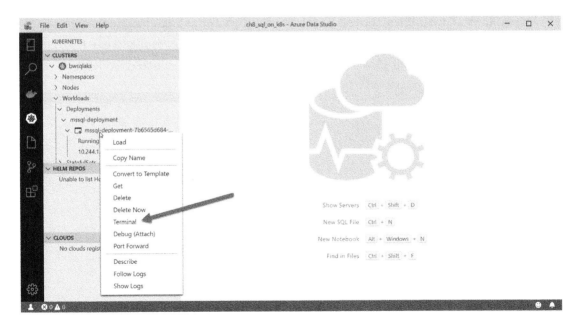

Figure 8-5. *Running a terminal session in a k8s pod*

The Terminal of ADS was displayed, and now I was in a Bash shell in the SQL Container of the pod. I was then able to navigate to /var/opt/mssql/log and dump out the ERRORLOG, as seen in Figure 8-6.

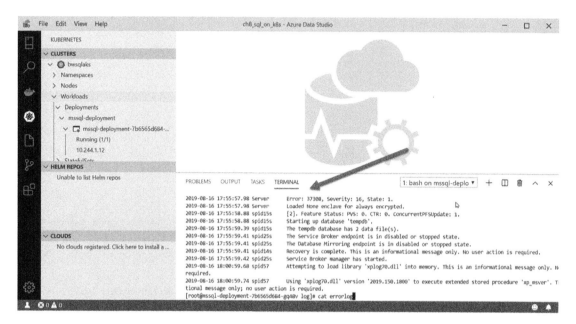

Figure 8-6. *Dumping out the ERRORLOG for a SQL Server pod in k8s*

I typed in exit to quit the terminal session. Another thing I discovered was the ability to reverse engineer a deployment to see what the YAML file looked like for that deployment. Using the right-click feature on the deployment, I selected Convert to Template, as seen in Figure 8-7.

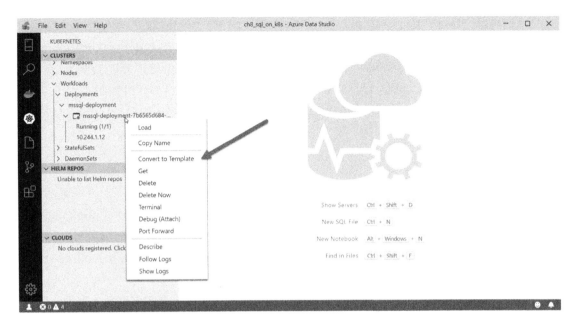

Figure 8-7. *Reverse engineering a k8s deployment*

I typed in the name of my YAML file, and I was presented with an editor to see the resulting YAML file.

I'm sure there are other nifty options with the k8s extension I have not explored yet, but will continue to use this with my journey with k8s.

Other kubectl Commands Include

kubectl has many other commands that are worth showing, including

kubectl top – This command on a node or pod basis displays metrics for memory and CPU. This could be helpful, for example, to see how much memory a pod is consuming or how much memory is left on a node.

kubectl cp – This command can be used to copy a file into the container file system for a pod. Just like docker cp, you could use this to copy in a backup file of a SQL Server database into the container writeable layer.

For example, given the example you deployed, assume the pod name is mssql-deployment-7b6565d684-92l8s in the mssql namespace and that you have downloaded the WideWorldImporters database sample (`https://github.com/ Microsoft/sql-server-samples/releases/download/wide-world-importers-v1.0/ WideWorldImporters-Full.bak`) to your local directory. The following command will copy the backup file into the SQL Server container so it can be restored:

```
kubectl cp ./WideWorldImporters-Full.bak mssql/mssql-deployment-7b6565d684-
92l8s:/var/opt/mssql
```

kubectl exec – This command allows you to execute a program in the namespace of the container in a pod. You would use this command much like docker exec to run a Bash shell for the container, or for SQL Server the sqlcmd utility, since that is part of the SQL Server container.

Based on the example I just showed you to copy in the WideWorldImporters backup, the following command could be used to restore the backup:

```
kubectl exec mssql-deployment-7b6565d684-92l8s -- /opt/mssql-tools/bin/sqlcmd
-S localhost -U SA -P "Sql2019isfast" -Q "RESTORE DATABASE WideWorldImporters
FROM DISK = '/var/opt/mssql/WideWorldImporters-Full.bak' WITH MOVE 'WWI_
Primary' TO '/var/opt/mssql/data/WideWorldImporters.mdf', MOVE 'WWI_UserData'
TO '/var/opt/mssql/data/WideWorldImporters_userdata.ndf', MOVE 'WWI_Log' TO
'/var/opt/mssql/data/WideWorldImporters.ldf', MOVE 'WWI_InMemory_Data_1' TO
'/var/opt/mssql/data/WideWorldImporters_InMemory_Data_1'"
```

This syntax took me a while to figure out; note here that you don't specify the namespace, so you must be in the context of the namespace for your pod. Also note the use of the -- syntax before specifying /opt/mssql/bin/sqlcmd which is used to separate arguments for kubectl and arguments for the program, which in this case is sqlcmd.

kubectl version – This command dumps out the version of kubectl. I've seen situations where users had problems with kubectl because it was older and not compatible with the version of the k8s cluster. This command prints out the versions of both the client and the server. Read more about version compatibility at `https:// kubernetes.io/docs/setup/release/version-skew-policy/`.

kubectl explain – This command displays documentation explaining information about k8s objects. Use a command like the following to find out more about YAML requirements for a ReplicaSet:

```
kubectl explain ReplicaSet
```

kubectl cluster-info dump – Stand back kubeheads (is that a term? If not, I just made one). This command will dump out a massive set of diagnostics. Use the --output-directory to create a set of diagnostic files. Be sure to use the --all-namespaces option to get diagnostics about all namespaces. This command dumps just about any log file that is part of the k8s cluster, including pods. I couldn't really find any specific documentation on what is in the logs, but, as I use k8s myself more over time, I will probably learn more (and become a kubehead).

The k8s Dashboard

The Kubernetes dashboard displays visual information about the k8s cluster. You can read all about the dashboard at `https://kubernetes.io/docs/tasks/access-application-cluster/web-ui-dashboard/`.

For AKS, you can read how to display the k8s dashboard for your cluster at `https://docs.microsoft.com/en-us/azure/aks/kubernetes-dashboard`. When I used the steps in this documentation page to launch the dashboard, my browser popped up with the UI. I then changed the namespace to mssql, and my screen looked like Figure 8-8.

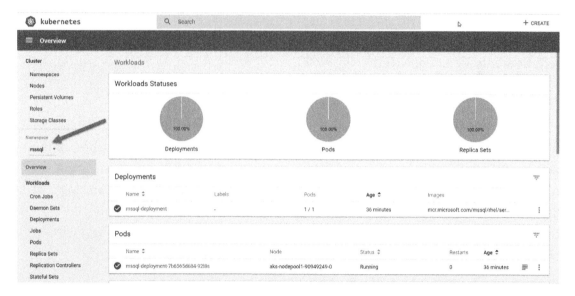

Figure 8-8. *The k8s dashboard*

Metrics and Logs with AKS

Using AKS has advantages because it is like a managed k8s platform. It includes built-in metrics, visualizations, and log view capabilities in the Azure Portal. Figure 8-9 shows some of the insights I can gain using the Azure Portal with my AKS cluster.

Figure 8-9. *Insights from the Azure Portal for AKS*

The next step in this chapter is to show you how built-in HA works with k8s and how it applies to SQL Server. If you are going to use the examples in the next section, don't remove any resources you've already configured. The script **cleanup.sh** can be used to clean up all resources, so you can use that if you *don't* plan to go through the examples in the next section.

SQL Server High Availability on k8s

One of the most beautiful aspects of k8s is the built-in feature set for high availability. Imagine having high availability for SQL Server with no clustering software required for you to install or maintain!

I talked about the term **ReplicaSet** earlier in the chapter, and now it is time to talk about its significance.

When you applied the SQL Server deployment in the previous section's example, the YAML file included this declaration:

```
replicas: 1
```

This declaration indicates to k8s to *always try to ensure* that one instance of the container in the pod, which in this case holds the SQL Server container, is always running. If the container crashes, then k8s will restart the container. If the pod dies, then k8s will spin up a new pod, and if the node dies, k8s will spin up a new pod on a new node, should one exist (and there are resources to allow it).

With SQL Server, when you combine a ReplicaSet with a LoadBalancer and persisted storage, this becomes a natural shared storage HA story. Consider Figure 8-10 as a visual representation of the deployment you created in the previous section.

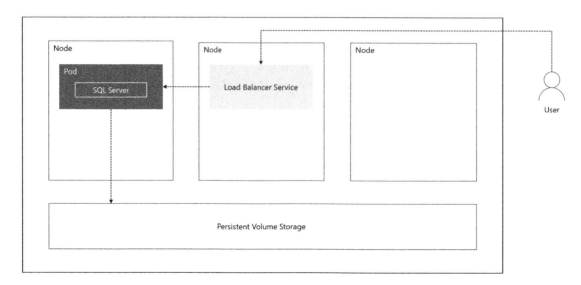

Figure 8-10. *Basic HA with SQL Server and k8s*

In this example, the user would connect to the Load Balancer which is bound to the pod holding the SQL Server Container (in reality the Load Balancer doesn't just live in a user node). If the SQL Server container crashed, you would only see a slight blip as k8s would spin up another container in the pod.

Consider what would happen if the pod had a problem, as seen in Figure 8-11.

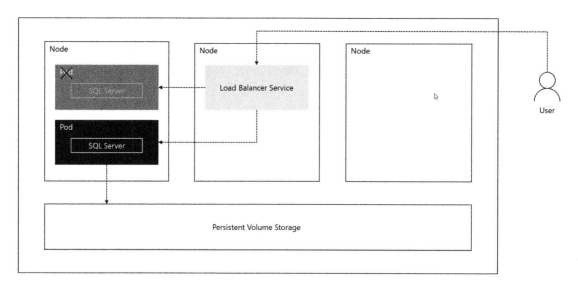

Figure 8-11. *A pod failure in k8s*

In this scenario, k8s would spin up another pod (most likely on the same node) which starts a new container. But notice the container still points to the PVC, which is bound to system and user databases. To SQL Server, it just sees existing system and user databases and starts up. The new pod would have a new private IP address, but the Load Balancer is automatically redirected to this new address. From the application point of view, it is a simple retry of the connection and all is well.

What if the node (it could be a VM) crashes, as seen in Figure 8-12.

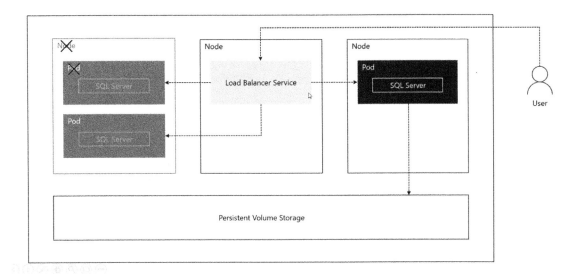

Figure 8-12. *A node failure in k8s*

k8s would detect this scenario and spin up a new pod on a new node. Even though the new pod has a new private IP address, the Load Balancer is still redirected to the new pod. This has a similar feel to Always On Failover Cluster Instance, except you didn't need to install any special clustering software.

Let's build on the previous chapter example to see how this works. All the scripts for this example can be found at **ch8_sql_on_k8s\ha**.

1. Run the following command or **step12_getpods.sh** to see the name of the pod, IP address, and node the pod is running on:

    ```
    kubectl get pods -o wide
    ```

Your results should look something like this:

```
NAME                                      READY  STATUS    RESTARTS
  AGE   IP            NODE                         NOMINATED NODE
  READINESS GATES
mssql-deployment-7b6565d684-8r7cc  1/1     Running  0
  91m  10.244.1.11  aks-nodepool1-90949249-0  <none>        <none>
```

2. Let's simulate a container failure by shutting down SQL Server.
   Run the following command or script **step13_crash_sql.sh** to shut
   down SQL Server, thereby stopping the container:

```
SERVERIP=$(kubectl get service | grep mssql-service |
awk {'print $4'})
PORT=31433
sqlcmd -Usa -PSql2019isfast -S$SERVERIP,$PORT -Q"SHUTDOWN WITH
NOWAIT"
```

3. Run the following command or script **step14_getpods.sh** to see
   everything is the same:

```
kubectl get pods -o wide
```

Your results should look the same as before as the container was
restarted in the same pod on the same node:

```
NAME                                      READY  STATUS    RESTARTS
  AGE   IP            NODE                         NOMINATED NODE
  READINESS GATES
mssql-deployment-7b6565d684-8r7cc  1/1     Running  1
  91m  10.244.1.11  aks-nodepool1-90949249-0  <none>        <none>
```

Run the following command to see the sequence of events:

```
kubectl get events
```

Your results should look something like:

```
LAST SEEN    TYPE      REASON    KIND    MESSAGE
16s          Normal    Pulled    Pod     Container image
"mcr.microsoft.com/mssql/rhel/server:2019-latest" already
present on machine
16s          Normal    Created   Pod     Created container
16s          Normal    Started   Pod     Started container
```

4. Try to connect to SQL Server and see that all is well using the following command or script **step15_testsql.sh**:

```
SERVERIP=$(kubectl get service | grep mssql-service |
awk {'print $4'})
PORT=31433
sqlcmd -Usa -PSql2019isfast -S$SERVERIP,$PORT -Q"SELECT
@@version"
```

You should see you can connect to SQL Server and display the version.

5. Test a pod failure with the following command or script **step16_pod_failure.sh**:

```
kubectl delete pod -l app=mssql
```

In this example, instead of using the pod by name, we can take advantage that we associated a label with the pod that is a name easy to remember.

You should see a message like this:

```
pod "mssql-deployment-7b6565d684-8r7cc" deleted
```

6. Check out the status of the pod including IP address with the following command or script **step17_getpods.sh**:

```
kubectl get pods -o wide
```

You can see from the output that the pod is now running on the same node (it could have been scheduled to a new node) with a new name and new IP address:

```
NAME                                       READY    STATUS     RESTARTS
    AGE       IP              NODE                    NOMINATED
NODE      READINESS GATES
mssql-deployment-7b6565d684-gq48v    1/1       Running    0
2m55s   10.244.1.12    aks-nodepool1-90949249-0    <none>
<none>
```

Check out the sequence of events using the following command:

```
kubectl get events
```

Your output will show the sequence of terminating the pod and creating a new one, similar to the following:

```
LAST SEEN   TYPE    REASON        KIND        MESSAGE
6m53s       Normal  Pulled        Pod         Container image "mcr.
microsoft.com/mssql/rhel/server:2019-latest" already present on machine
6m53s       Normal  Created       Pod         Created container
6m53s       Normal  Started       Pod         Started container
39s         Normal  Killing       Pod         Killing container with
id docker://mssql:Need to kill Pod
40s         Normal  Scheduled     Pod         Successfully assigned
mssql/mssql-deployment-7b6565d684-gq48v to aks-nodepool1-90949249-0
34s         Normal  Pulled        Pod         Container image "mcr.
microsoft.com/mssql/rhel/server:2019-latest" already present on machine
34s         Normal  Created       Pod         Created container
34s         Normal  Started       Pod         Started container
40s         Normal  SuccessfulCreate ReplicaSet Created pod: mssql-
deployment-7b6565d684-gq48v
```

7. Try to connect to SQL Server using the LoadBalancer service with the following command or script **step18_testsql.sh**:

```
SERVERIP=$(kubectl get service | grep mssql-service |
awk {'print $4'})
PORT=31433
sqlcmd -Usa -PSql2019isfast -S$SERVERIP,$PORT -Q"SELECT
@@version"
```

Because we are using a LoadBalancer bound to the pod, the connection remains the same, even though the pod has a new private IP address.

8. Clean up all resources by running the following commands or script **cleanup.sh**:

```
kubectl delete namespace mssql
kubectl config delete-context mssql
kubectl config use-context bwsqlaks
```

You have now seen the fundamental HA capabilities of SQL Server running in k8s. For the scenario where a node is no longer available, simulating a true crash of a node would require you to gain direct access to the VMs supporting a node and "crashing" it. However, you can see the behavior for how k8s would automatically schedule the SQL Server deployment based on the ReplicaSet definition by running the following command:

```
kubectl drain <nodename>
```

You can bring your node back online for scheduling (but it doesn't mean pods would be moved to that node) by running the following command:

```
kubectl uncordon <nodename>
```

Now let's examine how you can update SQL Server in k8s similar to how you updated a container in Chapter 7.

Updating SQL Server on k8s

You learned in Chapter 7 how to update a SQL Server container by "switching" containers backed by a persisted volume. The running container is stopped, and a new container, with a new CU build of SQL Server, is started – pointing to the same volume, which is mapped to the directory containing the system and user databases.

You can achieve the same in k8s. Only this time k8s will do all the work for you, given the right declarations. Let's go back and look at this section of the sql2019deployment. yaml file from the first exercise in this chapter:

```
spec:
  replicas: 1
  selector:
    matchLabels:
      app: mssql
  strategy:
    type: Recreate
```

Notice the strategy of type **Recreate**. Recreate declares to k8s that if the deployment is **updated** to stop and recreate the container. Another choice for a strategy type is **RollingUpdate**. We can't use this strategy with SQL Server unless we have some coordination with multiple SQL Server containers. We will talk about this concept, though, in the last section of this chapter, on Always On Availability Groups and k8s.

One way to update the deployment is to update the image of the container running in the pod. For SQL Server, this could mean updating to a new cumulative update, just like I showed you how to switch to a container with a new image in Chapter 7. And since we are using a persistent volume, the system and user database will be recognized by the new container using the updated image. k8s provides a method for you to do this *all in one command*. And there is a rollback story, too, since k8s tracks the update to the deployment as a *revision*.

Let's see this in action. All the scripts for this example can be found at **ch8_sql_on_k8s\update**. If you have run the previous examples, be sure to clean up all your existing resources using the **cleanup.sh** script found in either the **ha** or the **deploy** folder.

At the time of writing this book, we have not yet shipped a cumulative update for SQL Server 2019, so I'll use SQL Server 2017 in these examples. However, once we start shipping CU builds, you can use this same technique for SQL Server 2019.

1. First, we need to deploy a SQL Server pod, as we did in the first example in this chapter. Instead of going through all of those steps, I built one script that does it all, called **step1_deploysql.sh**. This script uses the following commands:

    ```
    kubectl create namespace mssql
    kubectl config set-context mssql --namespace=mssql
    --cluster=bwsqlaks --user=clusterUser_bwaks_bwsqlaks
    kubectl config use-context mssql
    kubectl apply -f sqlloadbalancer.yaml
    ```

```
kubectl create secret generic mssql --from-literal=SA_
PASSWORD="Sql2017isfast"
kubectl apply -f storage.yaml
kubectl apply -f sql2017deployment.yaml
```

The **storage.yaml** and **sqlloadbalancer.yaml** files are identical to the files used in the first example in this chapter. The **sql2017deployment.yaml** file is also the same, except for this section:

```
image:  mcr.microsoft.com/mssql/server:2017-CU10-ubuntu
```

This means our new pod with a container will use a SQL Server 2017 CU10 image for Ubuntu. If this image is not on the node that is deployed for the pod, k8s will have to pull the image first.

Note   To this date, I've not found a single easy method to pre-pull SQL Server images on all the k8s nodes, except to run pods using those images and then deleting the pods (the image will stay cached on the local node). There are other techniques out there, and one of them is to gain admin access to log in to the actual Linux node VMs and use docker directly to pull images.

Use the same techniques as in the first example to check that the pod and deployment are up and running. For example, run the following command:

```
kubectl get all
```

The status of the pod must be Running, and the LoadBalancer must have a valid External-IP address before you can continue.

2. Now we want to update the deployment by changing the image using the following command or script **step2_updatesql.sh**:

```
kubectl --record deployment set image mssql-deployment
mssql=mcr.microsoft.com/mssql/server:2017-latest-ubuntu
```

k8s will do all the work behind the scenes to stop the current container and start a new one (using the same arguments from the deployment) with the new image.

3. Use the following command or script **step3_checkstatus.sh** to *watch* the progress of the update. This command won't complete until the update of the container with the new image is complete and the container is running again:

```
kubectl rollout status deployment mssql-deployment
kubectl rollout history deployment mssql-deployment
```

When the new deployment is finished, your results should look something like this:

```
Waiting for deployment "mssql-deployment" rollout to finish:
0 out of 1 new replicas have been updated...
Waiting for deployment "mssql-deployment" rollout to finish:
0 out of 1 new replicas have been updated...
Waiting for deployment "mssql-deployment" rollout to finish:
0 out of 1 new replicas have been updated...
Waiting for deployment "mssql-deployment" rollout to finish:
0 of 1 updated replicas are available...
deployment "mssql-deployment" successfully rolled out
deployment.extensions/mssql-deployment
REVISION   CHANGE-CAUSE
1          <none>
2          kubectl deployment set image mssql-deployment mssql=mcr.
microsoft.com/mssql/server:2017-latest-ubuntu --record=true
```

4. You can make sure your pod is running again with this command or script **step4_getpods.sh**:

```
kubectl get pods -o wide
```

Your pod status should show as Running.

5. SQL Server will recognize the existing system and user databases,
    but will need to perform any necessary steps to update to the
    new CU build. Therefore, if you try to connect to SQL Server too
    quickly, you may get the following error:

    ```
    Sqlcmd: Error: Microsoft ODBC Driver 17 for SQL Server : Login
    failed for user 'sa'. Reason: Server is in script upgrade mode.
    Only administrator can connect at this time.
    ```

    Try executing the following command or script **step5_testsql.sh**
    until you see the new version of SQL Server:

    ```
    SERVERIP=$(kubectl get service | grep mssql-service |
    awk {'print $4'})
    PORT=31433
    sqlcmd -Usa -PSql2017isfast -S$SERVERIP,$PORT -Q"SELECT
    @@version"
    ```

6. Just like the example with containers in Chapter 7, you may want
    to roll back to the previous container. k8s provides a method
    to do this by changing the revision number. Run the following
    command to roll back to the previous CU build or use script
    step6_rollbacksql.sh:

    ```
    kubectl rollout undo deployment mssql-deployment --to-revision=1
    ```

7. Run the following command or script **step7_getpods.sh** to verify
    the pod is back to a Running state:

    ```
    kubectl get pods -o wide
    ```

8. Once the pod is Running, run the following command (or use the
    script **step8_testsql.sh**) to make sure you have rolled back to SQL
    2017 CU10:

    ```
    SERVERIP=$(kubectl get service | grep mssql-service |
    awk {'print $4'})
    PORT=31433
    sqlcmd -Usa -PSql2017isfast -S$SERVERIP,$PORT -Q"SELECT
    @@version"
    ```

You have now successfully updated a SQL Server container and rolled it back using the built-in capabilities of k8s to update images from a running container.

Use the script **cleanup.sh** to clean up all resources you deployed in this example in the chapter.

Using Helm Charts

The process of deploying a pod with a container in k8s is pretty straightforward, but, as you saw from the examples, there are a lot of steps involved. Wouldn't it be nice to deploy a container like SQL Server in a pod much like an installation occurs from a package manager (like yum on RHEL)?

Helm makes this possible. You can read about how to use Helm Charts at `https://helm.sh/`.

For SQL Server, a Helm Chart for SQL Server 2017 on Linux is available at `https://github.com/helm/charts/tree/master/stable/mssql-linux`.

When you install Helm in your k8s cluster, you will be able to deploy a SQL Server pod using a single command like this:

```
helm install --name sql-server stable/mssql-linux --set acceptEula.value=Y
--set sapassword=Sql2019isfast --set edition.value=Developer
```

The examples at `https://github.com/helm/charts/tree/master/stable/mssql-linux` include how to configure the installation with persistence and how to connect to the running pod using the built-in LoadBalancer that is deployed.

I think Helm has some great possibilities to simplify the k8s experience with SQL Server, so it will be interesting to continue looking into this technology in combination with k8s for deployment.

SQL Server Availability Groups on k8s

The built-in high availability solution for k8s fits well with the needs of SQL Server. However, there are a few issues with just using this approach for high availability for your database:

- If k8s must spin up a new pod and container, it is effectively a restart of SQL Server. A full recovery must be performed on all system and user databases. Depending on how the container was shut down (and if you are not using our new Accelerated Database Recovery option), this could lead to longer than expected times for the new SQL Server container to be usable (even though the pod is Running). A Running pod just means the sqlservr process is running, it doesn't mean SQL Server is actually available.

- The second issue is the time it may take to pull a new SQL Server image. If the SQL Server images are not pre-pulled on a node where a new pod is created for SQL Server, this can cause a delay in starting up the pod and making SQL Server available.

- k8s only *understands* the health of a container, pod, or node. It doesn't understand the health of a program running in the container. A SQL Server container could be running but not available (or the database not available) due to a SQL Server *health* issue.

  We built Always On Availability Groups to help reduce downtime for availability should a failover be required. Part of this technology is to recognize failover conditions outside of the health of the host for SQL Server. You can read more about these failover conditions at `https://docs.microsoft.com/en-us/sql/database-engine/ availability-groups/windows/flexible-automatic-failover- policy-availability-group`. In addition, we added in failover health for databases in Availability Groups, which you can read more about at `https://docs.microsoft.com/en-us/sql/ database-engine/availability-groups/windows/sql-server- always-on-database-health-detection-failover-option`.

- The fourth issue is that, with a single sqlservr pod, there is no concept of a replica. Only one pod at a time can access the system and user databases. It would be nice to have more than one SQL Server involved in the HA solution so that the other instances (replicas) could have read copies of the data, and all the containers would not rely on a single Persistent Volume Claim.

Therefore, it makes sense for us to find a way to combine the built-in HA of k8s with the SQL Server failover technology of Availability Groups. And we did just that during the preview of SQL Server 2019. You can see the full story of how we did this and how it works through this blog post by my colleague Sourabh Agarwal at

https://cloudblogs.microsoft.com/sqlserver/2018/12/10/
availability-groups-on-kubernetes-in-sql-server-2019-
preview/.

The methodology is that we use the k8s concept of a *StatefulSet* (read more at https://kubernetes.io/docs/concepts/ workloads/controllers/statefulset/) to deploy Availability Group replicas. We would also use the concept of an *operator* to orchestrate deployment of the Availability Group and to detect failover scenarios.

Furthermore, we designed this solution to use LoadBalancer services for both the primary and secondary replicas. This way an application could connect to the primary replica using the primary LoadBalancer, regardless of which replica was the primary. Also, another application, perhaps a reporting application, could connect to one or more read secondary replicas and use k8s to truly load balance the connections.

We also built a new container called an *AG Agent* living in the SQL Server pod to help detect and coordinate failover detection logic for SQL Server. Combined with a concept called a k8s *ConfigMap* (read more at https://kubernetes.io/docs/tasks/configure-pod-container/configure-pod-configmap/), the AG Agent and operator would help integrate failover decisions with the k8s cluster for scenarios outside the scope of k8s health (container, pod, or node).

All of this is based on components we built during the preview of SQL Server 2019; we announced that Availability Groups for k8s will not be part of the SQL Server 2019 release. However, Availability Groups are part of the HADR story for Big Data Clusters which you will learn about more in Chapter 10.

I talked to Ross Monster, lead developer of this feature. He told me the intention is to still invest in this feature in the future. Ross told me that our thinking is to still end up using the operator concept, AG Agent concept, and StatefulSet concepts, but the overall design may change. Once the Availability Group (AG) is deployed, it will behave just like an AG does outside of k8s, allowing you to read secondary replicas and have a similar failover experience. Again, the beauty of k8s with AGs is that no failover cluster software is required on your part to install or maintain.

If you want to see a lab exercise using the preview version of AG with k8s, take a look at Module 5 of the SQL Server 2019 on OpenShift lab at `https://github.com/microsoft/sqlworkshops/blob/master/SQLonOpenShift/sqlonopenshift/05_Operator.md`.

One concept Ross explained we are thinking about is that we could actually support a rolling update scenario. So instead of having to rely on switching containers manually and end up experiencing more downtime, we could potentially provide an almost no-downtime scenario to update a series of SQL Server containers in an Availability Group. This brave new world would act very similar to the code we built that Red Hat demonstrated at the May 2019 Summit. You can watch a video of this demonstration at `www.pscp.tv/RedHatOfficial /1vAGRWYPjngJl` and see this new world of operators and almost zero downtime updates of SQL Server in action.

Summary

I'm very confident containers and Kubernetes are a big part of the future of distributed and scalable computing. And we have built SQL Server to be a part of this future. In this chapter, you learned enough fundamentals of Kubernetes (k8s) to understand how to deploy SQL Server in a k8s cluster. You also were able to see the power of HA built into k8s and how SQL Server can take advantage of it. Just like you saw in Chapter 7 with containers, you can use k8s capabilities to update a SQL Server container in a pod with a new cumulative update and roll back if necessary. I briefly introduced you to Helm Charts, which represent a new method to deploy pods and containers in k8s using a package management approach.

Finally, I gave you a glimpse of the future of SQL Server with k8s as we integrate Availability Groups with k8s to provide a robust, integrated HA solution with SQL Server, including all the power of Availability Groups you see today. Chapters 7 and 8 are important building blocks for learning as you go through Chapter 10 for SQL Server Big Data Clusters.

SQL Server Data Virtualization

Data Virtualization is one of the most exciting capabilities we are delivering with SQL Server 2019. In this chapter, you will learn more how Data Virtualization is made possible in SQL Server 2019 through a technology called Polybase. This chapter, along with Chapters 6, 7, and 8, provides the foundation to learn about **SQL Server Big Data Clusters** in Chapter 10.

What Is Polybase?

Polybase is an innovative technology introduced in SQL Server 2016, and expanded in SQL Server 2019, to solve the problem of *data movement*. Data movement typically involves building expensive and complex Extract, Transform, and Load (ETL) processes from other data sources into SQL Server from other data sources. Polybase solves this challenge by implementing a solution for *Data Virtualization*, a term I will discuss and define as we move along. I'll discuss and define Data Virtualization through this chapter.

In this chapter, I'll walk you through the history of Polybase and how it provides Data Virtualization. I'll talk about how Polybase works behind the scenes, and the typical workflow for Polybase through the concept of *external tables*. And, like most of the chapters in this book, we will use examples to show you the details of how to use Polybase for your Data Virtualization needs.

You can use our documentation as a guide to also understand more about Polybase at `https://docs.microsoft.com/en-us/sql/relational-databases/polybase/polybase-guide`.

© Bob Ward 2019
B. Ward, *SQL Server 2019 Revealed*, https://doi.org/10.1007/978-1-4842-5419-6_9

The History of Polybase

Around 2011, Dr. David DeWitt and his team created a new project called *Polybase* (you can see the project web site at `http://gsl.azurewebsites.net/Projects/Polybase.aspx`). His team included Rimma Nehme (now of Azure CosmosDB fame) and Alan Halverson from the Jim Gray Systems Lab for Microsoft Research. The goal of this project was to create a new way to access data in Hadoop systems without coding MapReduce jobs (you can read more about MapReduce, which is very popular with those who use Hadoop, at `https://en.wikipedia.org/wiki/MapReduce`).

I interviewed David, who now works at MIT, about the history of Polybase. I asked him why he would try and create a new way to use MapReduce. He pointed me to a blog post he and Michael Stonebraker wrote, which you can find at `https://homes.cs.washington.edu/~billhowe/mapreduce_a_major_step_backwards.html`. The post describes multiple ways MapReduce represents an inferior approach to accessing data.

David and his team subsequently created the Polybase project to use the Parallel Data Warehouse (PDW) technology at Microsoft to access "big data" in Hadoop systems. PDW, now called Analytics Platform System (APS), is the precursor to Azure SQL Data Warehouse in the cloud. As David tells it, "...we could connect PDW to HDFS and use PDW's parallel query to give our customers the ability to use standard SQL instead of MapReduce. This would give customers the ability to access both their relational data and their external tables stored in HDFS in a single query."

The team created a paper for the technology, which you can read at `http://gsl.azurewebsites.net/portals/0/users/projects/polybase/polybasesigmod2013.pdf`. The paper appeared in the proceedings of the 2013 ACM SIGMOD conference. Polybase first appeared as a feature in PDW in mid-2012 and is still there today.

Figure 9-1 represents a visual diagram of the original Polybase concept.

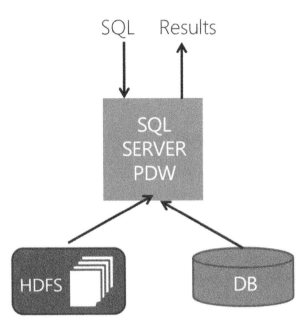

Figure 9-1. *The original Polybase concept from Jim Gray Systems Lab*

Fast forward to the development of SQL Server 2016. If Polybase can be used via SQL in PDW, why not SQL Server? In SQL Server 2016, we added the Polybase feature to access data in Hadoop systems using T-SQL. I often refer to this feature as "Polybase classic" (my term; not an official Microsoft term). You can use T-SQL to create what is called an *external table* to map over HDFS files, then query that external table like any other table. The "query" would be converted into a MapReduce Java program to run on the target Hadoop system.

I joined the engineering team right around the launch of SQL Server 2016, and I never really saw Polybase take off with our customers. I'm not sure exactly why, but part of the answer could be that customers would have to install Java – typically the Java Runtime Environment (JRE) from Oracle – on the same computer as SQL Server. It also could be that, back in 2016, SQL Server customers were just not ready to integrate with Hadoop, and Hadoop users wanted to segment themselves from relational databases.

In 2016, Microsoft acquired a company called Metanautix, which I mentioned in the opening chapter of this book. With this acquisition came ODBC technology to access data sources like SQL Server, Oracle, Teradata, and MongoDB. Folks like Travis Wright and Slava Oks saw the vision with these technologies, and so they expanded Polybase in

SQL Server 2019 to allow a user to use external tables to access not only Hadoop but also SQL Server, Oracle, Teradata, and MongoDB. And to add "icing to the cake," we added support for accessing *any data source* using an ODBC driver of your choice. I call this new capability **Polybase++** (again, this is my term, not Microsoft official).

What Is Data Virtualization?

I had not spent much time on Polybase for SQL Server 2016, but I knew the concepts. When I started pouring my time into speaking and training on SQL Server 2019, the term *Data Virtualization* (I think the first time I heard this term was from Travis Wright) was really the first time I dug more into Polybase.

Data Virtualization is defined in many ways, but you can read the "official" definition on Wikipedia at `https://en.wikipedia.org/wiki/Data_virtualization`. I like this specific sentence, where it says, "Unlike the traditional extract, transform, load ("ETL") process, the **data remains in place**, and real-time access is given to the source system for the data. This reduces the risk of data errors, of the workload moving data around that may never be used, and it does not attempt to impose a single data model on the data."

The key to Data Virtualization is the concept of *no data movement*. To be clear, "data" in this case is not to move from a source in their native format. Instead, retrieve data through a query or request it from the data source.

As part of the overall strategy for SQL Server 2019 to implement a solution for Data Virtualization, our hope and promise is that SQL Server is an excellent *center* for Data Virtualization. In other words, SQL Server 2019 can become the *data hub* for your organization.

Figure 9-2 is a slide often present to talk about the overall concept of Polybase, Data Virtualization, and SQL Server 2019.

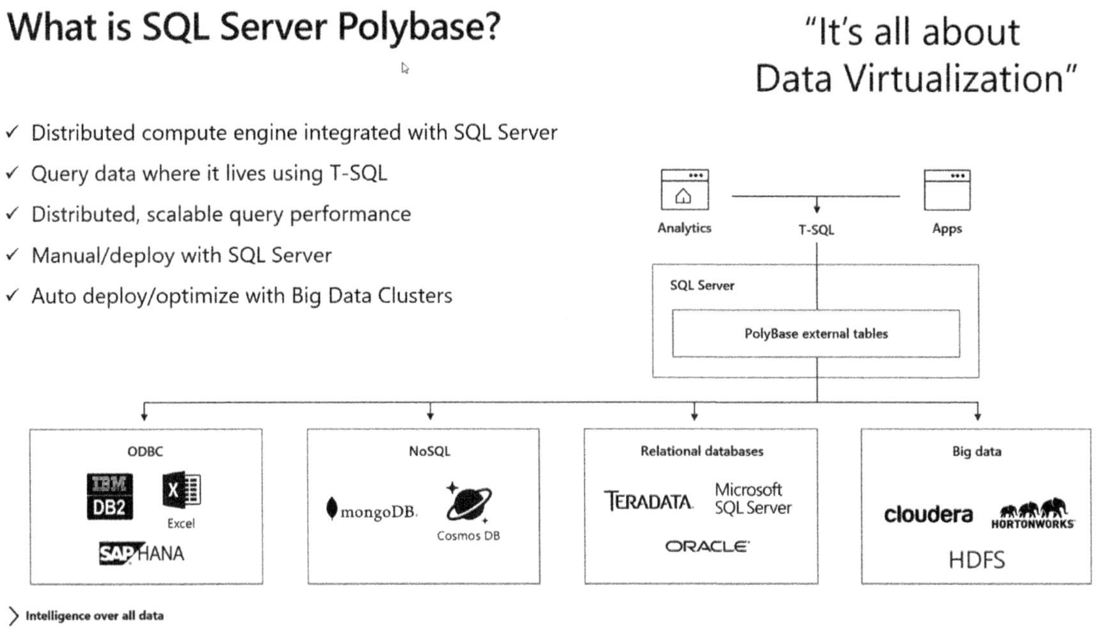

What is SQL Server Polybase?

"It's all about Data Virtualization"

✓ Distributed compute engine integrated with SQL Server

✓ Query data where it lives using T-SQL

✓ Distributed, scalable query performance

✓ Manual/deploy with SQL Server

✓ Auto deploy/optimize with Big Data Clusters

Figure 9-2. Polybase and Data Virtualization in SQL Server 2019

Look at all of these icons in the figure. With SQL Server 2019, you can run T-SQL queries against external tables based on data sources ranging from HDFS to Oracle, to CosmosDB, to SAP HANA. And here is the radical part: You can query these resources using T-SQL and join them to local SQL Server tables or to any other external table representing any of these other data sources.

On this slide, I attempt to simplify the definition of what Polybase is:

- **A distributed computing engine**

  Polybase contains software inherent to the original PDW design that integrated with SQL Server and provides its own distributed computing engine. I'll describe more about this component in the next section called "How Polybase Works."

- **Query data where it lives with T-SQL**

  This is the promise of Data Virtualization. Execute T-SQL queries to a local SQL Server and query data in other data sources without moving the data. Here is another point about Polybase for SQL Server 2019: The software required to query SQL Server, Oracle,

301

Teradata, and MongoDB is built-in to the installation of SQL Server. **No additional client software is required!**

- **Distributed, scalable query performance**

  Polybase provides more than just a method to "connect" to other data sources; linked servers can provide that. Because Polybase is an integrated distributed computing engine, it can provide scalable query performance. And a concept called scale-out groups provides the ability to distribute queries to data sources like Hadoop, SQL Server, and Oracle.

- **Manual/deploy with SQL Server**

  This sounds incredibly cool so far, so, is there a catch? Well, setting up Polybase does require some work, especially if you want to set up scale-out groups on Windows. Once you get Polybase deployed, there is not much configuration required. Setting up data source connections does require some work, as Polybase is only as good as your ability to gain access and connect to the data sources you represent with external tables.

- **Auto deploy/optimize with Big Data Clusters**

  As you will discover in Chapter 10, SQL Server Big Data Clusters will provide Data Virtualization, with Polybase deployed, and a deployed Hadoop cluster with optimized access to data in HDFS.

How Polybase Works

I often believe that understanding at some level how SQL Server capability works allows you to use it most effectively. If you have seen my talks at various conferences like the PASS Summit, you also know I have a reputation for presenting the internal aspects of SQL Server functionality. Therefore, when I was asked to present a few sessions at the SQL Bits 2019 conference in Manchester, UK, I picked Polybase as my topic. I wanted to study more about how Polybase works internally, especially how we built an architecture to access data sources like Oracle. I've had a long background in SQL Server, so was very familiar with the details of linked servers. How was Polybase different? I will talk more about a comparison of these technologies later in the chapter. A nice supplement to this chapter would be my talk at SQL Bits on this subject, which you can find at `https://sqlbits.com/Sessions/Event18/Inside_SQL_Server_2019_Polybase`.

The Polybase Workflow

Before I describe all the software components that are deployed with SQL Server to provide Polybase capabilities, I think you should know the *workflow* of using Polybase.

Figure 9-3 is a slide I often use to show the Polybase workflow in SQL Server.

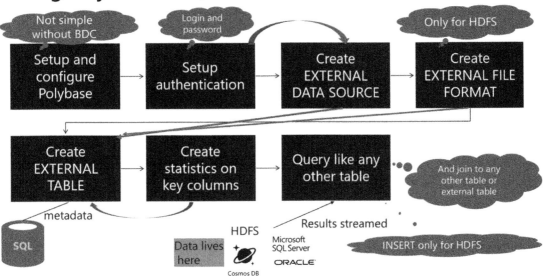

Figure 9-3. *The Polybase workflow in SQL Server*

Let me explain each of the pieces of this workflow:

Setup and configure Polybase – I'll talk more about the details of setup and configuration for Polybase in the section called "Prerequisites for the Examples." You can also read about the setup of Polybase for Windows at `https://docs.microsoft.com/en-us/sql/relational-databases/polybase/polybase-installation` and for Linux at `https://docs.microsoft.com/en-us/sql/relational-databases/polybase/polybase-linux-setup`.

Setup authentication – You must have a way to authenticate a connection to an external data source. Polybase only supports the concept of basic authentication, which means you must store some type of IDENTITY (or user) and SECRET (password or key) in SQL Server in order to access the external data source. This is an object called a *database scoped credential*, and it is encrypted with a SQL Server **MASTER KEY** object. You can read about database scoped credentials at `https://docs.microsoft.com/en-us/sql/t-sql/statements/create-database-scoped-credential-transact-sql`.

EXTERNAL DATA SOURCE – Think of an **EXTERNAL DATA SOURCE** as a T-SQL object similar to an ODBC data source. Create this one time for a data source you intend to use for one or more EXTERNAL TABLE definitions. You will see in the examples in this chapter that you will need connectivity information for an EXTERNAL DATA SOURCE. You can read about an EXTERNAL DATA SOURCE at `https://docs.microsoft.com/en-us/sql/t-sql/statements/create-external-data-source-transact-sql`. The CREDENTIAL value will be the name of the database scoped credential you created.

EXTERNAL FILE FORMAT – Relational and even noSQL data has structure, typically in the form of columns or fields. Data stored in Hadoop systems is typically semistructured. In order for SQL Server to access data in files in HDFS, you must specify a format, which is what **EXTERNAL FILE FORMAT** defines. This specification is unnecessary for data sources such as Oracle. You can read about an EXTERNAL FILE FORMAT at `https://docs.microsoft.com/en-us/sql/t-sql/statements/create-external-file-format-transact-sql`.

EXTERNAL TABLE – Think of an EXTERNAL TABLE like a virtual SQL Server table (more commonly known as a view). This means an EXTERNAL TABLE acts like a SQL Server table – metadata about the table is stored in catalog views, but the data or storage of the external table is at the data source itself. You can read about an EXTERNAL TABLE at `https://docs.microsoft.com/en-us/sql/t-sql/statements/create-external-table-transact-sql`. The DATA_SOURCE property when you create the external table will be the name of the external data source. For HDFS external tables, you will specify the external file format you created using the FILE_FORMAT property.

Statistics – To assist the query processor and the Polybase compute engine to generate an optimal query plan for external tables, you can create statistics stored in SQL Server based on columns from the external tables. You can read about creating statistics at `https://docs.microsoft.com/en-us/sql/t-sql/statements/create-statistics-transact-sql`.

Query – Once you have all these objects defined, you can run T-SQL queries against external tables, even joining them to local SQL Server tables or other external tables. The key concept is that the data lives at the external data source and is not loaded into SQL Server; only the metadata and statistics are stored in the SQL Server database. Queries against external tables are read-only except for Hadoop. SQL Server supports *ingestion* or INSERT into external tables based on Hadoop. You can read about Polybase queries at `https://docs.microsoft.com/en-us/sql/relational-databases/polybase/polybase-queries`.

SQL Server 2019 Polybase Architecture

Now that you see the objects and workflow to use Polybase for queries against external tables, let me describe the software components that power this capability before you try it out for yourself.

Note   Full credits to Stuart Padley, David Kryze, James Rowland-Jones, and UC for all the details behind the internals of Polybase which turned into the section you see in this chapter.

How External Tables Work

First, Figure 9-4 is the first visual I show when talking about how Polybase works.

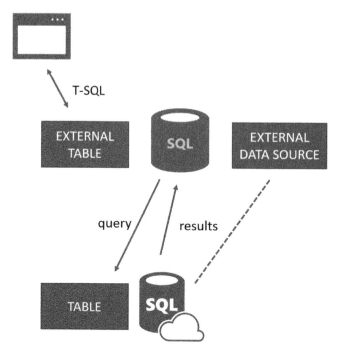

Figure 9-4. *How external tables work*

It is important to understand when using and studying Polybase that SQL Server only stores metadata for an EXTERNAL DATA SOURCE and EXTERNAL TABLE and *not the data.* Users run T-SQL queries referencing an EXTERNAL TABLE just like a SQL Server table. The EXTERNAL TABLE is mapped to an EXTERNAL DATA SOURCE for the true location of the data. SQL Server as a data hub will take the query against the EXTERNAL TABLE and submit a new query to the external data source using the driver that corresponds with that source. Results are sent back to SQL Server and eventually the original user. Another aspect of queries against external tables is the concept of *pushdown.*

Pushdown is the concept of pushing the responsibility of filtering data to an external data source. In Figure 9-4, if the external data source was Azure SQL Database and a query used a WHERE clause for query criteria, Polybase will attempt to push the query to Azure SQL Database, including the WHERE clause (it may not be an explicit WHERE clause for all data sources), so that the computation of obtaining the minimum amount of rows is done on the external data source. The opposite (and less efficient) approach would be to bring back all rows from an external table into SQL Server and let the SQL Server engine filter which rows are needed to satisfy a query. You can read more about pushdown computation with Polybase at `https://docs.microsoft.com/en-us/sql/ relational-databases/polybase/polybase-pushdown-computation`.

The Polybase Standalone Instance

Let's dig a little deeper into the architecture of Polybase using Figure 9-5.

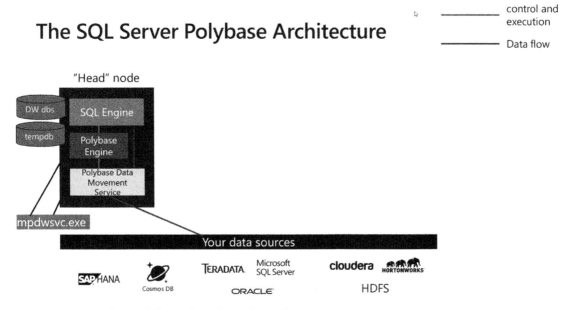

Figure 9-5. *The Polybase head node architecture*

Let me describe this figure more in the context of Windows, and then I'll discuss how we implement this on Linux.

When you deploy Polybase on Windows, you will have two choices to make:

Standalone PolyBase-enabled instance

Choose this option if you only want one SQL Server instance to be used for Polybase. All software needed for Polybase will be installed on this instance, and it will be considered the *head node.*

Use the SQL Server instance as part of a PolyBase scale-out group

Use this option to set up what is called a scale-out group. I'll describe more about a scale-out group later.

Figure 9-5 represents a standalone PolyBase-enabled instance scenario. Let me describe the components in this diagram:

Polybase Engine – The Polybase Engine is a Windows service with a program called mpdwsvc.exe. Notice in the diagram that the Polybase Engine is responsible for **control and execution**. In other words, the Polybase Engine is the coordinator for execution of external table queries. The SQL Server engine will coordinate with the Polybase Engine.

The Polybase Engine actually includes code from the Polybase functionality in PDW to support external tables. The mpdwsvc.exe is executed by the Windows Service using a parameter of **-dweng**. The communication between the Polybase Engine and SQL Server is through a local named pipe.

Polybase Data Movement Service (DMS) – Much like the name implies, the Polybase DMS is responsible for the data. This means the Polybase DMS will execute the queries against external data sources and transfer results back to the SQL Server engine. What is interesting is that the Polybase DMS is also implemented with the executable called mpdwsvc.exe but with the parameter **-dms**. On a server for the head node, you should see two processes called mpdwsvc.exe. This also means the Polybase DMS is the program that loads all the ODBC drivers or runs the Java code for MapReduce against Hadoop systems. The Polybase DMS also communicates with the SQL Server engine and the Polybase Engine over named pipes. The Polybase DMS service will stream data over the named pipe with the SQL Server engine to send back results from external data queries.

DW dbs – The Polybase feature requires its own metadata. When you install Polybase, you will find these databases installed on SQL Server: DWConfiguration, DWDiagnostics, and DWQueue. You should think of these databases as system databases for Polybase, so they need to be available for this feature to work. I won't go into the specifics of what is in each database, and we don't document these. I did find an interesting user who blogged about poking around the internals of these databases at `https://36chambers.wordpress.com/2019/04/03/polybase-revealed-the-dw-databases/`.

Tempdb – Polybase may use tempdb for intermediate query processing when executing external table queries. In addition, in order to ensure that the streaming of data is handled properly, Polybase will create tempdb tables as a "storage backing" to streaming of data (though it may never use that backing). In my use of Polybase, I have not seen significant use of tempdb; I just wanted you to be aware of tempdb usage – this way you are not surprised to see temporary table activity with Polybase.

Polybase also comes with a series of catalog views and Dynamic Management Views, and I'll use some of these in the examples in this chapter. You can see a list of these catalog views and Dynamic Management Views at `https://docs.microsoft.com/en-us/sql/relational-databases/polybase/polybase-troubleshooting`.

A Polybase Scale-Out Group

If you choose to set up a Polybase Scale-Out Group, multiple SQL Server instances can be used for query processing with scale out. See Figure 9-6 for a scale-out group configuration.

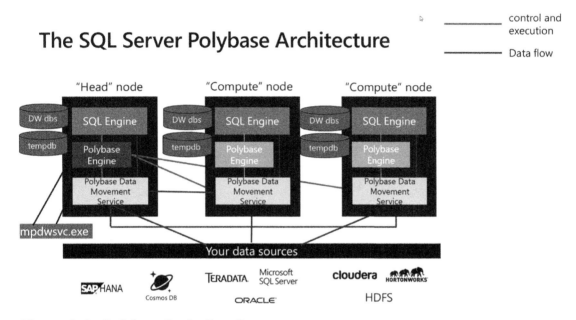

Figure 9-6. Polybase Scale-Out Groups

With Polybase Scale-Out Groups, you can enable Polybase on other SQL Server instances to be used for scale-out query processing. The other SQL Server instances that enable Polybase are called *Compute nodes*. Notice on compute nodes the Polybase Engine is not active. On Windows, the Polybase Engine service is installed, but it is disabled and not needed. The Polybase Engine on the head node does all the coordination across all nodes, while Polybase DMS services perform all the data exchange on each node. The reason we install the Polybase Engine on all nodes is so that a Compute node can become a head node if needed (e.g., if the current head node had a problem).

Scale-out groups can be most effective when SQL Server decides that using multiple instances can speed up a query to an external table. This could be very powerful for Hadoop systems, and scale-out groups were built with distributed Hadoop systems in mind. For other data sources, like SQL Server or Oracle, Polybase can detect partitions on these sources and use the scale-out group to query each partition on the target.

We call this capability *scale-out reads*, which you can read about at `https://docs.microsoft.com/en-us/sql/relational-databases/polybase/polybase-scale-out-groups?view=sql-server-ver15#scale-out-reads`.

Query Processing and Polybase

One of the great innovations of Polybase is that querying external tables is integrated into the SQL Server query processor. This means the SQL Server query processor *understands* when it is working with an external table and builds the right execution details to submit to the Polybase Engine so that operations like pushdown can be supported.

Later in the chapter, I'll show an example of what a remote query operator looks like for an external table query in the SQL Server engine.

How Does It Work on Linux?

SQL Server 2019 on Linux only supports a standalone Polybase instance (we will support a scale-out group concept with SQL Server Big Data Clusters, which you will read about in Chapter 10). In addition, Polybase for SQL Server 2019 on Linux does not support the generic ODBC connector for data sources.

Therefore, the architecture of Polybase is for the Polybase Engine and Polybase Data Movement Service to be implemented in the sqlservr process on Linux using the SQLPAL (for more details on the SQLPAL, see Chapter 6).

At the time I was writing this chapter, we were winding down the release of SQL Server, but still had not shipped Hadoop external table capabilities with SQL Server on Linux (outside of SQL Server Big Data Clusters). I expect this feature to make the final release of SQL Server 2019, but the concepts are the same as with Windows. It is possible we will have a separate Linux package for this capability, but it should be in the documentation at `https://docs.microsoft.com/en-us/sql/relational-databases/polybase/polybase-linux-setup`.

How Is This Different Than Azure?

Polybase exists now as a feature in SQL Server, Azure SQL Data Warehouse, and Analytics Platform System (APS, formerly Parallel Data Warehouse). However, the capabilities provided by each are different.

> **Note**   An EXTERNAL TABLE object does exist in Azure SQL Database, but it is not the Polybase feature per se (as of the release of SQL Server 2019). An external table in Azure SQL Database is used to support elastic queries. You can read more about elastic queries at `https://docs.microsoft.com/en-us/azure/sql-database/sql-database-elastic-query-getting-started`.

Polybase for Azure SQL Data Warehouse is all about using external tables for access to Hadoop or HDFS with sources like Azure Blob Storage or Azure Data Lake. Sources like SQL Server, Oracle, and so on are not supported for Azure SQL Data Warehouse. You can read more about Polybase with Azure SQL Data Warehouse at `https://docs.microsoft.com/en-us/sql/t-sql/statements/create-external-data-source-transact-sql?view=azure-sqldw-latest`.

Polybase for APS is similar to Azure SQL Data Warehouse, but is designed more for providing access to "on-premise" Hadoop systems. You can read about Polybase for APS at `https://docs.microsoft.com/en-us/sql/t-sql/statements/create-external-table-transact-sql?view=aps-pdw-2016-au7`.

Prerequisites for the Examples

Let's talk about some examples in the rest of the chapter. First, I'll give you some tips on deploying and configuring Polybase, and then some guidance on using the examples.

Setting Up and Enabling Polybase

To install Polybase for Windows, you can follow the steps in the documentation at `https://docs.microsoft.com/en-us/sql/relational-databases/polybase/polybase-installation`. The steps are very straightforward when choosing a standalone Polybase instance. One choice you do have to make is whether you want to use the **Java connector for HDFS**. If you do make this choice to support external tables for HDFS, you will have a choice to use the default Open Java we provide with SQL Server 2019 or install your own. The Open Java we provide is based on Zulu Java, which you can read about at `https://cloudblogs.microsoft.com/sqlserver/2019/07/24/free-supported-java-in-sql-server-2019-is-now-available/`).

Once you install Polybase on Windows, we will install a series of ODBC drivers (which we place in the **binn\Polybase\ODBC Drivers** directory). These drivers provide support for the built-in connectors to SQL Server, Oracle, Teradata, and MongoDB.

Once you install the Polybase feature, you must enable the feature with sp_configure as documented at `https://docs.microsoft.com/en-us/sql/relational-databases/polybase/polybase-installation?view=sql-server-ver15#enable`.

For SQL Server on Linux, we provide a separate package for Polybase, which you can read about how to configure and use at `https://docs.microsoft.com/en-us/sql/relational-databases/polybase/polybase-linux-setup`.

For scale-out groups, the process to set up gets very interesting. Since scale-out groups are only supported on Windows at this time, that is the only configuration you need to worry about for SQL Server 2019.

My experience with scale-out group deployment was fairly difficult. You can read all the steps in our documentation at `https://docs.microsoft.com/en-us/sql/relational-databases/polybase/configure-scale-out-groups-windows?view=sql-server-ver15`. Let me give you some initial thoughts before you go down this path:

- You will need a Windows domain, so if you don't have a domain controller, you will need to set one up.

- All the Windows services for the Polybase Scale-Out Group must be using the same domain service account. You have to configure this through setup or using the SQL Server Configuration Manager.

- You have to make some choices initially on head node and compute node. When you first install Polybase on all nodes using setup and choose the option **Use the SQL Server instance as part of a PolyBase scale-out group**, all nodes are candidates to be the head node. To get Polybase to work properly, you need to choose one of your computers as the head node. Then for the other nodes, you need to run a stored procedure to configure them as compute nodes, listing the name of the head node server and port (pay attention to the port you picked during setup, because you will need it here). The process to join as a compute node is documented at `https://docs.microsoft.com/en-us/sql/relational-databases/polybase/configure-scale-out-groups-windows?view=sql-server-ver15#add-other-sql-server-instances-as-compute-nodes`.

- You need to enable Polybase with sp_configure on all nodes and restart SQL Server.

- You also need to restart all Polybase services on all nodes. In fact, if the stored procedure doesn't do this automatically, you need to stop the Polybase Engine on the compute nodes. If all works well, the Polybase Engine service will be disabled on the compute nodes, but you should double-check this.

- Query the DMV **dm_exec_compute_nodes** to make sure all the nodes are the right status of HEAD or COMPUTE. You can read more about this DMV at `https://docs.microsoft.com/en-us/sql/relational-databases/system-dynamic-management-views/sys-dm-exec-compute-nodes-transact-sql`.

Using the Examples

Consider a possible scenario for the WideWorldImporters company in Figure 9-7.

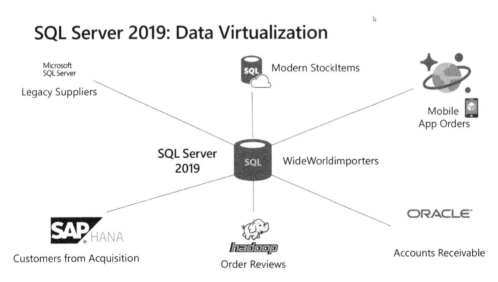

Figure 9-7. *The SQL Server data hub*

In this example, the WideWorldImporters (WWI) company uses SQL Server 2019, but wants to access data in these data sources:

SQL Server 2008R2 – The company has an older SQL Server system that stores an archive of suppliers. They don't want to touch this system but want to access this supplier information.

Azure SQL Database – A team in the company is looking to move to the cloud and build a new StockItems database using Azure. Teams in WWI want to see and join this StockItem data with existing ones in the SQL Server 2019 database without disrupting the new team's work.

Azure CosmosDB – Another team is piloting a mobile application for Orders and is experimenting with Azure CosmosDB. The WWI team wants to be able to look at these orders and join with data associated with the orders in the local database.

Oracle – The accounting software for the WWI is in Oracle. While WWI is considered a migration of this database to SQL Server, it is taking time for the migration project. In the meantime, the WWI knows that some data in the SQL Server database references data in Accounts Receivable. If they can get the right reasonable access to Oracle, they would like to join local SQL Server data with the Accounts Receivable data in Oracle, until the migration is complete.

Hadoop – A team at WWI is building a rating system on the company web site for customers to review the order experience. To accelerate the project, the development team is storing the order reviews in semistructured format using Azure Blob Storage. Teams at WWI want to run analytics on this data and join with local data in SQL Server.

SAP HANA – WWI recently acquired another company, Vandelay Industries (I was inspired by the fictional company from *Seinfeld*. See `https://seinfeld.fandom.com/wiki/Vandelay_Industries`). This company has data on their customers in SAP HANA. While the WWI team devises a migration strategy, they want to run analytics on these customers without having to move the data.

All of these scenarios are possible with Polybase in SQL Server 2019 and external tables. In fact, there is an example of each one of these in your examples in the **ch9_data_virtualization\sqldatahub** folder.

Using External Tables

Before I walk through some of the examples from the **sqldatahub** folder, let me explain the basic template you will consistently find in these examples. This template follows the general workflow of external tables, which I described in the section called "The Polybase Workflow." All Polybase objects are in the scope of a user database.

1. Create a MASTER KEY in the database.

2. Create a DATABASE SCOPED CREDENTIAL for authentication to the external data source.

3. Create an EXTERNAL DATA SOURCE to show the location of the data source. The CREDENTIAL property will be the name of the database scoped credential.

4. Create an EXTERNAL FILE FORMAT for HDFS data.

5. Create an EXTERNAL TABLE to map to the external data source target tables. The DATA_SOURCE property will be the name of the external data source. The FILE_FORMAT property (for HDFS only) will be the name of the external file format object.

6. Create local statistics on columns for the external table.

7. Query the EXTERNAL TABLE sometimes joining the table to local SQL Server tables or other external tables.

There is an excellent reference for all the T-SQL statement involved in creating Polybase objects at `https://docs.microsoft.com/en-us/sql/relational-databases/polybase/polybase-t-sql-objects`.

Tools and External Tables

Before I walk through the example scripts for the sqldatahub, you should know about tools support for external data sources and external tables.

SQL Server Management Studio (SSMS) supports creating external data sources and external tables through SSMS templates. Figure 9-8 shows an example of using SSMS to create an external data source.

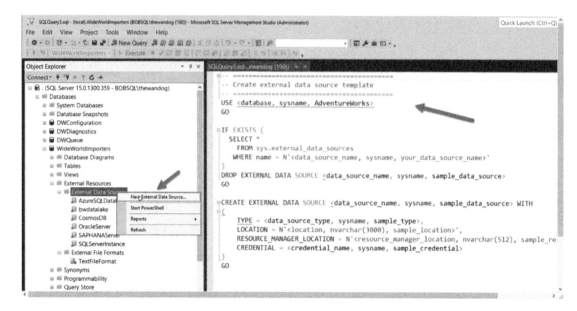

Figure 9-8. *Using an SSMS template to create an external data source*

The same concept applies to external tables.

Once you create external data sources and tables, you can use SSMS Object Explorer to browse these resources. Figure 9-9 shows an example of external data sources and file formats created in the WideWorldImporters database.

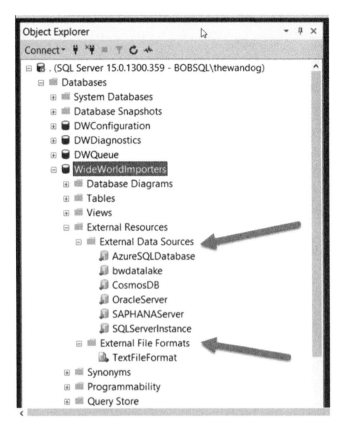

Figure 9-9. SSMS Object Explorer browsing external data sources and file formats

Azure Data Studio (ADS) also supports an External Table Wizard for SQL Server and Oracle data sources to walk you through the process of creating new external tables. You can read about this capability at `https://docs.microsoft.com/en-us/sql/relational-databases/polybase/data-virtualization`.

I'll walk you through the steps for setting up an external table for Azure SQL Database. For other sqldatahub examples, I'll point you to the script examples and explain a few points about each scenario.

Using an External Table with Azure SQL Database

One of the built-in connectors for SQL Server provides access to data sources for SQL Server, Azure SQL Database, and Azure SQL Data Warehouse.

I've provided example scripts based on the template steps I've described in the **ch9_data_virtualization\sqldatahub\azuredb** folder. I've provided both a T-SQL Notebook and T-SQL script to create and query external tables.

317

In order to use these scripts, the first thing you need to do is provision and get access to an Azure SQL Database. Use the statements in the **createazuredbtable.sql** script against your Azure SQL Database.

Once you have this set up, let's walk through each step and the results you should expect using the **azuredbexternaltable.sql** T-SQL script:

1. Run **Step 1** from the T-SQL script to change database context and create a master key to encrypt the database scoped credential:

```
-- Step 1: Create a master key to encrypt the database credential
USE [WideWorldImporters]
GO
CREATE MASTER KEY ENCRYPTION BY PASSWORD = 'SOme!nfo'
GO
```

2. Run **Step 2** to create a database scoped credential protected by the master key. You need to supply the login and password of the server for the Azure SQL Database you created:

```
-- Step 2: Create a database credential that stores the login and
password to the Azure SQL Server Database
-- IDENTITY = login
-- SECRET = password
CREATE DATABASE SCOPED CREDENTIAL AzureSQLDatabaseCredentials
WITH IDENTITY = '<login>', SECRET = '<password>'
GO
```

3. Run **Step 3** to create an external data source using the database scoped credential for authentication as the CREDENTIAL:

```
-- Step 3: Create an external data source
-- sqlserver is a keyword meaning the data source is a SQL Server,
Azure SQL Database, or Azure SQL Data Warehouse
-- The name after :// is the Azure SQL Server Database server.
Your SQL Server must be on the same vnet as the Azure SQL Server
Database or must pass through its firewall rules
CREATE EXTERNAL DATA SOURCE AzureSQLDatabase
```

```
WITH (
LOCATION = 'sqlserver://<azure sql database server URI>',
PUSHDOWN = ON,
CREDENTIAL = AzureSQLDatabaseCredentials
)
GO
```

There are a few things to notice about this script. The LOCATION
syntax includes a <type>:<connection information>, where the
type has these possible values:

- sqlserver

- oracle

- teradata

- mongodb

- obdc

The type will indicate to SQL Server which ODBC driver to use
for the external data source. For SQL Server, the connection
information for Azure SQL Database should be the URL for the
server (e.g., <server>..database.windows.net).

When you successfully create the external data source, you can see
a list of created sources using the **external_data_sources** catalog
view in the context of your user database.

Tip   Unfortunately, the external data source can be created without validating a
connection to the data source. If you get the name of the connection information
wrong, you won't know until you try to create the external table. The same issue
applies for the database scoped credential. If you don't supply the correct login and
password, you won't know this until you try to create an external table.

---

4. Run **Step 4** of the script to create a schema to hold external table objects. This is not required, but I like to use schemas to help organize objects, which also makes it very convenient for security purposes:

```
-- Step 4: Create a schema in the WideWorldImporters for the
external table
CREATE SCHEMA azuresqldb
GO
```

5. Run **Step 5** to create the external table using the external data source as specified in the DATA_SOURCE property:

```
-- Step 5: Create the EXTERNAL TABLE
-- Each column must match the column in the remote table
-- Notice the character columns use a collation that is compatible
with the target table
-- The WITH clause includes the name of the remote [database].
[schema].[table] and the external database source
CREATE EXTERNAL TABLE azuresqldb.ModernStockItems
(
        [StockItemID] [int] NOT NULL,
        [StockItemName] [nvarchar](100) COLLATE Latin1_General_100_
        CI_AS NOT NULL,
        [SupplierID] [int] NOT NULL,
        [ColorID] [int] NULL,
        [UnitPackageID] [int] NOT NULL,
        [OuterPackageID] [int] NOT NULL,
        [Brand] [nvarchar](50) COLLATE Latin1_General_100_CI_AS NULL,
        [Size] [nvarchar](20) COLLATE Latin1_General_100_CI_AS NULL,
        [LeadTimeDays] [int] NOT NULL,
        [QuantityPerOuter] [int] NOT NULL,
        [IsChillerStock] [bit] NOT NULL,
        [Barcode] [nvarchar](50) COLLATE Latin1_General_100_CI_AS NULL,
        [TaxRate] [decimal](18, 3) NOT NULL,
        [UnitPrice] [decimal](18, 2) NOT NULL,
        [RecommendedRetailPrice] [decimal](18, 2) NULL,
```

```
        [TypicalWeightPerUnit] [decimal](18, 3) NOT NULL,
        [LastEditedBy] [int] NOT NULL
)
 WITH (
 LOCATION='wwiazure.dbo.ModernStockItems',
 DATA_SOURCE=AzureSQLDatabase
)
GO
```

This is an important piece of the Polybase scenario, so I'll point out a few details:

- The number, names, and data types must match exact with the external data source table, but you can use any name you want on the SQL side both for the column names and the name of the table itself.

- Type mapping can be tricky. We have documentation to help you with defining SQL Server types to match up with corresponding external data source types at `https://docs.microsoft.com/en-us/sql/relational-databases/polybase/polybase-type-mapping`.

- The LOCATION syntax for the external table is how you map the external data source object. Each data source has a LOCATION that can be different to identify the data source object. In the case of SQL Server or Azure SQL Database, you should reference the table using the "three-part" convention of <database>.<schema>.<tablename>.

- Verification is performed when trying to create the external table for proper column matching, type mapping, and the use of any restricted types (I'll mention restrictions in the section later in the chapter called "Restrictions and Limitations").

Once created, you can see a list of external tables using the catalog view **sys.external_tables**. The **sys.objects** catalog view lists an external table with a type of USER_TABLE. The **sys.tables** catalog view has a column you can use, **is_external**, to identify which tables are external tables.

6. Run **Step 6** to create local statistics on key columns from the external table. This is not required, but recommended to help the query processor make smart decisions to support operations like pushdown computation:

```
-- Step 6: Create local statistics on columns you will use for
filters
CREATE STATISTICS ModernStockItemsStats ON azuresqldb.
ModernStockItems ([StockItemID]) WITH FULLSCAN
GO
```

7. Run **Step 7** to see a simple example of scanning all rows in an external table. In this example, there should only be one row returned if the query was successful:

```
-- Step 7: Just try to scan the remote table
SELECT * FROM azuresqldb.ModernStockItems
GO
```

Remote operators are built into the query processor to support queries against external tables using the Polybase service. Figure 9-10 shows an Actual Execution Plan for the query in Step 7, including the details of the remote operator.

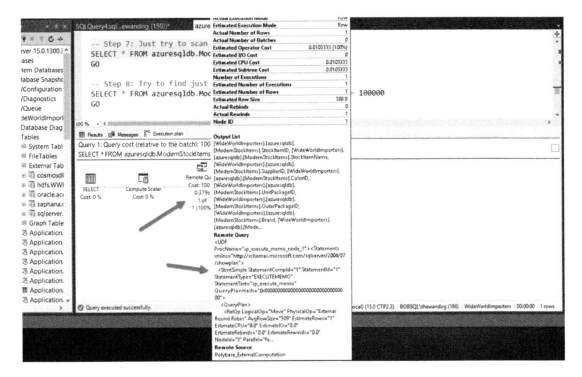

Figure 9-10. *The remote operator for external tables*

Polybase also comes with a series of Dynamic Management
Views that can be used to look at the execution of queries against
external tables.

sys.dm_exec_distributed_requests – Much like sys.dm_exec_
requests you can find out queries specific to Polybase. What is
nice about this DMV is that it holds the history of recent queries
and not just the active ones. The value in the **execution_id**
column is the key to use other DMVs to dig deeper into query
execution.

sysdm_exec_distributed_request_steps – This DMV will take the
execution_id from sys.dm_exec_distributed_requests and let you
look at specific steps in the execution of Polybase to process the
query against the external table. For an execution_id, each step
has a **step_index** value.

sys.dm_exec_distributed_sql_requests – This DMV shows more details for each step_index in sys.dm_exec_distributed_steps, including what compute node is executing the query (it could be the head and/or compute nodes for a scale-out query).

dm_exec_dms_workers – This DMV provides more details about execution with the Polybase Data Movement Service (DMS) for a specific execution_id and step_index. This DMV is important to see details of the connection to an external data source via the ODBC drivers, including possible error information.

8. Run **Step 8** to use a WHERE clause to filter results (and possibly use pushdown to the external data source):

```
-- Step 8: Try to find just a specific StockItemID
SELECT * FROM azuresqldb.ModernStockItems WHERE StockItemID = 100000
GO
```

9. Run **Step 9** to find all stockitems both on SQL Server 2019 and Azure SQL Database using a UNION:

```
-- Step 9: Use a UNION to find all stockitems for a specific
supplier both locally and in the Azure table
SELECT msi.StockItemName, msi.Brand, c.ColorName
FROM azuresqldb.ModernStockItems msi
JOIN [Purchasing].[Suppliers] s
ON msi.SupplierID = s.SupplierID
and s.SupplierName = 'Graphic Design Institute'
JOIN [Warehouse].[Colors] c
ON msi.ColorID = c.ColorID
UNION
SELECT si.StockItemName, si.Brand, c.ColorName
FROM [Warehouse].[StockItems] si
JOIN [Purchasing].[Suppliers] s
ON si.SupplierID = s.SupplierID
and s.SupplierName = 'Graphic Design Institute'
```

```
JOIN [Warehouse].[Colors] c
ON si.ColorID = c.ColorID
GO
```

The first part of the UNION involves a join between the external table and a local SQL Server table.

You have seen an example of using an external table for Data Virtualization with Azure SQL Database using the built-in connector for SQL Server. Read on for some information about the other examples in the sqldatahub folder.

Using Built-in Connectors for External Tables

These are the other examples which use the built-in connectors for external tables. Each example has a readme.md file with tips on setting up the external data source and scripts to build the data source object and populate data. They all follow the same template as the example for Azure SQL Database.

- **ch9_data_virtualization\sqldatahub\cosmosdb** – Use this for an example of using the MongoDB connector with Azure CosmosDB.

- **ch9_data_virtualization\sqldatahub\oracle** – Use this for an example of using the Oracle connector.

Tip   One issue that I ran into is that the value for the LOCATION property for the EXTERNAL TABLE for Oracle is case sensitive.

- **ch9_data_virtualization\sqldatahub\sql2008r2** – Use this for an example of using the SQL Server connector to an older version of SQL Server.

Note   This example requires a workaround for SQL Server 2008R2 which was not addressed at the time I wrote this chapter. As we were getting close to release, it was not clear how far back we would support SQL Server versions, since 2008R2 is out of support.

Using an External Table with HDFS

An example of using Polybase with HDFS and Azure Blob Storage can be found in the **ch9_data_virtualization\sqldatahub\hdfs** directory. The readme.md file included provides more information on how to set this up and how to use the example.

One big difference with external data sources with HDFS is the use of the LOCATION property with the external data source and the use of the TYPE property.

Here is an example of the T-SQL statement to create the external data source from the example:

```
CREATE EXTERNAL DATA SOURCE bwdatalake with (
    TYPE = HADOOP,
    LOCATION ='wasbs://<container>@<azure storage account name>',
    CREDENTIAL = AzureStorageCredential
)
GO
```

Unlike the other examples, a TYPE field is needed for HADOOP. In addition, the LOCATION property doesn't have a <type> like sqlserver. This is because the TYPE = HADOOP tells SQL Server the type of connector to use for HDFS.

Using External Tables with ODBC Connectors

The final example is for an external table for SAP HANA using the ODBC connector. Note that this example only works for SQL Server 2019 on Windows. You can find this example in the **ch9_data_virtualization\sqldatahub\saphana** directory.

In this example, the data source is different, as it requires the ODBC data source and connection string details. Here is the external data source creation for this example:

```
CREATE EXTERNAL DATA SOURCE SAPHANAServer
WITH (
LOCATION = 'odbc://<datasource>',
CONNECTION_OPTIONS = 'Driver={HDBODBC};ServerNode=<server>:<port>',
PUSHDOWN = ON,
CREDENTIAL = SAPHANACredentials
)
GO
```

> **Tip**   Here is an important tip for using the ODBC data connector with scale-out groups, because it caused me issues when I was first setting up these scenarios. You must install the ODBC driver you are using on each node of the scale-out group. If you don't, you may get intermittent errors when executing queries. This is because when you have a scale-out group, it is possible for any of the nodes to be used to execute the queries against the external data source, even if it is not a scale-out ready query.

We also have documentation to guide you with ODBC connectors at `https://docs.microsoft.com/en-us/sql/relational-databases/polybase/polybase-configure-odbc-generic`. I should tell you that ODBC connectors open up some interesting possibilities to use SQL Server as a data hub. I had one customer at a big event ask me about using Polybase with Office 365. I didn't know the answer, and wondered, "Is there an ODBC Driver for O365?" Turns out there is at `https://marketplace.visualstudio.com/items?itemName=CDATASOFTWARE.Office365ODBCDriver`. Stand back. Maybe you might see me one day creating a demo of SQL Server running queries against my Office mail!

Considerations for External Tables

Now that you have seen how Polybase works and gone through some examples, there are a few areas to consider when deciding whether you should use Polybase with SQL Server 2019.

A New Semantic Layer

I borrowed this concept from my colleague Travis Wright. The idea is that Polybase allows you to define objects by naming conventions under your control vs. having to use the naming conventions of objects from external data sources.

In other words, you can use the semantics of the policies and procedures you use with SQL Server. When you build external tables, you use SQL Server conventions, schemas, and securables under your control. Combine this with the ability to join with local SQL Server tables, use UNION to combine with local tables, and then create views on top of these constructs.

Also remember that Polybase is defined at the user database level, so all objects are secured and controlled by the owner of the user database.

External Tables vs. Linked Servers

One of the most frequent questions I get on Polybase and external tables is if they are different from linked servers, which have been in the product since SQL Server 7.0.

We have built a nice comparison of the technologies in our documentation at `https://docs.microsoft.com/en-us/sql/relational-databases/polybase/polybase-faq?view=sql-server-ver15#polybase-vs-linked-servers`.

The most noticeable difference is that linked servers are defined at the instance level, and use OLE-DB to access data from the other data source. Polybase is defined at the user database level and uses ODBC to access external data.

Restrictions and Limitations

The number one restriction that you need to know is that Polybase is, for the most part, a read-only solution (the exception is that you can use INSERT statements with external tables based on HDFS).

I also ran into a few problems with supported data types in SQL Server for an external table. The following data types are not supported with an EXTERNAL TABLE in SQL Server 2019:

- VARCHAR(MAX)

- GEOGRAPHY

- Computed Columns

- JSON

Summary

With the addition of new built-in connectors and support for ODBC, I believe Polybase will gain more adoption than when it was first released in SQL Server 2016. The possibility of now accessing and querying data to many different data sources without moving the data is compelling. In fact, even since I've presented the SQL Server 2019 story since September of 2019, this is one of the most asked about features of the new release from customers. The fact that you can query Oracle data through SQL Server and not have to install any special software on the SQL Server has opened up some eyes. It is possible for Polybase to become part of a *migration strategy from Oracle to SQL Server*. Take a look at this recording of a session I did with my colleague Amit Banerjee at Microsoft Ignite in 2019, where Amit shows how to use Polybase with SQL Server 2019 for an incremental migration strategy from Oracle to SQL Server (`https://myignite. techcommunity.microsoft.com/sessions/65955`).

It is important that you have read this chapter before moving to Chapter 10. That is because in Chapter 10 I will discuss a new solution with SQL Server 2019 that will involve the concept of Data Virtualization and Polybase called SQL Server Big Data Clusters.

CHAPTER 10

SQL Server Big Data Clusters

If you remember back to Chapter 1, I showed the key major new capabilities of SQL Server 2019. Figure 10-1 shows the first major feature at the top left-hand corner from Figure 1-3 in that chapter.

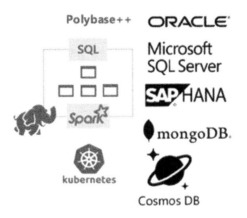

Figure 10-1. *Intelligence over all your data*

A more accurate representation of this infographic is *Intelligence over all your data*. This is because the functionality behind Figure 10-1 is more than just Polybase++. You will learn more about what I mean by Intelligence over all your data as you read through this chapter.

Figure 10-1 represents in a nutshell what is behind **SQL Server Big Data Clusters (BDC)**, but it can't possibly show their full potential. What started as Project Aris, which I described in Chapter 1, has become a *product within a product* and one of the most compelling stories of SQL Server 2019.

© Bob Ward 2019
B. Ward, *SQL Server 2019 Revealed*, https://doi.org/10.1007/978-1-4842-5419-6_10

Since I started in Chapter 1 by talking about Project Aris and this infographic in Figure 10-1, why is SQL Server Big Data Clusters way back in Chapter 10?

When I was planning this book, I originally had BDC as the first chapter, and the lead story to start off with a bang! However, as I thought more about how the book would play out, leaving this as one of the last chapters made sense for the following reasons:

- I wanted you to learn the fundamentals of SQL Server 2019 on Linux, Containers, Kubernetes, and Polybase to help you understand BDC. This is why those topics landed in Chapters 6, 7, 8, and 9.

- You will see that part of BDC is a **SQL Server Master Instance**. When you see the SQL Server Master Instance, I wanted you to already be familiar with what other core capabilities in SQL Server 2019 come with that component of BDC.

- BDC was a major effort and took many team members to design, build, and code. Therefore, it was the largest component of SQL Server 2019 to become fully functional during our CTP builds and preview releases. I wanted to wait as close as possible to the completion of the book to give you the most up-to-date and accurate information about BDC, what you can use it for, and how it works.

In this chapter, you are going to learn why BDC solves some interesting challenges for today's data professional:

- As I described in Chapter 9 on Polybase, data professionals need to access data sources in their organization outside of SQL Server. They would like to be able to access data from a variety of sources *with little or no data movement.*

- Many data professionals are looking into investing in *Big Data.* I'll talk more about some crisp details around the term Big Data in the next section, but when this term comes up, it usually involves a system powered by *Hadoop.*

- Some organizations have never invested in Hadoop, so would like guidance or even automation to deploy a Hadoop system to store unstructured or semistructured data. This data is usually *high-volume data*, while data stored in their SQL Server is considered *high-value data.*

- Furthermore, many organizations need more rigor around securing and managing a Hadoop system, much like they do with SQL Server today. They would like a complete ecosystem to build a *data lake* that is easily deployable, secure, and scalable and leverages the best of modern technology for both SQL Server and Big Data.

- Organizations want to invest more with Machine Learning (ML) and want to build and deploy ML applications that are scalable and secure and run close to the data sources that power the ML models. What I've heard customers say is that they want an *end-to-end Machine Learning platform*.

Figure 10-2 is a visual we have used to talk about the three major solution areas that Big Data Clusters attempt to solve.

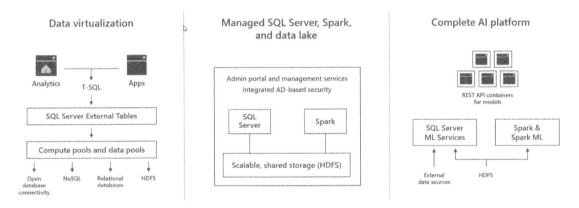

Figure 10-2. *Big Data Cluster solutions*

In this chapter, I intend to answer the following questions:

- **Why** did we call it Big Data Clusters?

- **What** functionality do you get when you deploy a Big Data Cluster?

- How do you **deploy** a Big Data Cluster?

- What is the architecture of Big Data Clusters, and **how does it work?**

- How do you **use** a Big Data Cluster?

- How do you use **Machine Learning** with a Big Data Cluster?

- How do you **manage and monitor** a Big Data Cluster?

This seems like enough for a book on its own, so I can't deep dive on everything. However, I'll explore some details that are not in the documentation but that I think you should know. I'll also give examples and tips from my perspective on why BDC is an important solution for SQL Server 2019.

Note   In this chapter, I will sometimes refer to statements or samples in a workshop produced by my colleague Buck Woody called **Workshop: SQL Server Big Data Clusters – Architecture**, which you can find at `https://github.com/Microsoft/sqlworkshops/tree/master/sqlserver2019bigdataclusters`. It is an excellent resource to supplement this chapter.

Why Big Data Clusters?

I'm sure our team has many reasons why they would say we called this solution SQL Server Big Data Clusters. For me, it is a very simple answer. We are deploying and combining three major technologies with this solution:

- **SQL Server** – SQL Server will be the hub for accessing data in the cluster. This is the full SQL Server product, with everything I've described in the book, running in a container based on a Linux OS image.

- **Big Data** – We are deploying Big Data technologies for you, like HDFS and Spark.

- **Cluster** – We use a Kubernetes cluster to deploy and run different containers to provide a complete end-to-end system.

As you read more over the next few sections of this chapter, the details will come together for you on how we are integrating these technologies.

I think it is important to describe my perspective on the term *Big Data* and why we felt it was important to include this in the solution for Big Data Clusters. My colleague Buck Woody at Microsoft wrote an excellent blog post on the topic of Big Data at `https://buckwoody.wordpress.com/2019/08/26/big-data-is-just-data/`.

I love this description of the term Big Data, "Big Data is any data you can't process in the time you want with the systems you have." What this means for SQL Server is that you may have data in your organization that is perhaps not the right fit for storing in a relational database management system (RDBMS) like SQL Server. There could be all types of reasons for this, including size, structure, data origin, and complexity, to transform into relational tables.

It was interesting to read the origins of the original Hadoop project. The founders of Hadoop originally wanted a file system to store massive amounts of data in a distributed fashion across a cluster of commodity hardware. They called this the Google File System (it is really a more complex story; you can read more about the history of Hadoop at `https://en.wikipedia.org/wiki/Apache_Hadoop#History`). The goal of that original project was to solve the problem Buck defined for the term Big Data.

With SQL Server Big Data Clusters, what we are really providing in my opinion is a *single system* that gives you *both worlds* of data storage and processing. We deploy SQL Server for you to store and access data stored in a relational format with tables. And we deploy a Hadoop distributed file system (HDFS) cluster, allowing you to store data in an unstructured or semistructured file format. The key ingredient that makes this system special is that they are *integrated*. With the help of Polybase, you can join tables from SQL Server (and other sources like Oracle, Teradata, and MongoDB) with HDFS files, in a seamless method and with scalable performance.

There is more to this story; in the next section, I'll describe exactly what value you get by deploying a SQL Server Big Data Cluster.

What Comes with Big Data Clusters?

I've described a SQL Server Big Data Cluster (BDC) as a product within a product. This is because when you deploy BDC, you get a wealth of valuable functionality including the following.

SQL Server 2019

BDC comes with a *complete* SQL Server 2019 instance running in a container using a Linux OS image. This means that all of the capabilities of SQL Server 2019 for Linux also come with BDC. This will include Active Directory authentication and High Availability with Always On Availability Groups.

Polybase

The Polybase feature for SQL Server with BDC is automatically installed and enabled. This means you get built-in connectors for SQL Server, Oracle, Teradata, MongoDB, and Hadoop. In addition, BDC comes with *special connectors* to access HDFS files and data caches within the cluster in an optimized method. Furthermore, even though SQL Server 2019 on Linux doesn't support Polybase Scale-Out Groups, BDC comes with an implementation of Polybase Scale-Out Groups using a concept called a *Compute Pool*, which I'll talk about more in the section "Big Data Cluster Architecture."

Hadoop Distributed File System (HDFS)

BDC will deploy a HDFS storage cluster using open source Apache Hadoop. You will have several different ways you can access files stored in the HDFS cluster in BDC, including Polybase through SQL Server. We also provide a method for you to mount your own external HDFS storage into the local HDFS storage in BDC, a concept we call *HDFS Tiering*.

Spark

BDC installs Apache Spark to provide another method to analyze and process data. I like Buck Woody's definition of Spark as, "Apache Spark is an analytics engine for processing large-scale data. It can be used with data stored in HDFS and has connectors to work with data in SQL Server as well." You will interact with Spark through Spark Jobs for data within the cluster. I'll talk more about using Spark with BDC in the section titled "Using Spark."

Data Cache

Our documentation says we provide a *data mart*, and I suppose that term is technically true. For me, what we are really providing is a *data cache*. I call it a data cache because we provide a special set of SQL Server instances optimized to store results from queries against Polybase external data sources. Think of the scenario where you want to *store a set of results*, refreshed weekly, for reporting purposes. Those results could come from Polybase queries using many different data sources, and our data cache in BDC is a perfect solution for that. We implement the data cache in a component called the *Data Pool*, which I'll explain in more detail in the section "Big Data Cluster Architecture."

Tools and Services

In order to help you deploy, use, and manage BDC, we have a set of tools available as part of the solution. You will find the Azure Data Studio tool, which you have used in this book, will be a key part of the overall BDC tool solution, including support for *Notebooks*. In addition, we deploy a set of containers as *services* to help coordinate and manage BDC. The documentation calls these services the *Controller*, and you will learn more how the Controller works in several sections of the chapter.

Endpoints

You will need the ability to connect to BDC for all types of tasks, so we provide a series of *Service endpoints*. This will include endpoints to connect to SQL Server, HDFS and Spark, and several management and monitoring services. You will learn more about service endpoints throughout the rest of this chapter.

Application Deployment

SQL Server Big Data Clusters allow you to execute code via T-SQL statements and Spark Jobs. SQL Server Machine Learning Services and Extensibility also allow you to run R, Python, and Java code integrated with SQL Server. Since BDC is deployed in a Kubernetes cluster, we want to provide a method for developers to deploy applications in BDC, provide an exposed interface to interact with those applications, and allow the application to access data sources connected in BDC, such as SQL Server tables and external tables. Therefore, BDC provides the concept of *Application Deployment* for you to deploy R, Python, MLeap, and SSIS applications. Application Deployment is a key element in using BDC as an end-to-end Machine Learning platform. I'll discuss more details about Application Deployment in the section "Using Big Data Clusters" later in this chapter.

Machine Learning

I told you one of the solutions BDC provides is an end-to-end Machine Learning platform. BDC does this through the following capabilities:

- SQL Server Machine Learning Services
- SparkML

- MLeap

- Machine Learning packages

- Application Deployment

I'll discuss these in more detail in the section "Machine Learning and Big Data Clusters" later in the chapter.

Look back at this list! Can you see now why SQL Server Big Data Clusters is a product within a product? This story gets better. Keep reading.

Note   Buck Woody's **Workshop: SQL Server Big Data Clusters – Architecture** has an excellent page describing BDC components in Module 2.0. Use this as another resource to study what is in BDC.

Prerequisites for the Examples

Before I begin the discussion about deployment, let me describe how to find the examples I'll be using in the chapter. Instead of providing specific examples and scripts, I'll be using several examples from the following sources:

- **SQL Server Samples GitHub Repo** – There are several examples I will use and talk about at `https://github.com/Microsoft/sql-server-samples/tree/master/samples/features/sql-big-data-cluster`.

- **SQL Server 2019 Big Data Cluster Workshop** – Buck Woody has some great examples I'll use at `https://github.com/Microsoft/sqlworkshops/tree/master/sqlserver2019bigdataclusters`.

Using these examples requires the following:

- A deployed SQL Server 2019 Big Data Cluster. At the time I wrote the chapter of this book, I was using SQL Server 2019 Release Candidate, which is very close to the final release of SQL Server 2019. I'll talk more about the requirements, including client tools, in the next section entitled "Deploying Big Data Clusters."

- A Windows, macOS, or Linux client to deploy and to run example scripts or T-SQL queries. Almost all of the tools used in deployment and in the examples run on Windows, macOS, and Linux. I also recommend you install and use Azure Data Studio (ADS), which you can download at `https://docs.microsoft.com/en-us/sql/azure-data-studio/download`. ADS and the use of notebooks are key to the successful use of Big Data Clusters.

Deploying Big Data Clusters

I'll show you my experiences deploying SQL Server Big Data Clusters so I can then show you the components and architecture. It was tough to decide whether to show you the architecture first or the deployment. I thought it was important to deploy first and then describe what is deployed, and I recommend you do the same.

Note   All of the software in a BDC is deployed as containers in a Kubernetes cluster. BDC relies on you deploying your own Kubernetes cluster, but tools are also provided to help deploy k8s as an option.

Plan the Deployment

Deployment requires some planning. Let me describe my experience to plan how I deployed BDC, as it could help you in your planning efforts. If you are planning a production deployment of BDC, I recommend you read through the section "Configuring Deployment for Production" later in this chapter.

Decide on k8s

The first decision to make when you will deploy BDC is choosing a Kubernetes (k8s) distribution and location. BDC supports deployment on k8s in a public cloud provider with **Azure Kubernetes Service** (AKS) or in your own Linux server or virtual machine deployment of k8s (e.g., if you have deployed k8s on your own with kubeadm). I expect the list of other well-known k8s providers to be supported with BDC to increase as we release SQL Server 2019 and beyond, including Azure Stack, Red Hat OpenShift, and others. At the time I wrote this book, you can technically deploy BDC on a k8s deployment on Windows Server, but this scenario will require Linux Virtual Machines running on Windows Server for k8s.

Our tools to deploy BDC will create a series of pods with containers (in most cases pods will have multiple containers) in k8s to support the BDC system. We will also deploy and use other k8s objects, such as Load Balancer, Persistent Volume Claim, ReplicaSet, and StatefulSet objects.

Once you decide your k8s choice, you can either deploy k8s yourself or use scripts we have built to deploy k8s and BDC together.

For either option, the basic requirement just to deploy for "dev/test" BDC is a Linux virtual machine (VM) or computer (in the case of AKS, choose the VM size) with these resources:

- 64Gb RAM.

- 8 CPUs (can be logical).

- For AKS, an Azure VM size that supports at least 24 disks.

- If you plan to deploy more than one BDC node, each node (VM) will need to meet these resource requirements.

Note   Slava Oks and I have talked about the need to reduce the footprint for a "Developer Edition" of BDC that doesn't require so much RAM. I told Slava that ideally I could deploy a BDC on my laptop just to test the basic capabilities.

Our scripts and notebooks choose an Azure VM default size of Standard_L8s_v2, but, as long as you pick an Azure VM for AKS with 64Gb, 8 CPUs, and 24 disks, the deployment should work. You can read more about Azure VM sizes at https://docs. microsoft.com/en-us/azure/virtual-machines/linux/sizes-general.

For my deployment experience, I'm going to use AKS and use a script we provide that will deploy an AKS cluster and BDC all in one step. I recommend as you plan your deployment you read the following documentation resources:

https://docs.microsoft.com/en-us/sql/big-data-cluster/deploy-get-started
https://docs.microsoft.com/en-us/sql/big-data-cluster/deployment-guidance

Pick the Client and Download Tools

Once you have decided on the k8s strategy, you need tools to deploy BDC. It is very important to ensure you have all the right tools installed on the client before you try to deploy BDC. The documentation provides a list of tools you will need at `https://docs.microsoft.com/en-us/sql/big-data-cluster/deploy-big-data-tools`. For my client, I chose my "laptop in the cloud." This means I installed Windows 10 in an Azure Virtual Machine and drove all of my BDC use in that VM.

This list of tools includes the following:

python – python is a key component used by several different tools and is available on all OS platforms. The azdata tool, required to install BDC, is written in python. I needed python as I used a python script to deploy AKS and BDC all in one step. For python for Windows, I just pull down the latest python build from `www.python.org/downloads/release/python-374/`.

kubectl – As you learned in Chapter 8, kubectl is a tool specifically designed to send requests to the k8s API server. This is your programming interface for Kubernetes.

I had already installed kubectl on my Windows machine; I checked the version and it was 1.14. The docs notes say, "You must use kubectl version 1.10 or later. Also, the version of kubectl should be plus or minus one minor version of your Kubernetes cluster." Since I'm using AKS, I checked the command to see what versions would be used in my AKS deployment and found that the highest version supported is 1.14.6 – so I should be good to go. You can find out more about checking if supported AKS versions are available on your cluster at `https://docs.microsoft.com/en-us/azure/aks/supported-kubernetes-versions`.

azdata – This tool, formerly called mssqlctl in early preview releases of SQL Server 2019, is *critical* to deploy and manage BDC. Written in python, you should think of azdata as the "kubectl" of BDC.

To verify I had azdata properly installed, I just ran `azdata` from the command line to see what the interface looked like. The results are shown in Figure 10-3.

```
 _ _ _   _ _    _ _ _  _ _ _  _ _ _
/ /\ | / / \| / / / / | / /\ | / / / |
/ /\/ / \|_/ / / / |  / /\/ | / /\/ |
/ / | \|_/ |_/ /_ /|_| / / | / / | |
/_/  |_ _|_ _|  /_/ |_ _| /_/  |_/_/  |_|
```

Welcome to the azdata CLI.

Use `azdata --version` to display the current version.
Here are the base commands:

```
    app      : Create, delete, run, and manage applications.
    bdc      : Select, manage, and operate SQL Server Big Data Clusters.
    login    : Log in to the cluster's controller endpoint.
    logout   : Log out of cluster.
    notebook : Commands for viewing, running, and managing notebooks from a terminal.
    sql      : The SQL DB CLI allows the user to interact with SQL Server via T-SQL.
PS C:\demos\bdc>
```

Figure 10-3. *The azdata CLI*

You can see the complete azdata reference at https://docs.microsoft.com/en-us/
sql/big-data-cluster/reference-azdata.

Azure Data Studio (ADS) – This cross-platform, open source tool can be used to
query, deploy, manage, and navigate data for BDC. While SQL Server Management
Studio (SSMS) can be used to connect to the SQL Server Master Instance in BDC, ADS
has features and extensions specifically designed for BDC, including Notebook support.

I used the ADS Insiders build from https://github.com/microsoft/
azuredatastudio#try-out-the-latest-insiders-build-from-master, but, I expect
that by the time SQL Server 2019 releases, you will have a public build of ADS with
everything you need for BDC. You can get the latest ADS build at https://docs.
microsoft.com/en-us/sql/azure-data-studio/download.

I also grabbed the latest SQL Server 2019 preview extension at https://docs.
microsoft.com/en-us/sql/azure-data-studio/sql-server-2019-extension and
installed the vsix file. (You can ignore the warning about third-party extensions because
the extension is from Microsoft.) It is hard to know if this is working or finished, but
give it a few minutes and you will see in the lower right-hand corner a message like,
"Completed installing the extension microsoft.sql-vnext."

az – If you are using AKS, you will need the Azure command-line interface to log in to
Azure and to deploy and manage AKS.

curl – curl stands for "Client URL" and is a popular tool to copy data from a specific URL,
often files stored on web sites. For me, curl comes with Windows 10. Curl is a great tool, not
only to copy remote scripts to use with BDC but also to copy data into the BDC HDFS cluster.

Deployment Method

Now that you know which type of k8s cluster you will deploy and have your required tools downloaded; you choose the method for deployment:

- A "single-step" method to deploy AKS and BDC using **python**, which you can find at `https://docs.microsoft.com/en-us/sql/big-data-cluster/quickstart-big-data-cluster-deploy`.

- A "single-step" Bash shell script to deploy k8s and BDC on your k8s cluster using **kubeadm**, which you can find at `https://docs.microsoft.com/en-us/sql/big-data-cluster/deployment-script-single-node-kubeadm`.

- Create your own AKS or k8s cluster first, and then deploy BDC using the **azdata** tool, which you can read about at `https://docs.microsoft.com/en-us/sql/big-data-cluster/deployment-guidance`.

- Use Azure Data Studio (ADS) to deploy BDC along with a new AKS cluster, to an existing AKS cluster, or to an existing k8s cluster you have deployed with kubeadm.

Figure 10-4 shows how to access this deployment experience in ADS.

Figure 10-4. *Choosing to deploy BDC in Azure Data Studio*

Figure 10-5 shows the experience to pick your deployment method.

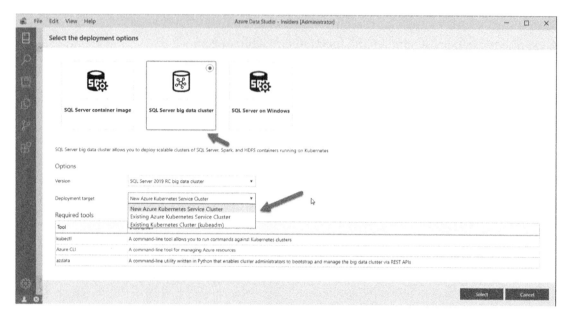

Figure 10-5. *Deployment options for BDC in Azure Data Studio*

Offline Deployment

I want to mention that if you need an offline deployment experience because your k8s cluster is not connected to the Internet (at least when you need to deploy BDC), we have documented how to pull our container images and deploy BDC on k8s. You will still need all the tools I've described in this chapter to deploy offline. You can read the details at https://docs.microsoft.com/en-us/sql/big-data-cluster/deploy-offline.

The BDC Deployment Experience

To give you my perspective on the BDC deployment experience, I'm going to deploy BDC on AKS and use the python script provided as a "one-step" solution. You can read the details of how to use this solution at https://docs.microsoft.com/en-us/sql/big-data-cluster/quickstart-big-data-cluster-deploy.

I chose the defaults except that I needed to deploy my AKS and BDC cluster in the eastus2 region.

The python script is effectively a wrapper for az and azdata. It uses your choices (or environment variables or defaults) to create an Azure Resource Group, an AKS cluster, and a BDC. BDC is created using the **aks-dev-test** configuration. This is a basic configuration for BDC that is well suited for a development or test scenario. I'll talk about configuration for production deployments in the section "Configuring Deployment for Production" later in this chapter.

Deployment takes time! There are many pods and containers to deploy for the BDC solution, and the process will take longer if you also deploy a k8s cluster. For me, the total deployment time using the python script with AKS was about 20 minutes, but I've seen it take up to an hour.

When you run the python script, you will get messages like

```
Creating azure resource group: <rgname>
<json details for the resource group>
Creating AKS cluster: <aks cluster name>
<json for the AKS cluster>
Creating SQL Big Data cluster:mssql-cluster
custom\bdc.json created
custom\control.json created
The privacy statement can be viewed at:
https://go.microsoft.com/fwlink/?LinkId=853010

The license terms for SQL Server Big Data Cluster can be viewed at:
https://go.microsoft.com/fwlink/?LinkId=2002534

Cluster deployment documentation can be viewed at:
https://aka.ms/bdc-deploy

NOTE: Cluster creation can take a significant amount of time depending on
configuration, network speed, and the number of nodes in the cluster.

Starting cluster deployment.
Waiting for cluster controller to start.
```

This last message, Waiting for cluster controller to start, is a key message and may be repeated several times. The *controller* is created first within the k8s cluster, and the *controller service* will be used to deploy the rest of the BDC.

You will then see a message like this:

```
Cluster controller endpoint is available at <ip address>:<port>
Cluster control plane is ready.
```

And soon you will see these messages:

```
Data pool is ready.
Master pool is ready.
Compute pool is ready.
Storage pool is ready.
Cluster deployed successfully.
```

This last message means both AKS and BDC are successfully deployed. I use the philosophy of "trust but verify," so, in the next section, I'll talk about how you can verify the deployment was successful and you are ready to use BDC.

Note   The name provided for `Creating SQL Big Data cluster:mssql-cluster` becomes the Kubernetes namespace for all objects created by BDC. Therefore, in my deployment, **mssql-cluster** is the k8s namespace.

Verify the Deployment

I used the following methods to perform a "sanity check" of a successful AKS and BDC deployment:

- Follow these steps to use **kubectl** to inspect the cluster:
  https://docs.microsoft.com/en-us/sql/big-data-cluster/
  quickstart-big-data-cluster-deploy?view=sqlallproducts-
  allversions#inspect-the-cluster.

- Log in to the cluster using **azdata**, find the controller endpoint, and then connect to SQL Server to make sure you can connect to SQL Server. Follow the steps at https://docs.
  microsoft.com/en-us/sql/big-data-cluster/deployment-
  guidance?view=sqlallproducts-allversions#endpoints.

Look for the endpoint called **SQL Server Master Instance Front-End**. The endpoint is the IP address and port to connect to SQL Server.

Follow the guidance at the following documentation page to connect to SQL Server in BDC with Azure Data Studio (ADS):

https://docs.microsoft.com/en-us/sql/big-data-cluster/
connect-to-big-data-cluster

My basic connection test to my BDC looked like Figure 10-6 in ADS.

Note   I used an Insider build of ADS at the time I deployed BDC so some of this interface may change as SQL Server 2019 is released

---

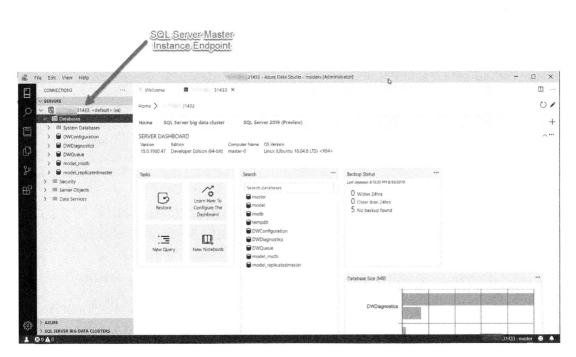

Figure 10-6. *Connect to SQL Server in BDC after deployment*

- Verify the overall status of BDC using the following command:

```
azdata bdc status show
```

The results for my BDC cluster looked like this:

```
Mssql-cluster: ready                                          Health Status:
                                                              healthy

===============================================================================
Services: ready                                              Health Status:
                                                              healthy

-------------------------------------------------------------------------------
Servicename  State  Healthstatus  Details

sql          ready  healthy       -
hdfs         ready  healthy       -
spark        ready  healthy       -
control      ready  healthy       -
gateway      ready  healthy       -
app          ready  healthy       -

Sql Services: ready                                          Health Status:
                                                              healthy

-------------------------------------------------------------------------------
Resourcename  State  Healthstatus  Details

master        ready  healthy       StatefulSet master is healthy
compute-0     ready  healthy       StatefulSet compute-0 is healthy
data-0        ready  healthy       StatefulSet data-0 is healthy
storage-0     ready  healthy       StatefulSet storage-0 is healthy

Hdfs Services: ready                                         Health Status:
                                                              healthy

-------------------------------------------------------------------------------
Resourcename  State  Healthstatus  Details

nmnode-0      ready  healthy       StatefulSet nmnode-0 is healthy
storage-0     ready  healthy       StatefulSet storage-0 is healthy
sparkhead     ready  healthy       StatefulSet sparkhead is healthy
```

Spark Services: ready   Health Status:
                                                               healthy

----

Resourcename	State	Healthstatus	Details
sparkhead	ready	healthy	StatefulSet sparkhead is healthy
storage-0	ready	healthy	StatefulSet storage-0 is healthy

Control Services: ready   Health Status:
                                                               healthy

----

Resourcename	State	Healthstatus	Details
controldb	ready	healthy	-
control	ready	healthy	-
metricsdc	ready	healthy	DaemonSet metricsdc is healthy
metricsui	ready	healthy	ReplicaSet metricsui is healthy
metricsdb	ready	healthy	StatefulSet metricsdb is healthy
logsui	ready	healthy	ReplicaSet logsui is healthy
logsdb	ready	healthy	StatefulSet logsdb is healthy
mgmtproxy	ready	healthy	ReplicaSet mgmtproxy is healthy

Gateway Services: ready   Health Status:
                                                               healthy

----

Resourcename	State	Healthstatus	Details
gateway	ready	healthy	StatefulSet gateway is healthy

App Services: ready   Health Status:
                                                               healthy

----

Resourcename	State	Healthstatus	Details
appproxy	ready	healthy	ReplicaSet appproxy is healthy

If everything is not healthy, consider using the following documentation to troubleshoot the cluster: https://docs. microsoft.com/en-us/sql/big-data-cluster/cluster-troubleshooting-commands.

Configuring Deployment for Production

My deployment experience used a *configuration*, shipped with the azdata tool, designed for a development or test cluster. A configuration for azdata is defined through JSON files and is used to control various types of resource definitions within the cluster. You can see the list of these configurations by using the command:

```
azdata bdc config list
```

The JSON files for configuration look very much like the Kubernetes YAML files I showed you in Chapter 8. In this case, the JSON files have a format recognized by the azdata tool (much like the YAML have a format recognized by kubectl).

In order to see what options are possible for you to configure your BDC deployment, you can run a command like the following to see how the aks-dev-test default configuration is deployed:

```
azdata bdc config init --source aks-dev-test --target custom
```

This command creates a new folder called custom and stores in this directory files called **bdc.json** and **control.json**. You can make changes to these files and run a command like this to create a new BDC with these desired configuration settings:

```
azdata bdc create --config-profile custom --accept-eula yes
```

There is a discussion of this method in the documentation at https:// docs.microsoft.com/en-us/sql/big-data-cluster/deployment- guidance?view=sqlallproducts-allversions#customconfig. In order to understand how to make changes to the BDC JSON files, you need to understand more of the architecture, which I'll describe in the next section titled "Big Data Cluster Architecture." I expect then you will need to come back to this section and look closer at the JSON files and techniques to modify them accordingly. Once you have some idea of what to change, you can use these guidelines in our documentation on how to make changes to the BDC JSON files https://docs.microsoft.com/en-us/ sql/big-data-cluster/deployment-custom-configuration. The complete deployment configuration reference for BDC JSON files can be found at https://docs.microsoft. com/en-us/sql/big-data-cluster/reference-deployment-config. You should also examine our "auto-deploy" scripts for Python and bash to see how k8s and BDC can be created.

python – https://docs.microsoft.com/en-us/sql/big-data-cluster/
quickstart-big-data-cluster-deploy

bash – https://docs.microsoft.com/en-us/sql/big-data-cluster/deployment-
script-single-node-kubeadm

These scripts assume one Kubernetes (k8s) node. You will likely want to use multiple nodes in a production k8s cluster. You can then decide how to place various components of BDC on specific k8s nodes at https://docs.microsoft.com/en-us/sql/big-data-cluster/deployment-custom-configuration.

One other important aspect to configure BDC for production is storage. Our documentation provides guidance on how to configure BDC storage to match your k8s storage configuration for production at https://docs.microsoft.com/en-us/sql/big-data-cluster/concept-data-persistence. Every pod that has stateful storage in BDC uses a separate Persistent Volume Claim (PVC). You can get a list of all PVC objects in BDC by executing the following command:

```
get PersistentVolumeClaim --namespace=mssql-cluster
```

Two other important aspects of deploying BDC in production are Security and High Availability which I'll describe more in sections "Security" and "High Availability" later in this chapter.

Big Data Cluster Architecture

I'll use my deployed BDC to describe more details about the architecture. I described what comes with BDC, but that was more of a "capability list" of components. The architecture is interesting to study because you can see exactly what pods and containers we have installed. Your knowledge from Chapters 7 and 8 will become important here.

Note   If you want to jump into using BDC, go to the next section called "Using Big Data Clusters." I consider this section on architecture the "Level 400" section of the chapter. You can always come back and read this section after going through aspects of using BDC. You should know that we have built BDC so that you don't have to know every detail of the architecture. And any of the details in this section of the chapter are subject to change. I'll show you some details that are "behind the scenes" and those certainly could change over time.

Let's use Figure 10-7 as the overall architecture of SQL Server Big Data Clusters (BDC).

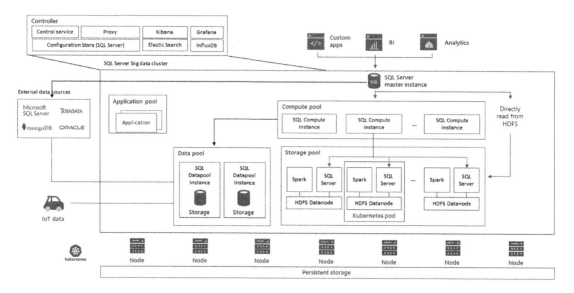

Figure 10-7. *The SQL Server Big Data Cluster architecture*

Notice that in this visual the term *pool* is used. A pool is a logical term in BDC that represents a collection of pods that serve a specific purpose in BDC. I've mentioned some of these pools previously in the chapter like Compute Pool and Data Pool. I'll describe more of what pods and containers make up these pools in this section.

Let's break down each piece of Figure 10-7 to describe the BDC architecture, using various commands and visuals. One way to break down the architecture is from a *k8s perspective.*

When I run this command, I get a list of all the pods deployed by BDC on my single node k8s cluster:

```
kubectl get pods --namespace mssql-cluster
```

The result is this list of pods and their status:

NAME	READY	STATUS	RESTARTS	AGE
appproxy-q8zkk	2/2	Running	0	24h
compute-0-0	3/3	Running	0	24h
control-vjwjf	3/3	Running	0	24h
controldb-0	2/2	Running	0	24h
controlwd-l8fmp	1/1	Running	0	24h
data-0-0	3/3	Running	0	24h
data-0-1	3/3	Running	0	24h
gateway-0	2/2	Running	0	24h
logsdb-0	1/1	Running	0	24h
logsui-f42ln	1/1	Running	0	24h
master-0	3/3	Running	0	24h
metricsdb-0	1/1	Running	0	24h
metricsdc-gtrxn	1/1	Running	0	24h
metricsui-kwh4q	1/1	Running	0	24h
mgmtproxy-nc8tl	2/2	Running	0	24h
nmnode-0-0	2/2	Running	0	24h
sparkhead-0	4/4	Running	0	24h
storage-0-0	4/4	Running	0	24h
storage-0-1	4/4	Running	0	24h

Based on this list and the concepts I've described to this point, you can probably guess how some of the pods map to Figure 10-7. The numbers in the READY column show you how many containers are running in each pod. This means that a simple BDC cluster for "dev/test" has ~43 containers!

Let's use this list to map pods in the k8s cluster to Figure 10-7 components, including the concept of *pools*.

SQL Server Master Instance

The SQL Server Master Instance is represented by the pod **master-0**. The main container running in this pod is a SQL Server Linux container. You can use the following command to get details of how BDC deploys a SQL Server container:

```
kubectl describe pod master-0 --namespace mssql-cluster
```

One important aspect of how we have organized BDC is the use of labels with Kubernetes. I described how to use a label in Chapter 8 with SQL Server and k8s. Look at this section of the output from the preceding command:

```
Labels:                 MSSQL_CLUSTER=mssql-cluster
                        app=master
                        controller-revision-hash=master-7bbc4d95fb
                        mssql.microsoft.com/sql-instance=master
                        plane=data
                        role=master-pool
                        statefulset.kubernetes.io/pod-name=master-0
                        type=sqlservr
```

You can see how we use some of these labels to map to terms in the BDC. For example, these two labels are interesting:

```
plane=data
role=master-pool
```

If you run the following command, you can see all the pods in the "data plane":

```
get pods --namespace mssql-cluster -lplane=data
```

On my BDC, I get the following output:

NAME	READY	STATUS	RESTARTS	AGE
appproxy-q8zkk	2/2	Running	0	24h
compute-0-0	3/3	Running	0	24h
data-0-0	3/3	Running	0	24h
data-0-1	3/3	Running	0	24h
master-0	3/3	Running	0	24h
nmnode-0-0	2/2	Running	0	24h
sparkhead-0	4/4	Running	0	24h
storage-0-0	4/4	Running	0	24h
storage-0-1	4/4	Running	0	24h

This list represents most of the major components in Figure 10-7, with the exception of the **Controller**, which I'll describe later in the next section called "Controller."

If you look further at the output of the kubectl describe pod command earlier, you will see the details of the SQL Server container, starting with:

```
Containers:
  mssql-server:
```

If you look back at Chapter 8, the important components involved in a pod for SQL Server in k8s were

- Container image
- Persistent Volume Claim
- Secret
- Load Balancer
- ReplicaSet

The output from the kubectl describe command earlier shows all of these components.

You can see the **container image** for the SQL Server container (remember I was using SQL Server 2019 Big Data Clusters release) in this section:

```
Image:          mcr.microsoft.com/mssql/bdc/mssql-server-data:2019-RC1-ubuntu
```

Later in the output you will see a list of *mounts* which describe persisted storage mounts to **PersistentVolumeClaim** objects.

Notice this mount:

```
/var/opt from data (rw)
```

And this Volume

```
Volumes:
  data:
    Type:        PersistentVolumeClaim (a reference to a
                 PersistentVolumeClaim in the same namespace)
    ClaimName:   data-master-0
    ReadOnly:    false
```

If you remember in Chapter 8, I showed you how to map a SQL Server directory like /var/opt to a PVC object.

You can run this command to see the details of the PVC object:

```
describe PersistentVolumeClaim data-master-0 --namespace=mssql-cluster
```

From this output, you can see this PVC object is bound to the default **StorageClass** for AKS and is 15Gb. That is not very big, of course, to store your SQL Server data, but this is just a test cluster. If you need to change these sizes for a custom configuration, you can read how to do this in our documentation at https://docs.microsoft.com/en-us/sql/big-data-cluster/concept-data-persistence.

The **secret** for SQL Server in Chapter 8 was used to control the sa password to connect to SQL Server. The deployment for BDC includes an environment variable called **MSSQL_SA_PASSWORD**, which I was prompted for using the python deployment script. For the SQL Server Master Instance, we create a secret called **mssql-sa-password**.

If you remember in Chapter 8, I showed you how to create a **LoadBalancer** service for SQL Server in a pod to connect to SQL Server. Our BDC deployment tool creates one for the SQL Server Master Instance. To see the exact objects for this service, you can run the following command:

```
kubectl get service --namespace=mssql-cluster -lrole=master-pool
```

The output will show you the **master-svc-external service** along with an External IP and port.

The final component for the SQL Server pod is a **ReplicaSet**. I showed you in Chapter 8 how a ReplicaSet provides "basic HA" for k8s for SQL Server. For BDC, we use a concept called a **StatefulSet**, which gives similar HA functionality as a ReplicaSet, but with more capabilities. StatefulSet objects are used for all pods in BDC except for the Controller. StatefulSet objects allow for pod ordering and scale and are a key component to allow for robust High Availability with BDC. I'll talk more about High Availability for BDC in the section "High Availability" later in this chapter.

If you look at the output of the kubectl describe command, you will see this section:

```
Controlled By:     StatefulSet/master
```

You can get more information about how we define the StatefulSet by running this command:

```
kubectl describe StatefulSet master --namespace=mssql-cluster
```

You will also notice there are two other containers in the master-0 pod:

```
collectd:
fluentbit:
```

These containers are part of every pod in BDC and are used to help collect logs and metrics used in managing and monitoring BDC.

Our documentation has information about the SQL Server Master Instance at `https://docs.microsoft.com/en-us/sql/big-data-cluster/concept-master-instance`. I'll talk more about how to use the SQL Server Master Instance in the section "Using Big Data Clusters" later in this chapter.

Controller

The *Controller* is a logical term that represents a collection of pods and containers. You can find a list of pods in the Controller with the following command:

```
kubectl get pods --namespace mssql-cluster -lplane=control
```

Here is the list of pods on my BDC deployment:

```
NAME              READY   STATUS    RESTARTS   AGE
control-vjwjf     3/3     Running   0          38h
controldb-0       2/2     Running   0          38h
controlwd-l8fmp   1/1     Running   0          38h
gateway-0         2/2     Running   0          38h
logsdb-0          1/1     Running   0          38h
logsui-f42ln      1/1     Running   0          38h
metricsdb-0       1/1     Running   0          38h
metricsdc-gtrxn   1/1     Running   0          38h
metricsui-kwh4q   1/1     Running   0          38h
mgmtproxy-nc8tl   2/2     Running   0          38h
```

The Controller is also called the *control plane*, much like the Kubernetes concept of a control plane (`https://kubernetes.io/docs/concepts/#kubernetes-control-plane`). Figure 10-8 shows a closeup of the components of the control plane for BDC.

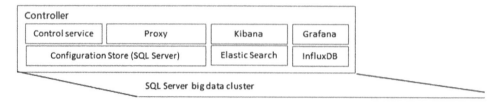

Figure 10-8. *BDC control plane*

You should think of the Controller as a set of services that are used to *manage* BDC. One of the tasks for management is deployment, and the Controller is used to help deploy BDC. Once azdata deploys the Controller, the Controller "takes over" and deploys other components of BDC. All pods running in the control plane use the k8s concept of a ReplicaSet for basic high availability.

One of the most important components of the Controller is the *controller service* (also listed as control service in Figure 10-8). The controller service is effectively the API server for BDC. This service accepts REST APIs to perform all types of operations for BDC including deploy, manage, Data Virtualization, and more. You will interact with the controller service using several different methods, including azdata, T-SQL external tables, and Azure Data Studio (ADS).

At the time of writing, there is no public documentation on the protocol of using the controller service for specific APIs. All APIs are accessible using azdata, Azure Data Studio (ADS), and T-SQL statements.

Tip   Azure Data Studio (ADS) is capable of connecting and interacting with BDC without azdata. Therefore, REST API examples to interact with the controller service exist in its open source code at `https://github.com/microsoft/azuredatastudio`. While you read these examples in the source, I don't recommend you rely on them, as we may change them. Furthermore, there is no method for you to install a program and gain access with certificates within BDC.

The other pods in the control plane implement services that support connectivity to various services (proxy), Kibana and Elasticsearch for logging, Grafana and InfluxDB for metrics and monitoring, and a SQL Server to store BDC "metadata."

The SQL Server container to store metadata is a normal SQL Server instance, but it is "private." In other words, you never connect to this instance. The controller container uses this SQL Server to read important data for management and health, but also for HDFS querying capabilities.

I love to find out how things work, so I used the following techniques to run a Bash shell inside this special SQL Server container. The name of the pod hosting this container is called **controldb-0**.

I used the following command to run a Bash shell and connect to the SQL Server container:

```
kubectl exec -it controldb-0 --namespace=mssql-cluster -- /bin/bash
```

This connects me to the first container in the pod which is SQL Server. As it turns out, we build this SQL Server image based on our core SQL Server image, which has sqlcmd installed.

I need the sa password to use sqlcmd, but it is not the sa password used to connect into the SQL Server Master Instance. It is a private password used only by the controller. I found out we store the secret for the sa password inside the container at /var/run/secrets/credentials/mssql-sa-password/password. Using that password string, I connected with sqlcmd and found these databases installed in the container: **health_system**, **controller**, and **hive_metastore**. These are databases used internally by BDC. This is an example of a SQL Server container used for internal BDC functionality vs. the SQL Server Master Instance which is used for normal SQL Server purposes plus Data Virtualization with HDFS and other data sources.

Storage Pool

I described in Chapter 9 how Polybase allows you to access data sources outside of SQL Server, including HDFS data. Polybase access to HDFS translates T-SQL queries into Java MapReduce jobs to access the HDFS data.

BDC deploys its own HDFS cluster for you to access HDFS data both through Polybase and also directly using a **Knox Gateway** (https://knox.apache.org/) through the Controller.

Figure 10-9 gives a closer view of how a HDFS cluster is deployed in BDC as a *Storage Pool.*

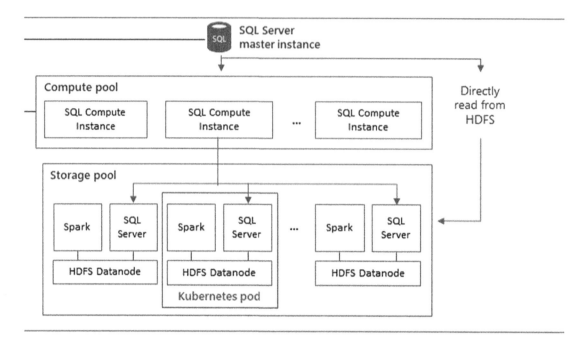

Figure 10-9. *The BDC Storage Pool*

The Storage Pool is made up of one or more k8s pods. By default, using the aks-dev-test configuration, two Storage Pool pods are deployed. If you look at pods in the Storage Pool with `kubectl describe`, you will see they are bound together with the label `role=storage-pool`. You can scale more Storage Pool pods using custom configuration by specifying a Replicas count.

In my list of pods deployed on BDC, these pods represent the Storage Pool:

```
storage-0-0     4/4     Running   0          24h
storage-0-1     4/4     Running   0          24h
```

Storage Pool pods are part of their own StatefulSet, so, in the case of two Replicas from BDC configuration, you get two pods in a single StatefulSet.

Each pod in the Storage Pool holds four containers (collectd and fluentbit are installed) including a pod for **Hadoop** components and one for **SQL Server**. The pod for Hadoop components (the container name is called Hadoop) runs YARN and HDFS. YARN is a resource manager for Hadoop components run in the cluster including Spark Jobs (you can read more about YARN at `https://hadoop.apache.org/docs/current/hadoop-yarn/hadoop-yarn-site/YARN.html`). HDFS provides Hadoop distributed file system functionality. BDC also deploys an HDFS Name Node use to store metadata and control access to the HDFS cluster.

Part of the capabilities of YARN and HDFS is distributed computing and storage, which means when you interact and use the Storage Pool through T-SQL and Spark, your compute and storage is part of a built-in distributed system.

The SQL Server container serves a special purpose in the BDC system. Note the connector in Figure 10-9 that says, "Directly Read from HDFS." This note means that the SQL Server container in the Storage Pool pods can read data directly from HDFS storage, including file types like csv and parquet. You don't connect to these SQL Server containers directly; they are used internally within BDC to optimize access to HDFS files in the BDC cluster. The Controller service redirects external table queries to HDFS in BDC to these SQL Server instances (which may be through the Compute Pool).

If you have your own HDFS system, you can mount this into the Storage Pool using a concept called HDFS Tiering. You can read about HDFS Tiering at `https://docs.microsoft.com/en-us/sql/big-data-cluster/hdfs-tiering`.

Compute Pool

Figure 10-9 in the previous section for Storage Pool also shows the concept of a *Compute Pool*. The Compute Pool is a StatefulSet of pods that implement the **Polybase Scale-Out Group** I discussed in Chapter 9.

The Compute Pool can be scaled by customizing the configuration of the BDC deployment using the Replicas count. By default, the aks-dev-test configuration only deploys one Compute Pool pod (the documentation also calls this instance).

If the Compute Pool is present, all external table queries through BDC will use the Compute Pool. The Controller redirects all external table queries for data sources in BDC through the Compute Pool.

In the case of my BDC deployment, the Compute Pool is implemented by this pod and uses the label `role=compute-pool`.

```
compute-0-0        3/3      Running   0          43h
```

Data Pool

The Data Pool implements one or more pods for the data cache functionality I discussed in the section "What Comes with Big Data Clusters?" By default, the aks-dev-test configuration for BDC deploys two pods for the Data Pool. In my BDC deployment, these pods are represented by:

```
data-0-0          3/3      Running   0        43h
data-0-1          3/3      Running   0        43h
```

The Data Pool consists of one or more pods using the label `role=data-pool` in a StatefulSet, each with a SQL Server container. Your access to SQL Server in the Data Pool is through Polybase external tables from the SQL Server Master Instance.

When you create external tables in the SQL Server Master Instance using the external data source for the Data Pool, SQL Server will create a database in each pod of the Data Pool, with the same name as the scope of the external table in the SQL Server Master Instance. Furthermore, we create a table with the same name as the external table name.

This means your interaction with the Data Pool is all through external tables in the SQL Server Master Instance. On each SQL Server in pods for the Data Pool, we will create a database and table to match your external table. In addition, we automatically shard or partition data (not using SQL Server partitions) as you insert data into the Data Pool (using round robin by default), and we build a clustered columnstore index on each table in each pod of the Data Pool to optimize read access. This means our Compute Pool can be used to access this data in a scalable fashion across the shards. The Data Pool cannot be modified; you can only ingest (INSERT) or query data. Since it is a cache, this means you must drop the external table and repopulate it when you are ready to refresh the cache. The Controller redirects specific external table requests to the SQL Server instances in the Data Pool (which may be through the Compute Pool).

Application Pool

The Application Pool is a collection of pods deployed based on the creation of an **application** in BDC. Figure 10-10 represents the area of BDC for the Application Pool.

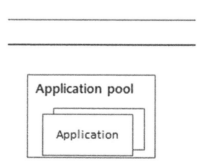

Figure 10-10. *The Application Pool in BDC*

When you use BDC interfaces to create an application with a YAML file, the controller service will dynamically create a ReplicaSet of pods with your application running in a container. Python, MLeap, and SSIS are the types currently supported.

There is another pod representing the application proxy, including a load balancer, which allows you to connect to the application running in the pool, both from within the BDC and from the outside world through a service endpoint:

```
appproxy-<id>
```

You can read more about the Application Deployment architecture in BDC at `https://docs.microsoft.com/en-us/sql/big-data-cluster/concept-application-deployment`.

Using Big Data Clusters

In this section, I'll review various use cases for Big Data Clusters (BDC). One of the first things you will want to do is **log in to BDC** using azdata. Technically, you do not have to log in to access some resources in BDC, but using azdata to log in gives you context to access all the service endpoints in a simple fashion.

In order to log in to BDC, you need the controller service endpoint, which is the LoadBalancer IP address and port for the controller service pod. On my AKS deployment, I was able to get the controller service endpoint by using the following command:

```
kubectl get svc controller-svc-external -n mssql-cluster
```

I can now give the azdata tool the proper context to use in various scenarios using the following command:

```
azdata login --controller-endpoint https://<ip-address-of-controller-svc-external>:30080 --controller-username admin
```

I was prompted for my password (this is the password I provided when prompted by the python script in the section titled "The BDC Deployment Experience"). When the login was successful, I saw the following message:

```
Logged in successfully to `https://<ip-address>:30080`
```

With this context, I can use azdata for many purposes. The first thing I want to do is to get a list of other service endpoints to use BDC. I'll use this command to retrieve those endpoints:

```
azdata bdc endpoint list -o table
```

My list looked like the following:

```
         Protocol

-----------------------------------------------------  -----------------------
-----------------------------------  -----------------  -------
Gateway to access HDFS files, Spark                    https://<knox-ip>:30443
                             gateway            https
Spark Jobs Management and Monitoring Dashboard         https://<knox-ip>:30443/
gateway/default/sparkhistory  spark-history      https
Spark Diagnostics and Monitoring Dashboard             https://<knox-ip>:30443/
gateway/default/yarn          yarn-ui            https
Application Proxy                                       https://<appproxy-ip>:
30778                         app-proxy          https
Management Proxy                                        https://<mgmt-ip>:30777
                             mgmtproxy          https
Log Search Dashboard                                   https://<mgmt-ip:30777/
kibana                        logsui             https
Metrics Dashboard                                      https://<mgmt-ip>:30777/
grafana                       metricsui          https
Cluster Management Service                             https://<cluster-ip>:
30080                         controller         https
SQL Server Master Instance Front-End                   <sql-ip>,31433
                             sql-server-master  tds
HDFS File System Proxy                                 https://<knox-ip>:30443/
gateway/default/webhdfs/v1    webhdfs            https
Proxy for running Spark statements, jobs, applications https://<knox-ip>:30443/
gateway/default/livy/v1       livy               https
```

I substituted in some names to represent the actual IP address on my cluster:

- **<knox-ip>** – This is the IP address of the Knox Gateway which, as you can see in this list, is used for multiple purposes. The Knox Gateway is used to access HDFS files (**webhdfs**), run Spark Jobs (**livy**), view Spark Job History (**spark-history**), and monitor Spark Jobs (**yarn-ui**).

- **<appproxy-ip>** – This is the IP address used to connect to applications deployed in BDC.

- **<sql-ip>** – This is the IP address to connect to the SQL Server Master Instance.

- **<cluster-ip>** – This is the IP address for the controller service.

You can also get all the endpoint IP address and ports using kubectl, but only azdata gives you specific details like how to access **webhdfs** and **livy**.

Azure Data Studio (ADS) now offers a BDC management experience including the ability to see a list of endpoints.

Figure 10-11 shows an example of BDC endpoints using ADS.

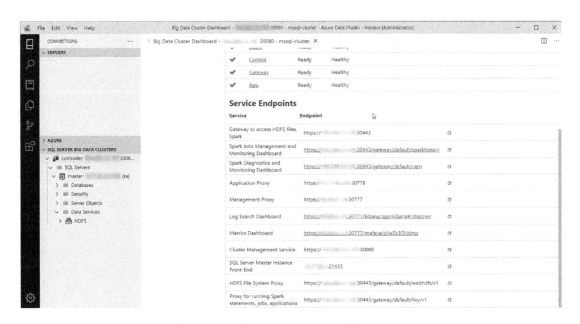

Figure 10-11. *BDC endpoints in Azure Data Studio*

The documentation at `https://docs.microsoft.com/en-us/sql/big-data-cluster/concept-security`, which is also shown in Figure 10-12, shows the common BDC endpoints.

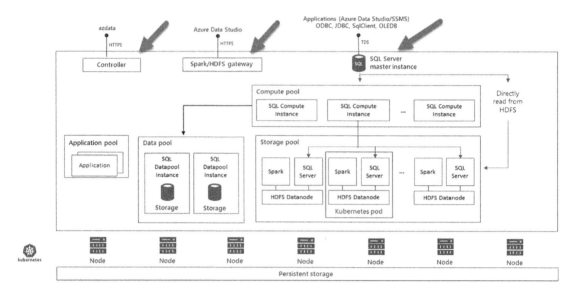

Figure 10-12. *Common BDC endpoints*

Using Data Virtualization

One important usage of BDC is to access data from external data sources using Polybase, as I've described in Chapter 9.

Polybase with BDC provides the same functionality as Polybase for Linux, including built-in connectors for SQL Server, Oracle, Teradata, MongoDB, and HDFS.

BDC provides a *twist* to this functionality through two additional built-in connectors unique to BDC:

- **sqlhdfs** – This connector allows you to access HDFS data within the Storage Pool.

- **sqldatapool** – This connector allows you to access data specifically stored in the Data Pool.

Here are example T-SQL scripts to create external data sources within your database to access these built-in connectors:

```
IF NOT EXISTS(SELECT * FROM sys.external_data_sources WHERE name =
'SqlDataPool')
    CREATE EXTERNAL DATA SOURCE SqlDataPool
    WITH (LOCATION = 'sqldatapool://controller-svc/default');
```

```
IF NOT EXISTS(SELECT * FROM sys.external_data_sources WHERE name =
'SqlStoragePool')
    CREATE EXTERNAL DATA SOURCE SqlStoragePool
    WITH (LOCATION = 'sqlhdfs://controller-svc/default');
```

Notice the URI for the LOCATION is a specific location for the controller service. The controller service directs requests for external tables based on these sources to the respective pool through the Compute Pool if it is deployed.

Our documentation has an example on how to use an external table with BDC to access Oracle data at `https://docs.microsoft.com/en-us/sql/relational-databases/polybase/data-virtualization`. You will need an Oracle instance to use this example. You can also use examples I've provided in Chapter 9 from the **ch9_data_virtualization\sqldatahub** folder.

Note   The only two examples you cannot use from this folder are hdfs and saphana. HDFS data is accessed in BDC through the sqlhdfs connector. ODBC connectors are not currently supported for BDC which is required for SAP HANA.

What I think you might find more interesting is to use the samples to access data through the **sqlhdfs** and **sqldatapool** connectors.

I recommend you first load sample data for using BDC through the instructions in the following documentation page at `https://docs.microsoft.com/en-us/sql/big-data-cluster/tutorial-load-sample-data`. I went through these instructions and had no issues loading this data. In this example, you will load csv files directory into HDFS using curl. This example uses the **WebHDFS** (`https://hadoop.apache.org/docs/r1.0.4/webhdfs.html`) endpoint from the Knox Gateway, which is called **HDFS File System Proxy**.

Once you have loaded your data, you can now go through the tutorial to access HDFS data at `https://docs.microsoft.com/en-us/sql/big-data-cluster/tutorial-query-hdfs-storage-pool`. You might also find it interesting to try the External Table Wizard that comes with Azure Data Studio as another way to create the external table mapped to HDFS data in BDC at `https://docs.microsoft.com/en-us/sql/relational-databases/polybase/data-virtualization-csv`.

It is possible you will need to ingest data directly into HDFS in BDC from sources such as IOT devices. Our documentation has examples on how to interact directly with HDFS in BDC at `https://docs.microsoft.com/en-us/sql/big-data-cluster/data-ingestion-curl`.

In addition, Azure Data Studio includes the capability to browse and work with files in HDFS directly, as you can see in Figure 10-13.

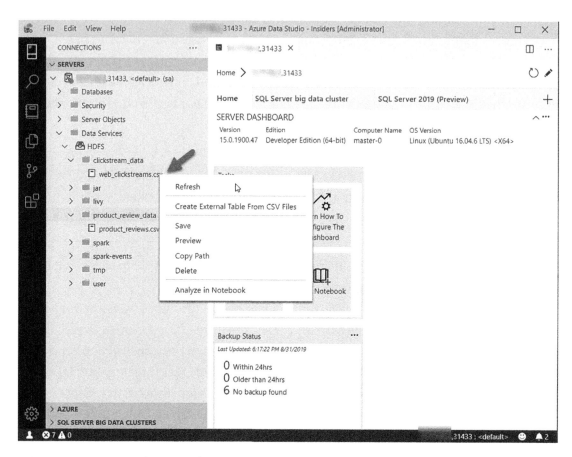

Figure 10-13. *Working with HDFS in BDC with Azure Data Studio*

Buck Woody built a workshop called SQL Server **Big Data Clusters – Architecture** and has a set of Notebooks you can use with ADS to see how Data Virtualization works with BDC. You can try out these Notebooks at `https://github.com/microsoft/sqlworkshops/tree/master/sqlserver2019bigdataclusters/SQL2019BDC/notebooks`, using tutorial 00, 01, and 02 for fundamental Data Virtualization notebooks.

Using the Data Pool

I've described the Data Pool in this book as a data cache. The process to use the Data Pool is to ingest or insert data based on queries from other data sources, which could be SQL Server Master Instance tables, external data sources from HDFS, or any other Polybase connector.

Data is automatically sharded across pods in the Data Pool and optimized for read access with clustered columnstore indexes.

I recommend you go through the example in our documentation to see the basics of using Data Pool at `https://docs.microsoft.com/en-us/sql/big-data-cluster/ tutorial-data-pool-ingest-sql`.

Buck Woody's workshop in tutorial 03 shows how to use the Data Pool in BDC at `https://github.com/microsoft/sqlworkshops/blob/master/ sqlserver2019bigdataclusters/SQL2019BDC/notebooks/bdc_tutorial_03.ipynb`.

Using Spark

Spark (`https://spark.apache.org/`) is a computing engine that is often used in Hadoop systems. BDC automatically provides capabilities to run Spark Jobs for various application needs. There are several ways to run Spark Jobs with BDC which I'll discuss in this section. You can run through some of these examples to see how Spark works with BDC. If you are new to Spark, you need to first consider why you would want to use Spark before embarking submitting Spark Jobs to BDC. There are some very good scenarios where Spark can be an effective method for processing data in HDFS, which is why we included Spark as part of the overall BDC solution. You will also find Spark to be a common solution to use in Machine Learning scenarios, which I'll talk more about in the section later in this chapter titled "Machine Learning and Big Data Clusters."

Run Spark Jobs from Azure Data Studio

One scenario where Spark can be useful is ingestion of data from HDFS in the Storage Pool into tables and in the Data Pool in BDC.

One method to run a Spark Job is to use Azure Data Studio connected directly to the SQL Server Master Instance. Figure 10-14 shows an example of how to run a Spark Job using Azure Data Studio (ADS).

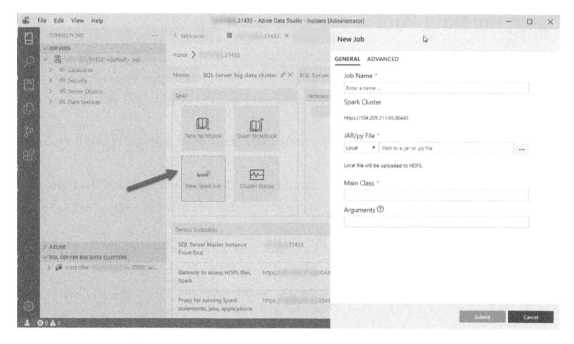

Figure 10-14. *Submitting a Spark Job in Azure Data Studio*

There is more information about submitting Spark Jobs directly with ADS at `https://docs.microsoft.com/en-us/sql/big-data-cluster/spark-submit-job`.

Running Spark Jobs from Other Tools

We also support submitting Spark Jobs against BDC with a tool called **IntelliJ** which you can read at `https://docs.microsoft.com/en-us/sql/big-data-cluster/spark-submit-job-intellij-tool-plugin`. You can also submit Spark Jobs with BDC using **Visual Studio Code** which you can read about at `https://docs.microsoft.com/en-us/sql/big-data-cluster/spark-hive-tools-vscode`. In both of these scenarios, you will use the **Gateway to access HDFS files, Spark** endpoint to connect to BDC to run Spark Jobs.

BDC also provides a REST endpoint for submitting Spark Jobs called **Livy** (`https://livy.apache.org/`). The Livy endpoint is provided through a proxy as part of the <knox-ip> called **Proxy for running Spark statements, jobs, applications**.

Perhaps the most common method for you to use Spark within the context of BDC is through Notebooks with Azure Data Studio (ADS). Up until this chapter of the book, I've shown you many examples using Notebooks with ADS using a *kernel* for SQL. ADS supports kernels for other language environments, including

- PySpark3

- PySpark

- Spark | Scala

- Spark | R

- Python

In any of these scenarios, you will connect to the SQL Server Master Instance with a notebook. ADS will handle submitting the Spark Jobs from the Notebook through the Knox Gateway to properly run the Spark Job in BDC. Any Python or R code in these notebooks will run on your local computer.

MSSQL Spark Connector

We provide another method to run Spark Jobs through the MSSQL Spark Connector. This connector talks to the SQL Server Master Instance, uses SQL Bulk Copy APIs for writes, and has a familiar JDBC interface. You can read more about the MSSQL Spark Connector and how to use it with BDC at `https://docs.microsoft.com/en-us/sql/big-data-cluster/spark-mssql-connector`.

Deploying and Using Applications

I described in the section "Big Data Cluster Architecture" how the Application Pool works in BDC including documentation on how to deploy an application in BDC.

We supply the "runtime" for applications written in R and Python, as well as applications that support MLeap (`https://mleap-docs.combust.ml/`) and SSIS packages. A developer will supply the code and a YAML file specifying how to run the application, and BDC will run a ReplicaSet of containers for the application code.

Once applications are deployed, they are always "running" as a container. If you want to consume or execute the application code, you can use the **azdata** command with the **app** option. You can see the azdata app reference at `https://docs.microsoft.com/en-us/sql/big-data-cluster/reference-azdata-app`.

BDC also provides another method to consume the deployed applications through a REST web interface. By default, all deployed applications have this capability through a protocol called **Swagger** (https://swagger.io/).

The best way to wrap your head around how this all works is to see the examples we have provided at https://github.com/Microsoft/sql-server-samples/tree/master/samples/features/sql-big-data-cluster/app-deploy.

Security

At the time I wrote this chapter, BDC only supported basic authentication, which means logins and passwords. All the service endpoints that come from the controller, Knox, and SQL Server Master Instance require a login and password.

All communication between pods within the cluster occurs with private communication channels using k8s secrets (which in themselves have logins and passwords) and self-signed certificates.

It is our intention by the time we release Big Data Clusters for SQL Server 2019 to support Active Directory (AD) authentication within BDC for all the service endpoints. This includes connecting to the SQL Server Master Instance, Controller Service, and Knox Gateway.

I expect all the details for how to join BDC to a domain, how to deploy BDC with the necessary AD information, the process to add AD users, and how to log in to BDC with an AD account will be in our documentation at https://docs.microsoft.com/en-us/sql/big-data-cluster/concept-security.

High Availability

As I've mentioned in the chapter, pods in BDC are deployed using a k8 StatefulSet or ReplicaSet. This provides *built-in HA* for the k8s platform should a container, pod, or node fail (node failure would only work with a multi-node k8s deployment).

While this form of *basic HA* is helpful for SQL Server, it would be better to use our Always On Availability Group (AG) technology that includes read replicas and SQL Server health detection.

When you deploy BDC, you have the option of enabling *hadr*. Enabling hadr will create an Availability Group by default in BDC and includes the **system databases** in the AG. Multiple pods in a StatefulSet are created to support this deployment.

Using this configuration, we also create endpoints to connect to the primary and secondary replicas of the AG. Since system databases are included as part of the AG, your primary connection is a connection to the SQL Server Master Instance primary, like an AG listener. If a failover occurs, this endpoint will stay connected to whatever replica becomes the new primary. Secondary read-only replica connections are also supported through a separate endpoint.

Take a look at our documentation for how to enable hadr and some of the ramifications of using this type of deployment at `https://docs.microsoft.com/en-us/sql/big-data-cluster/deployment-high-availability`.

Jupyter Books for SQL Server Big Data Clusters

Jupyter Books (`https://jupyter.org/jupyter-book/intro.html`) provide a mechanism to build a collection of notebooks. Azure Data Studio (ADS) provides a Jupyter Book of notebooks to help monitor, manage, and troubleshoot SQL Server Big Data Clusters. All of these notebooks are based on actual Troubleshooting Guides (TSG) used by the SQL Server engineering team!

Figure 10-15 shows a look at Jupyter Books for SQL Server Big Data Clusters.

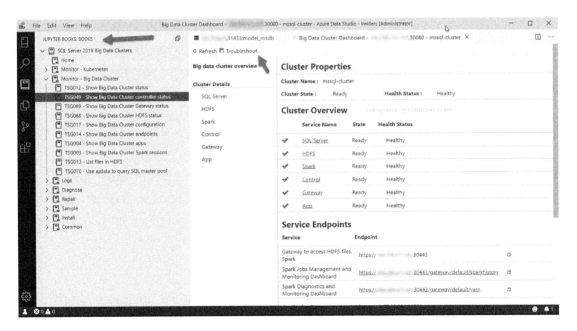

Figure 10-15. *Jupyter Books for SQL Server Big Data Clusters*

Machine Learning and Big Data Clusters

One of the promises of SQL Server Big Data Clusters (BDC) is an *end-to-end Machine Learning platform.* Consider the workflow in Figure 10-16.

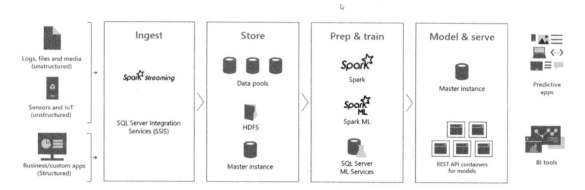

Simplified management and analysis through a unified deployment, governance, and tooling

Figure 10-16. *Machine Learning in Big Data Clusters*

You can do all of this within BDC! Ingest data from different types of data sources, both structured and unstructured, with Spark and SSIS. You can store this data in BDC with Data Pools, HDFS, or even the SQL Server Master Instance. Some of your data for your Machine Learning models may exist in external data sources outside of BDC such as Azure, SQL Server, Oracle, Teradata, and MongoDB. BDC gives you access to any of this data using T-SQL.

You can now prep and train your Machine Learning model using Spark, SparkML, and/or SQL Server Machine Learning Services (ML). You can then expose your model as a *Machine Learning application* using SQL Server ML with T-SQL or as an application with a REST interface in the Application Pool. The Application Pool provides an interesting method for developers since it is all based on your code with declarative YAML and containers. This means it could become a great candidate for a *Continuous Integration/Continuous Delivery* (CI/CD) development model.

Machine Learning Packages

One huge advantage for data scientists using BDC and SQL Server 2019 is all of the Machine Learning Packages we ship when you deploy the product. I asked Dr. Rony Chatterjee, a Senior Program Manager on our team, how I could discover all of these installed ML packages. He gave me the following T-SQL query I could run on SQL Server 2019 or BDC to see these packages:

```
EXEC sp_execute_external_script
@language=N'Python',
@script=N'
import pkg_resources
import pandas
OutputDataSet = pandas.DataFrame([(d.project_name, d.version) for d in pkg_
resources.working_set])'
```

I ran this query on my deployed BDC, and there were well over 160+ Machine Learning packages!

Using Examples

I believe you should review and even try out some examples to see what is possible with Machine Learning and SQL Server Big Data Clusters (BDC):

- **SparkML** – We have an example of using Spark and Spark ML with BDC to predict income levels based on past census data in the United States. You can see this example at `https://docs.microsoft.com/en-us/sql/big-data-cluster/spark-create-machine-learning-model`.

- **BDC Applications** – There are several ML application examples using Application Deploy you can use at `https://github.com/microsoft/sql-server-samples/tree/master/samples/features/sql-big-data-cluster/app-deploy`.

- **The Buck Woody Example** – Buck Woody and I were doing some training for a customer in spring of 2019, and Buck brought up a very cool real-world example for Machine Learning (ML). The idea is that the mythical company WideWorldImporters has trucks that ship temperature-sensitive products. The trucks have cooling systems powered by batteries. A big problem is that the cooling systems in the trucks can fail due to battery lifecycles. The batteries are supposed to last 3 months, but in many cases they fail earlier. The company wants to build a predictive ML model to determine when a battery may need to be replaced – based on dynamic factors of the truck and cargo, instead of the fixed 3-month cycle.

  Buck has a specific Notebook you can use to see this example at `https://github.com/microsoft/sqlworkshops/blob/master/sqlserver2019bigdataclusters/SQL2019BDC/notebooks/bdc_tutorial_05.ipynb`. You need to follow all the Notebooks to use this tutorial at `https://github.com/microsoft/sqlworkshops/tree/master/sqlserver2019bigdataclusters/SQL2019BDC/notebooks`. When Buck and I were doing this training, one of the customers remarked something to the effect of, "Finally someone has explained to me a practical, real-world example for Machine Learning, and I've learned I can use Big Data Clusters to implement it."

Managing and Monitoring Big Data Clusters

You can see there are many components and moving parts to SQL Server Big Data Clusters (BDC). There are many considerations to monitor and manage BDC including managing your Kubernetes cluster, SQL Server, and other BDC components.

Managing Kubernetes (k8s)

If you look at what we have built with BDC, it is effectively an *application powered by Kubernetes*. While we have specific capabilities to help you manage the BDC application, you still must be prepared to manage your k8s cluster. For development and testing of BDC, this is probably not an issue for you, but, to run BDC in production, you must plan for how your k8s cluster will be managed and monitored independent of BDC. I cannot begin to emphasize how important it is to understand how to ensure your k8s cluster is properly managed and functioning at a healthy level. The entire BDC solution depends on it.

I recommend the following resources for managing k8s:

- Look at our documentation for managing Azure Kubernetes Service (AKS) at `https://docs.microsoft.com/en-us/azure/aks/best-practices`.

- I highly recommend this book which also includes some great information on the internals of k8s: `https://learning.oreilly.com/library/view/managing-kubernetes/9781492033905/`.

I also provided tips and techniques to manage and monitor a k8s cluster in Chapter 8 in the section "Tips with k8s."

Managing and Monitoring Big Data Clusters

Besides standard management and monitoring of the SQL Server Master Instance through SQL Server diagnostics such as Dynamic Management Views (DMVs) and Extended Events, we have provided a series of tools and resources to help you specifically manage and monitor the SQL Server Big Data Cluster (BDC).

- **Azure Data Studio (ADS) Big Data Cluster Dashboard**

    ADS ships with a BDC dashboard to help you look at the health of the BDC cluster including all its components. Figure 10-17 shows an example of the ADS BDC Dashboard.

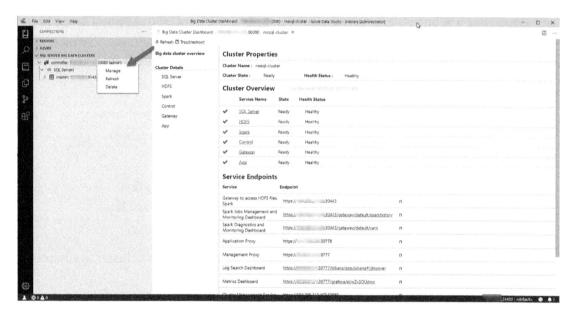

Figure 10-17. *The Azure Data Studio Big Data Cluster Dashboard*

You can click one of the Cluster Details like **SQL Server** and see the status of the SQL Server Master Instance, Compute, Data, and Storage Pool. We have implemented a *liveness probe* (`https://kubernetes.io/docs/tasks/configure-pod-container/configure-liveness-readiness-probes/`) into each pod in BDC to feed the overall health status of all the BDC components. You can read more about the Big Data Cluster dashboard at `https://docs.microsoft.com/en-us/sql/big-data-cluster/manage-with-controller-dashboard`.

- **Grafana Metrics**

Using this context, you can drill into Metrics showing a Grafana (`https://grafana.com/`) dashboard powered by components in the Controller. Figure 10-18 shows the Grafana dashboard for the SQL Server Master Instance.

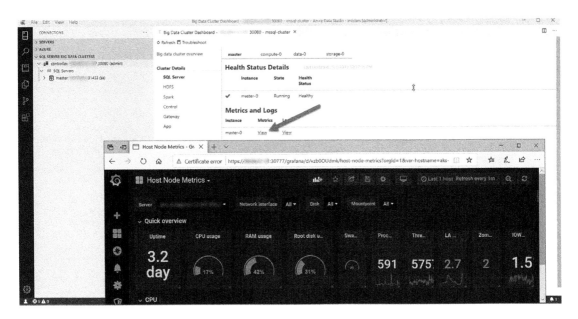

Figure 10-18. *Grafana dashboard for SQL Server Big Data Clusters*

- **Kibana and Elasticsearch**

  Every major component of BDC has a Grafana dashboard and a
  Kibana (https://en.wikipedia.org/wiki/Kibana) visualization
  of Elasticsearch (www.elastic.co/), with logs for deeper
  troubleshooting and analysis. Figure 10-19 shows a Kibana
  visualization of Elasticsearch logging from the SQL Server Master
  Instance through the ADS Big Data Cluster Dashboard.

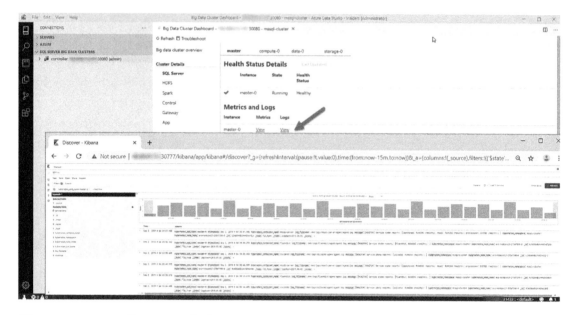

Figure 10-19. *Kibana and Elasticsearch for logs with BDC*

- **Using azdata with SQL Server**

  While Kubernetes allows you to interact with containers with
  a command like kubectl exec, the azdata program allows you
  to interact with SQL Server using the sql option of azdata as
  documented at `https://docs.microsoft.com/en-us/sql/big-`
  `data-cluster/reference-azdata-sql`. This allows you to execute
  T-SQL commands against the SQL Server Master Instance as well
  as access the sqlcmd "shell." Remember azdata is like the kubectl
  program for BDC; you can see the complete reference at `https://`
  `docs.microsoft.com/en-us/sql/big-data-cluster/reference-`
  `azdata`.

- **Kubernetes (k8s) and BDC Troubleshooting**

  Read through my discussion of k8s commands in Chapter 8,
  but we also have some tips on our documentation at `https://`
  `docs.microsoft.com/en-us/sql/big-data-cluster/cluster-`
  `troubleshooting-commands`. Don't forget to also use our SQL Server
  Troubleshooting Guides which I described earlier in this chapter in
  the section "Jupyter Books for SQL Server Big Data Clusters."

Summary

While SQL Server 2019 is radical, SQL Server Big Data Clusters is *revolutionary*. Who would have thought a product some consider just a relational database engine includes an entire solution for your own *data lake, Data Virtualization*, and an *end-to-end Machine Learning platform*, all built on top of Kubernetes?

Think about the technologies we have deployed for Big Data Clusters:

- SQL Server

- Polybase

- HDFS

- Spark

- Livy

- Kibana

- Elasticsearch

- Grafana

- InfluxDB

- Notebooks

- Machine Learning with R and Python

- Java Extensibility

- Always On Availability Groups

All of this is powered by a control plane with our "API Server" or controller serviced to deploy, manage, and power a Big Data Cluster built on Kubernetes.

This is my opinion, but why not just hear from a customer who has already seen the promise of this solution:

"Building and deploying our vertical AI-solution for clinical radiology combines very diverse implementation paradigms, data formats, and regulatory requirements. SQL Server 2019 Big Data Clusters allowed us to accommodate and integrate all aspects from one shared platform – for our data scientists with their deep learning as well as for our software engineers who wire up workflows, security, and scalability.

At runtime, our healthcare customers benefit from simple containerized deployment and maintenance while being able to move our solution between on-prem and the cloud easily." – René Balzano, Founder and CEO of Balzano.

This quote is from our blog we posted when we released Big Data Clusters for SQL Server 2019 as a Release Candidate at `https://cloudblogs.microsoft.com/sqlserver/2019/08/29/sql-server-2019-release-candidate-refresh-with-big-data-clusters/`. I look forward to many other customers that believe Big Data Clusters is just the revolutionary solution they need to power their business.

CHAPTER 11

The Voice of the Customer and Migration

I hope by the time you have reached this chapter, you can appreciate the incredible amount of innovation that has gone into SQL Server 2019. And if you have read all of the first ten chapters, you probably have the feeling of "information overload." I've had several folks who have attended my presentations in the past feel like their "brain is melting." If you feel that way up to this point of the book, I accomplished one of my goals. I wanted this book to be more than just a review of SQL Server 2019, because anyone can get that from the documentation. I wanted this to be a comprehensive look at the SQL Server 2019 release.

   With all these capabilities to solve modern data challenges, is there anything left to talk about? Well, yes, in fact, there is. I'll conclude this book by discussing the "pile of features" (I'm borrowing that term from my colleague Conor Cunningham) we built into SQL Server 2019 based on customer feedback. I'll also talk about methods, tools, and techniques for you to use when migrating to SQL Server 2019.

The Voice of the Customer

Everything you have read in this book so far is one way or another influenced by our customers. In this section, I'll show you a collection of enhancements for SQL Server 2019 which came directly from feedback and requests from customers, through escalations from Microsoft Support, our own internal testing, or engineering interaction directly with customers. If you have never seen the feedback channel directly to the product team, you can check it out at `https://aka.ms/sqlfeedback`. I've provided for you in this section a list of enhancements organized into three areas:

- **Performance** – SQL Server database engine performance enhancements designed to help all or specific workloads run faster.

© Bob Ward 2019
B. Ward, *SQL Server 2019 Revealed*, https://doi.org/10.1007/978-1-4842-5419-6_11

- **User experience** – These are enhancements to improve how the SQL Server product is used or configured.

- **Diagnostics** – These are enhancements designed to improve troubleshooting or diagnosing SQL Server problems.

Performance Enhancements

Our engineering team is always looking to improve performance in the core database engine and seeks opportunities through customer observation, Microsoft support escalations, and often through investigations using benchmark testing. These experiences and observations contributed to the following changes in the core database engine:

- **Reduced compilations for temporary tables**

    One design pattern to use temporary tables is to create the temporary table in one *scope* and use it in another. For example, you could create a temporary table in a batch and then try to use the temporary table in a stored procedure called by the batch. This would normally result in a recompilation of the stored procedure that references the temporary table. In SQL Server 2019, by default, we are able to avoid a recompilation in this scenario. While this improvement may not make the workload significantly faster, it can help an overall application use SQL Server, because lowering the number of recompilations can reduce the overall CPU usage of SQL Server.

- **Indirect checkpoint scalability**

    Indirect checkpoints are the new default method for database checkpoints, as you can read at `https://docs.microsoft.com/en-us/sql/relational-databases/logs/database-checkpoints-sql-server`. We discovered through some benchmark testing and customer feedback that heavy modification workloads could cause stalls in the SQL Server engine, leading to a condition called a non-yielding scheduler. We typically only saw these problems on larger systems with many CPUs, leading us to believe it was a scalability problem. SQL Server 2019 made improvements in the database engine to avoid this problem.

- **Concurrent PFS updates**

  PFS pages are special pages within a database file that SQL Server uses to help locate free space when allocating space for an object. (You can read an older blog post by Paul Randal when he worked at Microsoft to explain PFS pages at `https://blogs.msdn.microsoft.com/sqlserverstorageengine/2006/07/08/under-the-covers-gam-sgam-and-pfs-pages/`.)

  Page latch contention on PFS pages is something that is commonly associated with tempdb, but it can also occur on user databases when there are many concurrent object allocation threads. This improvement changes the way that concurrency is managed with PFS updates so that they can be updated under a shared latch, rather than an exclusive latch. This behavior is on by default in all databases (including tempdb) starting with SQL Server 2019.

  As customers adopt SQL Server 2019, I'm very interested to see the effectiveness on TempDB concurrency with TempDB memory-optimized metadata (discussed in Chapter 2) combined with this enhancement.

- **Worker stealing**

  I call this improvement the "Slava special" named after Slava Oks. We have seen over the years one weakness of the SQLOS scheduler is scheduler contention for worker threads. What a cool system SQLOS could become if we could dynamically change worker threads for a given task to a different scheduler if we detect a contention problem. Under the covers, we have begun to implement such a system, on a limited scale. SQL Server supports the concept of parallel redo for recovery. Dong Cao is the lead developer of this work and has blogged about parallel redo and the internals of redo on Always On Availability Group secondary replicas at `https://blogs.msdn.microsoft.com/sql_server_team/sql-server-20162017-availability-group-secondary-replica-redo-model-and-performance/`. Dong has implemented the concept of worker stealing behind the scenes, only for parallel redo on secondary replicas. If our tests continue to be successful, I look for a day when we can implement this change to the core scheduling in SQLOS across the engine for all types of workloads.

User Experience

We have worked on a set of improvements designed to help the user experience across error messages, setup, and configuration of SQL Server.

- **Verbose truncation warnings**

  Do you know what one of the most voted customer feedback requests of all time with SQL Server is? It is to improve the following error message:

  ```
  String or binary data would be truncated
  ```

  This error message, which is error message number 8152, happens when you attempt to insert or update data in a column where the value to insert or update exceeds the size of the target column. The problem with this message is *there is no context* – it does not provide the name of the table, the column, or the piece of data that would be truncated.

  In SQL Server 2019, the default behavior for an application is to receive error message number 2628, which looks like this:

  ```
  String or binary data would be truncated
  in table '%.*ls', column '%.*ls'.
  Truncated value: '%.*ls'
  ```

  Pam Lahoud of SQL Tiger Team fame blogs about this improvement, including examples, at https://blogs.msdn.microsoft.com/sql_server_team/string-or-binary-data-would-be-truncated-replacing-the-infamous-error-8152/.

  In this blog, she calls out that you can use trace flag 460 in SQL Server 2017 to take advantage of this better error message.

SQL Server 2019 also has a database option to change the default behavior for this error message, which you can read about at `https://docs.microsoft.com/en-us/sql/t-sql/statements/ alter-database-scoped-configuration-transact-sql?#verbose- truncation.`

- **Memory and parallel options during setup**

  Two of the most common instance configuration options to change after installation of SQL Server are "*max server memory*" and "*max degree of parallelism.*"

  Given how often these are changed, we have now put in options during the setup of SQL Server on Windows to choose these configuration options.

  Figure 11-1 shows the setup option to configure parallelism.

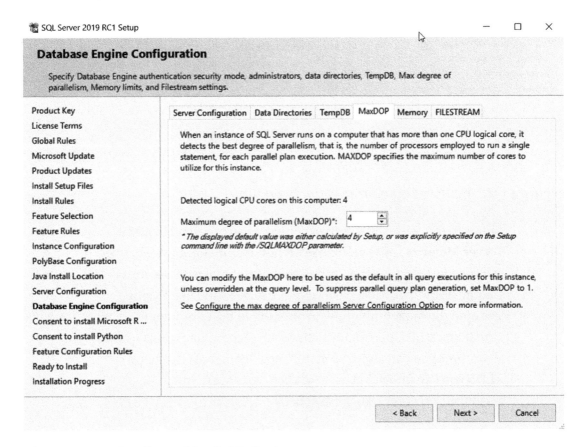

Figure 11-1. *Configure MaxDOP during setup*

Figure 11-2 shows the configuration option for memory during setup.

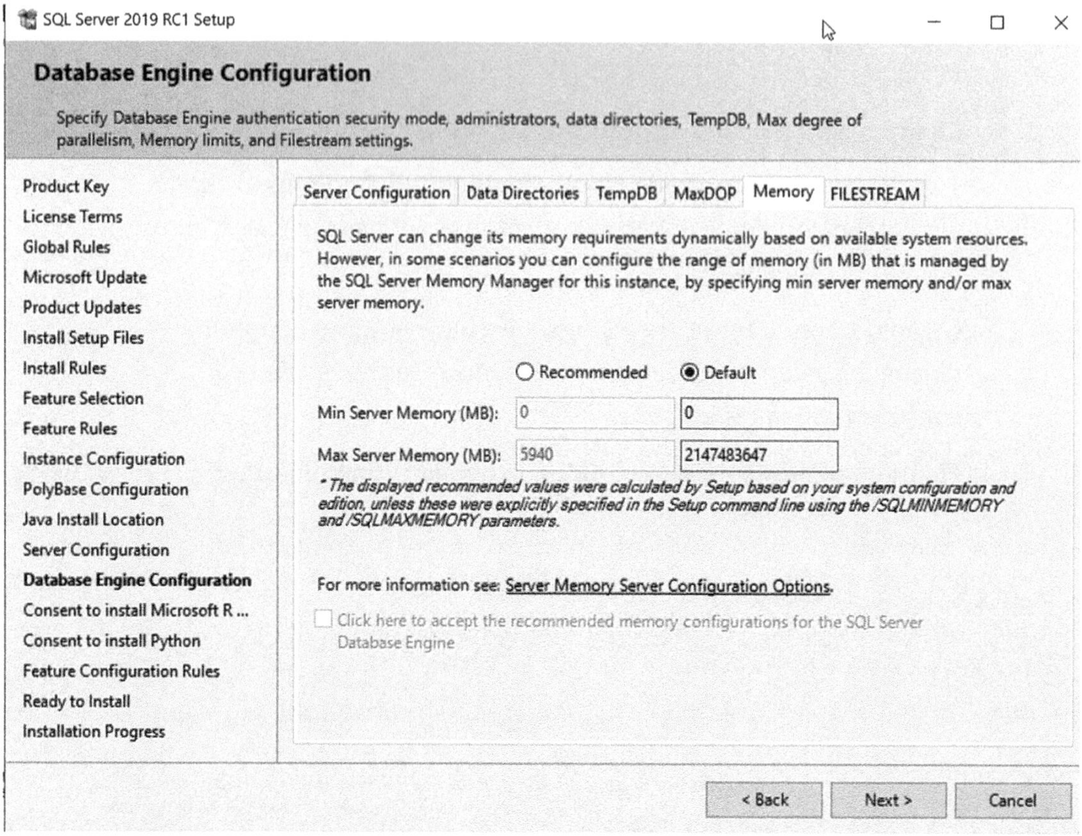

Figure 11-2. *Memory configuration during setup*

Notice in this figure, SQL Server setup has recommended a **Max Server Memory (MB) value**. We do not document how we arrive at a specific value, and you can use whatever makes sense for your environment. Most customers we have found use a value less than the maximum physical memory of the computer or virtual machine. I personally believe the recommendations use algorithms you can also find in the Tiger Team tools BPCheck, which you can find at `https://github.com/microsoft/tigertoolbox/tree/master/BPCheck`.

- **Memory grant percent in Resource Governor**

  I described in Chapter 2 a performance problem that can occur
  due to large memory grants. One solution that can help control
  large memory grants is to use Resource Governor with the
  REQUEST_MAX_MEMORY_GRANT_PERCENT option. One
  issue with this option is that the possible values are in whole
  integer numbers from 1 to 100, representing a percentage of the
  maximum memory value for SQL Server. Even 1% of 1TB is 10Gb,
  which may be too much memory to allow to memory grants. SQL
  Server 2019 now allows REQUEST_MAX_MEMORY_GRANT_
  PERCENT to be a floating-point value, which means it can accept
  values < 1.0.

  You can read more about the use of REQUEST_MAX_MEMORY_
  GRANT_PERCENT at https://docs.microsoft.com/en-us/sql/
  relational-databases/resource-governor/change-workload-
  group-settings.

- **Columnstore Index compression estimation**

  SQL Server includes a system procedure to help estimate
  savings for page and row compression called **sp_estimate_
  data_compression_savings**. SQL Server 2019 now enhances
  this procedure to show estimated compression for the use of
  columnstore indexes and options for columnstore archive. You
  can read more about the use of this procedure with these options
  at https://docs.microsoft.com/en-us/sql/relational-
  databases/system-stored-procedures/sp-estimate-data-
  compression-savings-transact-sql.

Diagnostics

Diagnostics and troubleshooting used to be my world at Microsoft for 20+ years while
I worked in Microsoft Support. I still love to see new diagnostic capabilities added to
the product, even if they seem minor. What may seem minor to some can provide huge
benefits to others.

- **You too can be Paul Randal**

Paul Randal has been a long-time friend of mine, both when he worked in Microsoft SQL Server engineering and in his long career as the CEO of SQLskills along with his wife, Kimberly Tripp. Paul and I both have reputations for internals knowledge, and examining the internals of database pages (sometimes called "page cracking") is an important skill to have. Both of us have for years used the undocumented and unsupported DBCC PAGE command to "hack" a database page. With SQL Server 2019 comes a pair of system objects to help examine the header of a database page:

dm_db_page_info – This is a system function to return a page header as a one-row result of columns for each field in the page header. You can read about this system function at https://docs.microsoft. com/en-us/sql/relational-databases/system-dynamic-management-views/sys-dm-db-page-info-transact-sql.

The required input for this function is information to identify a page, which is the **database id, file id, and page number**. There are some scenarios where the identifier for a page shows up in the result of column like from a DMV. One example is the **wait_resource** of dm_exec_requests. A page identifier from wait_resource is in the form of a *page resource string* which is <dbid>:<fileid>:<pageid>. The system function **fn_PageResCracker** takes a page resource string as input and returns a db_id, file_id, and page_id result.

Therefore, you can run a T-SQL statement like this:

```
SELECT page_info.*
FROM sys.dm_exec_requests AS d
  CROSS APPLY sys.fn_PageResCracker(d.page_resource) AS r
  CROSS APPLY sys.dm_db_page_info(r.db_id, r.file_id, r.page_
  id,'DETAILED')
    AS page_info;
```

This will extract page header details from a page resource. For a concurrency scenario like a page latch wait, this technique can be useful to find out what object belongs to the page for the latch wait.

If you go back to Chapter 2, you will find I provided you an example to use this technique to see which table was involved in tempdb page latch waits:

```
USE tempdb
GO
SELECT object_name(page_info.object_id), page_info.*
FROM sys.dm_exec_requests AS d
  CROSS APPLY sys.fn_PageResCracker(d.page_resource) AS r
  CROSS APPLY sys.dm_db_page_info(r.db_id, r.file_id, r.page_
  id,'DETAILED')
    AS page_info
GO
```

Pam Lahoud also wrote a very nice blog post on this small but important engine enhancement, which you can read at `https://blogs.msdn.microsoft.com/sql_server_team/sql-server-2019-ctp-2-0-new-features-introducing-the-page-cracker-aka-sys-dm_db_page_info/`.

- **Diagnostics on statistics**

   Statistics are a very important part of query performance. Statistics can be updated using a synchronous or asynchronous method, where synchronous means that the query must wait for the stats to be updated, and asynchronous means the query can continue, but the statistics will be updated in the background. Synchronous statistics updates can, in some cases, cause a SELECT statement to take longer than normal. SQL Server 2019 provides some diagnostics to give you granular information on waiting for synchronous statistics updates:

   WAIT_ON_SYNC_STATISTICS_REFRESH – This is a new `wait_type` found in **dm_os_wait_stats**. It shows the accumulated instance-level time spent on synchronous statistics refresh operations.

   dm_exec_requests – The command column of sys.dm_exec_requests will show the value of `SELECT (STATMAN)` if a query is waiting for a synchronous statistics update operation to complete prior to continuing query execution.

- **Query Store enhancements**

  Query Store is an important capability for performance tuning, benchmarking, and troubleshooting. In Chapter 2, I showed some examples of using the Query Store to compare differences in query performance with Intelligent Query Processing.

  The capabilities of Query Store have been enhanced to include the following:

  Forcing fast-forward and static cursors – Query Store now supports forcing plans that include fast-forward and static cursors.

  Custom capture policy for the Query Store – Some customers have had issues using Query Store with certain types of workloads. In SQL Server 2019, we have added more parameters to help with granular control over what is captured by the Query Store. You can find these new options explained using the QUERY_CAPTURE_POLICY in the documentation at `https://docs.microsoft.com/en-us/sql/t-sql/statements/alter-database-transact-sql-set-options`. What better way to interpret how to use the options than from the SQL Server community. There may be no one I know who is more passionate about Query Store than Erin Stellato, and she has an excellent blog talking about these new options at `www.sqlskills.com/blogs/erin/query-store-in-sql-server-2019-ctp-3-0/`.

- **Plan cache granular control**

  There are some cases where you want to manually clear a query or procedure from plan cache. One scenario might be to force a query to be recompiled. You can use the ALTER DATABASE SCOPED CONFIGURATION option CLEAR PROCEDURE_CACHE to clear plan cache for all queries and objects related to a database. Starting in SQL Server 2019, you can clear a plan cache using this statement based on a *plan_handle*. You can find a plan_handle using a DMV like dm_exec_query_stats.

- **DBCC CLONEDATABASE enhancements**

  DBCC CLONEDATABASE can be used for troubleshooting
  purposes to collect the schema and statistics from a database,
  but without user data, into a new database. This can allow you to
  investigate the estimated query plan for a database without having
  to copy all of the actual data.

  SQL Server 2019 enhances DBCC CLONEDATABASE by collecting
  statistics for columnstore indexes, which you can read more about
  at `https://docs.microsoft.com/en-us/sql/t-sql/database-`
  `console-commands/dbcc-clonedatabase-transact-sql`.

Tip   Since DBCC CLONEDATABASE captures all data in system tables (i.e., the
metadata), this includes data for the Query Store. This means you can examine
Query Store performance data offline from the main user database.

What About Business Intelligence?

The SQL Server product comes with Business Intelligence (BI) capabilities, including
SQL Server Analysis Services (SSAS) and SQL Server Reporting Services (SSRS).

Both SSRS and SSAS are part of the SQL Server license for various editions of SQL
Server (SSAS is only part of Enterprise and Standard).

SSRS has no new enhancements in SQL Server 2019. It is important to keep in
mind that Power BI Report Server, which is updated at a different pace than SQL Server
releases, is part of the Enterprise Edition license for SQL Server. You can read more about
Power BI Report Server at `https://docs.microsoft.com/en-us/power-bi/report-`
`server/get-started#licensing-power-bi-report-server`.

SSAS does offer new capabilities in SQL Server 2019; you can read about these
enhancements at `https://docs.microsoft.com/en-us/sql/sql-server/what-s-new-`
`in-sql-server-ver15?#analysis-services`.

Migration to SQL Server 2019

As you make the decision to migrate to SQL Server 2019 for one, many, or all of your instances, it always makes sense to have a plan for migration. In this section, I'll talk about tools and resources that can be helpful to you as you make decisions and build a plan for migration to SQL Server 2019.

The Pam and Pedro Show

This is not a new TV series, but it does sound like one. It represents the methodology that my colleagues Pam Lahoud and Pedro Lopes have been speaking and training customers and the community about how to plan for a successful migration to newer releases of SQL Server. Pam and Pedro call this process **Modernizing the Right Way**. Instead of trying to repeat all of the information Pam and Pedro have used for their training, why not watch it yourself on video? I highly recommend you sit back and watch at your own pace this video on YouTube, a 1-hour presentation by Pam and Pedro on this topic: `www.youtube.com/watch?v=5RPkuQHcxxs`.

I have also used a slide in my presentations about the flow of migration and tools you may want to consider using, as seen in Figure 11-3.

Migrate to the Modern SQL Server

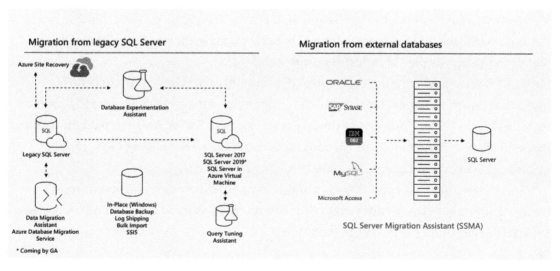

Figure 11-3. *The migration flow and tools for SQL Server*

Pam and Pedro talk about tools as part of their training. I'll spend the rest of the chapter reviewing this flow and the tools in Figure 11-3.

Database Migration Assistant

The **Database Migration Assistant (DMA)** is a free tool available for you to download and run on a Windows computer to assess the configuration and code for an existing instance of SQL Server and to see any possible issues you might face migrating to newer versions. Pedro shows you a walkthrough of this tool in the video I've referenced earlier, but let me also give you some more details about the tool and why I think you should strongly consider using it.

DMA is much more than its predecessor tool, Database Upgrade Advisor. DMA has these major capabilities:

- Assess possible migration *blockers* for your SQL Server (DMA also supports Amazon Relational Database Service (RDS) as a source) migration. This includes options to see what using various database compatibility level options will provide for you as part of the migration. These blockers can include breaking changes, behavior changes, and deprecated features. I'll discuss more details about these terms in the section "Database Compatibility."

- Discover new features in a new version of SQL Server based on an assessment of your current deployment; DMA is smart enough to recognize features that might provide you benefits. Some examples of new feature recommendations include columnstore indexes, Always Encrypted, Transparent Data Encryption (TDE), and Dynamic Data Masking.

- Although not specifically related to SQL Server 2019, DMA will also assess migration issues with SSIS packages when migrating to Azure SQL Database.

- DMA will also support performing the migration of your database to various target types like SQL Server 2019. I only recommend you use this for very small migrations or to test a migration of your database.

Even though DMA is a tool built to run on Windows, you can use this tool for many different sources and targets, including SQL Server on Windows and Linux, Azure SQL Database, Azure SQL Database Managed Instance, and SQL Server in Azure Virtual Machine.

Figure 11-4 shows the possible targets for an assessment and migration using DMA 4.4.

Figure 11-4. *Targets supported for DMA*

There are a few other nice aspects of DMA you should be aware of:

- DMA is a graphical tool on Windows, but also offers a command-line interface (CLI) so you can use it in automation scenarios. You can read more about the DMA CLI at `https://docs.microsoft.com/en-us/sql/dma/dma-commandline`.

- If you want to run an assessment for a large number of SQL Server instances, our migration team has provided a method to store the information in a database for the purpose of reporting, which you can read about at `https://docs.microsoft.com/en-us/sql/dma/dma-consolidatereports`.

- With this data warehouse of assessment data, you can now build Power BI reports on this data. The migration team has also provided a GitHub repo for Power BI reports at `https://docs.microsoft.com/en-us/sql/dma/dma-powerbiassesreport`.

Pedro Lopes has a nice walkthrough demo of using DMA in the YouTube video link I pointed you to previously in this chapter in the section "The Pam and Pedro Show."

We have a great database migration team, and you will find some of their blog posts on the topic very valuable at `https://techcommunity.microsoft.com/t5/Microsoft-Data-Migration/bg-p/MicrosoftDataMigration`.

Database Experimentation Assistant

Assessing the migration of your database and SQL Server deployment is based on the configuration of your SQL Server and databases (including your T-SQL code like stored procedures). However, this assessment is fairly static for possible issues to migrate your SQL Server.

Therefore, one important piece of the migration is performance. Executing as much performance testing of your SQL Server application is one of the most critical aspects to a successful migration. **Database Experimentation Assistant (DEA)** can be a very powerful tool to help you achieve that goal. The goal is to use DEA to tell you what queries from your application will run better, worse, or the same on the new target version of SQL Server. In addition, DEA can tell you if any queries might fail, for example, due to a compatibility issue.

The DEA documentation can be found at `https://docs.microsoft.com/en-us/sql/dea/database-experimentation-assistant-overview`, including a pointer to download the tool. The tool is free and runs on Windows, but can be used to assess migrations to SQL Server on Linux.

To use DEA correctly, it is possible you will need up to four SQL Server instances:

- The source SQL Server to capture your workload

- Two target SQL Servers to replay the captured workload traces

- One SQL Server to store analysis and run reports (you need a database to store the results, so it could actually exist on one of the target SQL Server instances)

The basic flow for using DEA is as follows:

1. Back up the database on the source SQL Server.

2. Capture a trace of your workload using the DEA tool, which can use SQL Server Trace or Extended Events. SQL Server Trace is required if you are capturing a workload on a SQL Server version earlier than SQL Server 2012, because Extended Events does not

have the required events in SQL Server 2008. DEA does support SQL Server 2005, but you must use SQLTrace (you must use SQLTrace for any SQL Server version prior to 2012).

In order to make the best use of the DEA tool, you need to capture a trace of your workload that is representative of the application. The DEA tool allows for captures that range from 5 minutes up to 3 hours. You may have a test server where you can capture a trace for your application, or you may need to run it against the production SQL Server.

3. Prepare replaying traces by restoring the backup in Step 1 to two target SQL Server instances:

    Target Server #1 – A version of SQL Server that is the same as the source from the captured trace in Step 2. You generally do not want to use your production SQL Server.

    Target Server #2 – The new version of SQL Server you are migrating toward, which can be SQL Server on Linux.

    You should set up these SQL Server instances with environments as close to identical as possible in terms of CPU, Memory, disk speeds, and SQL Server configurations.

4. Use the DEA tool to replay the captured trace from Step 2 on both target SQL Servers. The DEA tool will ask for a location to save a trace of the replay.

5. Use the DEA tool to analyze the two captured replay traces so you can compare performance or possible errors from queries in the trace. The DEA tool will prompt you for a SQL Server database to store the analysis results and the location of the replayed traces from Step 4.

Tip   Earlier versions of DEA required you to use a feature in SQL Server called Distributed Replay. You can still use that method, but, as of DEA version 2.6, you can use the **InBuilt** replay method. The InBuilt replay method internally uses a tool called ostress.exe (I introduced you to this tool in Chapter 2). It is still a famous tool within the SQL Server team and community and was developed by my lifetime friends at Microsoft, Keith Elmore and Robert Dorr.

I highly recommend you take a look at DEA before you perform any major migration of SQL Server. Pedro Lopes has a nice walkthrough demo of DEA reports in the YouTube video link I pointed you to previously in this chapter in the section "The Pam and Pedro Show."

Here are a few tips and notes about using the DEA tool:

- DEA comes with reporting tools to view an analysis of the replays. You can read more about DEA reports at https://docs.microsoft.com/en-us/sql/dea/database-experimentation-assistant-view-report.

- DEA also allows you to automate execution from a command-line interface (CLI), which you can read more about at https://docs.microsoft.com/en-us/sql/dea/database-experimentation-assistant-run-command-prompt.

Upgrading to SQL Server 2019

After you perform all of your assessments and you are ready to proceed with an upgrade, you have the following choices.

In-Place Upgrade

This is the process of directly upgrading SQL Server by running setup on the same computer as the SQL Server installation. While this process is completely supported by Microsoft for enterprise production installations, I don't recommend it, except in the case of rolling upgrades, which I'll discuss later in this chapter. This is not an official Microsoft position, but my own recommendation based on years of experience working with customers in Microsoft Support. Even if you choose this option, ALWAYS ensure you have a complete backup of your SQL Server databases from the previous version of SQL Server before you perform the upgrade. In fact, I actually recommend you capture a complete image of the server or virtual machine, so that you could rapidly roll back the exact snapshot of your production server should that be needed.

Note   SQL Server on Linux also supports an in-place upgrade by changing the repository to the new version of SQL Server and running a package manager update (e.g., yum update mssql-server).

There is a variation of an in-place upgrade called a *rolling upgrade*. You can use this method with Always On Failover Cluster Instance or Always On Availability Groups. I'll discuss this option in the section "Live Migration."

Don't forget about the possible upgrade scenario using containers as I described in Chapter 7, in the section "A New Way to Update SQL Server."

Restore a Database

This is perhaps the most common method to upgrade SQL Server (outside of a rolling upgrade). The SQL Server engine understands how to *upgrade* a database when it is restored (technically SQL Server knows how to upgrade a database when it is brought online which is how an in-place upgrade works). Therefore, many customers choose to install SQL Server on a different computer or virtual machine for a migration and restore their databases from an older version of SQL Server.

It is not possible to restore an upgraded database from a major version back down to an older major version. For example, you cannot restore a backup from SQL Server 2019 to SQL Server 2017 (but as I showed you in Chapter 7, you can switch between cumulative updates within a major version).

For SQL Server 2019, you will be able to restore databases from SQL Server 2008 or later. This includes the ability to restore from SQL Server on Windows to a SQL Server 2019 on Linux, since databases are fully compatible across operating system platforms. If you have a database backup from a version of SQL Server prior to SQL Server 2008, you will need to perform a "jump" process by restoring the backup to a supported version of SQL Server (as early as 2008), then back up from there and perform another restore to SQL Server 2019.

One of the key pillars to help reduce problems with migration is that when a database is restored to a new version of SQL Server, **the database compatibility level is retained** from the older SQL Server version. I'll discuss more about this concept in the section later in the chapter called "Database Compatibility."

SQL Server Integration Services (SSIS) or Bulk Import/Export

Another method to migrate your database to SQL Server 2019 is to export and import the data using SQL Server Integration Services (SSIS) or other tools for bulk export/import.

I've seen some customers use this method when they need to perform transformations or structural changes to the overall database design or schema. In other words, instead of just moving the database "as is," some customers *migrate the application* with a move to a new version of SQL Server. This includes changes to the database schema. Another technique I've seen for transformation is to restore the database from a previous version and then run build code on the new version of SQL Server to redesign certain tables or stored procedures.

Live Migration

Restoring a database requires downtime for the application and users. What if your business requirements require a very small amount of downtime? In these scenarios, you may consider using some techniques, such as

- **Rolling upgrade**

  One popular option if you are using an Always On Failover Cluster Instance or Always On Availability Group is a rolling upgrade. Both of these options are possible with SQL Server 2019, and a rolling upgrade is one of the reasons customers use these High Availability solutions.

  Always On Failover Cluster Instance supports rolling upgrades, provided the SQL Server version on the current cluster is supported for an in-place upgrade scenario. You can read more about rolling upgrades for an Always On Failover Cluster Instance at https://docs.microsoft.com/en-us/sql/sql-server/ failover-clusters/windows/upgrade-a-sql-server-failover- cluster-instance.

  Always On Availability Groups are only supported back to SQL Server 2012, since that is the first version where this technology was available. This rolling upgrade option has many options and is probably the most preferred method for an enterprise live migration scenario for SQL Server. You can read about this option at `https://docs.microsoft.com/en-us/sql/database-engine/availability-groups/windows/upgrading-always-on-availability-group-replica-instances`.

SQL Server 2017 also introduced a new feature for Availability Groups called *Clusterless* Availability Groups. A Clusterless Availability Group does not require underlying failover clustering software. It is also possible to perform a live migration using this technology, and it could be one of your best options to migrate from SQL Server 2017 to SQL Server on Linux. You can read more about this option at `https://docs.microsoft.com/en-us/sql/linux/sql-server-linux-availability-group-cross-platform`.

- **Log Shipping**

   A more basic method for a live migration is to use Log Shipping. Log Shipping is a simple technology that uses SQL Server database and transaction log backups and restores to synchronize data to a secondary SQL Server. You can read about Log Shipping at `https://docs.microsoft.com/en-us/sql/database-engine/log-shipping/about-log-shipping-sql-server`. This is a form of a *manual* rolling upgrade that does not require any Always On technologies.

   You can read through the process of upgrading with Log Shipping at `https://docs.microsoft.com/en-ca/sql/database-engine/log-shipping/upgrading-log-shipping-to-sql-server-2016-transact-sql`.

- **Replication**

   Our documentation provides details on how to upgrade a complete SQL Server replication topology at `https://docs.microsoft.com/en-us/sql/database-engine/install-windows/upgrade-replicated-databases`. One interesting idea (I was inspired by Amit Banerjee on this idea when we visited a customer together) is to use SQL Server Replication for a live migration, even if you don't need replication as a strategy.

Since a subscriber in a replication topology can be a newer version of SQL Server than the distributor and publisher, you could use the subscriber as your new primary. In other words, you could set a subscriber with SQL Server 2019, with an older version of SQL Server as the distributor and publisher. As your apps and users are writing against the older publisher, your SQL Server 2019 subscriber has all the latest data. When you are ready for a cutover, disable replication and point all users to the new SQL Server 2019 database (which *was* the subscriber). It sounds simple, but there will be some downtime, and it may be painful to set up and disable replication. Disabling replication does not remove data in the subscriber database, and this is documented at `https://docs.microsoft.com/en-us/sql/relational-databases/replication/disable-publishing-and-distribution`.

Database Compatibility

Database compatibility is designed to *provide backward compatibility* as you migrate to a newer version of SQL Server. You should use the following resource for all terminology and details about database compatibility: `https://aka.ms/dbcompat`.

One of the first things you should understand is how database compatibility levels correspond to the default level for a SQL Server version. You can see this list at `https://docs.microsoft.com/en-us/sql/t-sql/statements/alter-database-transact-sql-compatibility-level?#syntax`. As an example, the default database compatibility level of SQL Server 2012 is 110.

Note   I've been asked before why the dbcompat levels don't line up with the name or version label of the SQL Server release. This is because SQL Server has an internal version number, and the dbcompat levels line up with that version number. SQL Server 2012 is really version 11.x (see @@VERSION) so the dbcompat level is 110. Confusing, I realize, but we name releases a bit differently from how we version them.

If you restore a database backup from SQL Server 2012 to SQL Server 2019, SQL Server will keep the database compatibility level at 110. The intention of this design is for you to have confidence that your application, queries, and behavior against the database will behave just like it was running on SQL Server 2012. The difference is you can now take advantage of new features in the new release of SQL Server (there is an exception to this in that we sometimes use database compatibility to enable new functionality).

I mentioned in the preceding section on Database Migration Assistant (DMA) that the DMA tool would look for migration problems using the following terms: breaking changes, behavior changes, and deprecated features. Let me define these terms in relation to the use of database compatibility for backward compatibility.

Breaking changes is defined as *behavior changes* that can result in a different outcome. In some cases, a breaking change is protected by using a database compatibility level on a new version of SQL Server. In other cases, a breaking change is not protected by database compatibility level. Confusing? I understand how you feel. Fortunately, the most recent versions of SQL Server have very few breaking changes that are not protected. The good news is that the DMA tool is designed to help detect these issues.

To find out a list of breaking changes with each SQL Server version, start at this documentation page `https://docs.microsoft.com/en-us/sql/t-sql/statements/ alter-database-transact-sql-compatibility-level?#using-compatibility- level-for-backward-compatibility` and scroll down for the section that starts with the sentence, "Breaking changes introduced in a given SQL Server version…" This section includes pointers to breaking changes in all SQL Server versions back to SQL Server 2012.

There are some behavior changes used with database compatibility level that are designed to correct a problem or enable new functionality. One example of this is the Intelligent Query Processing capability I discussed in Chapter 2, which is enabled with database compatibility 140 or 150.

Deprecated functionality is protected by database compatibility level. Deprecated functionality includes features or behavior that we do not intend to enhance in the future. Microsoft may remove this functionality in any new release. **Discontinued** functionality means we have removed a feature or behavior from a release of SQL Server, so database compatibility will not help. Discontinued functionality starts as deprecated first. Fortunately, we have made decisions in recent releases to not discontinue anything. However, I personally would not rely on deprecated functionality, especially for new projects. The SQL Server documentation to find deprecated functionality is easier with recent releases. Use the following documentation link to find deprecated and discontinued functionality in recent releases: `https://docs. microsoft.com/en-us/sql/database-engine/sql-server-database-engine- backward-compatibility`. To go further back, you will have to switch to an older release

of the documentation. For example, this is the documentation link for SQL Server 2014:
`https://docs.microsoft.com/en-us/sql/database-engine/sql-server-database-engine-backward-compatibility?view=sql-server-2014`.

With this in mind, how good is database compatibility level to maintain backward compatibility when migrating to a new version of SQL Server? It is good enough that Pedro Lopes is hoping you will bet on it. And he is hoping to convince many Independent Software Vendors (ISV) to do the same. Pedro's vision is for application developers to *certify* their application on a database compatibility level instead of on a version of SQL Server. If you listen closely to Pedro on the video link I provided in "The Pam and Pedro Show" section, he says, "Microsoft will stand by Database Compatibility" as a certification model by

- Full functional protection if the DMA tool comes back clean with
  no errors.

  This means no breaking changes for your application if you pick
  an appropriate database compatibility level that comes back with
  no errors.

- Query plan shape protection on similar hardware

  This means the structure of a query plan (i.e. operators and
  their flow) should not change on similar hardware where you
  ran the query on a previous version using the same database
  compatibility level on the new version of SQL Server.

To this date, our experience is that these bold statements are holding true with our customers.

Here is my summary of what you can expect for backward compatibility as you think of migrating to SQL Server 2019:

- If you have been using a discontinued feature, your application might
  break after migrating.

- If you have been using a deprecated feature, you should be fine. But
  I would make plans to move away from relying on this deprecated
  functionality.

- Start with the database compatibility (dbcompat) level that matches
  the SQL Server version you were migrating from. If you are on SQL
  Server 2012, keep your dbcompat at 110 as a starting point.

405

Note   The biggest change in database compatibility (dbcompat) level that could affect query performance was 120. This is because we introduced a fairly large change to the query optimizer called the Cardinality Estimation (CE) model. If you migrated to a newer version of SQL Server and needed to use a dbcompat of 120 or higher, but experience issues related to the CE model, you can disable the CE mode using the LEGACY_CARDINALITY_ESTIMATION option of ALTER DATABASE SCOPED CONFIGURATION.

- Keep this dbcompat level in your production SQL Server 2019 instance, or perform a test migration to SQL Server 2019, and do further testing with newer dbcompat levels to look for any issues with your application. In the next section, I'll discuss a tool called **Query Tuning Assistant** that can aid you in these efforts. You can use the DMA tool to see the configuration assessment of various dbcompat levels for SQL Server 2019 for your database.

A few other comments about database compatibility (dbcompat) and backward compatibility:

- You can see a complete list of differences in behavior between dbcompat levels starting at this documentation link: `https://docs.microsoft.com/en-us/sql/t-sql/statements/alter-database-transact-sql-compatibility-level?#differences-between-compatibility-level-140-and-level-150`. You start here and scroll down to see differences, all the way back to 90 (SQL Server 2005).

- Database compatibility does not affect breaking changes at the SQL Server instance level. So as good as our commitment is to use dbcompat as a mechanism to certify an application, if the application uses any SQL Server instance level functionality, you need to ensure this is well tested. Instance level functionality could be anything from the use of system catalog views, system Dynamic Management Views, SQL Agent, Linked Servers, or T-SQL statements that affect the entire instance of SQL Server and are not scoped to a database.

Query Tuning Assistant and Post Migration

At various times in 2018, I kept seeing e-mails to our teams from Pedro Lopes about a project he was working on called TUNA. At least that is how I kept remembering the project name. What the name of the project really was, I came to find out, was **TunA.** TunA stands for **Tun**ing **A**ssistant.

If you remember back to the previous section, where I talk about recommendations for database compatibility, I mention the idea of testing your application against a new database compatibility level as part of our migration.

Let's review back to the video from "The Pam and Pedro Show" section earlier in this chapter. About 40:40 into the video, you will see Pedro talk about **Post Migration**. What he means here is that there are steps you can take to optimize your workload after you migrate to a newer version of SQL Server, *assuming* you kept your *source* database compatibility level from the previous version of SQL Server.

Pedro proposes a methodology using Query Store to compare workload performance before and after a change to database compatibility level. This method comes from the documentation with Query Store as a usage scenario, called **Keep performance stability during the upgrade to newer SQL Server**, which you can read at `https://docs.microsoft.com/en-us/sql/relational-databases/performance/query-store-usage-scenarios?#CEUpgrade`.

Now comes in the TunA project. Pedro and team built functionality into the SQL Server Management Studio (SSMS) tool in version 18.x called the **Query Tuning Assistant (QTA).** QTA allows you to automate the process of using the Query Store to assess and fix any query performance issues when moving to a new database compatibility level.

Figure 11-5 shows the QTA workflow.

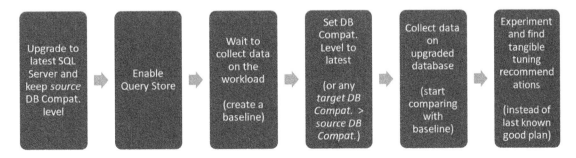

Figure 11-5. *The QTA workflow*

Using the QTA tool with SSMS provides you expert advice when query performance may be worse under a new database compatibility level, after a migration to a newer version of SQL Server. The resulting recommendations may involve a change to the query, such as the use of query options. All of the recommendations are based on documented advice. It's like having "Pedro Lopes in a box."

I thought about putting a sample of QTA in this chapter, but, instead, why not just use the extremely well put together sample Pedro Lopes has on GitHub. You can download and use this example from `https://github.com/microsoft/tigertoolbox/blob/master/Sessions/Winter-Ready-2019/Lab-QTA.md`.

Running in Azure Virtual Machine

When you make the decision to deploy or migrate to SQL Server 2019, you may want to consider using SQL Server 2019 in the cloud. One option to run SQL Server 2019 in the cloud is with Azure Virtual Machine (which is known as an Infrastructure as a Service or IAAS environment).

Azure Virtual Machine (VM) allows you to focus on the deployment of the operating system (Windows or Linux) and SQL Server and not worry about the hardware platform and infrastructure.

Azure VM is known as one of the most frictionless methods to move to the cloud for SQL Server, because your interaction with SQL Server is just like a virtual machine in your data center or your environment.

In reality, that is not 100% true, because there are choices you have to make that are specific to Azure, including machine sizes, storage, networking, and security. We have guidance in our documentation about all of these choices at `https://docs.microsoft.com/en-us/azure/virtual-machines/windows/sql/virtual-machines-windows-sql-server-iaas-overview`.

We also provide automation with Azure Virtual Machine that you may not be aware of. This includes automated backups for SQL Server and automated patching for both the operating system and SQL Server. You can read about automated backups at `https://docs.microsoft.com/en-us/azure/virtual-machines/windows/sql/virtual-machines-windows-sql-automated-backup-v2` and automated patching at `https://docs.microsoft.com/en-us/azure/virtual-machines/windows/sql/virtual-machines-windows-sql-automated-patching`.

In the summer of 2019, we announced three important updates in Azure that are helpful for managing SQL Server in Azure Virtual Machine:

- A new Azure portal experience, called **Azure SQL**, which simplifies creating and managing assets related to SQL Server in the cloud.

  Figure 11-6 shows the new Azure SQL portal experience.

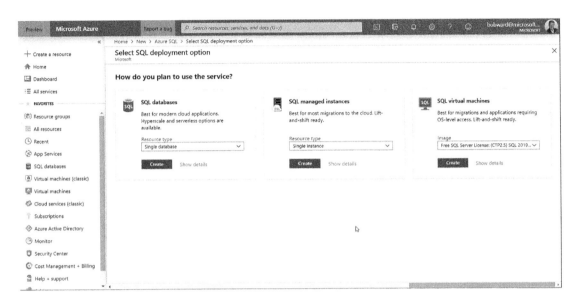

Figure 11-6. *The Azure SQL portal experience*

- A method to **register your Azure Virtual Machine (VM) with SQL Server** with our resource provider. This registration applies to scenarios where you install SQL Server in an Azure Virtual Machine instead of using the gallery images. It unlocks your SQL Server in Azure VM to take advantage of Azure Hybrid Benefits, compliance, automated backup, and automated patching. You can read more about this capability at https://docs.microsoft.com/en-us/azure/ virtual-machines/windows/sql/virtual-machines-windows-sql- register-with-resource-provider.

- Azure announced the general availability of **Ultra Disk Storage** or **Ultra SSD**. Ultra SSD provides low-latency, extremely fast performance in the cloud, which matches very well to I/O-intensive SQL Server workloads. You can read about the announcement for Ultra SSD at `https://azure.microsoft.com/en-us/blog/announcing-the-general-availability-of-azure-ultra-disk-storage/`. If you want to see Ultra Disk Storage in action with SQL Server, check out the recording of this Microsoft Ignite session in 2018: `https://azure.microsoft.com/en-us/resources/videos/ignite-2018-running-high-performance-workloads-in-azure-with-ultra-ssds-the-next-gen-azure-managed-disk/`. If you look about 46 minutes into this recording, you might recognize this presenter as he shows SQL Server performance with Ultra Disk Storage.

SQL Server Migration Assistant

Some of you reading this book may not be using SQL Server or may have other assets in your organization for other database products such as Oracle, mySQL, and DB2. I covered in Chapter 9 how to use Polybase to access these data sources. But what if you want to migrate your database and application from these products to SQL Server?

We have a free tool to assist you with migrations to SQL Server (and Azure) from other "third-party" database solutions. This tool is called the **SQL Server Migration Assistant**. The right-hand side of Figure 11-3 shows the possibilities with this tool. You can read more about this tool, how to deploy it, and how to use it successfully for a migration at `https://docs.microsoft.com/en-us/sql/ssma/sql-server-migration-assistant`.

Figure 11-7 shows a screenshot of using SSMS to migrate from Oracle.

Figure 11-7. Using SSMS to migrate from Oracle to SQL Server

SSMA comes as a series of tools, one for each type of third-party product supported for migration. Like DMA and DEA, SSMS also has a command-line interface (CLI). You can read more about the syntax of SSMS for Oracle at https://docs.microsoft.com/en-us/sql/ssma/oracle/command-line-options-in-ssma-console-oracletosql.

Summary

In this chapter, I've shown numerous enhancements to SQL Server 2019 based on customer feedback and our experiences working directly with customers. Each of these may not seem like major enhancements, but, collectively, they represent key innovation to enhance the performance, user experience, and diagnostics of SQL Server.

I've also discussed how to plan and execute a migration to SQL Server 2019 including tools, strategies, and the use of database compatibility for functional and performance protection.

This chapter marks the end of our journey together in this book with SQL Server 2019. I hope you have enjoyed reading and learning about SQL Server 2019 as much as I enjoyed writing about it. For many of you, this will really be the beginning of your journey with SQL Server 2019. For me, you will continue to hear me speak and talk about SQL Server 2019. But I'll also be looking into the future for our next release, our rapid pace of work in the cloud, and the next set of innovation that makes SQL Server a truly unique product in the industry.

Index

A

Aborted transaction map, 130
Accelerated database recovery (ADR),
  116, 125
  fast rollback and aggressive log
    transaction, 136
  long active transactions, 126
  performance/size, 139–141
  PVS, 129, 141, 142
    log records, 133, 135
    off-row storage, 130
    phases, 131, 133
    recovery process, 130
    snapshot isolation, 129
  speeding up recovery, 137, 139
  SQL process, 127–129
  tracking, 142
    extended events, 143
  usage, 144
Active Directory (AD) authentication,
  186, 238
Adaptive Query Processing (AQP), 21
Aggressive log truncation, 127
Always encrypted, 11
  architecture, 89
  attestation service, 91
  client application, 89
  secure enclaves, 90–92
  SQL Server 2016, 89

Apache Spark, 5
Application Programing
  Interface (API), 252
APPROX_COUNT_DISTINCT()
  function, 57
Architecture, BDC
  controller, 357
    ADS, 358
    application pool, 362, 363
    compute pool, 361
    control plane, 358
    data pool, 361, 362
    server container, 359
    service, 358
    storage pool, 359–361
  k8s perspective, 352, 353
  pool, 352
  SQL server master instance, 353–357
Aris cluster, 5
Attestation Service, 91
Availability Group (AG), 372
Availability groups
  enchancements, 123
  concepts, 124
  read/write connection
    redirection, 124, 125
  synchronous replicas, 124
Azure Data Studio (ADS), 14, 211, 317,
  339, 358
Azure Kubernetes Service (AKS), 250, 254

413

B

Bare metal computer, 199
Bash shell scripts, 210
Batch mode, rowstore, 49–51
Big data clusters (BDC), 3, 6
    ADS, 365
    application deployment, 337
    architecture (*see* Architecture, BDC)
    controller service endpoint, 337, 363
    data cache, 336
    deployment (*see* Deployment, BDC)
    HDFS, 335, 336
    high availability, 372
    high-value data, 332
    IP address, 365
    Jupyter Book, 373
    Kubernetes (k8s), 376, 377
    ML, 337, 374
        examples, 375, 376
        packages, 375
    managing/monitoring, 377
        ADS, 378
        azdata, 380
        Grafana metrics, 378
        kibana and
          elastic search, 379
    master instance, 332
    polybase, 336
    security, 372
    service endpoints, 337
    solutions, 333
    sources, 338, 339
    spark, 336
    SQL Server 2019, 335
    Swagger, 372
    technologies, 334
Breaking/behavior changes, 404
Business Intelligence (BI), 393

C

Cardinality estimation (CE), 20
Certificate management, 88, 112–114
Change data capture (CDC), 13, 177, 184
Columnstore indexes, 49
Command-line interface (CLI), 252, 396
Complete durability, 181
Compute nodes, 309
Constant time recovery (CTR), 125
Containers, SQL Server
    AD Authentication, 238
    application, 229
    bin/libs, 198
    capability, 195
    CMD statement, 204
    command-line tools, 203
    concept, 195
    concept of isolation, 196
    consistent, 197
    COPY command, 204
    cumulative update, 225–228
    daemon program, 204
    db-init.sh, 231, 233
    db-init.sql, 232, 233
    debugging technique, 206
    deployment, 212–224
    directory, 205
    docker, 198
    Docker magic, 200–201
    editions/licensing, 242, 243
    efficient, 198
    entrypoint.sh, 231, 232
    -e parameters, 205
    EXPOSE command, 204
    FROM command, 204
    high availability, 239
    hosting, 199, 200
    host OS, 198

image, 196

isolated manner, 196

lifecycle, 201–203

lightweight, 197

Linux users, 211

macOS users, 211

non-root containers, 238, 239

operating system, 196

packages, 242

performance, 236, 237

persisted storage, 198

portable, 196

replication, 233–236

resource control, 239, 240

RUN command, 204

security, 238

server/database configuration, 241

startup sequence, 206

virtual machines, 195

windows users, 211

working, 206–209

Continuous integration/continuous
delivery (CI/CD), 374

COUNT() function, 57

D

Data nodes, 5

Database compatibility, 403

backward, 405, 406

certification model, 405

Database Experimentation Assistant (DEA)

flow, 397, 398

instances, 397

tool, 399

Database Migration Assistant (DMA), 404

capabilities, 395

targets, 396

Database scoped credential, 304

Data classification

accept classification
recommendations, 99

auditing, 105–110

data sensitivity details, 108

information_type, 93

launching tool, 97

manually adding, 102

report, 100

saving accepted
recommendations, 100

SSMS, 98

tool, 94

T-SQL, 104

view columns, 96

WHERE clause, 110

wizard in SSMS, 92

Data Movement Service (DMS), 308, 324

Data platform, 2

Data pool, 336, 369

data_sensitivity_information, 94, 105

Data virtualization, 5, 10

built-in connectors, 366

concept, 300

definition, 300–302

external tables, BDC, 367

HDFS in BDC, working, 368

polybase, 301

T-SQL scripts, 366

Deployment, BDC

configuration, 350, 351

experience, 344–346

Kubernetes (k8s) distribution, 339, 340

method, 343, 344

offline, 344

sanity check, 346–349

tools, 341, 342

Deployment options, Kubernetes
   AKS, 254
   Azure Stack, 254
   cloud providers, 255
   Minikube, 253
   open source, 253
   Red Hat OpenShift, 254
   Windows Server, 254
Deployment, SQL Server
   ADS, 219, 224
   dockerpowershell directory, 212
   RHEL container, 213
   WideWorldImporters backup file, 212
Deprecated functionality, 404
Development servers, 197
Diagnostics, 389–393
Discontinued functionality, 404
Distributed Transaction Coordinator
      (DTC), 13, 151, 176
Docker-compose.yml file, 230, 231
DockerDesktopVM, 199
Docker inspect command, 208
Docker magic
   control groups, 200
   Namespace, 200
   readable layer, 201
   union file system, 200
   volume, 201
   writeable layer, 201
Dynamic Management Function (DMF), 68
Dynamic Management
      Views (DMVs), 61, 179, 377

E

Edge constraints, 155
Elastic Kubernetes Service (EKS), 255
Enclaves, 90, 91

Encrypting connections, 88
Encrypting data, 89
End-to-end encryption mechanism, 89
Extensibility framework, 159
External resource pool, 164
External tables
   Azure SQL database, 317–325
   built-in connectors, 325
   HDFS, 326
   vs. linked servers, 328
   ODBC connector, 326, 327
   restrictions/limitations, 328
   scope, 315
   semantic layer, 327, 328
   tools, 315–317
Extract, Transform,
      and Load (ETL), 5, 184, 297

F

Failover Cluster Instance (FCI), 112
Fast and consistent
      database recovery, 126

G

General Data Protection
      Regulation (GDPR), 12, 88
Go application, 150
Go language, 149
Google Kubernetes
      Engine (GKE), 255
Graph database
   data and metadata, 152
   enhancements
      edge constraints, 155
      MERGE with graph tables, 156
      SHORTEST_PATH, 155

MATCH keyword, 152
nodes and edges, 152
social network, 153, 154
SQL Server, 153, 154

H

Hadoop distributed file
        system (HDFS), 335
Hash joins operation, 24
Hash Match operator, 57
HDFS Tiering, 336
Helm charts, 249
High Availability Disaster
        Recovery (HADR), 123
Host Guardian Service (HGS), 91
Hybrid Buffer Pool, 82
HyperLogLog, 57

I

Independent Software Vendors (ISV), 405
In-Memory Database
    features, 74
    hybrid buffer pool, 82
    page latch, 79, 80
    persistent memory, 82
    technical support article, 76
    Tempdb metadata, 75, 76
    Tempdb system, 80
In-Memory OLTP, 151
Instantaneous transaction rollback, 127
Intelligent performance, new
        enhancements, 19
Intelligent Query Processing (IQP)
    family tree, 22
    faster query plan, 48
    methods, 24

slower query plan, 46
steps, 23
table variable estimation, 47, 49
table variable use, 45
top resource consuming report, 44

J

Java Runtime Engine (JRE), 170, 192
Java Runtime Environment (JRE), 299

K

kubectl, 252
Kubernete (k8s), 5
Kubernetes (k8s)
    availability, 292–295
    Azure Cloud Shell, 258
    dashboard, 279, 280
    deployment options, 253–255
    extension
        ERRORLOG, 276
        namespace setting, 275
        terminal session, 275
        Visual Studio Code, 273
        YAML file, 274
    Helm Charts, 249, 292
    high availability, 281–287
    hosting containers, 249
    internal comments, 252
    kubectl commands, 277–279
    kubectl distribution, 255–257
    load balancer, 256
    metrics/logs, 280, 281
    mobile user, 259
    objects
        cluster, 251
        node, 251

Kubernetes (k8s) (*cont.*)
    pod, 251
    PVC, 251
    secret, 251
    service, 251
    storage class, 251
  references, 250
  reverse engineering, 277
  SQL Server deployment, 257–273
  storage class, 255
  updating SQL Server, 287–292
kubespray, 253

L

Languages and drivers, 148–150
Last-page insert contention, 83–85
Latch convoy, 83
launchpadd, 190
Libcontainer, 201
Lifecycle, container
  build command, 202
  client, 202
  compose, 202
  engine, 201
  pull command, 202
  push command, 202
  run command, 203
Lightweight profiling, 62
Lightweight query profiling, 61, 62
  active query, 65, 66
  better query, 73, 74
  nested loops, 67, 68
  problem query, 71–73
  SSMS, 64, 65, 69, 70
  usage, 62, 63
Linux
  AD, 186, 187

CDC, 184
deployment enchancements, 180, 181
deployment, SQL ML services, 187–189
DTC, 176, 184–186
extensibility framework/language
    extensions, 192
feature parity, 177, 178
launchpadd
  mssql_satellite login, 191
  R script, 190
  T-SQL script, 190
platform enchancements, 178
  dm_os_ring_buffers, 179
  memory notifications, 179
pmem, 182
polybase to SQL Server, 13
releases, 181, 182
replication, 183
SQLPAL, 176
SQL server architecture, 175
Linux Containers for
    Windows (LCOW), 199
Live query stats, 61
Log Sequence Number (LSN), 128
Log Shipping, 402

M

Machine Learning, 13
MATCH, 152
Max Server Memory (MB) value, 388
Memory-based hardware, 81
Memory grants
  excessive
    properties, 40, 41
    sa login, 37–39
  feedback, 25
  healed itself, 26

operations, 24
problems, 25
underestimated
    estimates *vs.* actuals, 30
    feedback properties, 36
    hash join tempdb spill, 31
    query plan, 29
    query plan properties, 33
    SELECT operator, 32, 35
underestimated
    query plan properties, 34
    T-SQL script, 27–29
Memory notifications, 179
Memory-optimized tables, 75
Metanautix, 5
Microsoft Container Registry, 210
Microsoft Distributed Transaction
        Coordinator (MSDTC), 184
Mission-critical availability, 12
Modern data developer
    graph database (*see* Graph database)
    languages and drivers, 148–150
    ML Services (*see* SQL Server Machine
        Learning Services)
    platforms and editions, 151
    UTF-8 Support, 157, 158
Modern Data Platform
    ADS, 14
    customer support, 14
    data virtualization, 10
    developers, 12, 13
    investment, 13, 14
    mission-critical availability, 12
    performance, 11
    security, 11
Modern development platform, 12, 13
mssql-java-lang-extension.jar, 169

mssql-launchpadd, 189
mssql-mlservices-packages-py, 188
mssql-mlservices-packages-r, 188

N

National Vulnerability Database (NVD), 88
nchar and nvarchar data types, 157
Non-root containers, 209

O

off-row storage, 130
Online index maintenance, 116, 117
    clustered columnstore, 123
    creation, 118–123
    prerequisites, example, 118
    resumable index rebuild operation, 117
Open Container Initiative (OCI), 201

P

Paging file, 31
Parallel data warehouse, 4
Parallel Data Warehouse (PDW), 298
Performance, 11
Performance enhancements, 384–386
Persistent memory (pmem), 182, 183
Persistent Version Store (PVS), 141, 142
Persistent Volume
        Claim (PVC), 251, 265, 293, 351
Polybase
    Azure, 310
    data movement, 297
    data virtualization, 297
    external tables work, 305, 306
    history, 298–300

Polybase (*cont.*)
    Linux, 193, 310
    prerequisites (*see* Prerequisites, polybase)
    scale-out group, 309
    standalone instance, 307, 308
    workflow, 303–305
Post migration, 407
Prerequisites, polybase
    setting up and enabling, 311, 312
    WWI, 314
Program managers (PM), 166
Project SQL Server Seattle, 2
Pushdown, 306

Q

Query processing and polybase, 310
Query Processor (QP), 21
Query profiling infrastructure, 61
Query Tuning Assistant (QTA), 406, 407

R

Red Hat Enterprise Linux (RHEL), 13, 182, 206
Relational database, 151
Relational database management system (RDBMS), 335
Resource Governor, 164
RevoScaleR, 159
Ring buffer dynamic management views, 179, 180

S

Seattle project, 2, 3
Secure enclaves, 11, 90

Security, 11, 12
    always encrypted (*see* Always encrypted)
    capabilities, 87, 88
    certificate management, 112–114
    challenges, 87, 88
    data classification (*see* Data classification)
    features, 88
    GDPR, 88
    TDE pause and resume, 111, 112
Sensitivity classifications, 105–110
Server/database configuration, 241
SHORTEST_PATH() T-SQL syntax, 155
Short-transaction optimization, 142
Software Guard Extensions (SGX), 90
Sort operation, 24
Spark, 4, 369
    ADS, 369, 370
    MSSQL spark connector, 371
    running with tools, 370, 371
SQL Platform Abstraction Layer (SQLPAL), 175
SQL Server 2016 R Services, 159
SQL Server 2019
    Azure VM, 408, 409
    deploy and configure, 15
    key functionality, 9
    migrate from Oracle, 411
    migration
        DEA, 397
        DMA, 395
        flow and tools, 394

upgrading
  databases, restore, 400
  in-place/rolling, 399, 400
  Log Shipping, 402
  replication, 402
  rolling, 401
  SSIS, 401
SQL Server Analysis
    Services (SSAS), 393
SQL Server Audit, 105
SQL Server development hub, 149
SQL Server Integration Services (SSIS)/
    bulk export/import, 401
SQL Server Machine
    Learning Services
  architecture, 160
  deeper dive, 161, 162
  extensibility architecture, 160
  extensibility framework, 159
  features, 165
  models, 159
  radical, 165
  scalable machine learning
      programs, 160
  security, isolation,
      and governance, 163–165
SQL Server Management Studio (SSMS),
    14, 64, 92, 95, 118, 179,
    235, 315, 407
SQL Server powers Azure
    SQL Database, 9
SQL server replication, Linux, 183
SQL Server Reporting
    Services (SSRS), 393
SQL server workshops, 16
Standard profiling, 61
Sys.sleep(), 191

T

Table variable deferred compilation, 43
Tabular Data Stream (TDS) protocol, 112
Transparent Data Encryption (TDE), 87,
    89, 111, 238, 395
Troubleshooting Guides (TSG), 373
T-SQL BEGIN DISTRIBUTED
    TRANSACTION statement, 184
T-SQL Language
  extensibility framework, 167, 168
  Java extension, tutorial, 170–173
  language extension, 174
T-SQL notebook, 43
T-SQL query, 162
T-SQL statements, 94
Tuning Assistant (TunA), 407

U

Ultra Disk Storage, 410
Union file system, 200
User-defined function (UDF), 52
  Actual Execution Plan, 53–55
  APPROX_COUNT_DISTINCT, 60
  COUNT and DISTINCT, 59
  Execution Plan, inlining, 57
  Execution Plan, not inlined, 56
  types, 52
User experience, 386, 387
  MaxDOP, 387
  memory configuration, 388, 389
UTF-8 Support
  unicode encoding, 156
  nchar and nvarchar data types, 157
  Windows, Linux, and containers, 158
UTF-16, 157

V

varchar data types, 157

Verbose truncation warnings, 386

Virtualization-based security (VBS)
        memory enclaves, 90

virtual machine (VM), 195, 340

W, X, Y, Z

WideWorldImporters (WWI), 314

Windows containers, 243–246

Windows Subsystem for Linux (WSL), 199

Worker stealing, 385